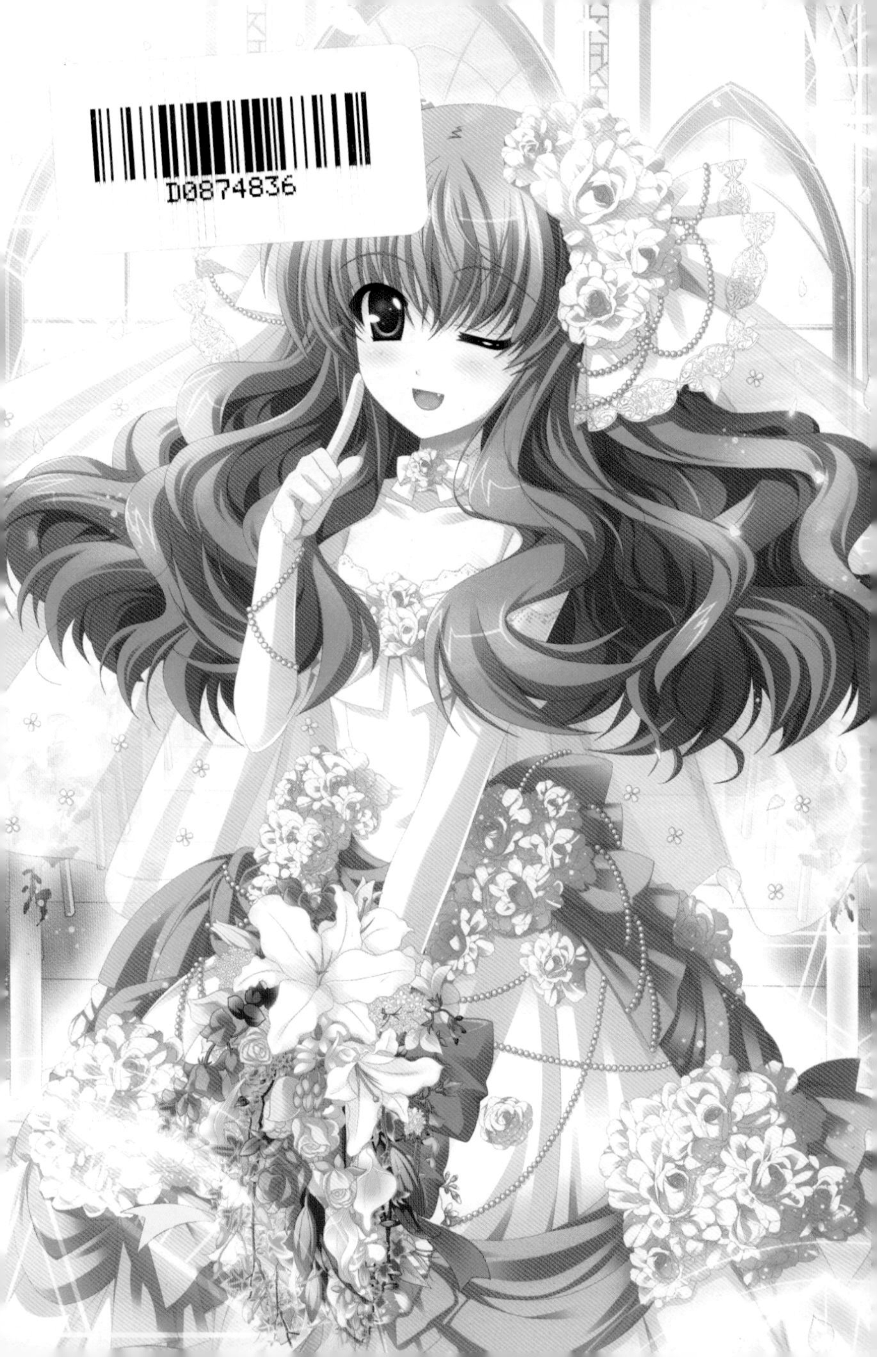

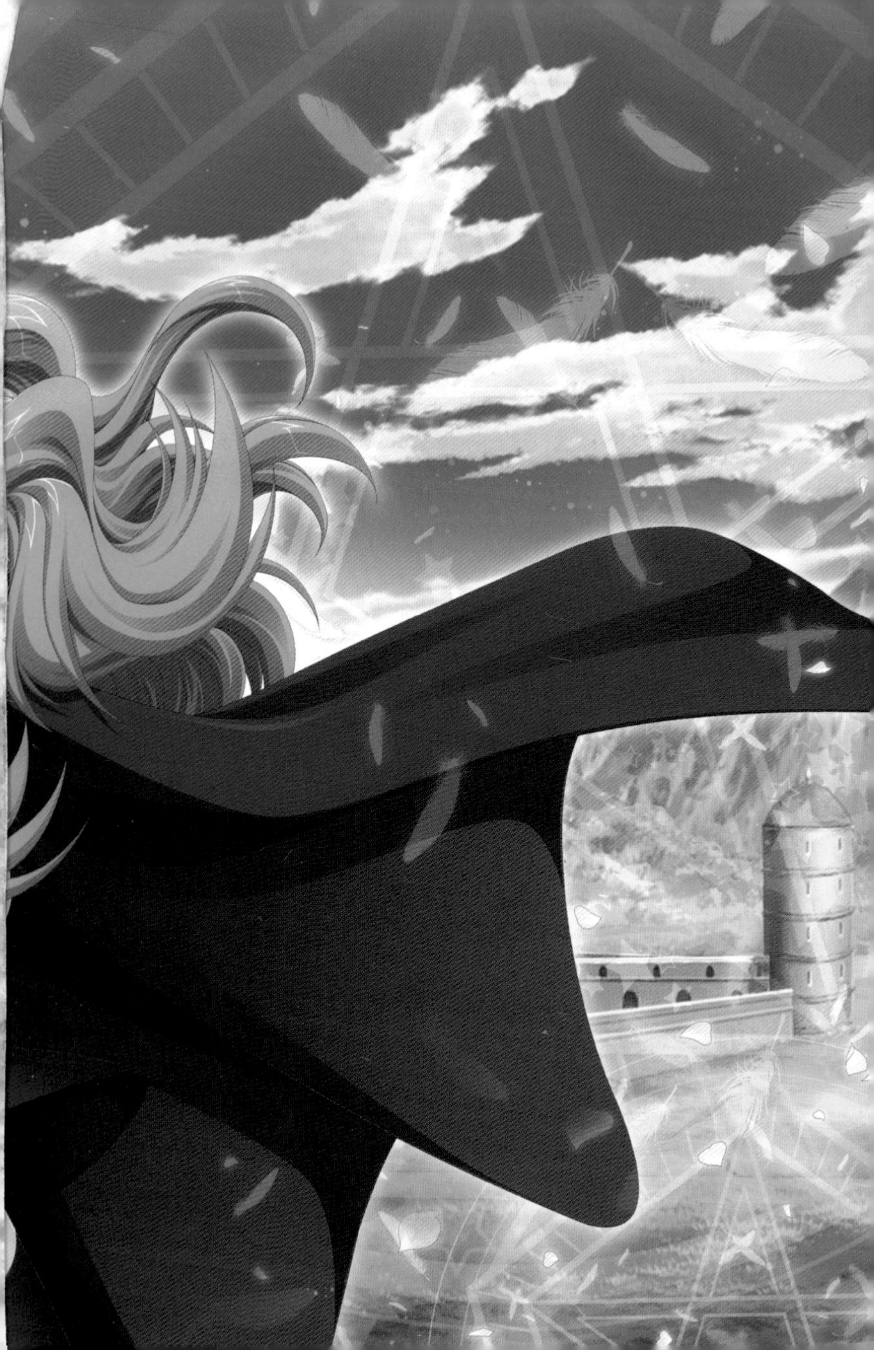

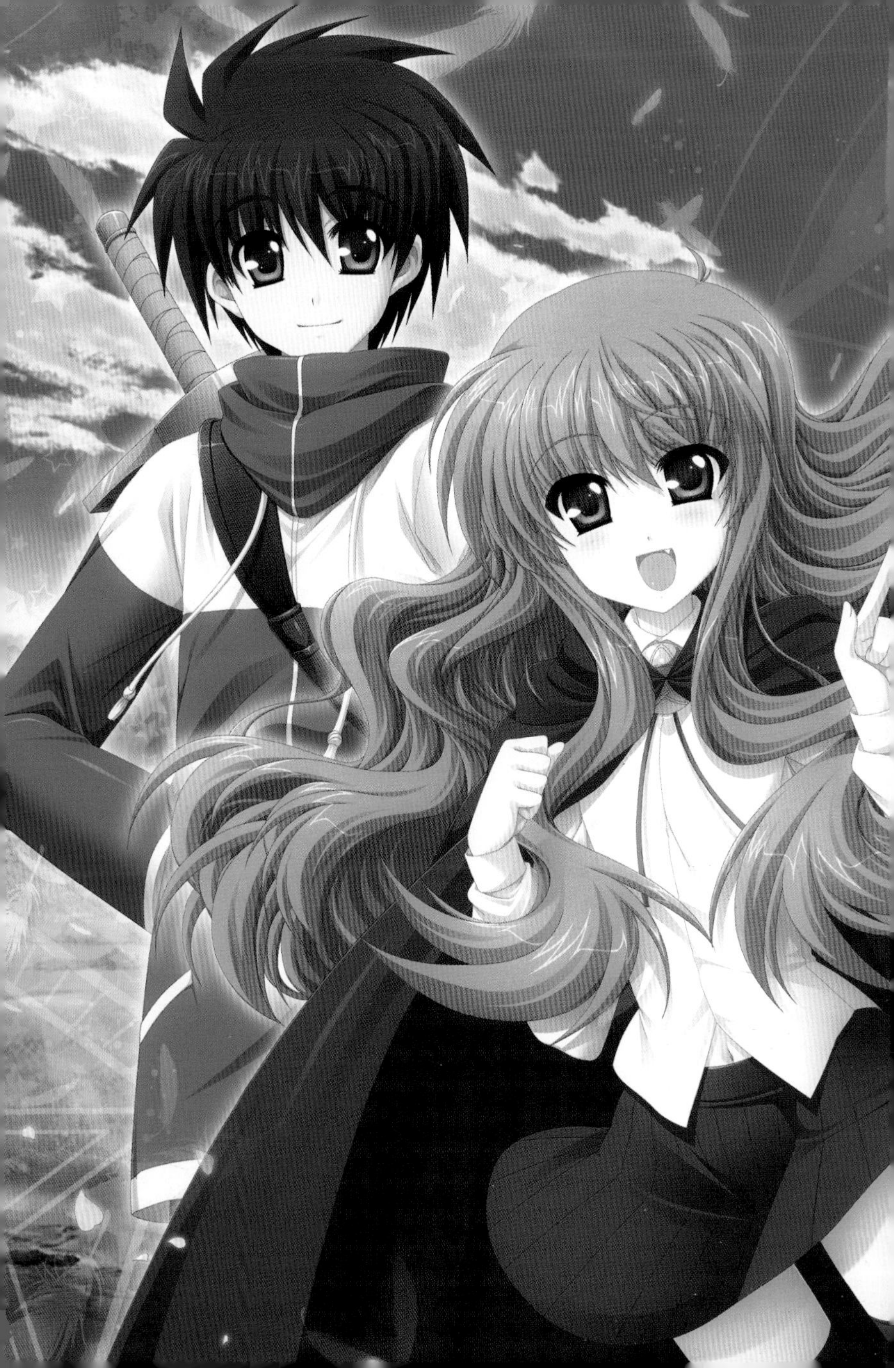

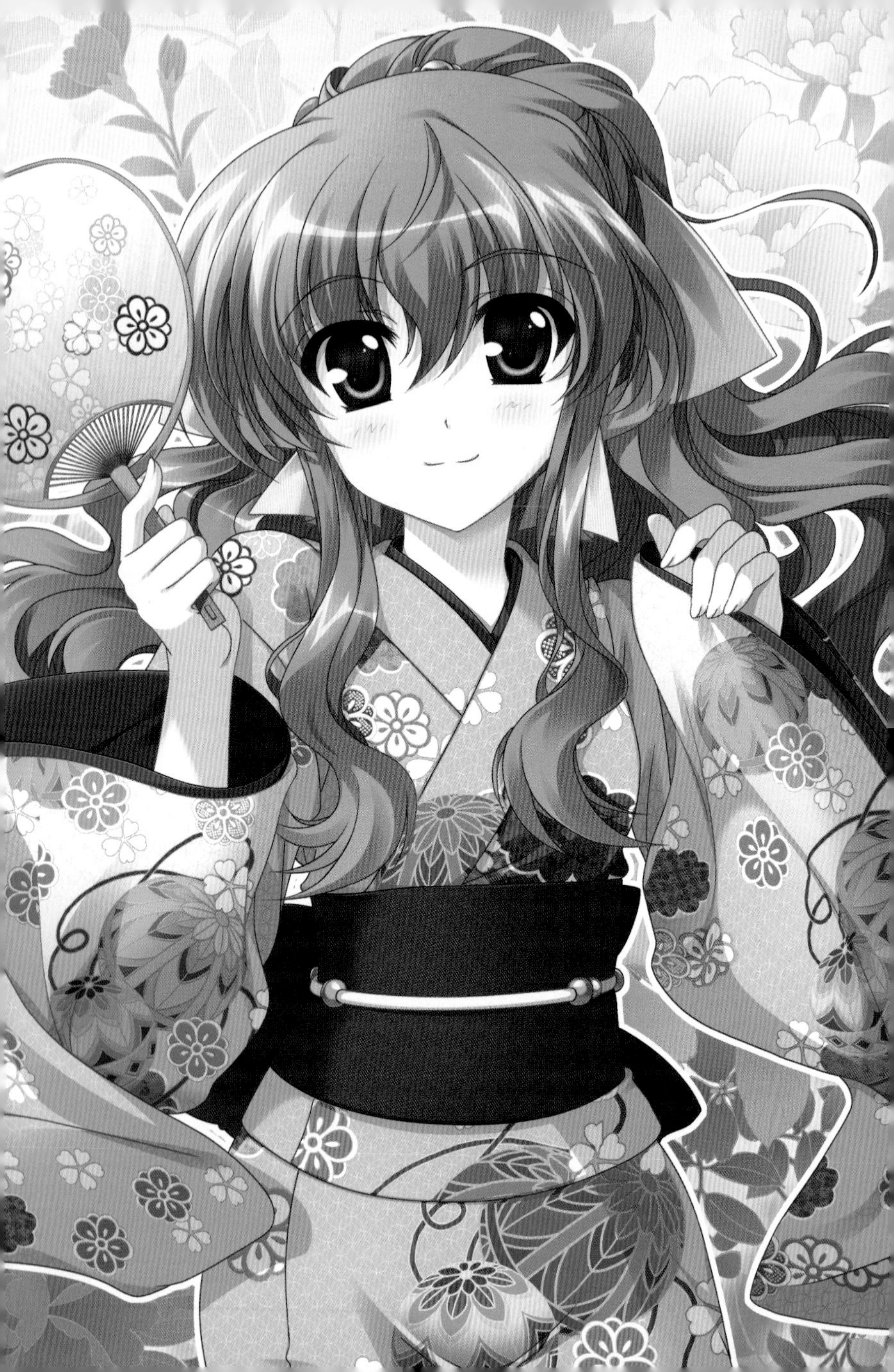

ZERO'S FAMILIAR Chevalier

4

Art: Yukari Higa
Story: Noboru Yamaguchi
Character Design: Eiji Usatsuki

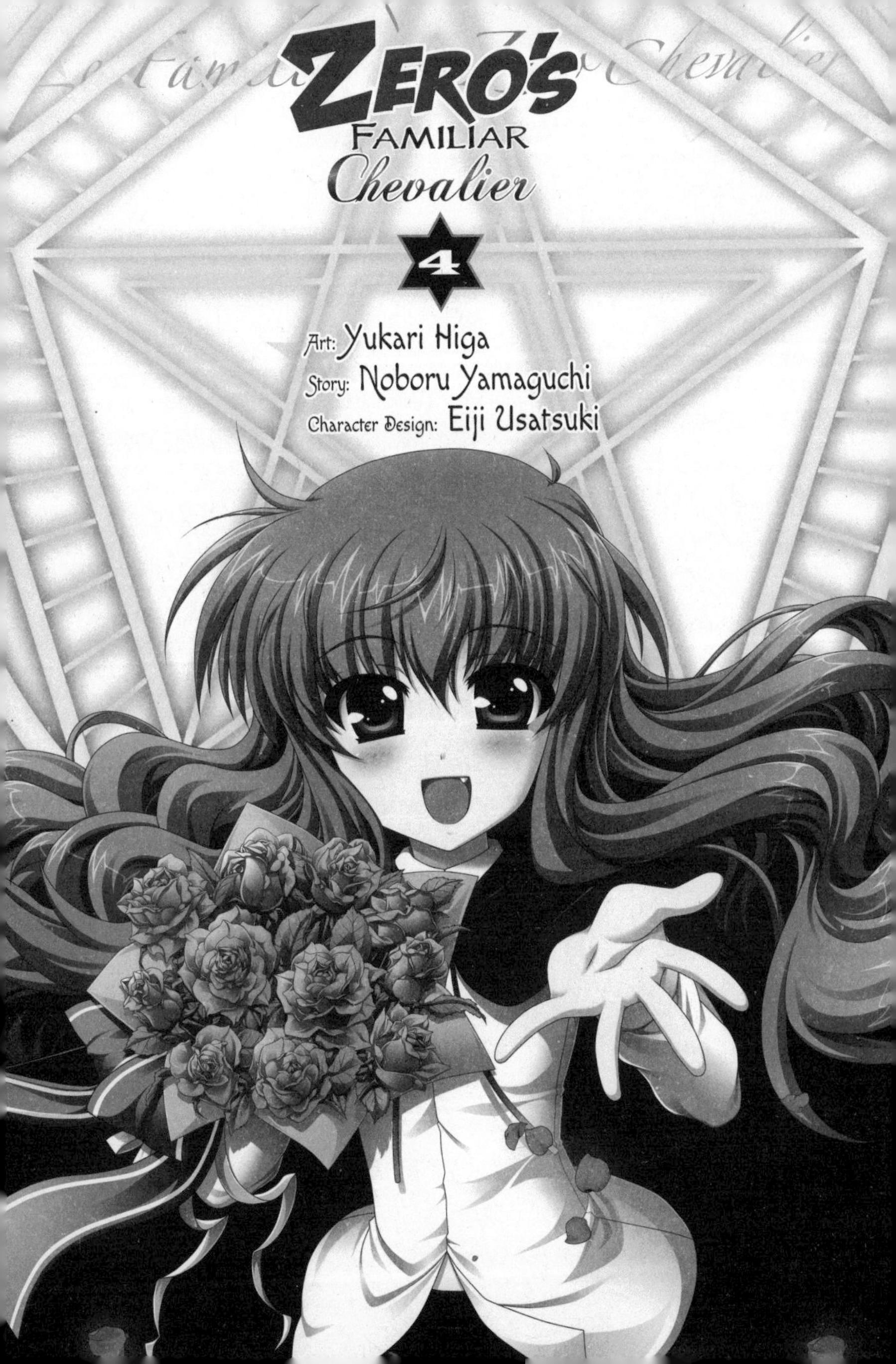

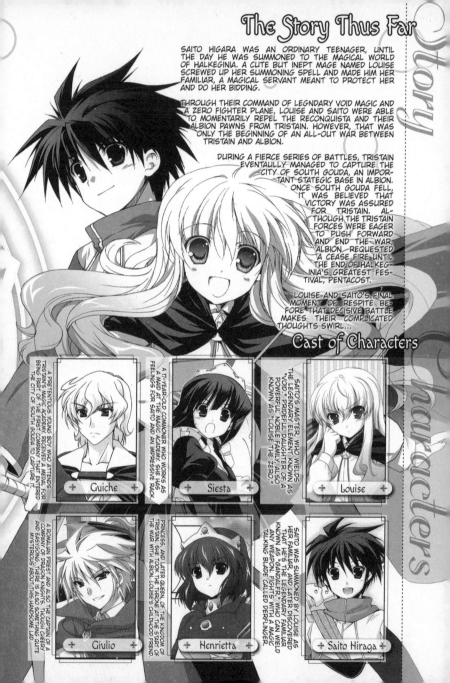

The Story Thus Far

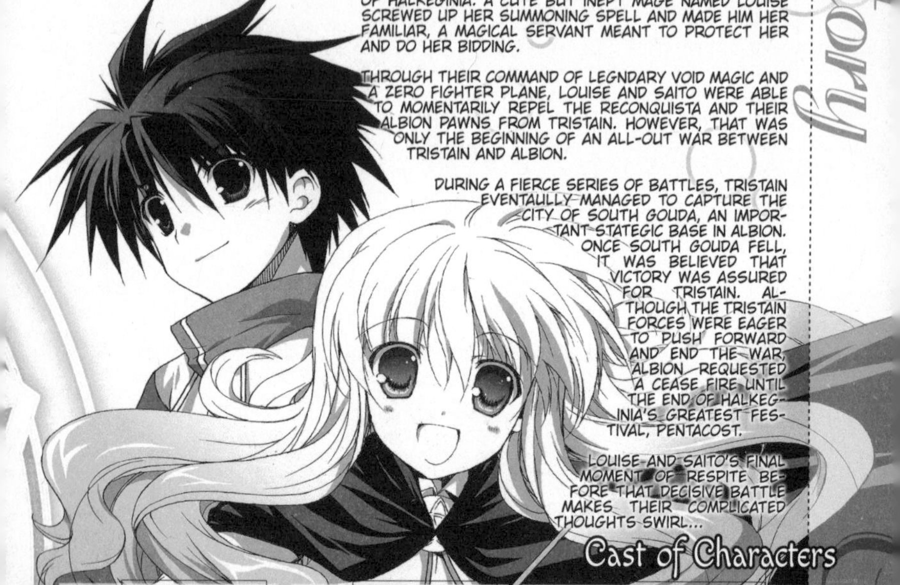

SAITO HIGARA WAS AN ORDINARY TEENAGER, UNTIL THE DAY HE WAS SUMMONED TO THE MAGICAL WORLD OF HALKEGINIA. A CUTE BUT INEPT MAGE NAMED LOUISE SCREWED UP HER SUMMONING SPELL AND MADE HIM HER FAMILIAR, A MAGICAL SERVANT MEANT TO PROTECT HER AND DO HER BIDDING.

THROUGH THEIR COMMAND OF LEGNDARY VOID MAGIC AND A ZERO FIGHTER PLANE, LOUISE AND SAITO WERE ABLE TO MOMENTARILY REPEL THE RECONQUISTA AND THEIR ALBION PAWNS FROM TRISTAIN. HOWEVER, THAT WAS ONLY THE BEGINNING OF AN ALL-OUT WAR BETWEEN TRISTAIN AND ALBION.

DURING A FIERCE SERIES OF BATTLES, TRISTAIN EVENTAULLY MANAGED TO CAPTURE THE CITY OF SOUTH GOUDA, AN IMPORTANT STATEGIC BASE IN ALBION. ONCE SOUTH GOUDA FELL, IT WAS BELIEVED THAT VICTORY WAS ASSURED FOR TRISTAIN. ALTHOUGH THE TRISTAIN FORCES WERE EAGER TO PUSH FORWARD AND END THE WAR, ALBION REQUESTED A CEASE FIRE UNTIL THE END OF HALKEGINIA'S GREATEST FESTIVAL, PENTACOST.

LOUISE AND SAITO'S FINAL MOMENT OF RESPITE BEFORE THAT DECISIVE BATTLE MAKES THEIR COMPLICATED THOUGHTS SWIRL...

Cast of Characters

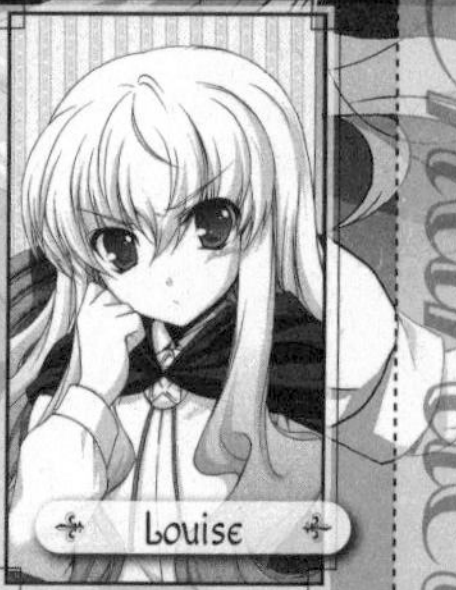

Louise

SAITO'S MASTER, WHO WIELDS THE LEGENDARY ELEMENT KNOWN AS "VOID." PRIDEFUL DAUGHTER OF A POWERFUL NOBLE FAMILY, ALSO KNOWN AS "LOUISE THE ZERO."

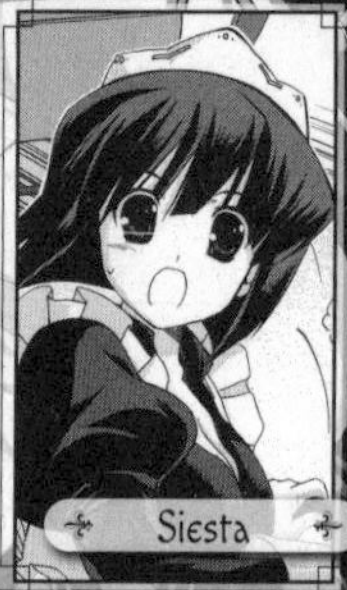

Siesta

A 17-YEAR-OLD COMMONER WHO WORKS AS A MAID AT THE MAGIC ACADEMY. SHE HAS FEELINGS FOR SAITO AND AN IMPRESSIVE RACK.

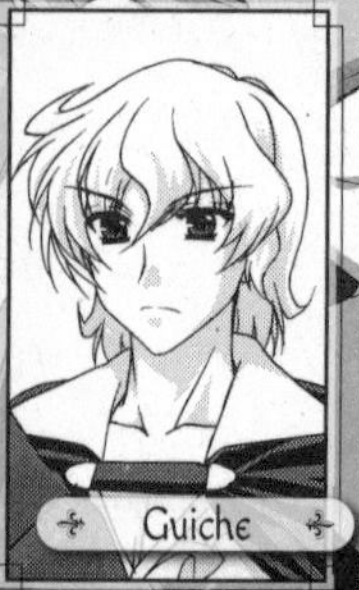

Guiche

A PRETENTIOUS YOUNG BOY WHO ATTENDS TRISTAIN'S MAGIC ACADEMY. RECEIVED A MEDAL FOR BEING PART OF THE FIRST COMPANY THAT ENTERED THE CITY OF SOUTH GOUDA TO CAPTURE IT.

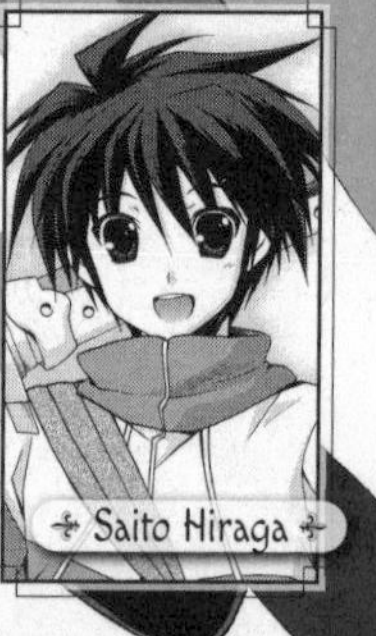

Saito Hiraga

SAITO WAS SUMMONED BY LOUISE AS HER FAMILIAR, AND LATER DISCOVERED THAT HE'S THE LEGENDARY FAMILIAR KNOWN AS "GANDALFR," WHO CAN WIELD ANY WEAPON. FIGHTS WITH A MAGIC TALKING BLADE CALLED DERFLINGER.

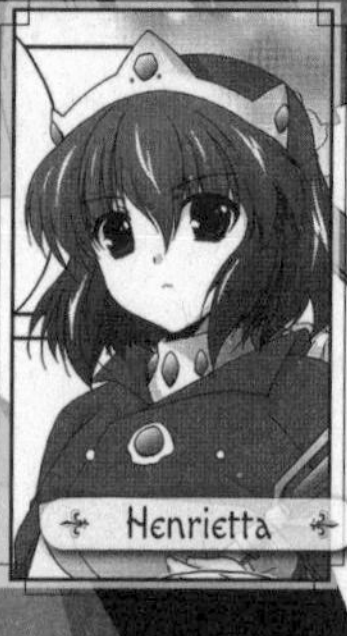

Henrietta

PRINCESS, AND LATER QUEEN, OF THE KINGDOM OF TRISTAIN. SHE TOOK THE THRONE AT THE START OF THE WAR WITH ALBION. LOUISE'S CHILDHOOD FRIEND.

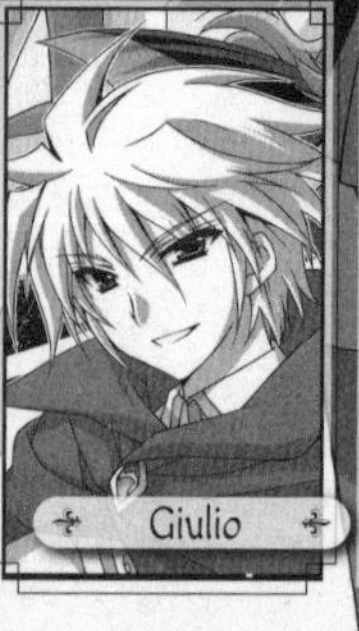

Giulio

A ROMALIAN PRIEST AND ALSO THE CAPTAIN OF A COMPANY OF DRAGON KNIGHTS. THOUGH CHEERY AND EASYGOING, THERE IS ALSO SOMETHING QUITE MYSTERIOUS ABOUT THIS HANDSOME LAD.

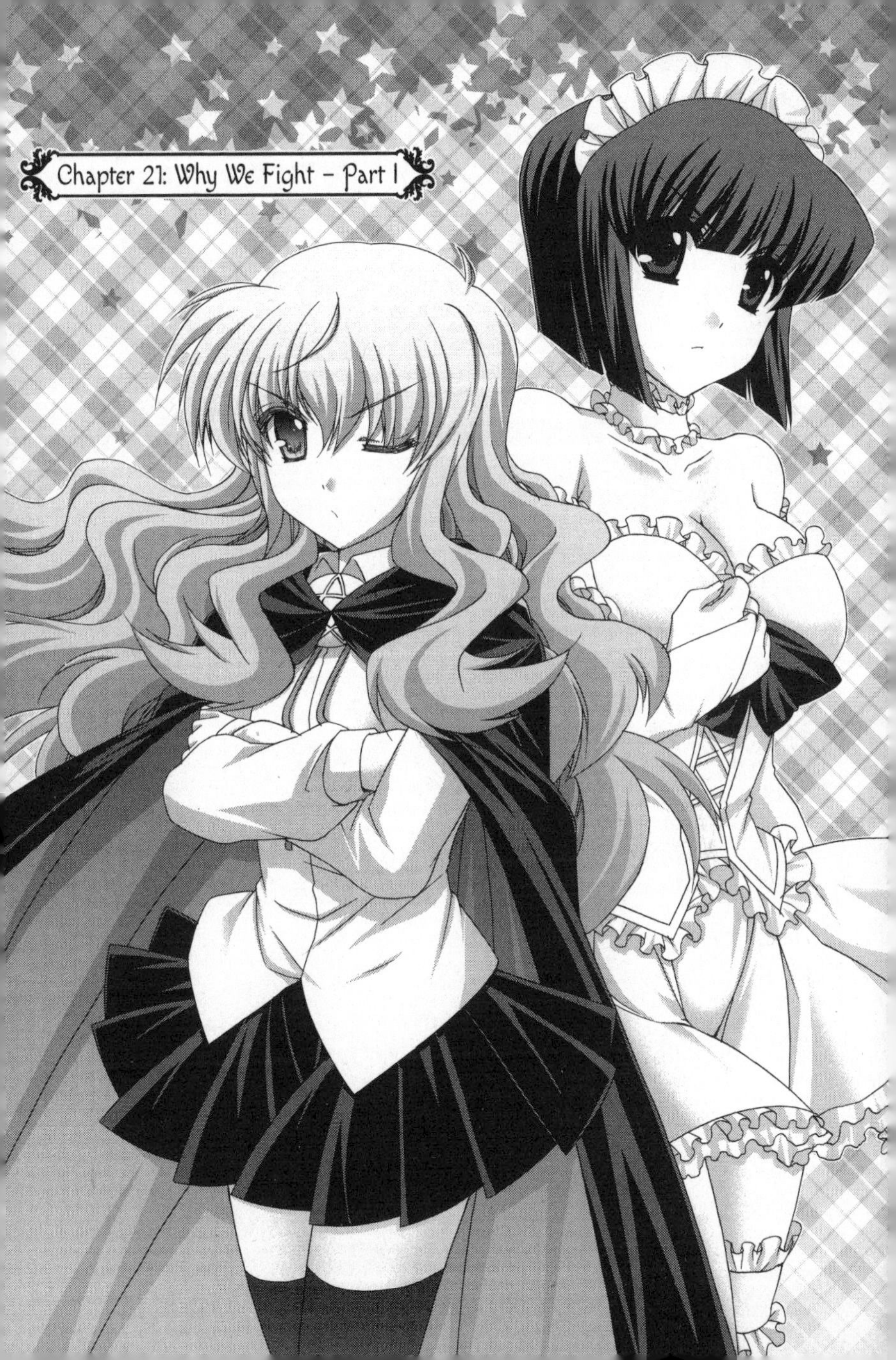
Chapter 21: Why We Fight – Part I

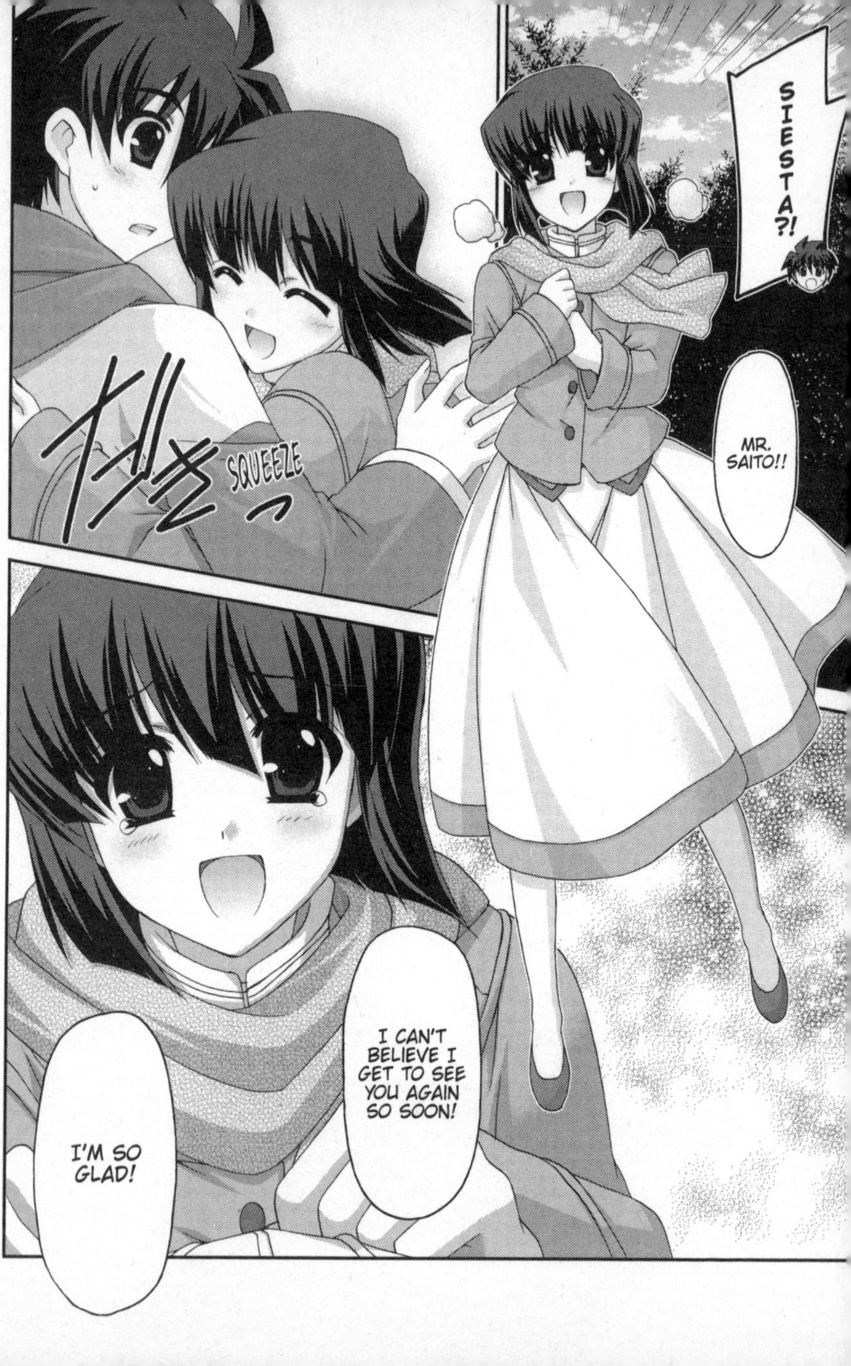

SIESTA?!
MR. SAITO!!
SQUEEZE
I CAN'T BELIEVE I GET TO SEE YOU AGAIN SO SOON!
I'M SO GLAD!

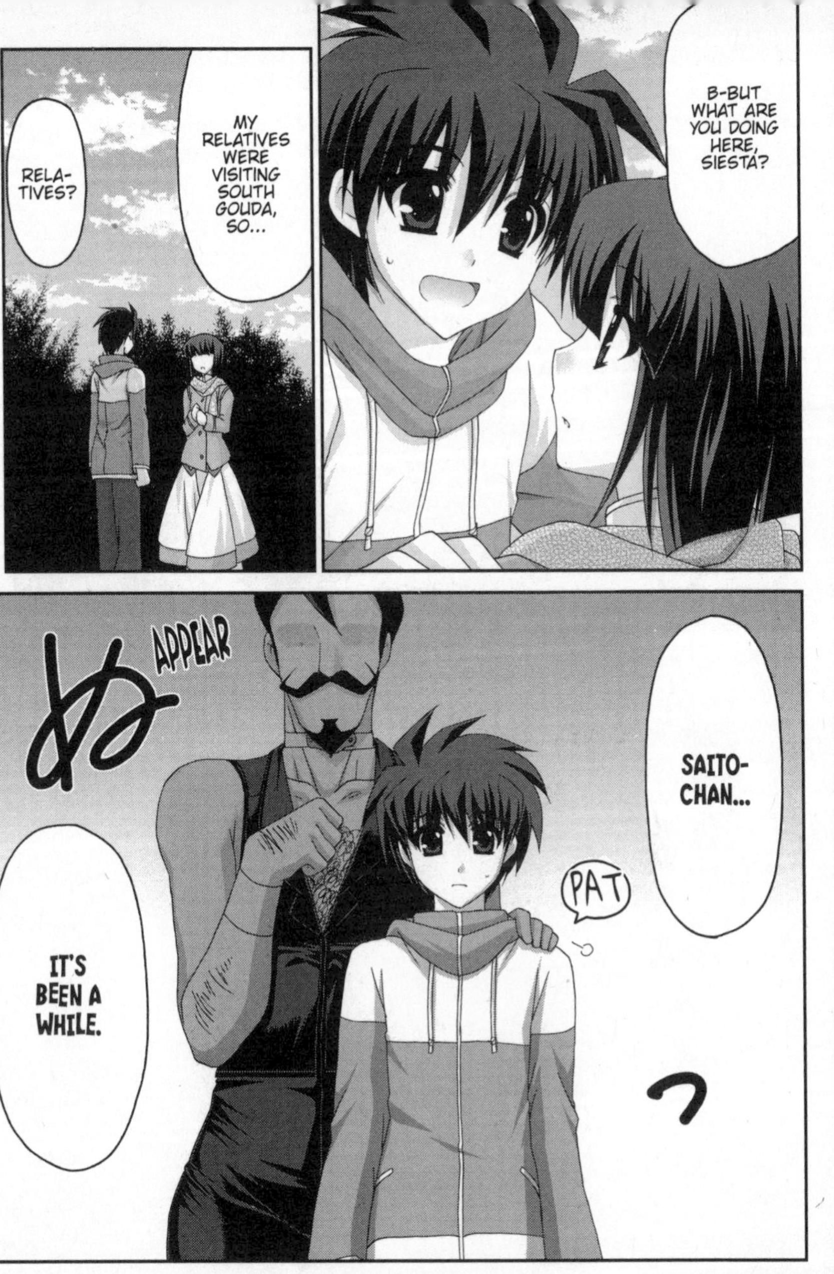
B-BUT WHAT ARE YOU DOING HERE, SIESTA?
MY RELATIVES WERE VISITING SOUTH GOUDA, SO...
RELA-TIVES?
SAITO-CHAN...
PAT
ぬ
APPEAR
IT'S BEEN A WHILE.

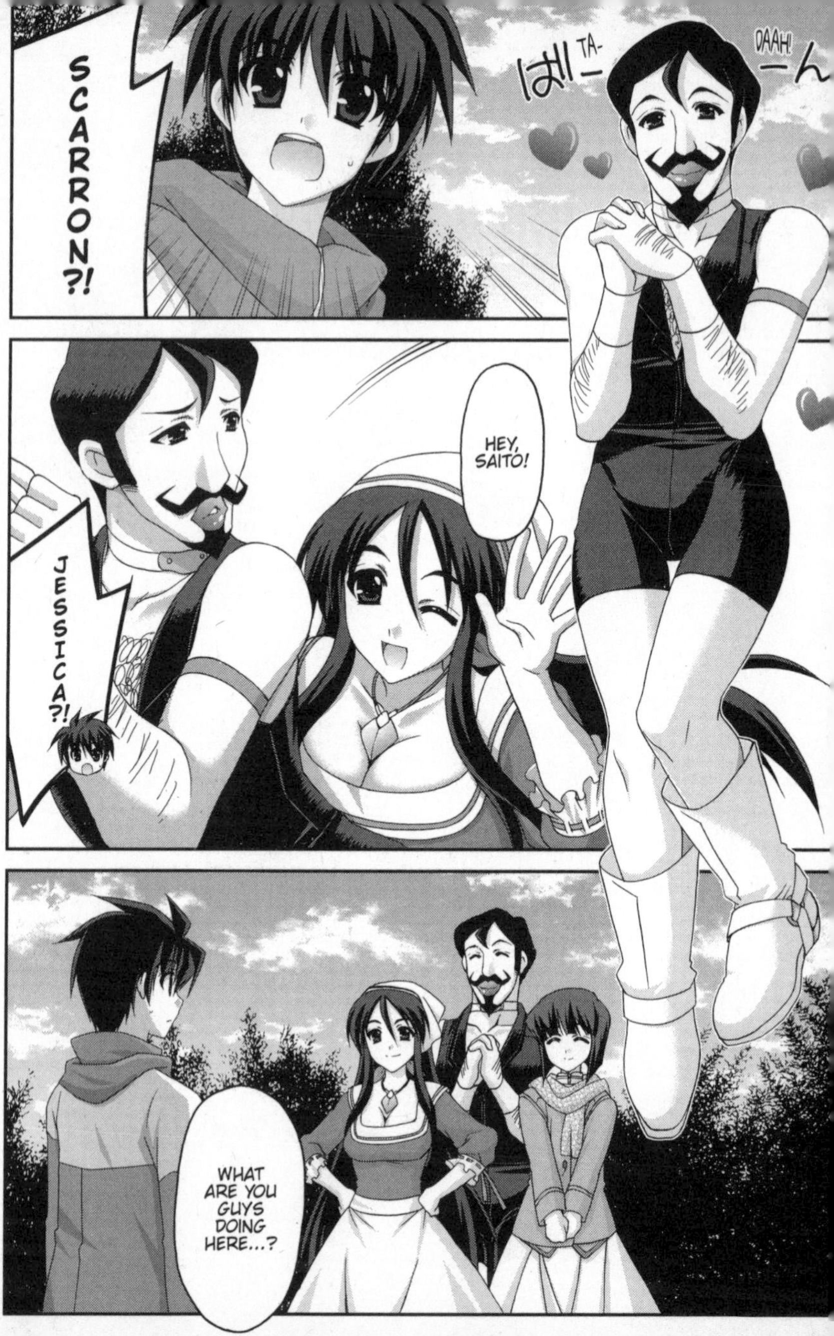
ぱ!ーーん
TA-DAAH!
SCARRON?!
HEY, SAITO!
JESSICA?!
WHAT ARE YOU GUYS DOING HERE...?

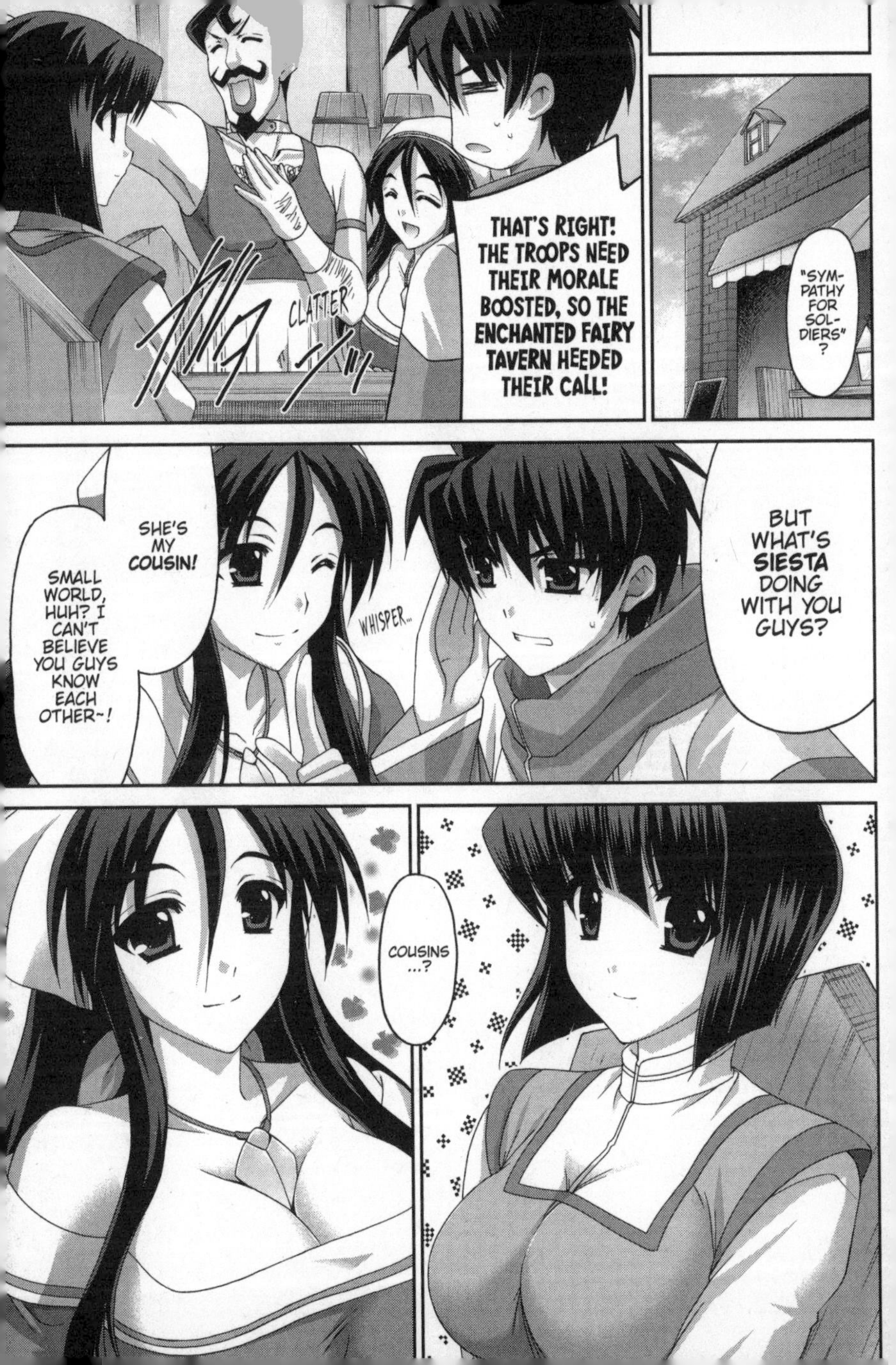
"SYMPATHY FOR SOLDIERS"?
THAT'S RIGHT! THE TROOPS NEED THEIR MORALE BOOSTED, SO THE ENCHANTED FAIRY TAVERN HEEDED THEIR CALL!
CLATTER
BUT WHAT'S SIESTA DOING WITH YOU GUYS?
WHISPER...
SHE'S MY COUSIN!
SMALL WORLD, HUH? I CAN'T BELIEVE YOU GUYS KNOW EACH OTHER~!
COUSINS ...?

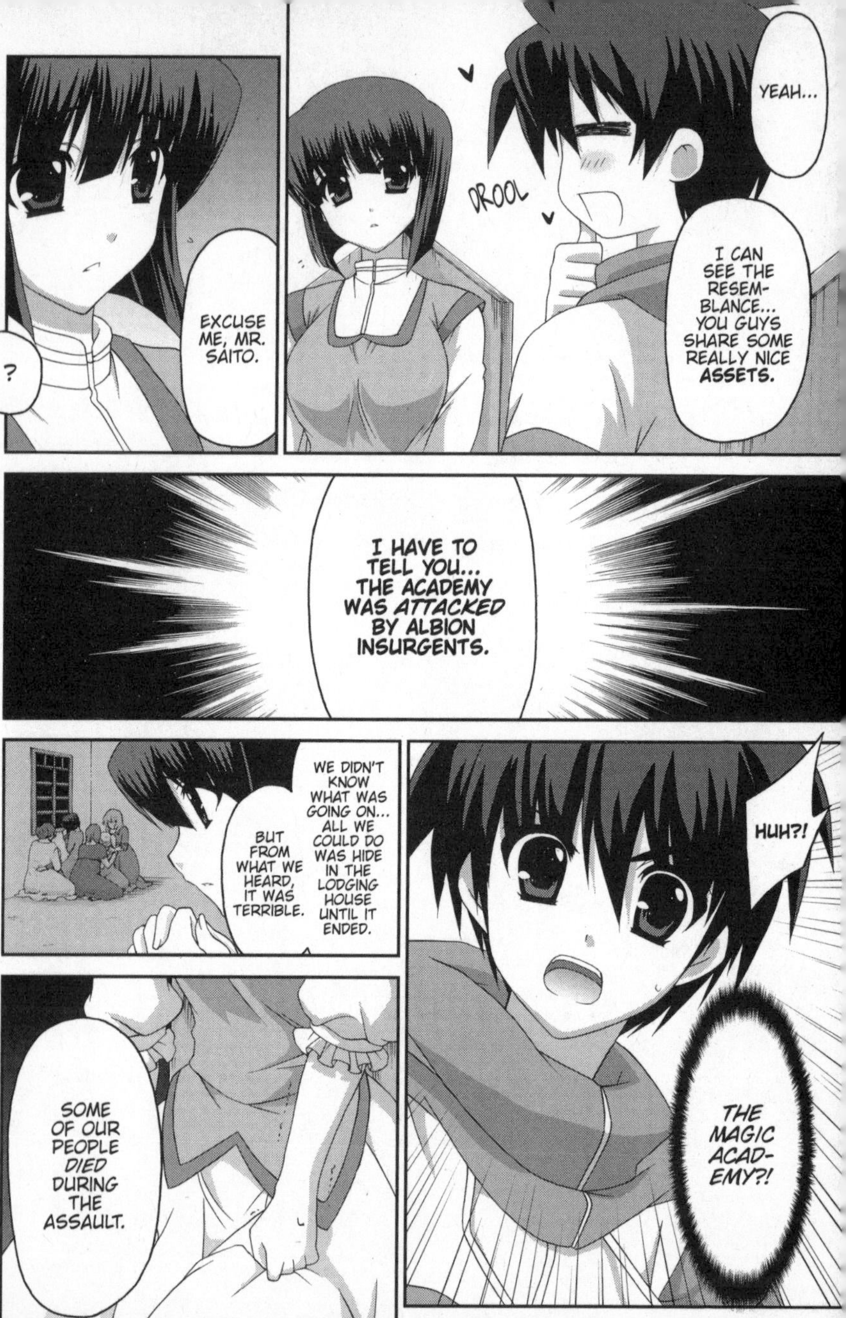

YEAH...
DROOL
I CAN SEE THE RESEMBLANCE... YOU GUYS SHARE SOME REALLY NICE **ASSETS.**
EXCUSE ME, MR. SAITO.
?
I HAVE TO TELL YOU... THE ACADEMY WAS *ATTACKED* BY ALBION INSURGENTS.
HUH?!
THE MAGIC ACADEMY?!
WE DIDN'T KNOW WHAT WAS GOING ON... ALL WE COULD DO WAS HIDE IN THE LODGING HOUSE UNTIL IT ENDED.
BUT FROM WHAT WE HEARD, IT WAS TERRIBLE.
SOME OF OUR PEOPLE *DIED* DURING THE ASSAULT.

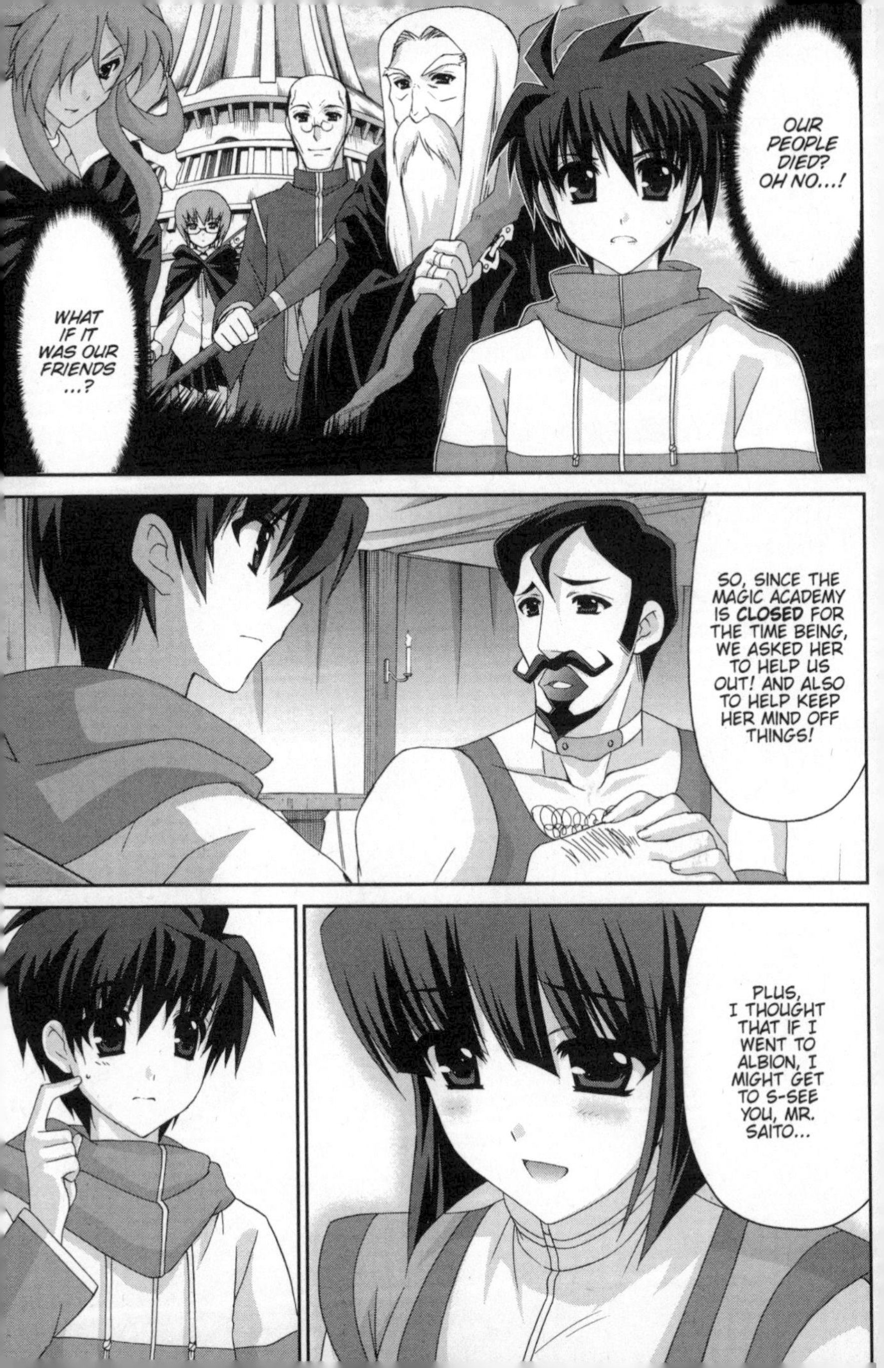
OUR PEOPLE DIED? OH NO...!
WHAT IF IT WAS OUR FRIENDS ...?
SO, SINCE THE MAGIC ACADEMY IS **CLOSED** FOR THE TIME BEING, WE ASKED HER TO HELP US OUT! AND ALSO TO HELP KEEP HER MIND OFF THINGS!
PLUS, I THOUGHT THAT IF I WENT TO ALBION, I MIGHT GET TO S-SEE YOU, MR. SAITO...

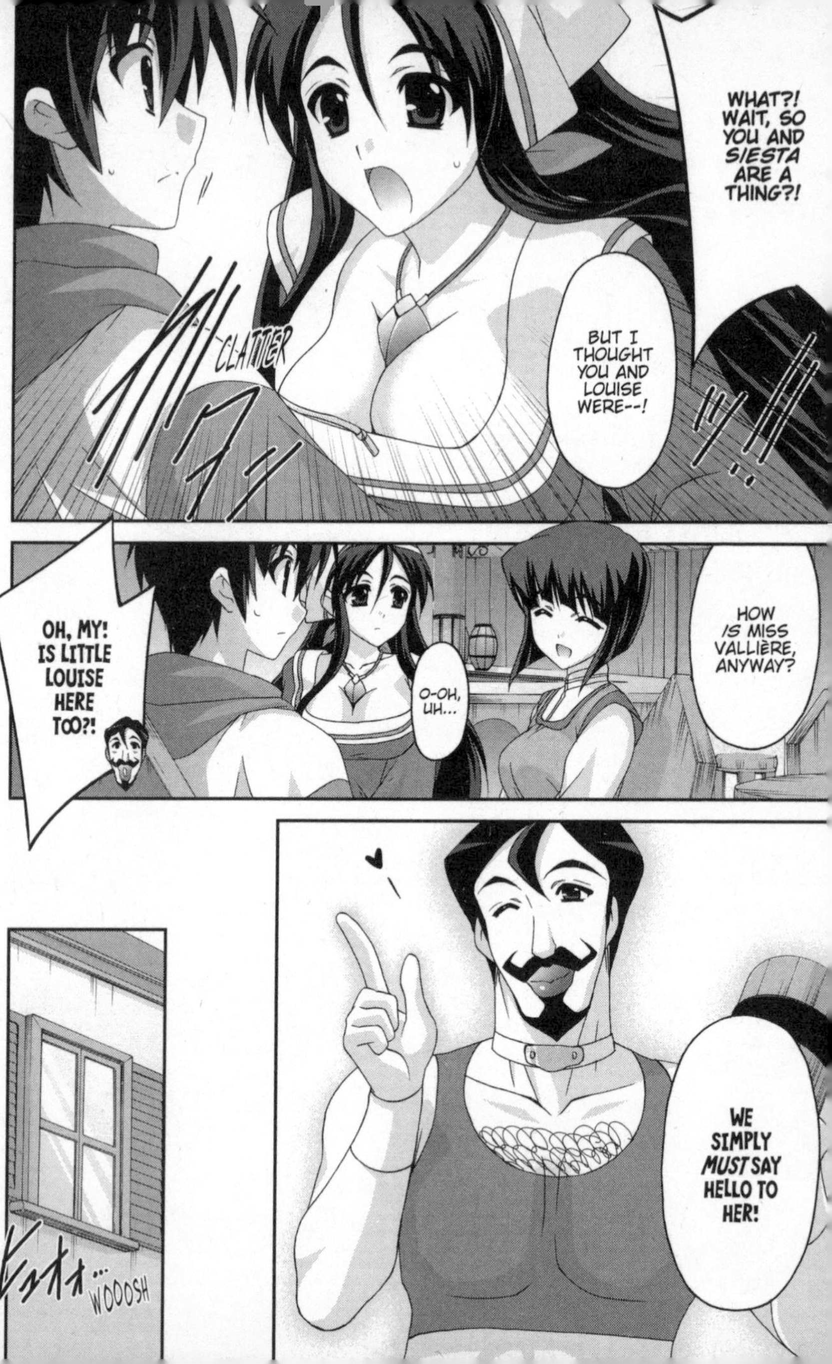
WHAT?! WAIT, SO YOU AND SIESTA ARE A THING?!
BUT I THOUGHT YOU AND LOUISE WERE--!
CLATTER
HOW IS MISS VALLIÈRE, ANYWAY?
O-OH, UH...
OH, MY! IS LITTLE LOUISE HERE TOO?!
WE SIMPLY MUST SAY HELLO TO HER!
WOOOSH

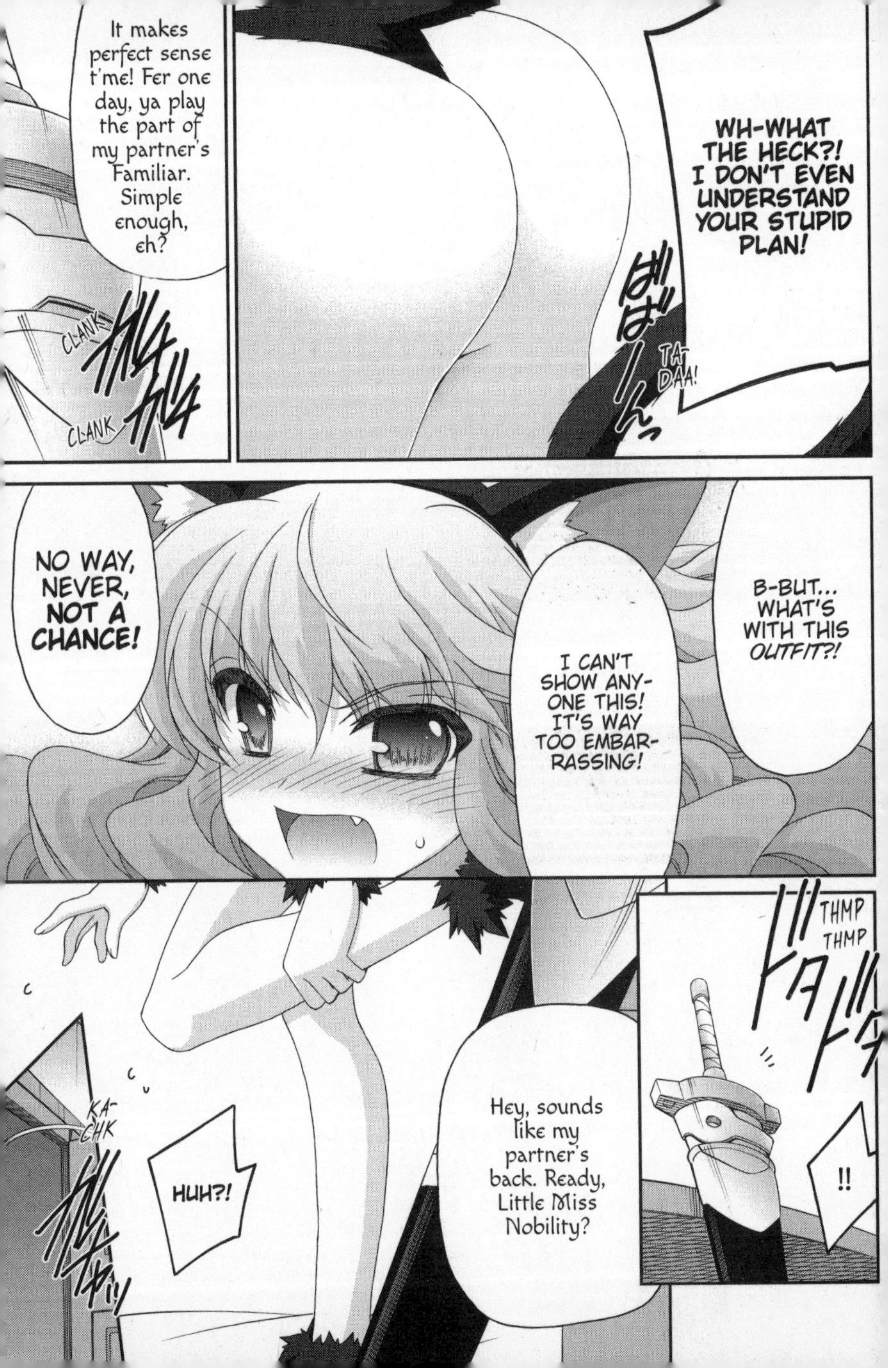
WH-WHAT THE HECK?! I DON'T EVEN UNDERSTAND YOUR STUPID PLAN!
TA-DAA!
It makes perfect sense t'me! Fer one day, ya play the part of my partner's Familiar. Simple enough, eh?
CLANK
CLANK
B-BUT... WHAT'S WITH THIS *OUTFIT?!*
I CAN'T SHOW ANY-ONE THIS! IT'S WAY TOO EMBAR-RASSING!
NO WAY, NEVER, NOT A CHANCE!
THMP THMP
!!
Hey, sounds like my partner's back. Ready, Little Miss Nobility?
HUH?!
KA-CHK

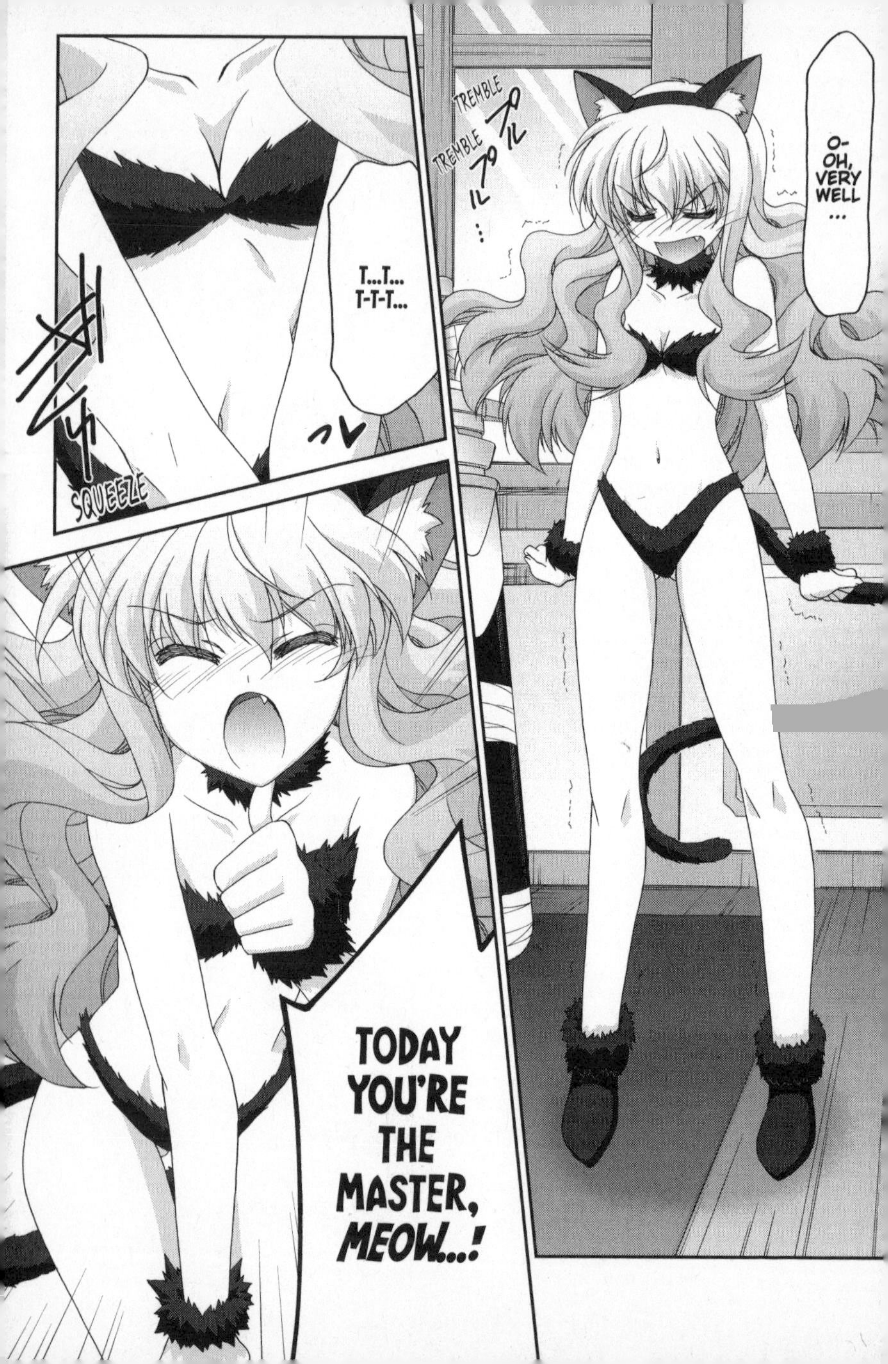
O-OH, VERY WELL...
TREMBLE
TREMBLE
T...T... T-T-T...
SQUEEZE
TODAY YOU'RE THE MASTER, MEOW...!

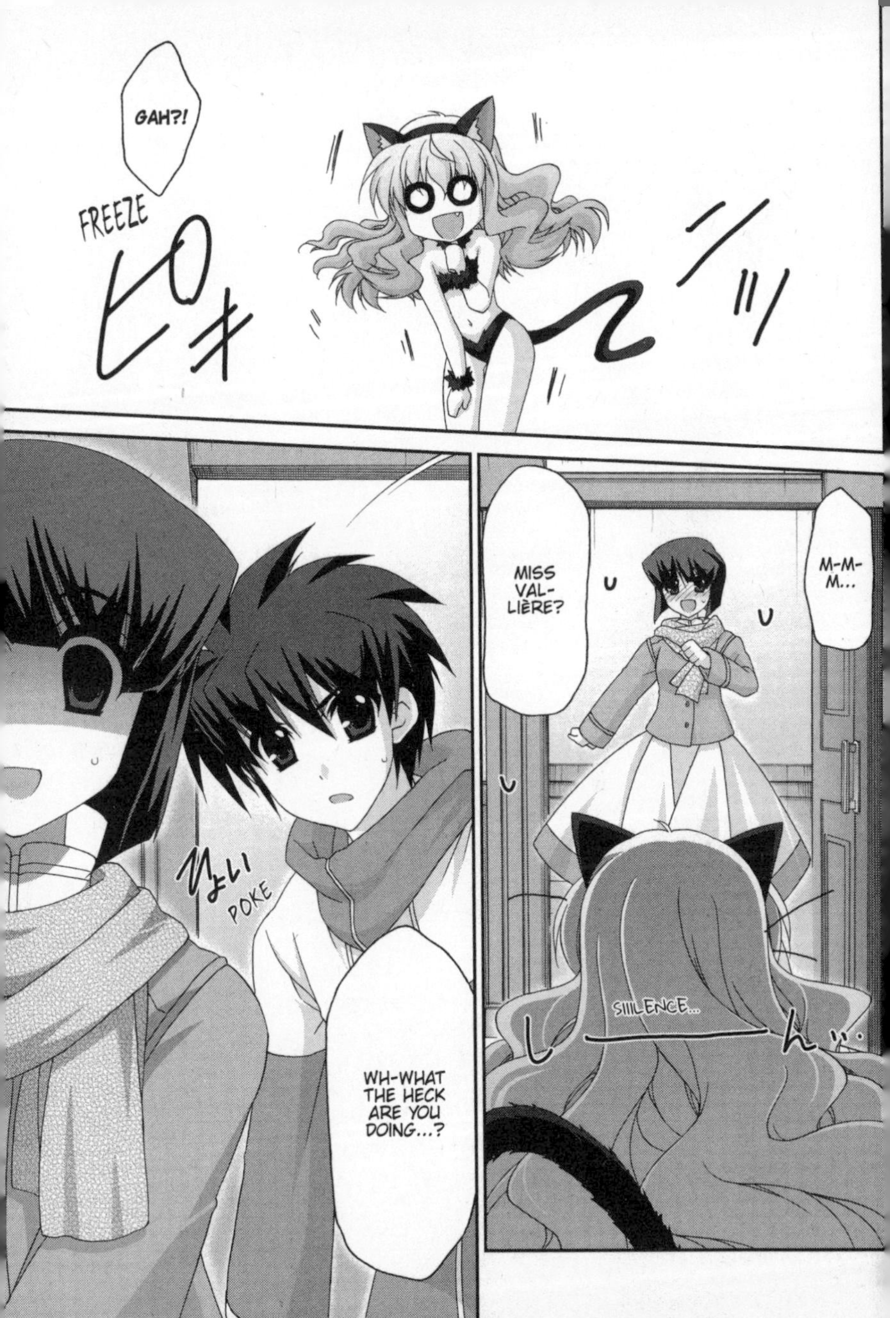
GAH?!
FREEZE
ピキーン
M-M-M...
MISS VAL-LIÈRE?
SIIILENCE...
しーーん
ひょい
POKE
WH-WHAT THE HECK ARE YOU DOING...?

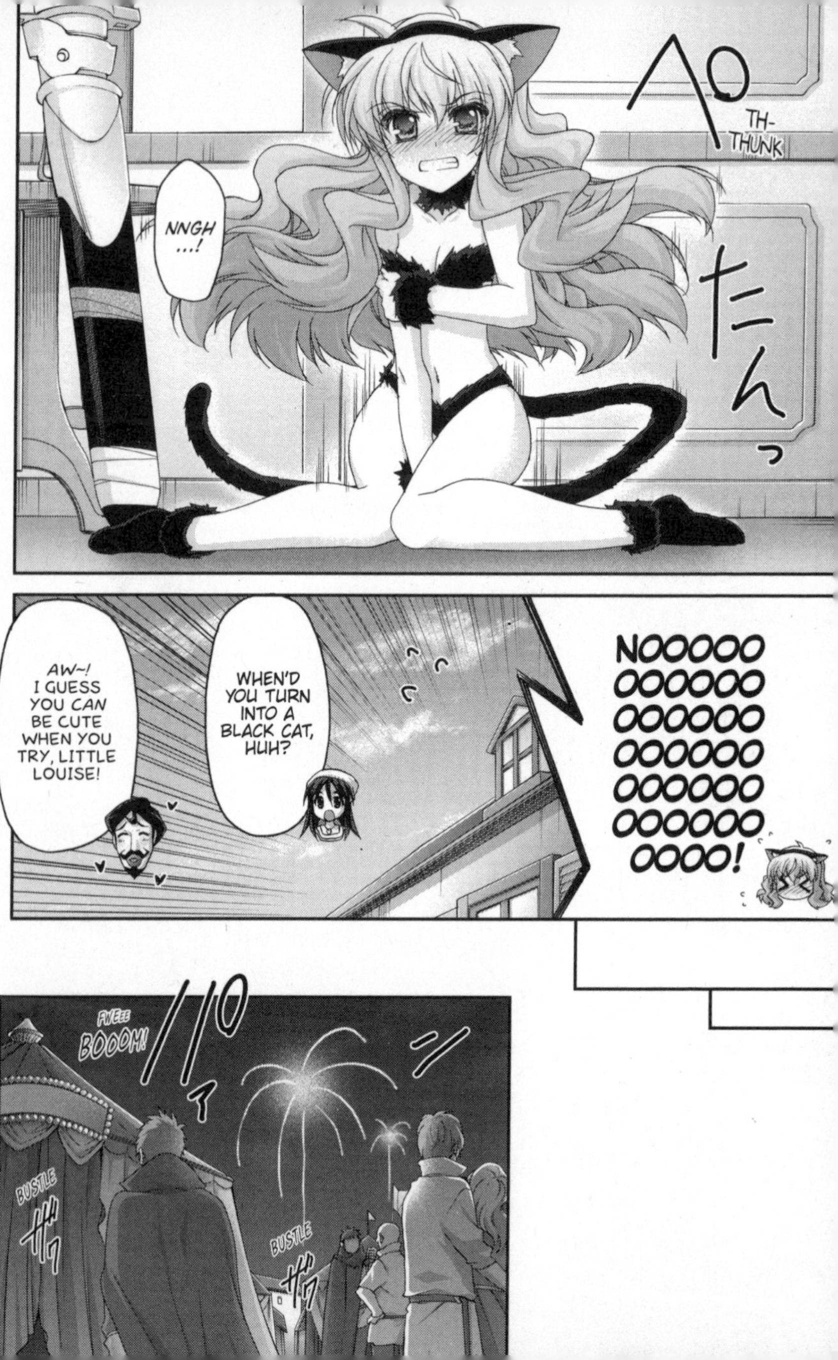
TH-THUNK
NNGH ...!
NOOOOOOOOOOOOOOOOOOOOOOOOOOOOOOOOOOOOOOOOOOOO!
WHEN'D YOU TURN INTO A BLACK CAT, HUH?
AW~! I GUESS YOU CAN BE CUTE WHEN YOU TRY, LITTLE LOUISE!
FWEEE BOOOM!
BUSTLE
BUSTLE

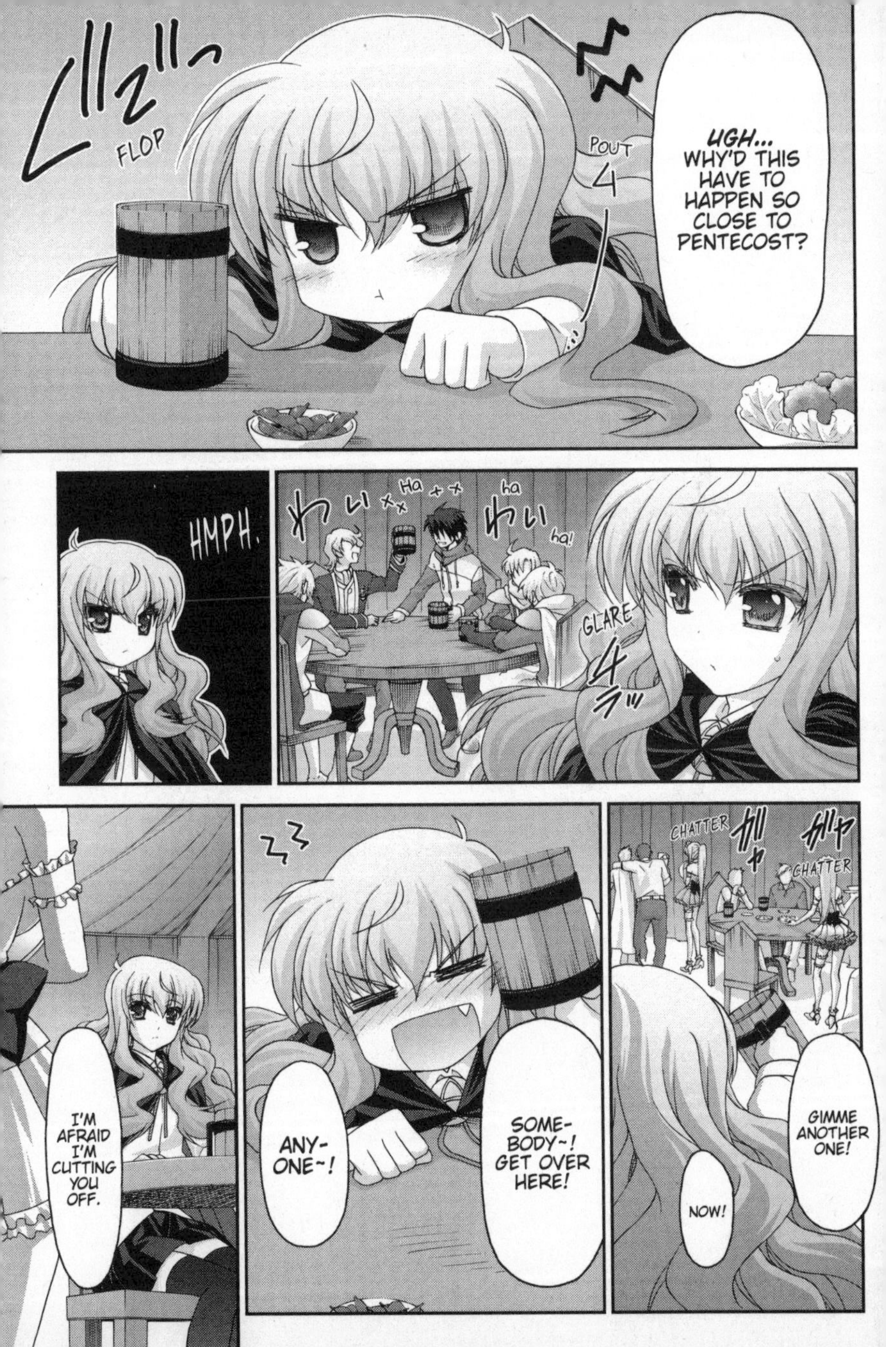
UGH... WHY'D THIS HAVE TO HAPPEN SO CLOSE TO PENTECOST?
POUT
FLOP
ha
わい
ha!
Ha
わい
GLARE
HMPH.
CHATTER
CHATTER
GIMME ANOTHER ONE!
NOW!
SOME-BODY~! GET OVER HERE!
ANY-ONE~!
I'M AFRAID I'M CUTTING YOU OFF.

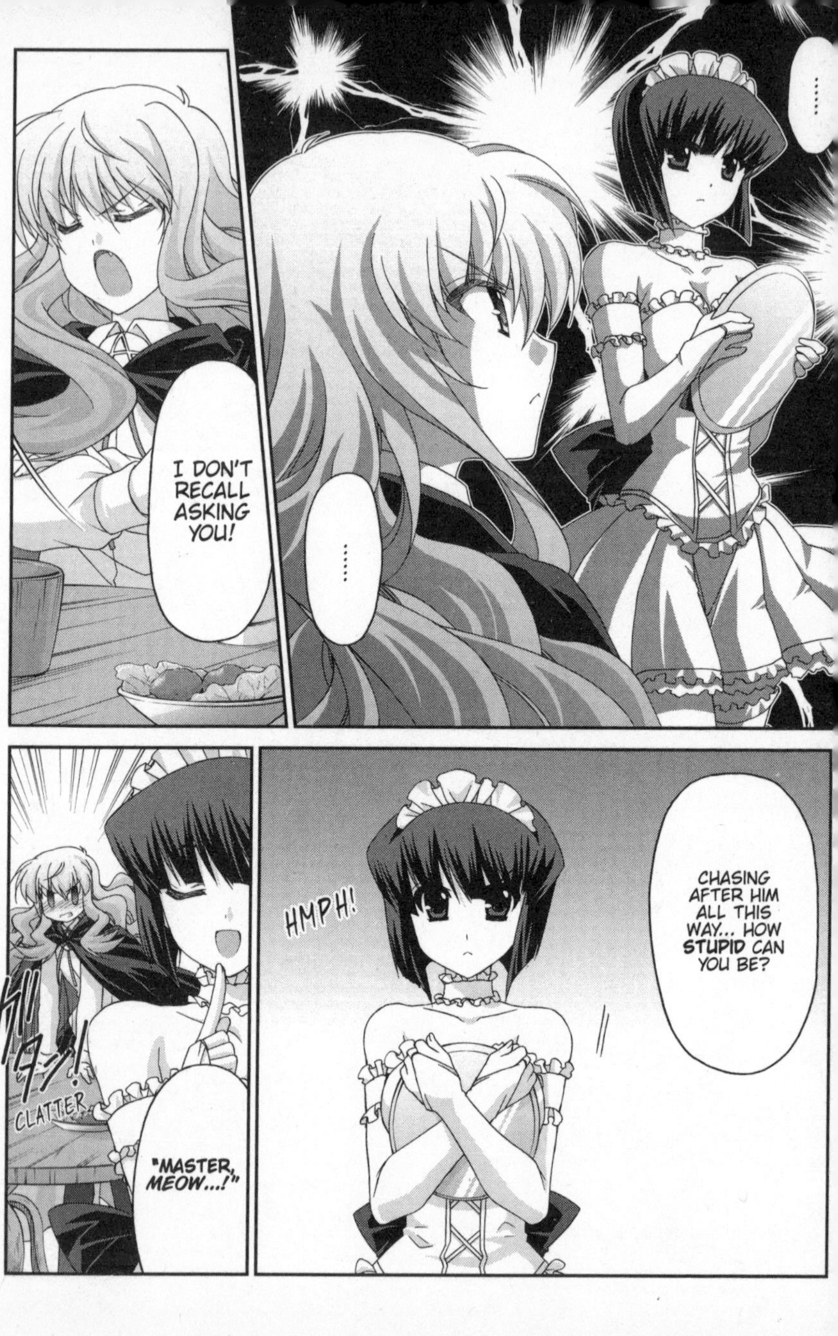
......
......
I DON'T RECALL ASKING YOU!
CHASING AFTER HIM ALL THIS WAY... HOW STUPID CAN YOU BE?
HMPH!
"MASTER, MEOW...!"
CLATTER

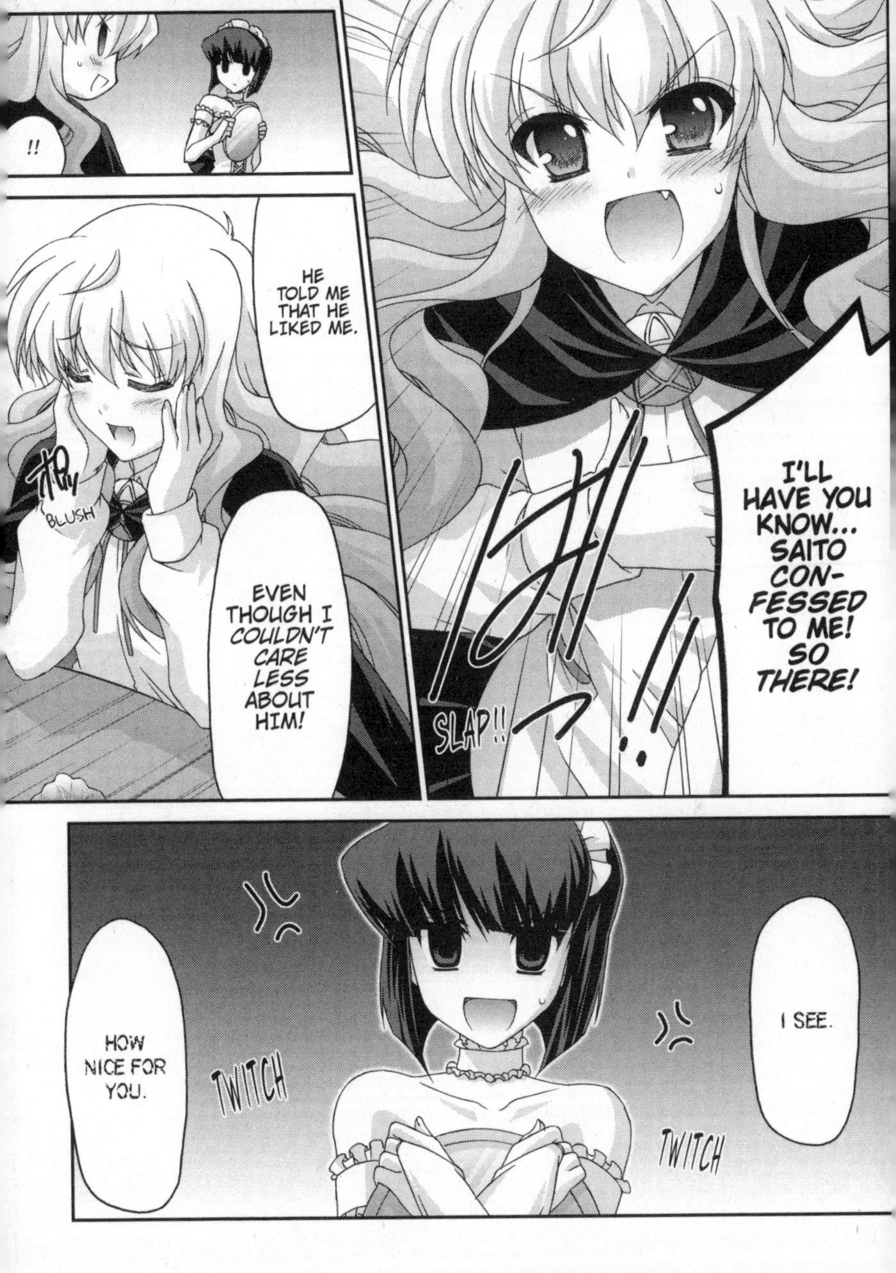
I'LL HAVE YOU KNOW... SAITO CONFESSED TO ME! SO THERE!
SLAP!!
!!
HE TOLD ME THAT HE LIKED ME.
EVEN THOUGH I COULDN'T CARE LESS ABOUT HIM!
BLUSH
I SEE.
TWITCH
TWITCH
HOW NICE FOR YOU.

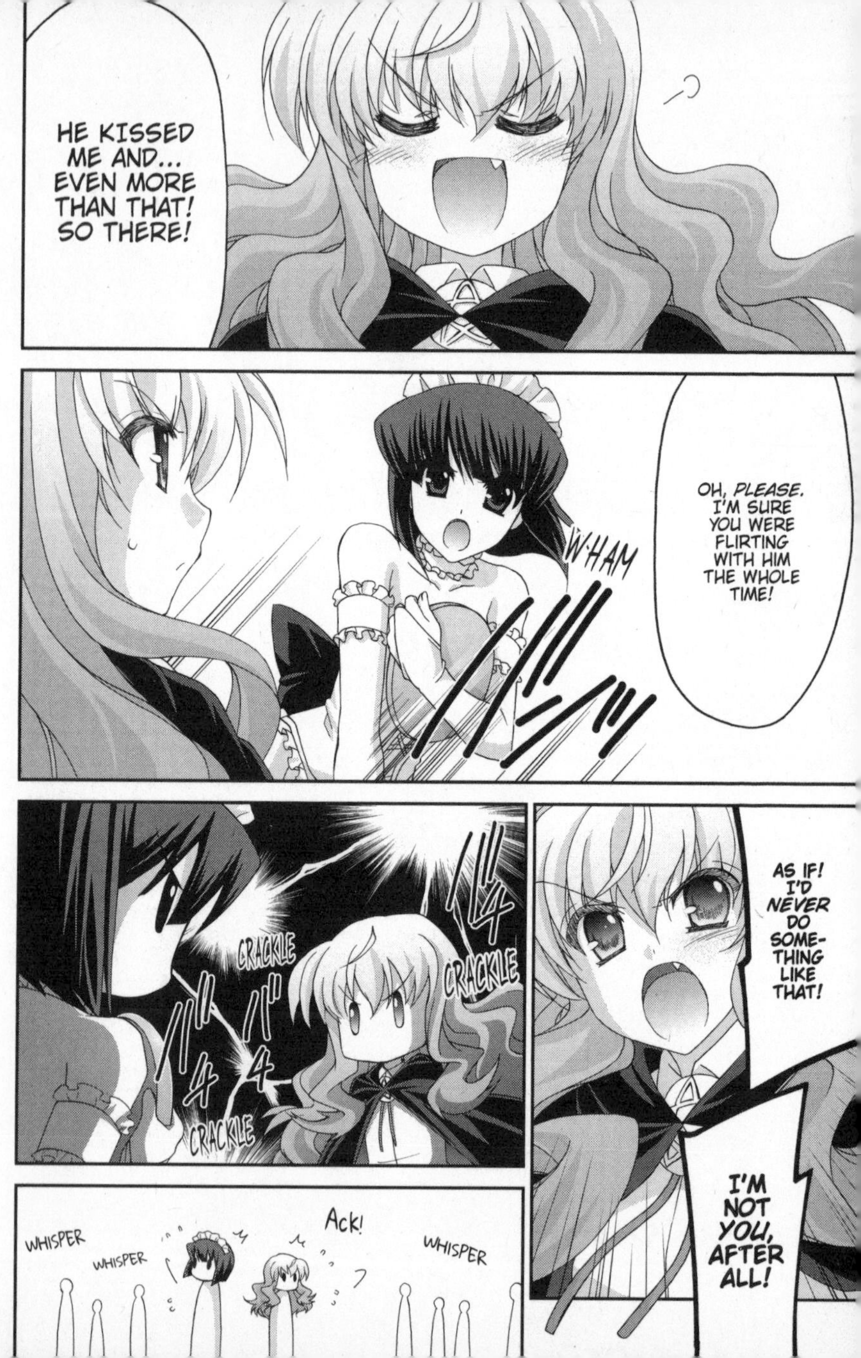
HE KISSED ME AND... EVEN MORE THAN THAT! SO THERE!
OH, *PLEASE*. I'M SURE YOU WERE FLIRTING WITH HIM THE WHOLE TIME!
WHAM
AS IF! I'D *NEVER* DO SOME-THING LIKE THAT!
I'M NOT *YOU*, AFTER ALL!
CRACKLE
CRACKLE
CRACKLE
WHISPER
WHISPER
Ack!
WHISPER

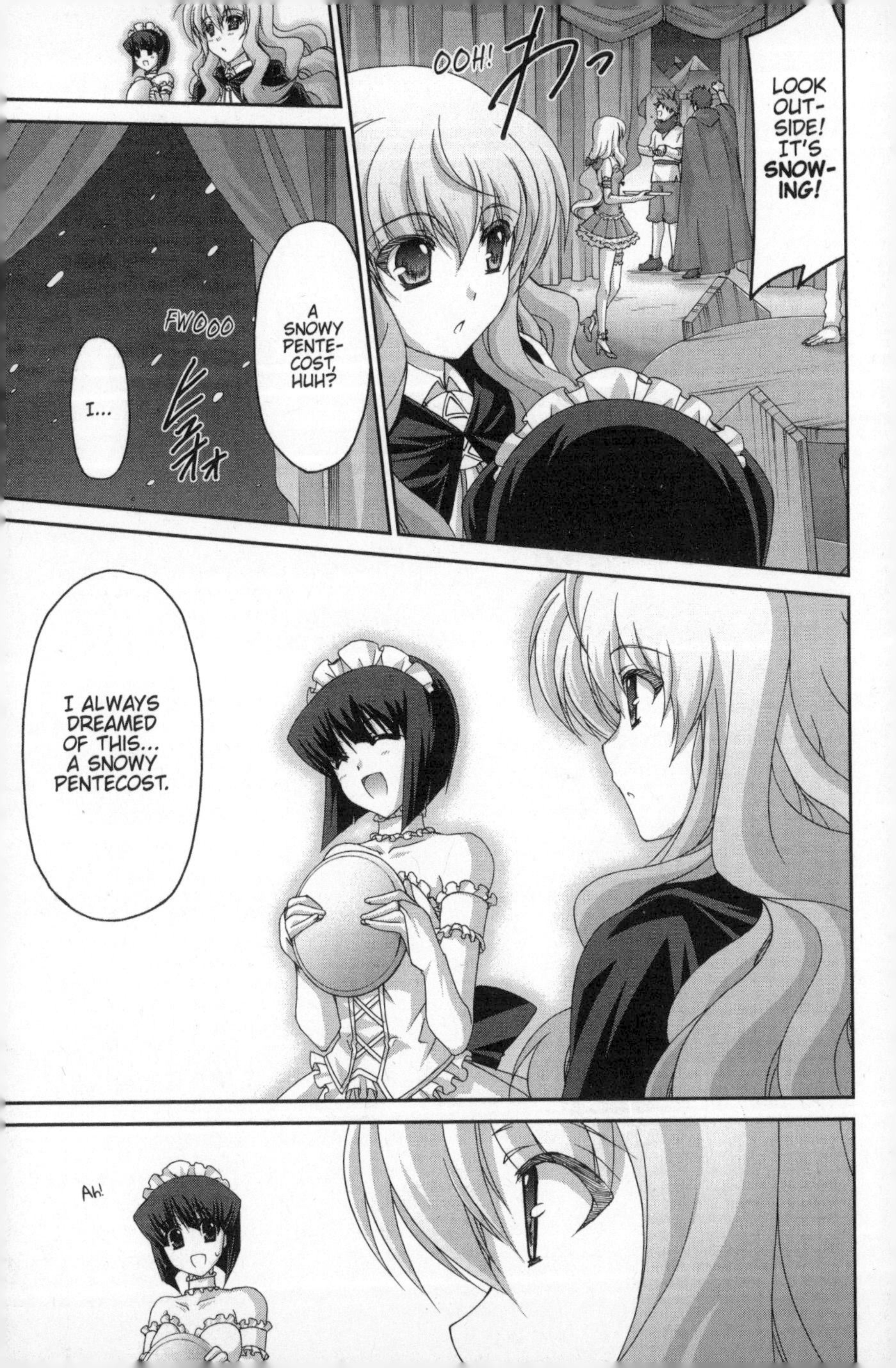
LOOK OUT-SIDE! IT'S SNOW-ING!
OOH!
わっ
A SNOWY PENTE-COST, HUH?
FWOOO
ヒュオオ
I...
I ALWAYS DREAMED OF THIS... A SNOWY PENTECOST.
Ah!

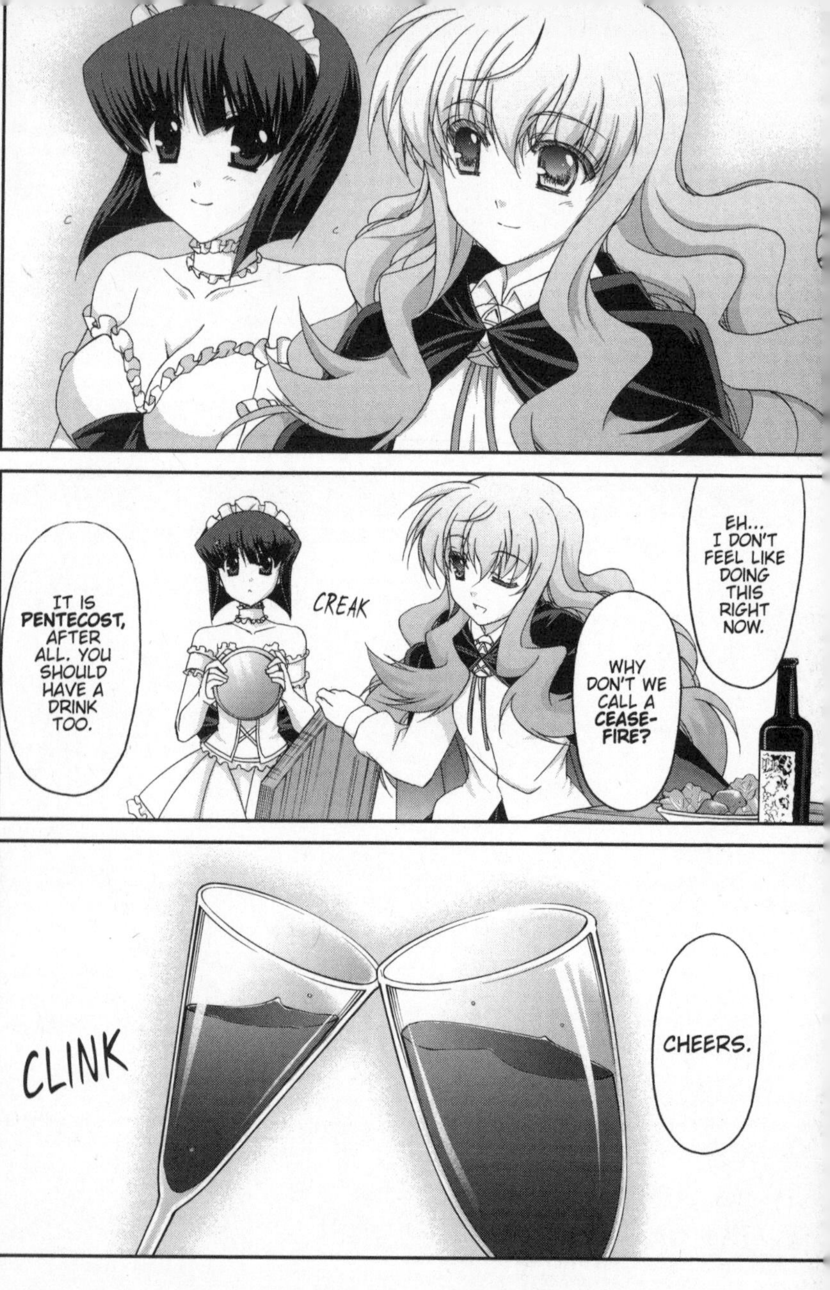
EH... I DON'T FEEL LIKE DOING THIS RIGHT NOW.
WHY DON'T WE CALL A CEASE-FIRE?
CREAK
IT IS PENTECOST, AFTER ALL. YOU SHOULD HAVE A DRINK TOO.
CHEERS.
CLINK

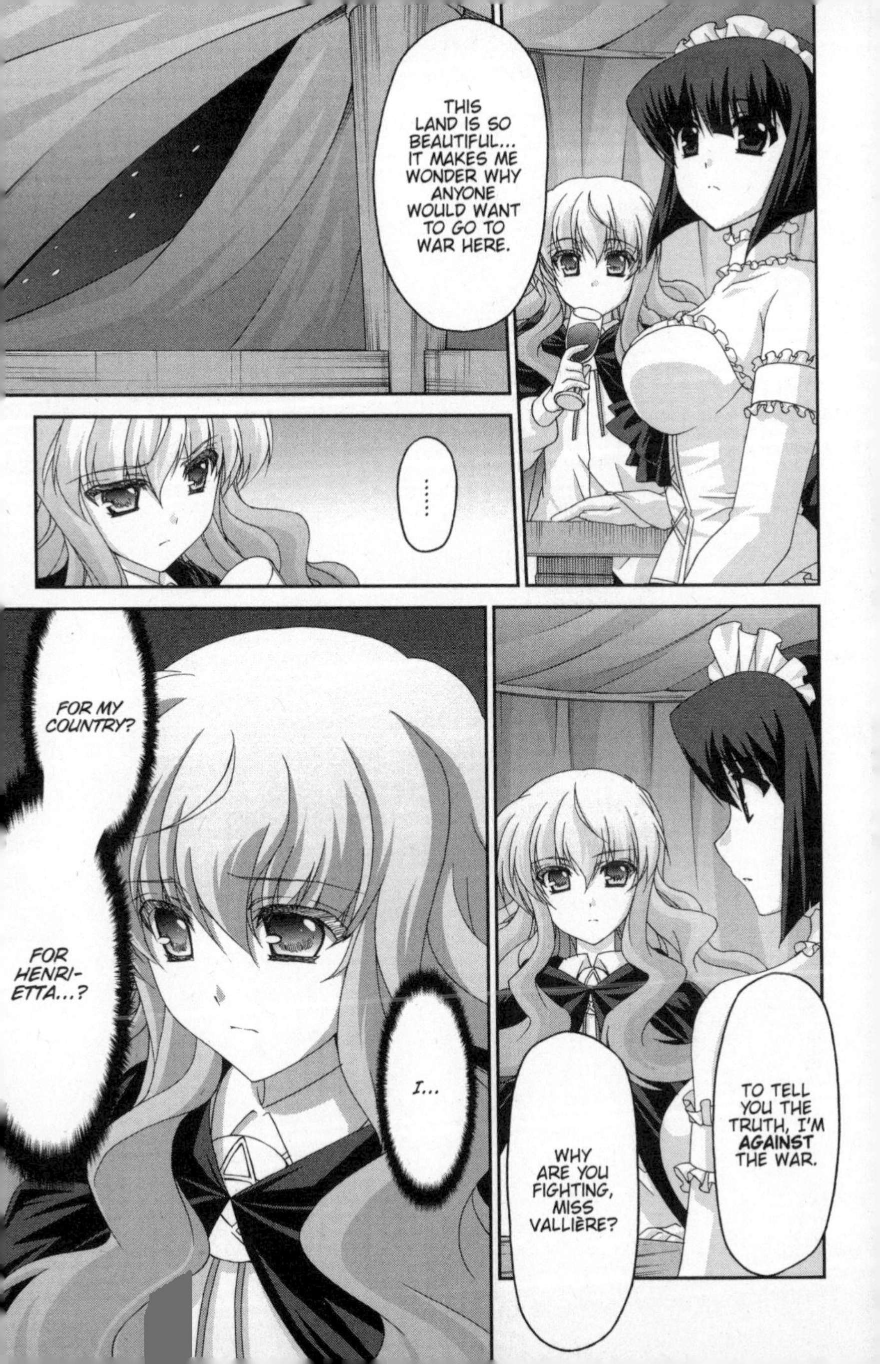
THIS LAND IS SO BEAUTIFUL... IT MAKES ME WONDER WHY ANYONE WOULD WANT TO GO TO WAR HERE.
......
TO TELL YOU THE TRUTH, I'M **AGAINST** THE WAR.
WHY ARE YOU FIGHTING, MISS VALLIÈRE?
FOR MY COUNTRY?
FOR HENRIETTA...?
I...

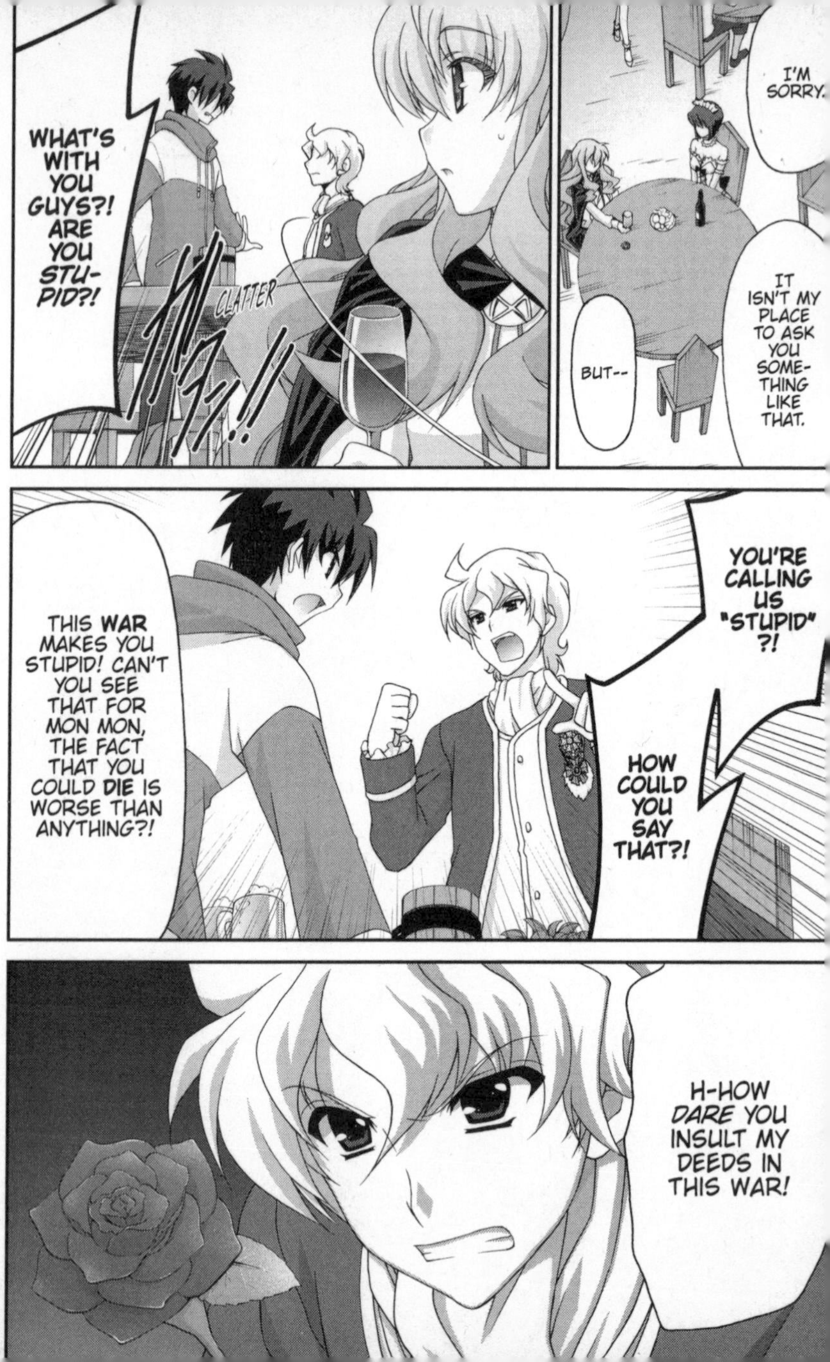
I'M SORRY.
IT ISN'T MY PLACE TO ASK YOU SOMETHING LIKE THAT.
BUT--
WHAT'S WITH YOU GUYS?! ARE YOU STUPID?!
CLATTER
YOU'RE CALLING US "STUPID"?!
HOW COULD YOU SAY THAT?!
THIS WAR MAKES YOU STUPID! CAN'T YOU SEE THAT FOR MON MON, THE FACT THAT YOU COULD DIE IS WORSE THAN ANYTHING?!
H-HOW DARE YOU INSULT MY DEEDS IN THIS WAR!

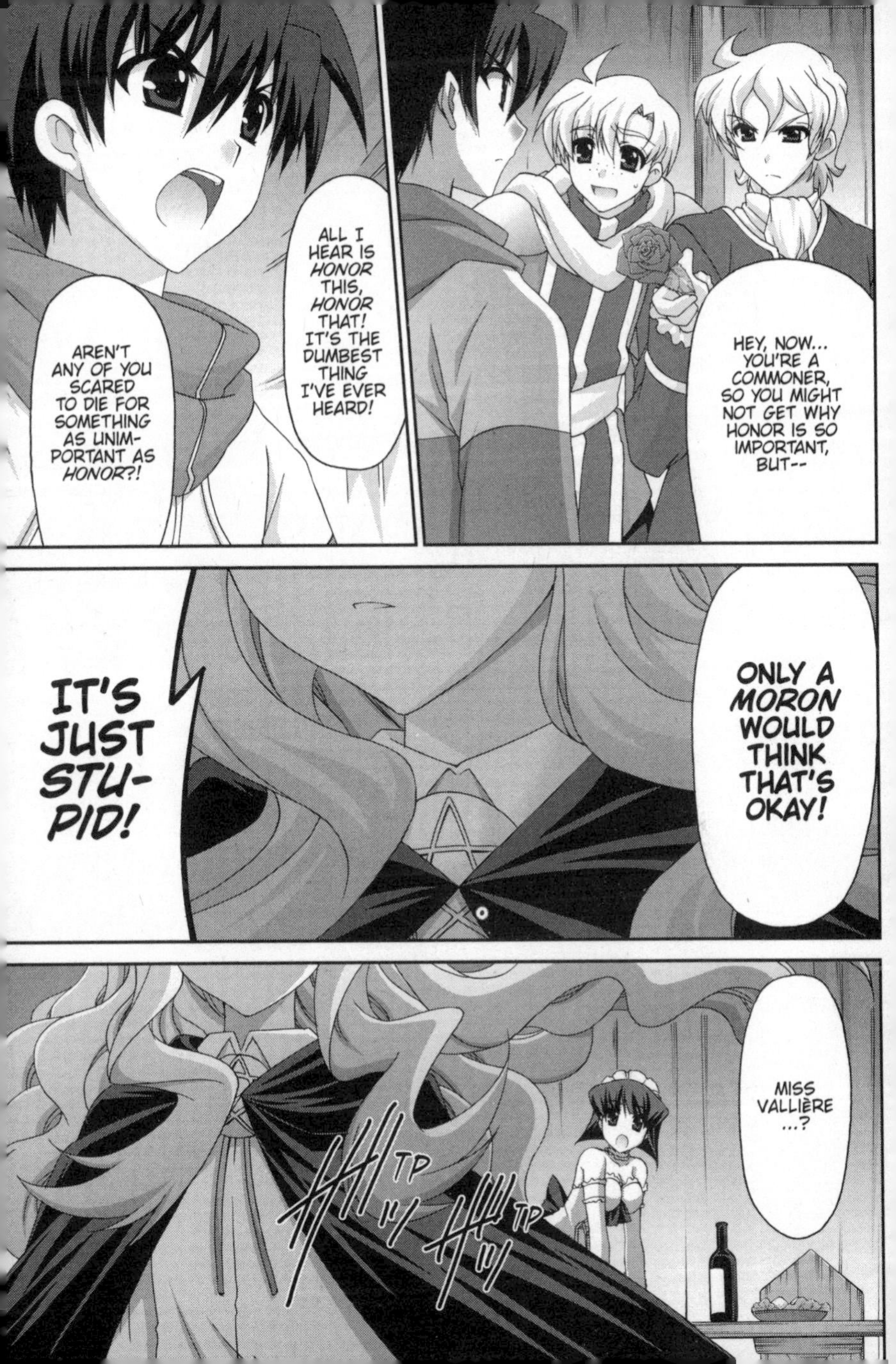
HEY, NOW... YOU'RE A COMMONER, SO YOU MIGHT NOT GET WHY HONOR IS SO IMPORTANT, BUT--
ALL I HEAR IS *HONOR* THIS, *HONOR* THAT! IT'S THE DUMBEST THING I'VE EVER HEARD!
AREN'T ANY OF YOU SCARED TO DIE FOR SOMETHING AS UNIMPORTANT AS *HONOR*?!
ONLY A *MORON* WOULD THINK THAT'S OKAY!
IT'S JUST STU-PID!
MISS VALLIÈRE ...?
TP
TP

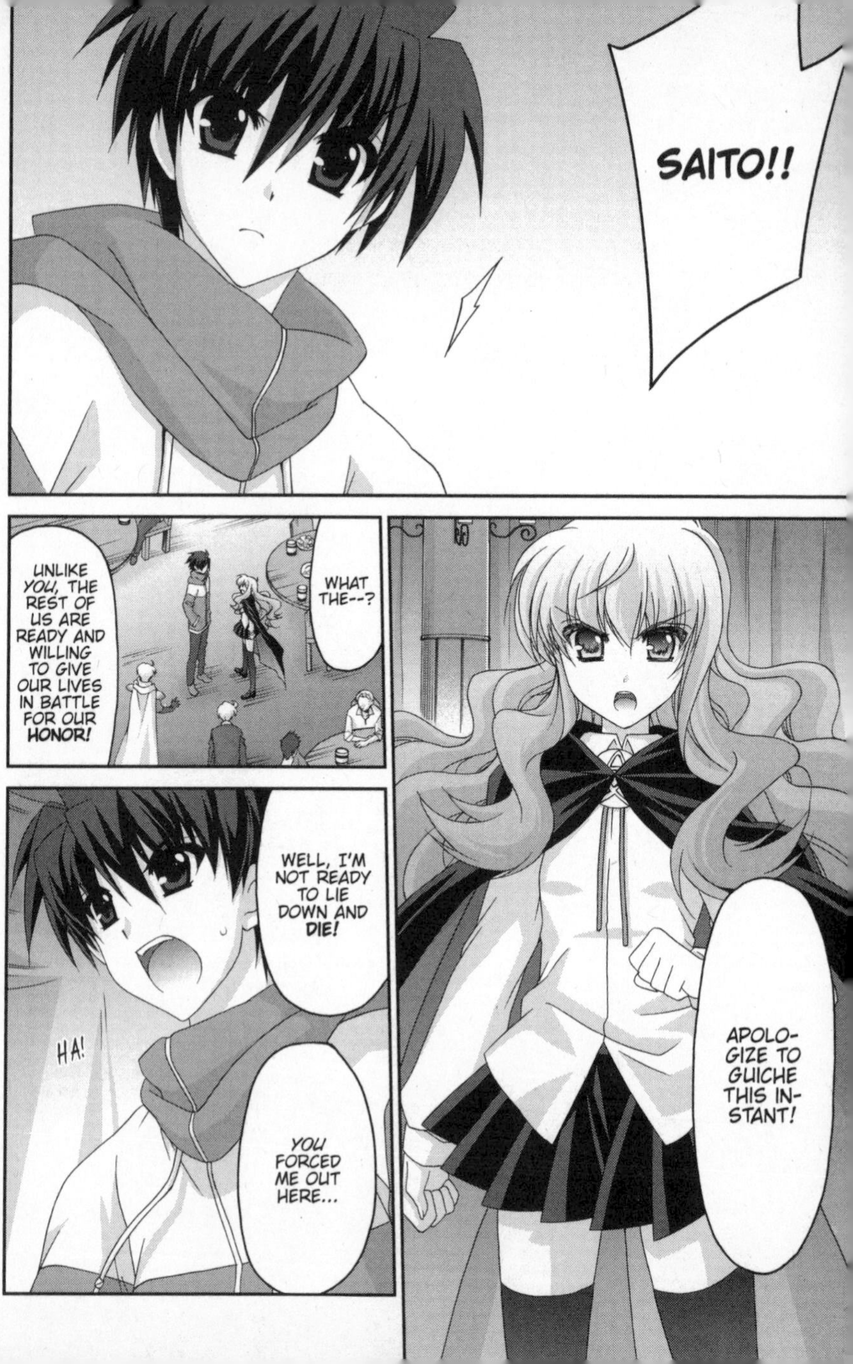
SAITO!!
APOLO-
GIZE TO
GUICHE
THIS IN-
STANT!
WHAT THE--?
UNLIKE YOU, THE REST OF US ARE READY AND WILLING TO GIVE OUR LIVES IN BATTLE FOR OUR HONOR!
WELL, I'M NOT READY TO LIE DOWN AND DIE!
HA!
YOU FORCED ME OUT HERE...

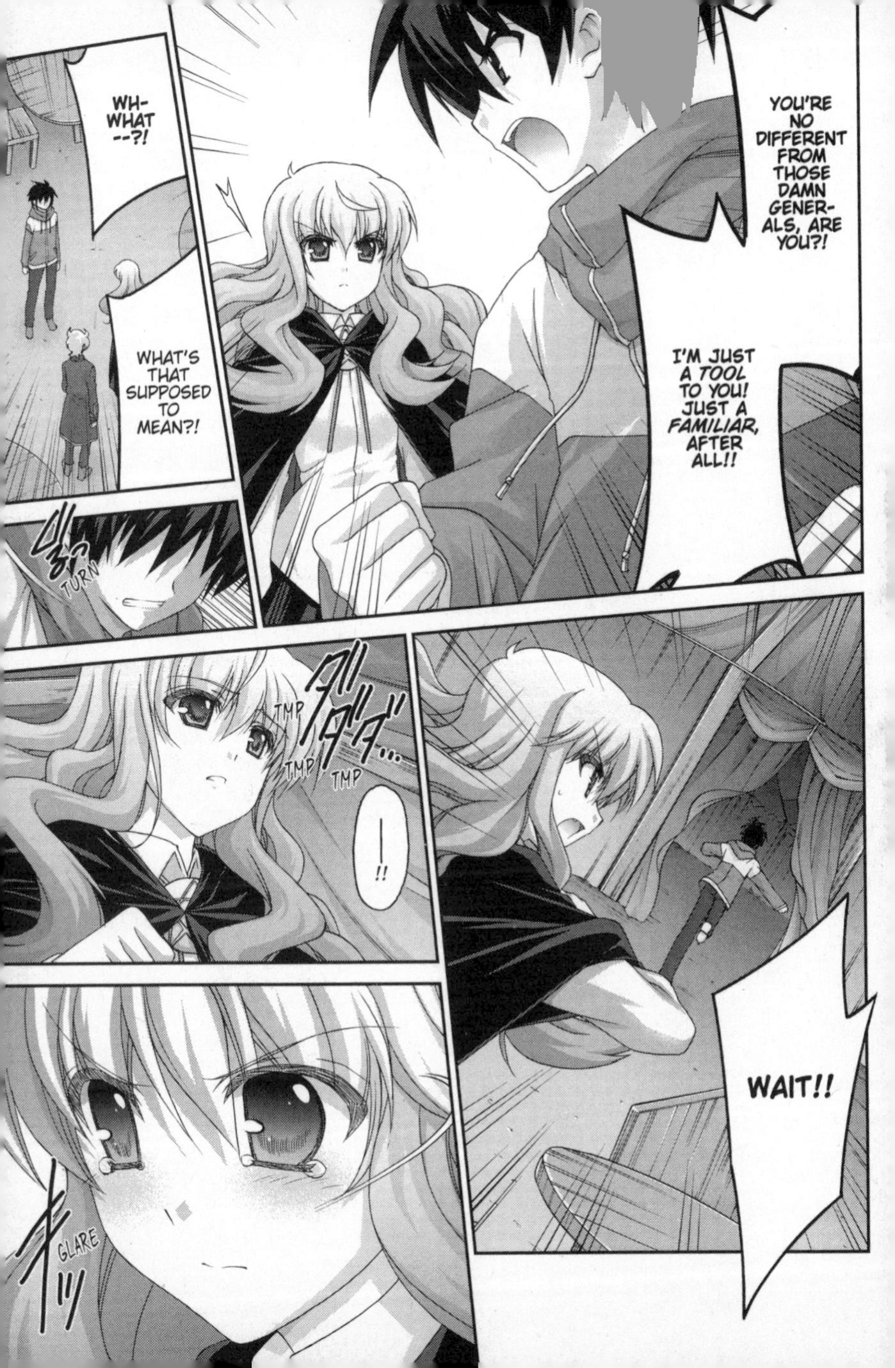
YOU'RE NO DIFFERENT FROM THOSE DAMN GENER-ALS, ARE YOU?!
I'M JUST A *TOOL* TO YOU! JUST A *FAMILIAR*, AFTER ALL!!
WH- WHAT --?!
WHAT'S THAT SUPPOSED TO MEAN?!
TURN
WAIT!!
TMP
TMP TMP
—!!
GLARE

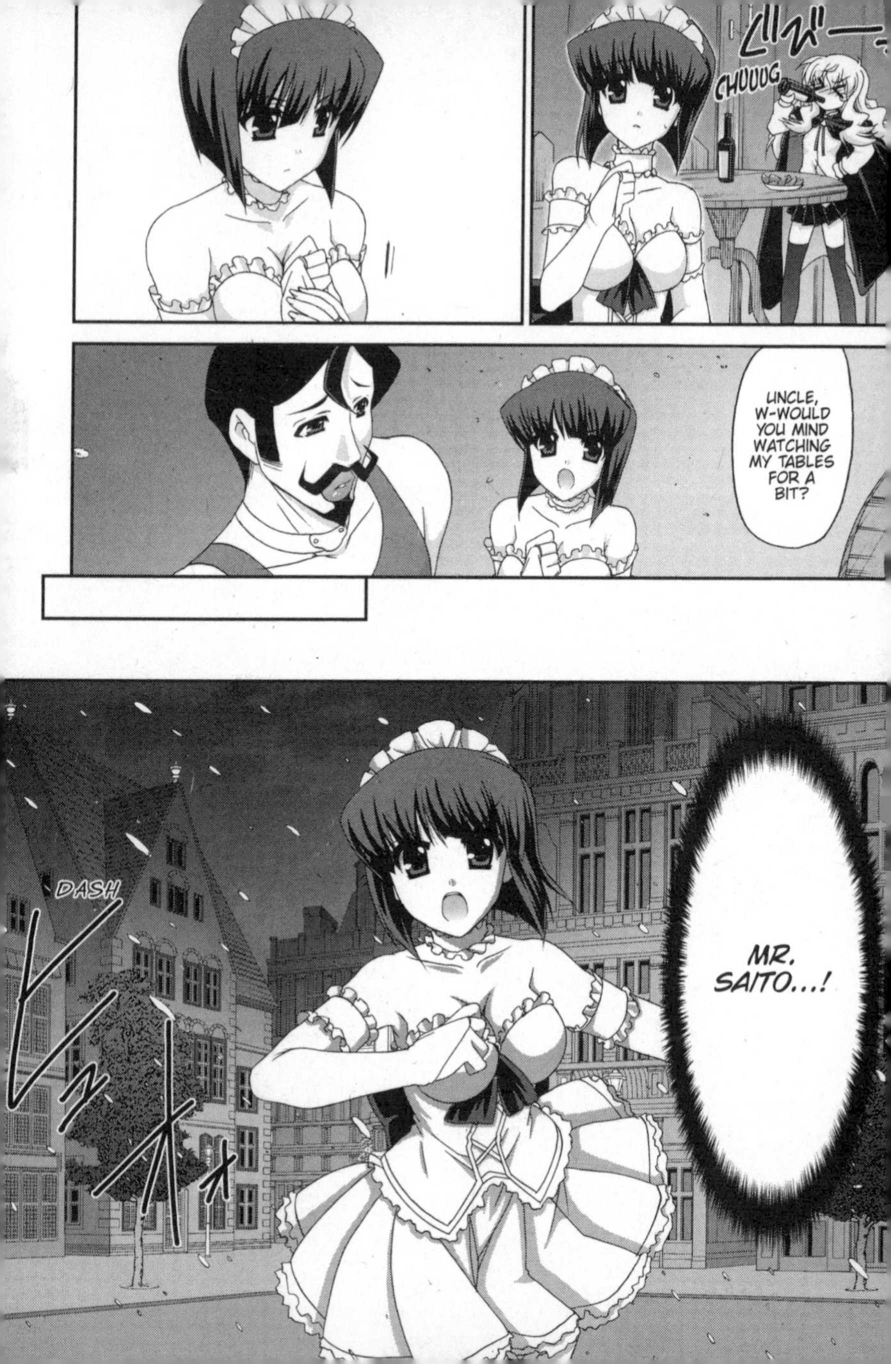
CHUUUG
UNCLE, W-WOULD YOU MIND WATCHING MY TABLES FOR A BIT?
MR. SAITO...!
DASH

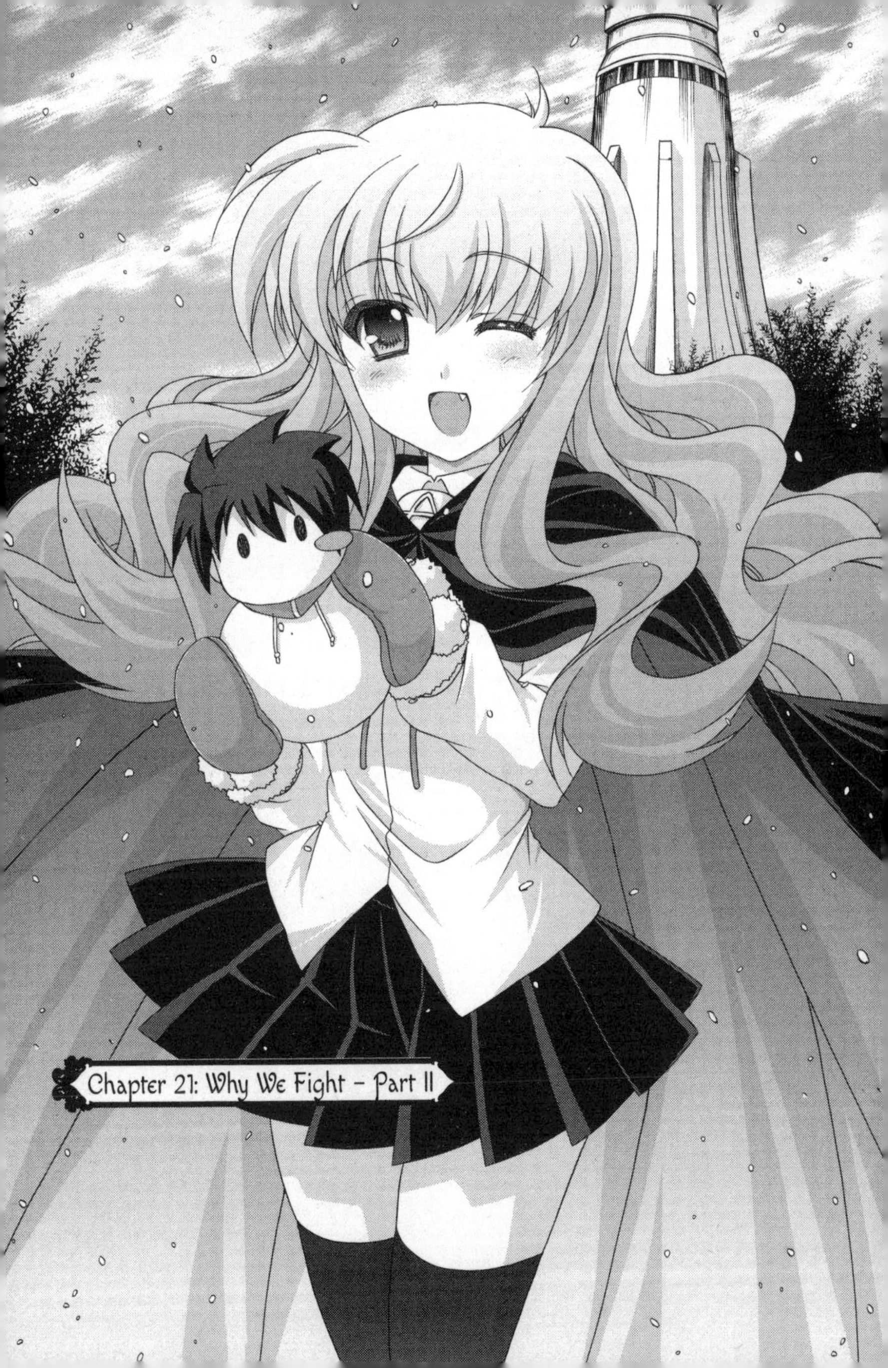
Chapter 21: Why We Fight - Part II

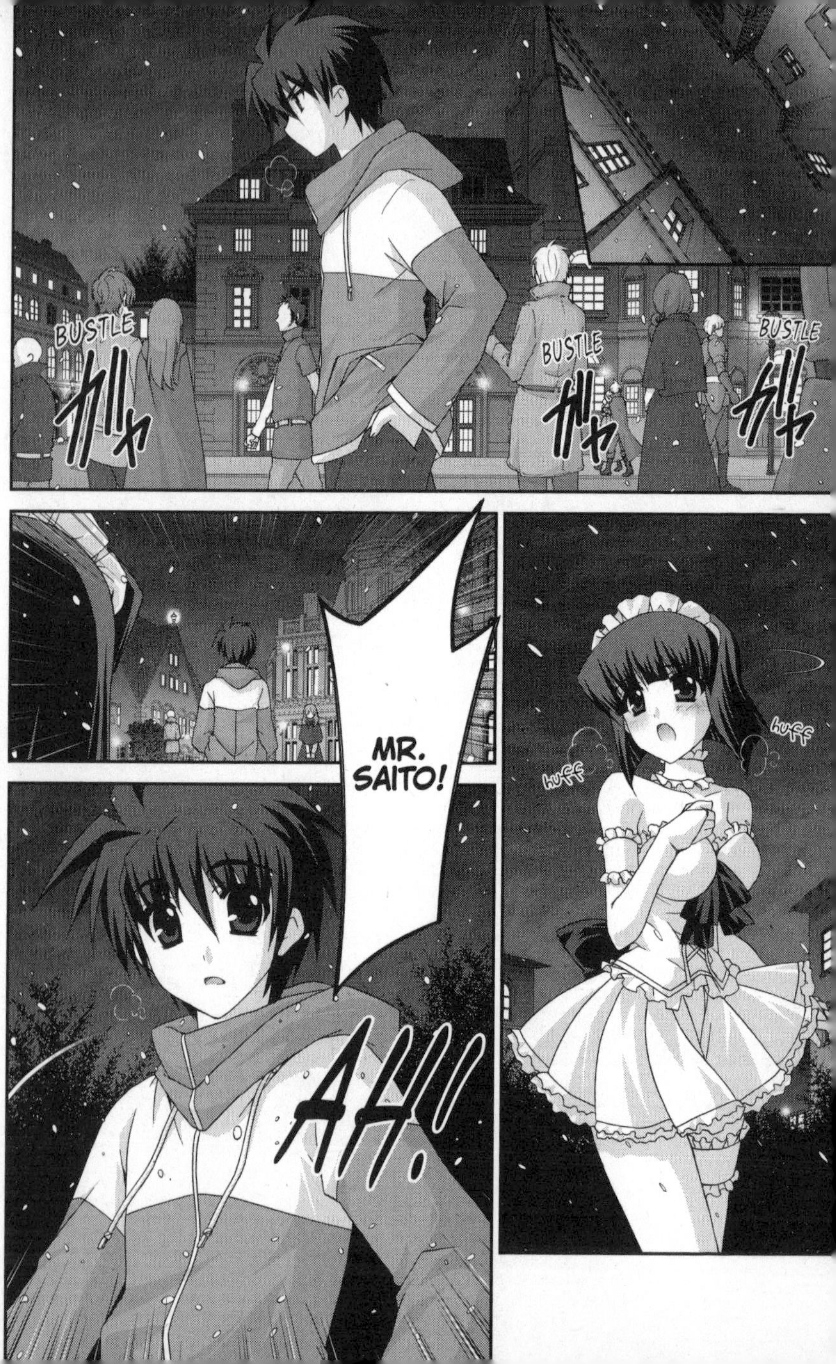
BUSTLE
BUSTLE
BUSTLE
MR. SAITO!
huff
huff
AH!

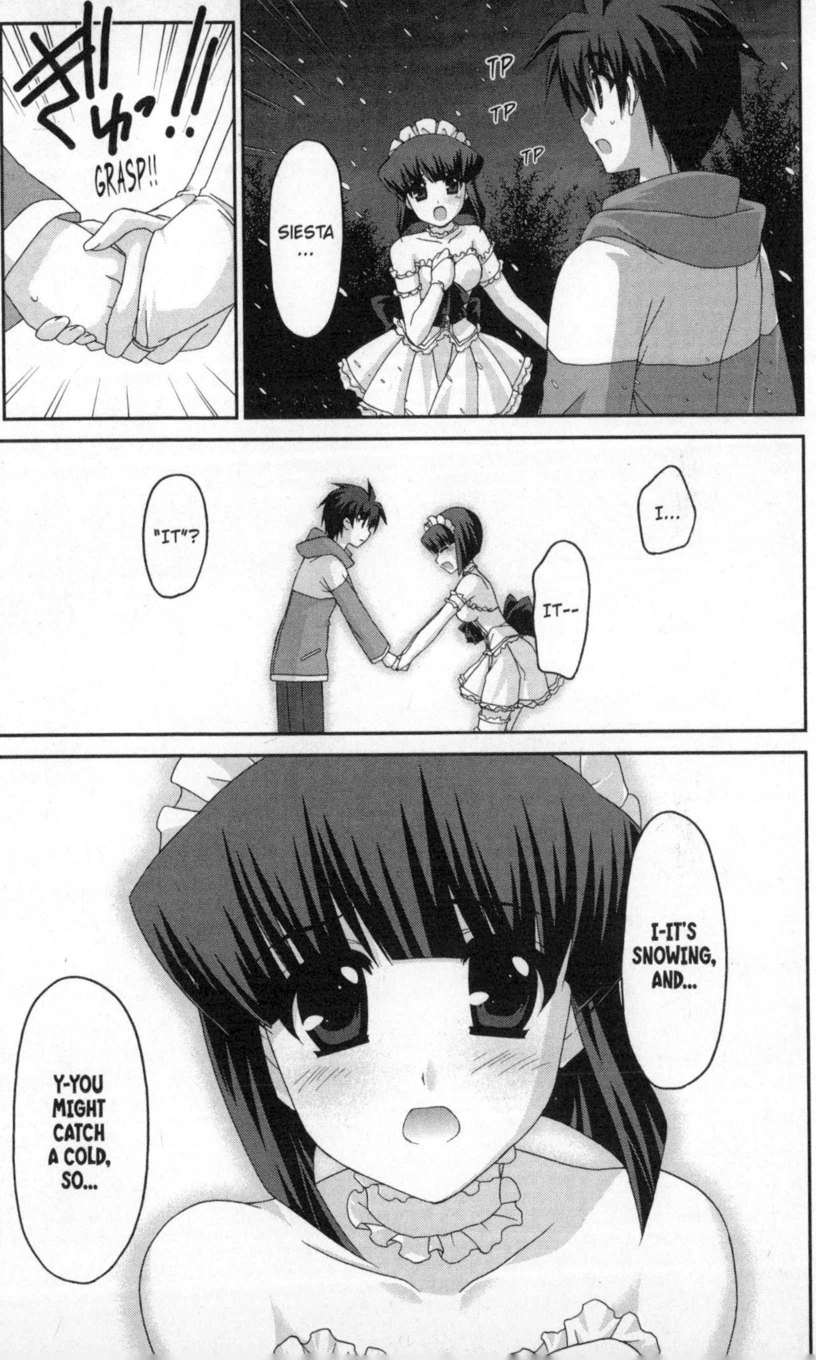

TP TP TP
SIESTA ...
ぎゅっ!!
GRASP!!
I...
IT--
"IT"?
I-IT'S SNOWING, AND...
Y-YOU MIGHT CATCH A COLD, SO...

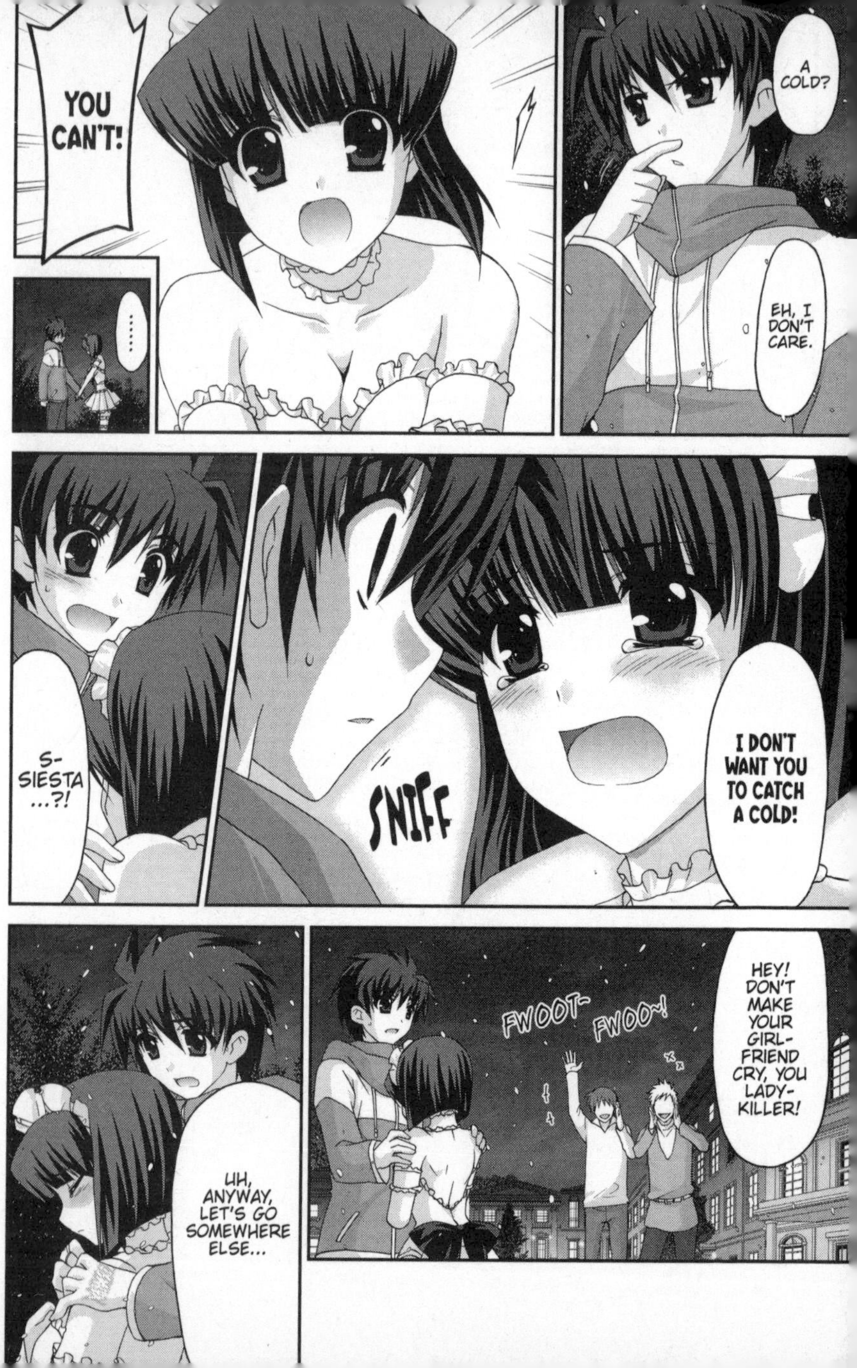
A COLD?
EH, I DON'T CARE.
YOU CAN'T!
......
I DON'T WANT YOU TO CATCH A COLD!
SNIFF
S-SIESTA ...?!
HEY! DON'T MAKE YOUR GIRLFRIEND CRY, YOU LADY-KILLER!
FWOOT-FWOO~!
UH, ANYWAY, LET'S GO SOMEWHERE ELSE...

BUSTLE

BUSTLE

I'M SORRY.

CLATTER

MAN, I CAN'T BELIEVE THEY CHARGE A GOLD ECU FOR A CRAPPY ROOM LIKE THIS.

WHAT'S WRONG?

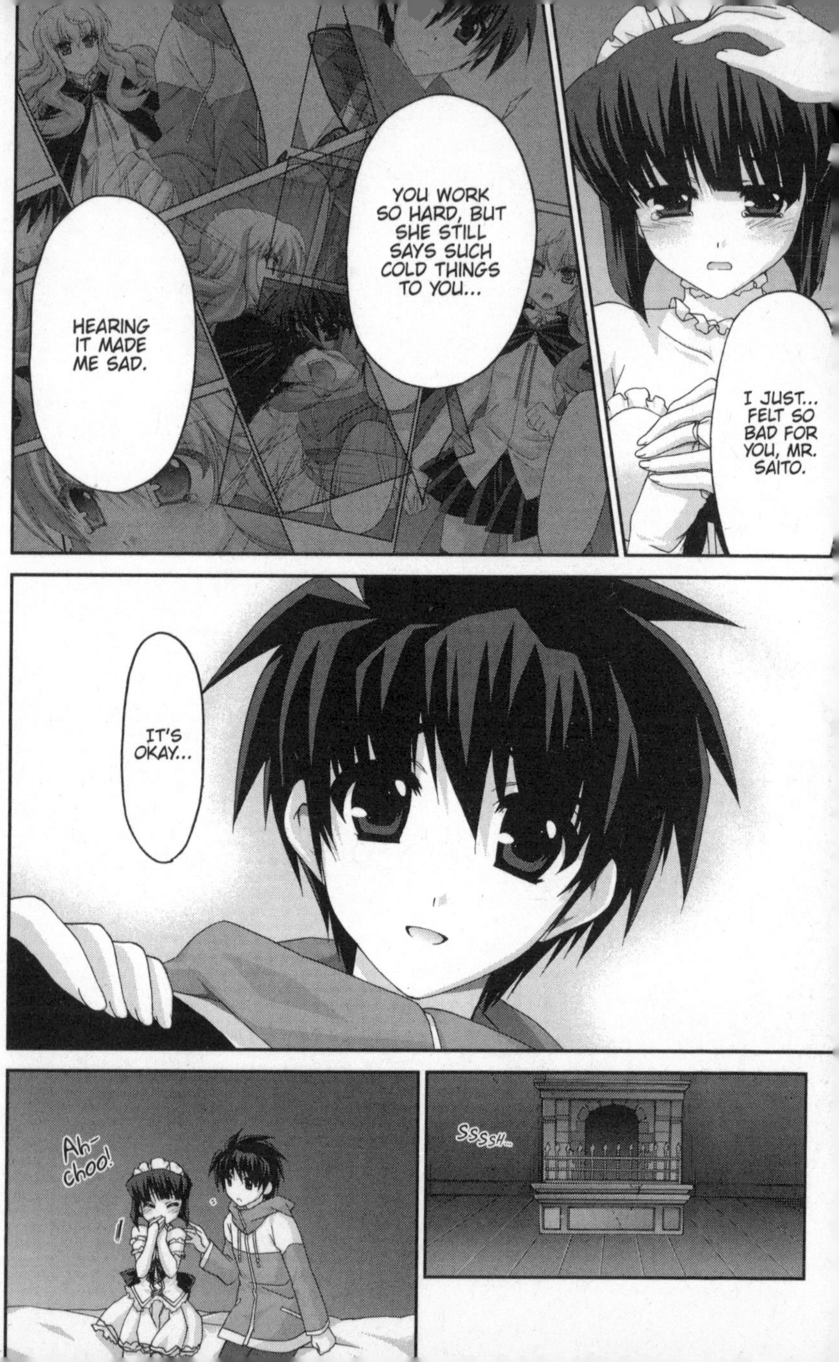
I JUST... FELT SO BAD FOR YOU, MR. SAITO.
YOU WORK SO HARD, BUT SHE STILL SAYS SUCH COLD THINGS TO YOU...
HEARING IT MADE ME SAD.
IT'S OKAY...
SSSSH...
Ah-choo!

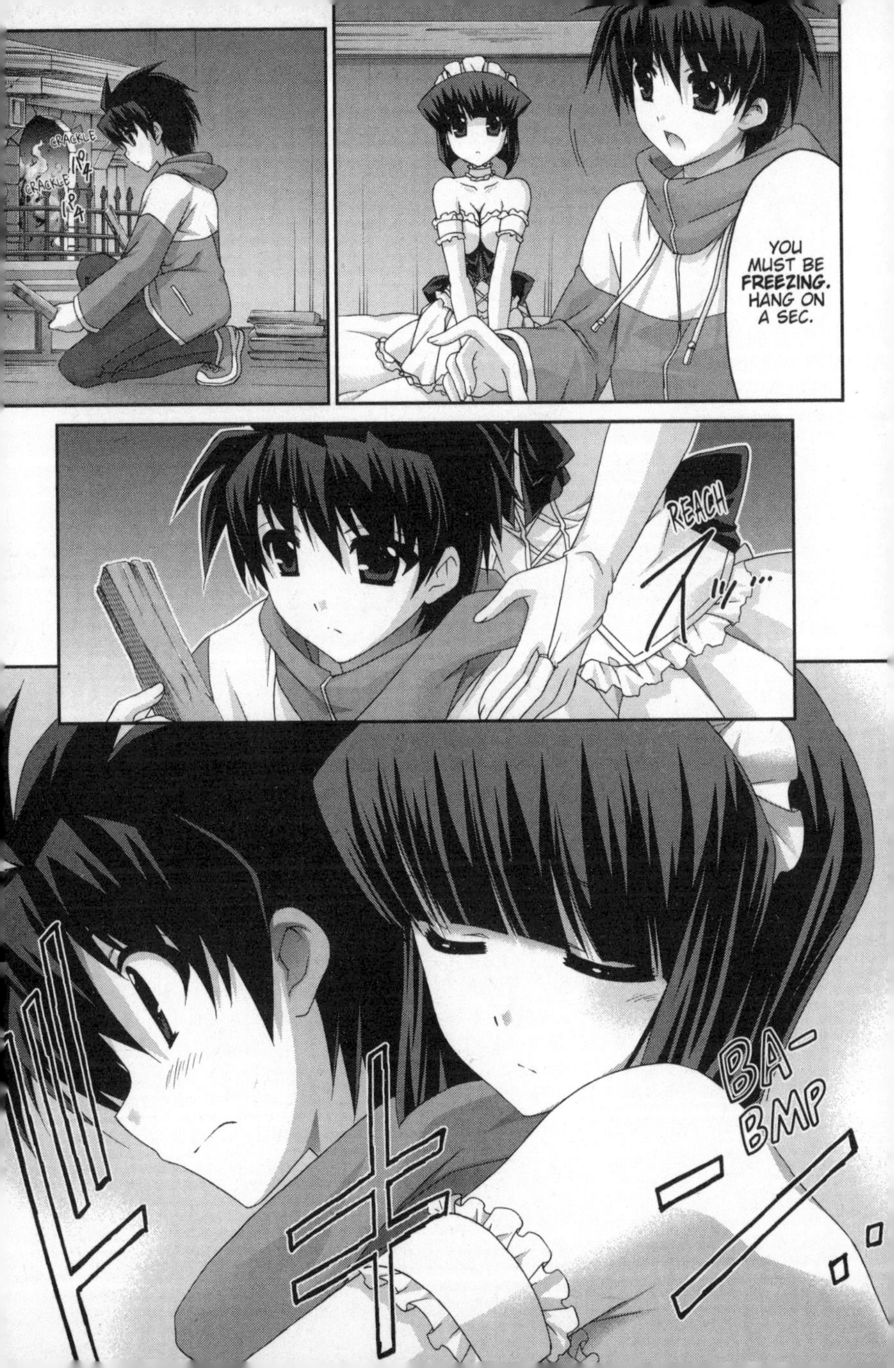
YOU MUST BE FREEZING. HANG ON A SEC.
CRACKLE
CRACKLE
REACH
BA-BMP

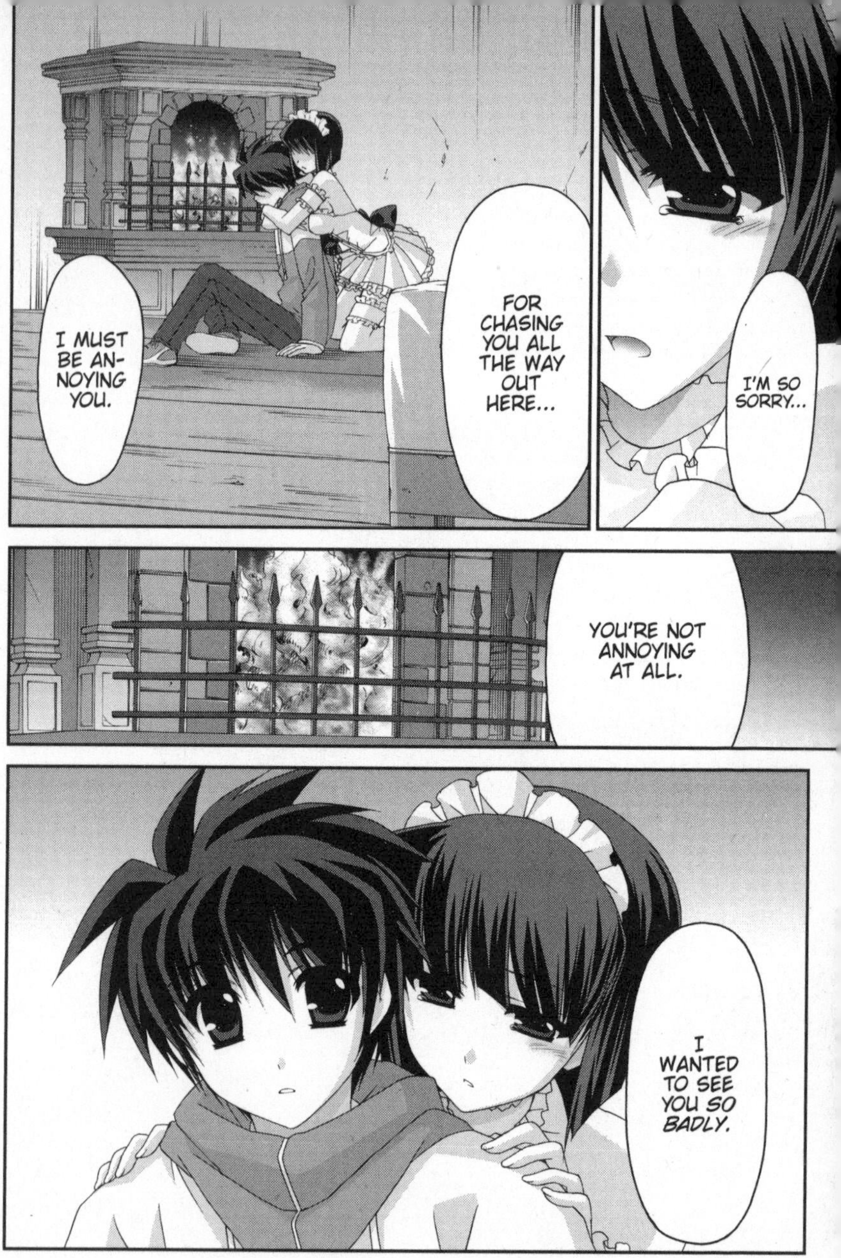
I'M SO SORRY...
FOR CHASING YOU ALL THE WAY OUT HERE...
I MUST BE AN-NOYING YOU.
YOU'RE NOT ANNOYING AT ALL.
I WANTED TO SEE YOU SO BADLY.

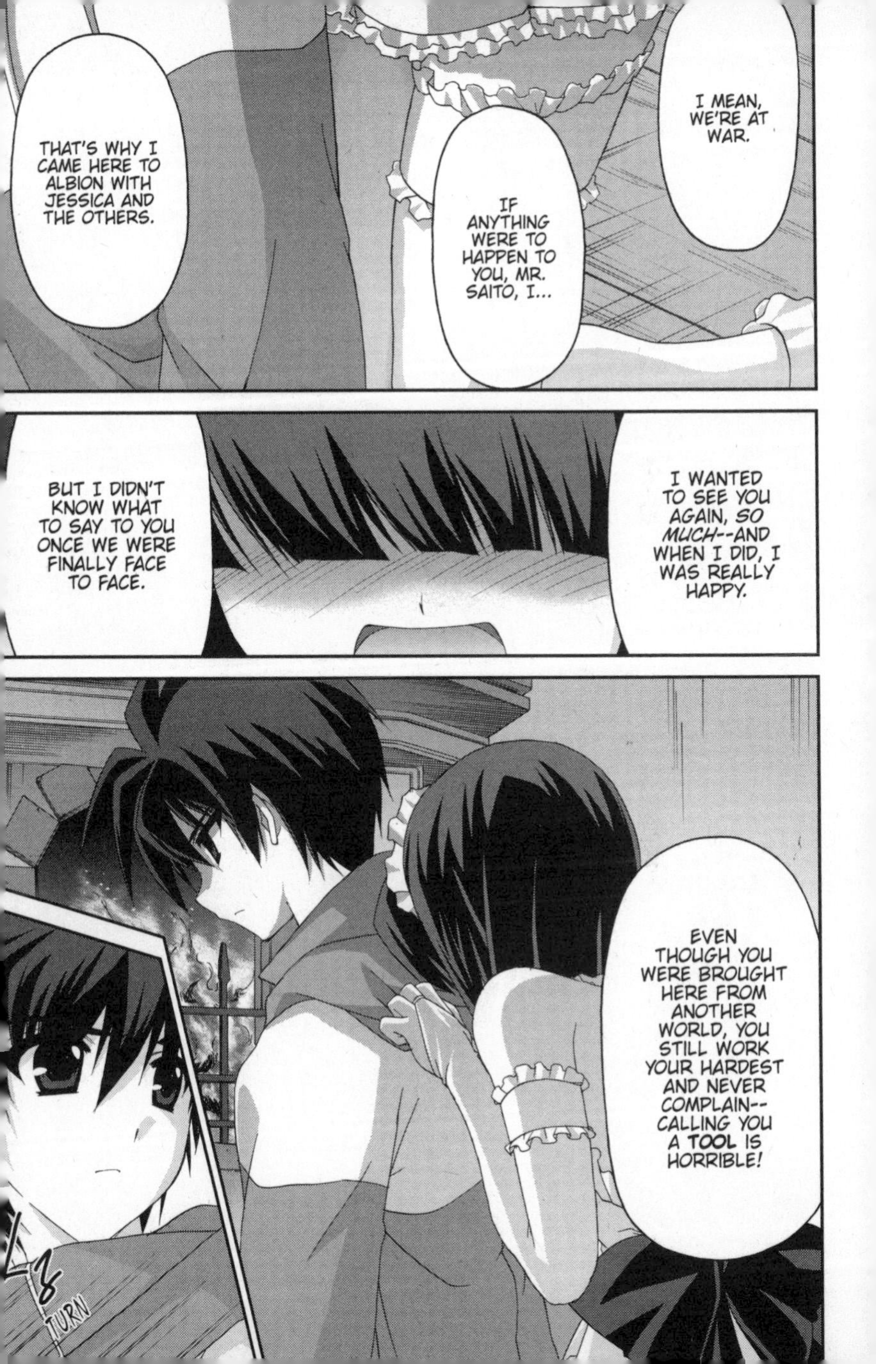
I MEAN, WE'RE AT WAR.
IF ANYTHING WERE TO HAPPEN TO YOU, MR. SAITO, I...
THAT'S WHY I CAME HERE TO ALBION WITH JESSICA AND THE OTHERS.
I WANTED TO SEE YOU AGAIN, *SO MUCH*--AND WHEN I DID, I WAS REALLY HAPPY.
BUT I DIDN'T KNOW WHAT TO SAY TO YOU ONCE WE WERE FINALLY FACE TO FACE.
EVEN THOUGH YOU WERE BROUGHT HERE FROM ANOTHER WORLD, YOU STILL WORK YOUR HARDEST AND NEVER COMPLAIN--CALLING YOU A **TOOL** IS HORRIBLE!
TURN

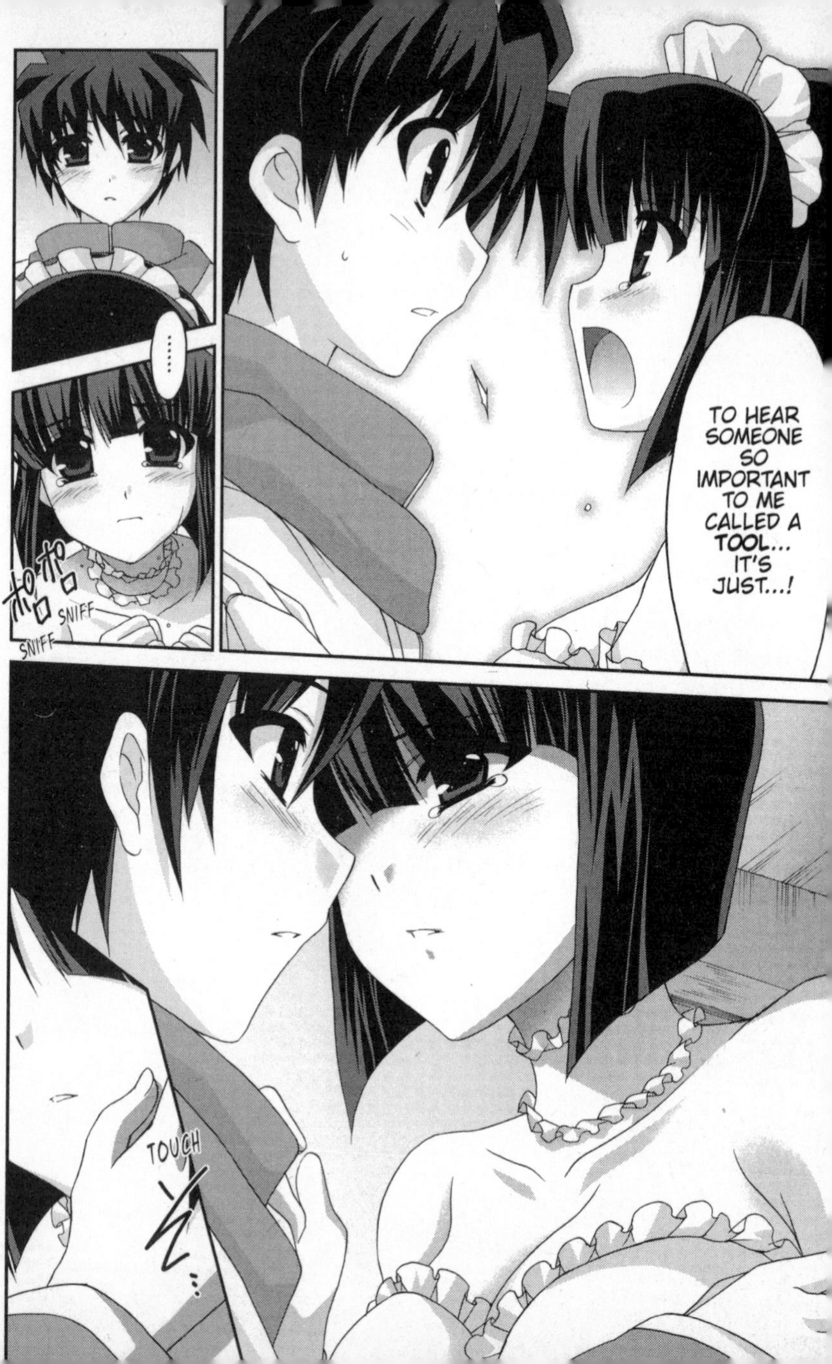
TO HEAR SOMEONE SO IMPORTANT TO ME CALLED A TOOL... IT'S JUST...!
......
ポロポロ
SNIFF
SNIFF
TOUCH

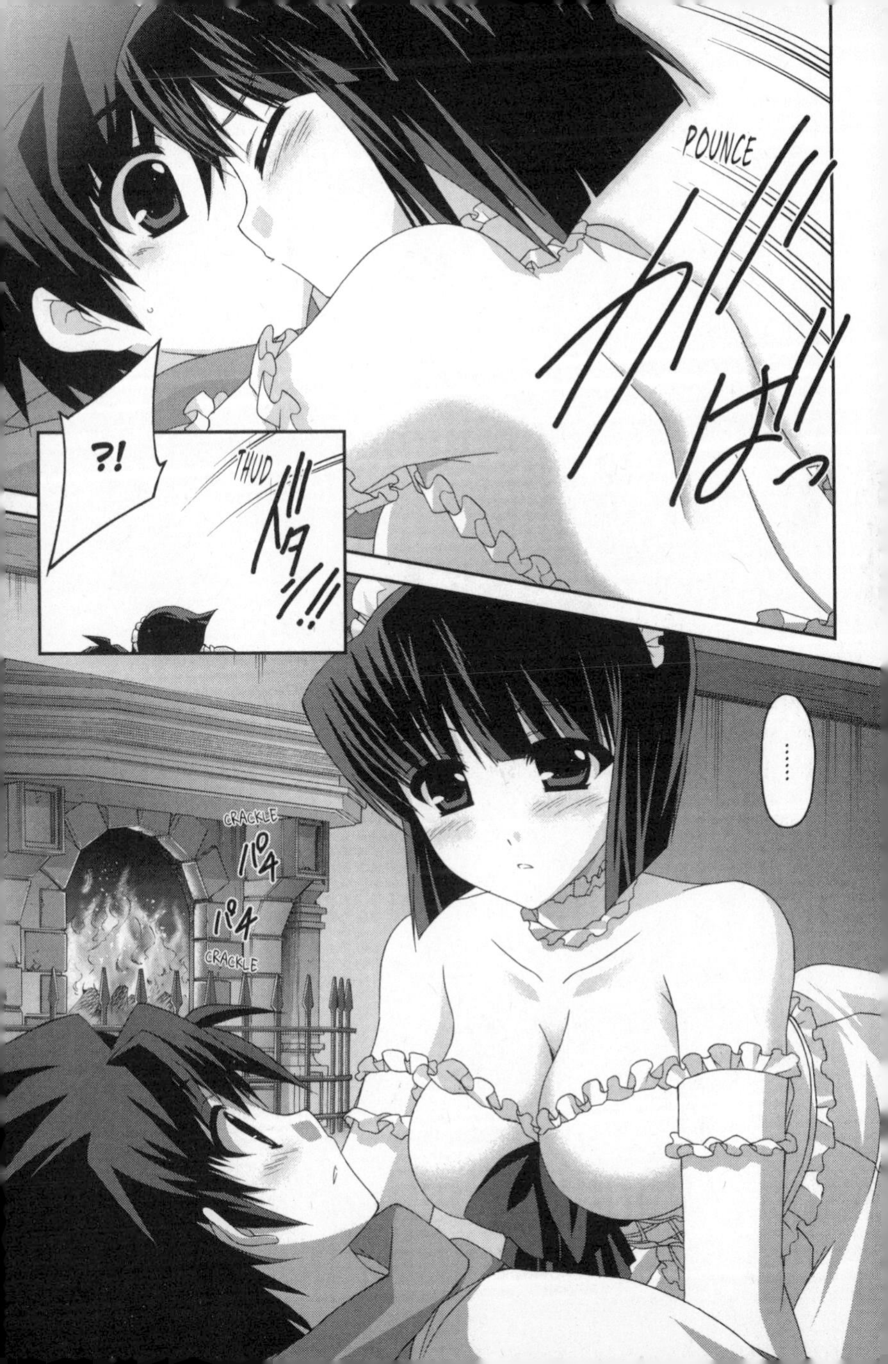

POUNCE
がばっ
?!
THUD
ドサッ!!!
......
CRACKLE
パチ
パチ
CRACKLE

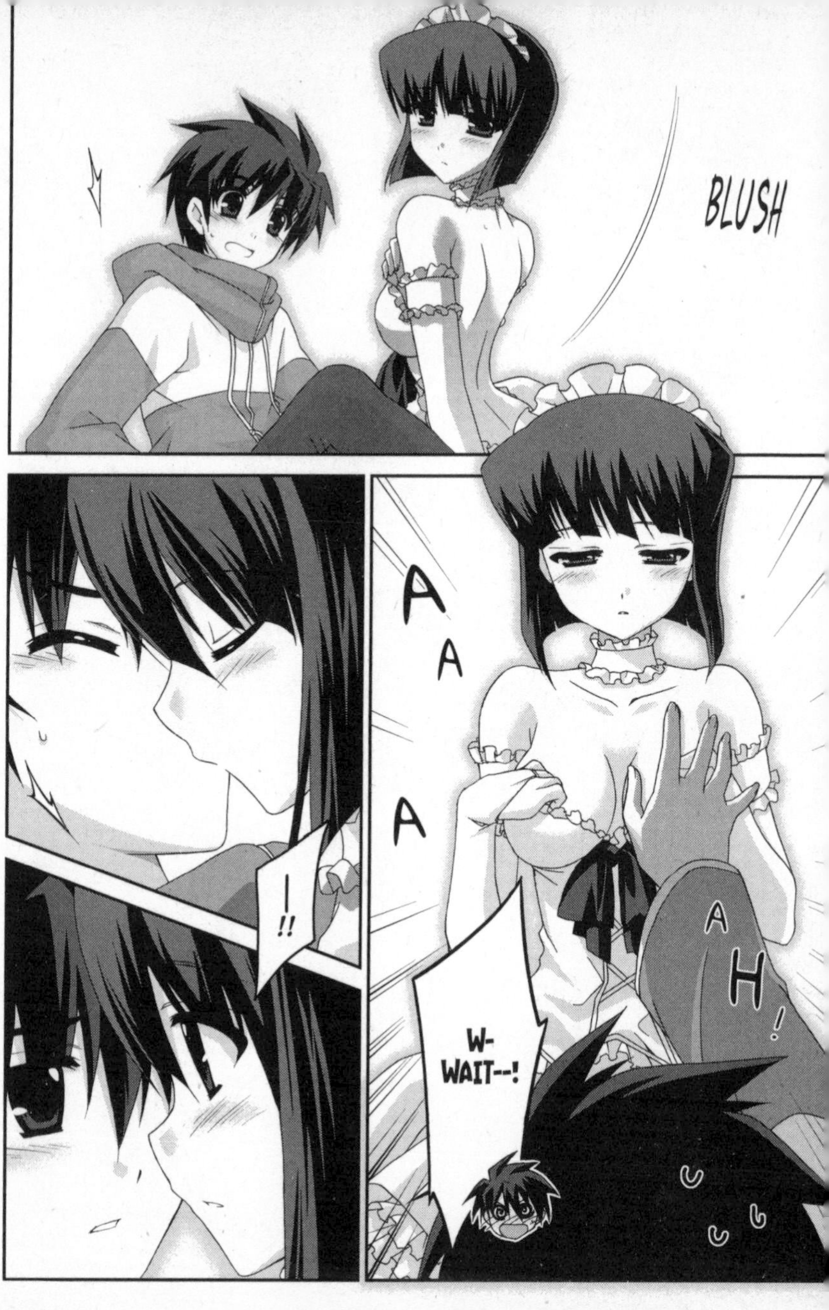
BLUSH
A
A
A
AH!
W-
WAIT--!
!
!!

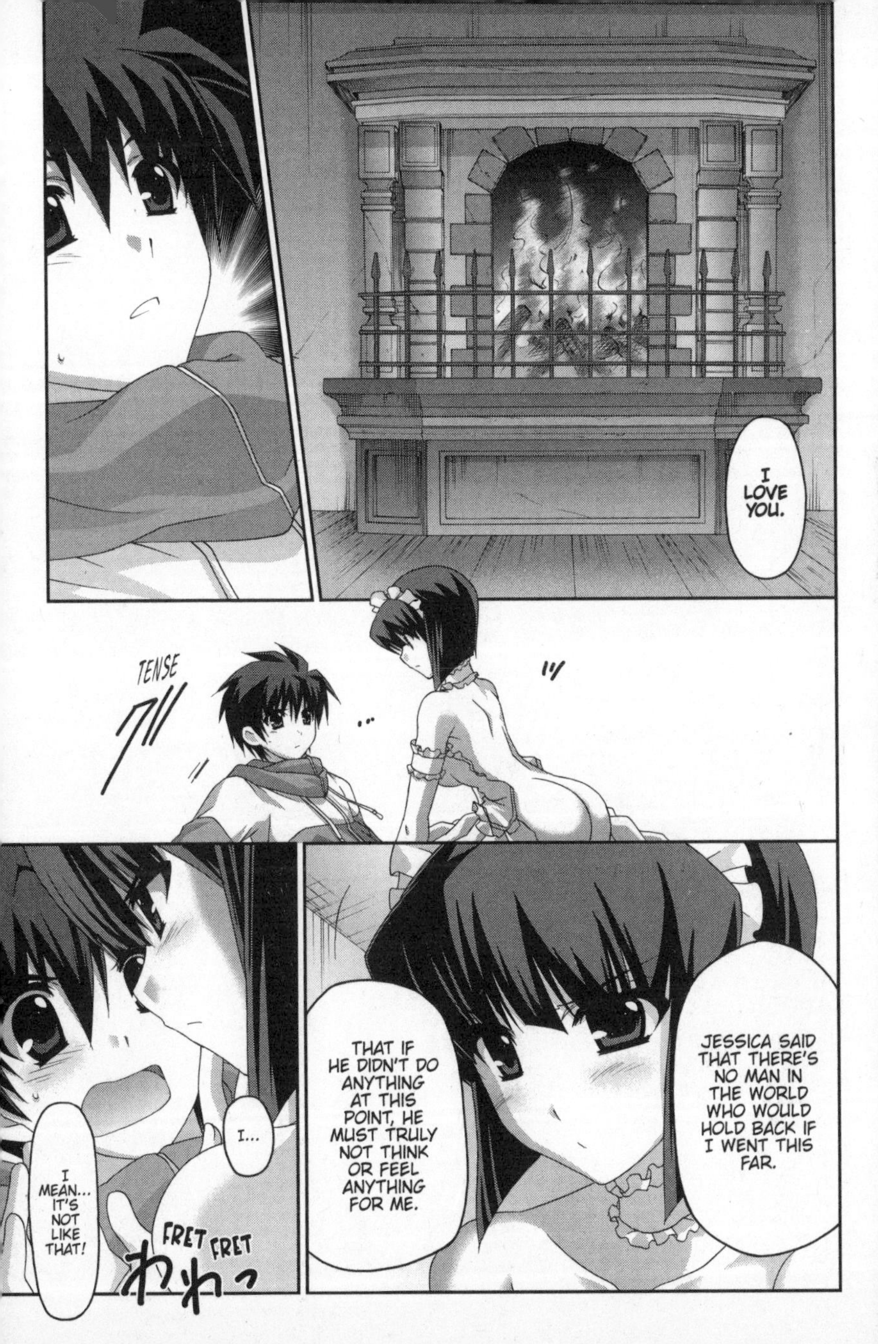
I LOVE YOU.
TENSE
...
JESSICA SAID THAT THERE'S NO MAN IN THE WORLD WHO WOULD HOLD BACK IF I WENT THIS FAR.
THAT IF HE DIDN'T DO ANYTHING AT THIS POINT, HE MUST TRULY NOT THINK OR FEEL ANYTHING FOR ME.
I...
I MEAN... IT'S NOT LIKE THAT!
FRET FRET
わわっ

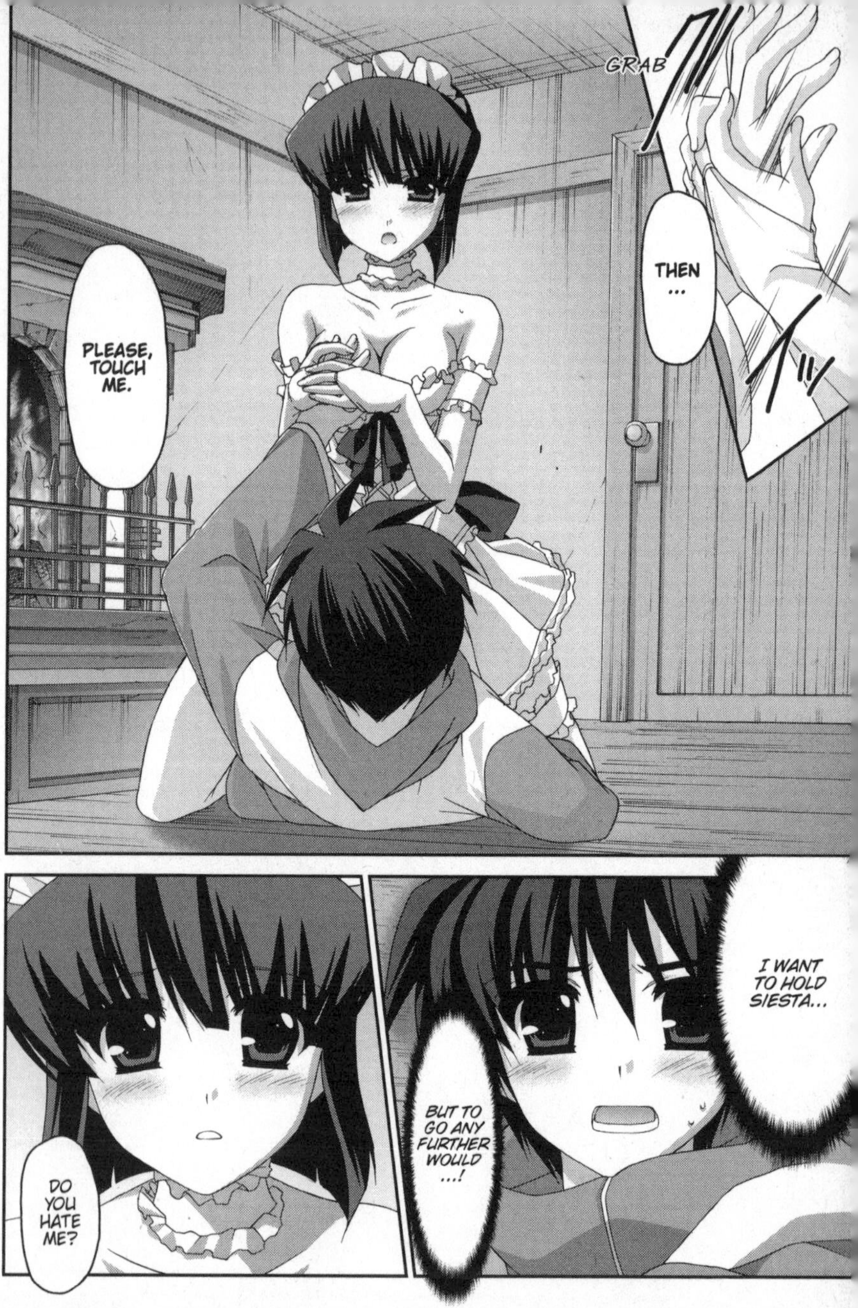
GRAB
THEN ...
PLEASE, TOUCH ME.
I WANT TO HOLD SIESTA...
BUT TO GO ANY FURTHER WOULD ...!
DO YOU HATE ME?

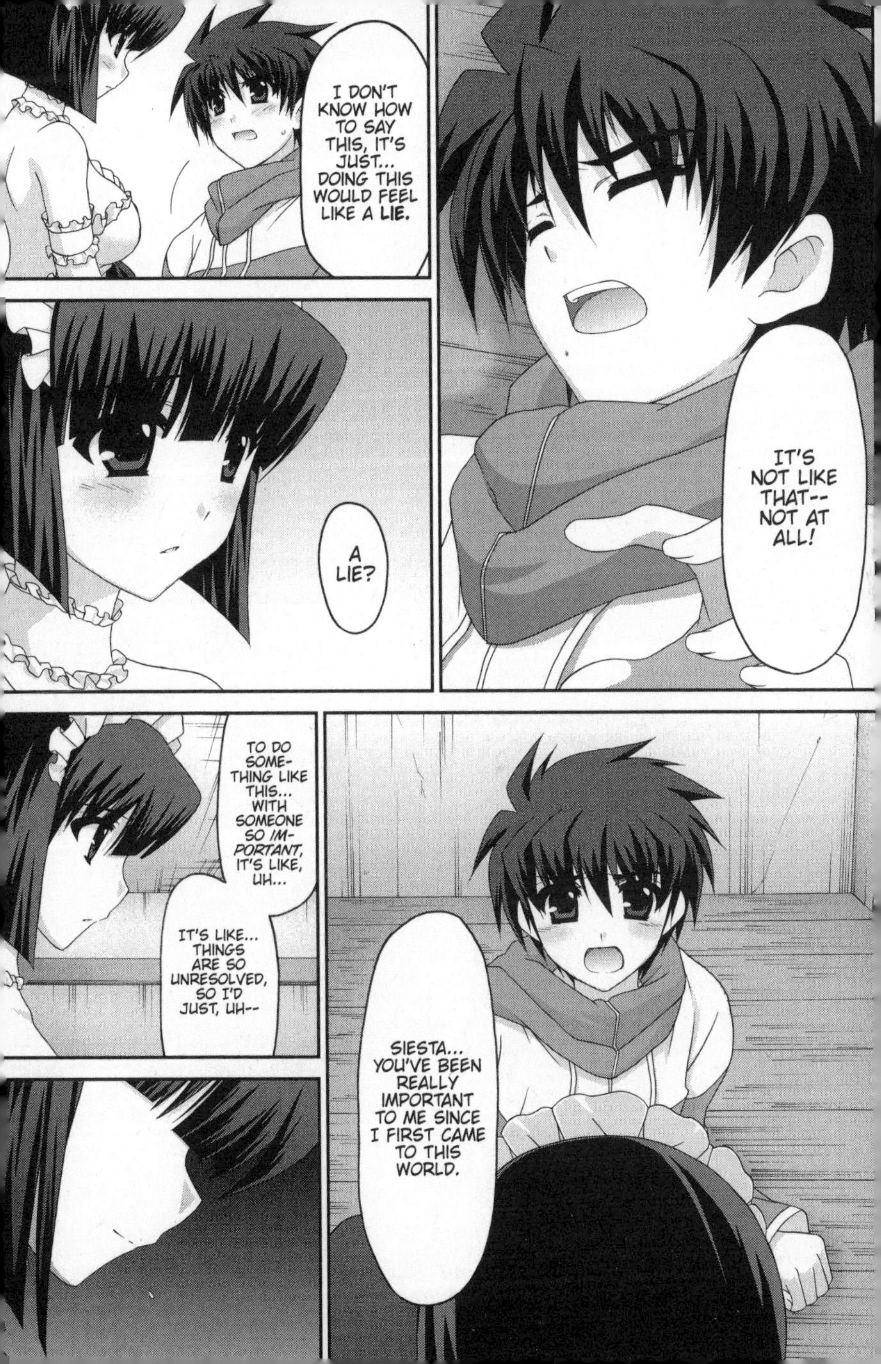
IT'S NOT LIKE THAT-- NOT AT ALL!
I DON'T KNOW HOW TO SAY THIS, IT'S JUST... DOING THIS WOULD FEEL LIKE A **LIE.**
A LIE?
SIESTA... YOU'VE BEEN REALLY IMPORTANT TO ME SINCE I FIRST CAME TO THIS WORLD.
TO DO SOME-THING LIKE THIS... WITH SOMEONE SO *IM-PORTANT*, IT'S LIKE, UH...
IT'S LIKE... THINGS ARE SO UNRESOLVED, SO I'D JUST, UH--

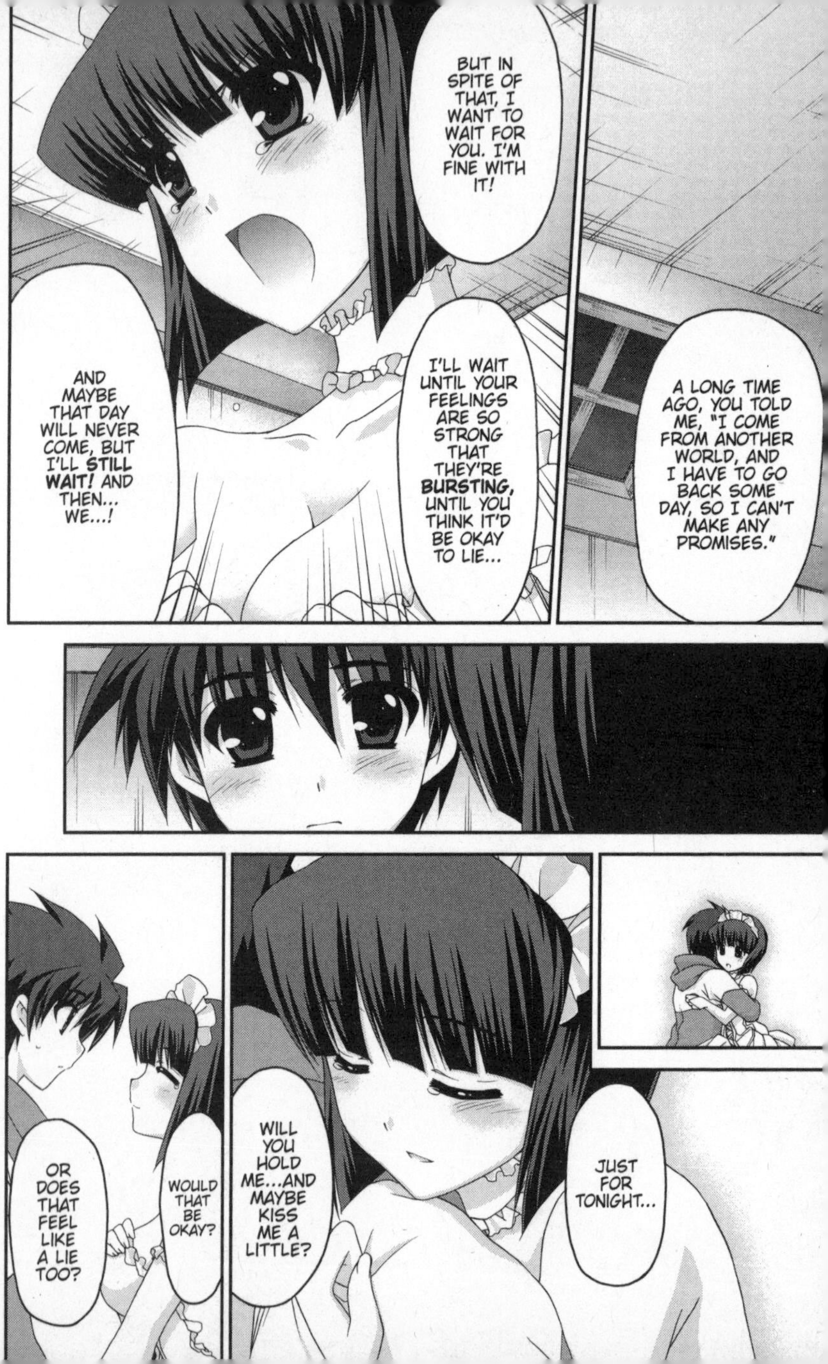
A LONG TIME AGO, YOU TOLD ME, "I COME FROM ANOTHER WORLD, AND I HAVE TO GO BACK SOME DAY, SO I CAN'T MAKE ANY PROMISES."
BUT IN SPITE OF THAT, I WANT TO WAIT FOR YOU. I'M FINE WITH IT!
I'LL WAIT UNTIL YOUR FEELINGS ARE SO STRONG THAT THEY'RE **BURSTING,** UNTIL YOU THINK IT'D BE OKAY TO LIE...
AND MAYBE THAT DAY WILL NEVER COME, BUT I'LL **STILL WAIT!** AND THEN... WE...!
JUST FOR TONIGHT...
WILL YOU HOLD ME...AND MAYBE KISS ME A LITTLE?
WOULD THAT BE OKAY?
OR DOES THAT FEEL LIKE A LIE TOO?

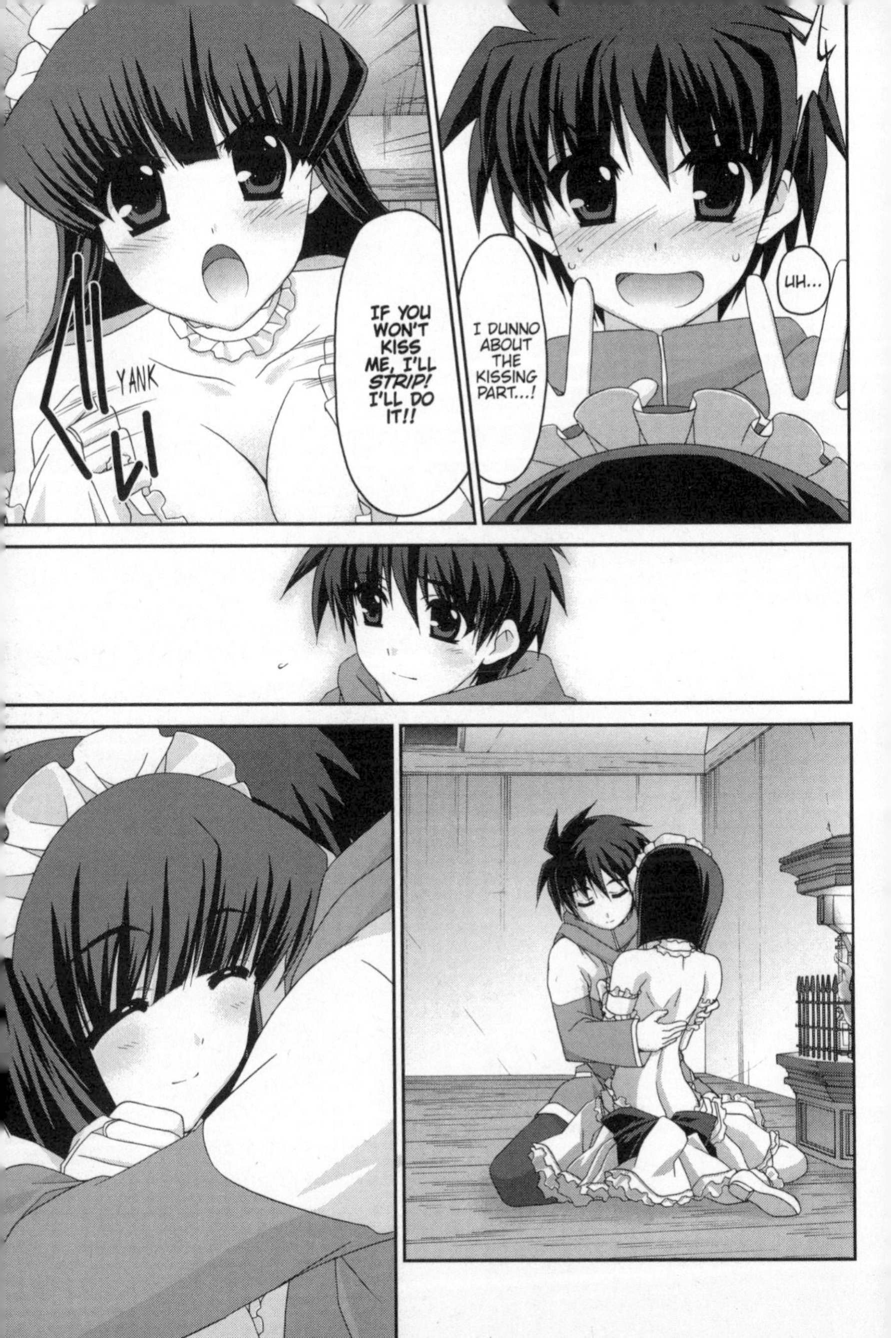
UH...
I DUNNO ABOUT THE KISSING PART...!
IF YOU WON'T KISS ME, I'LL *STRIP!* I'LL DO IT!!
YANK

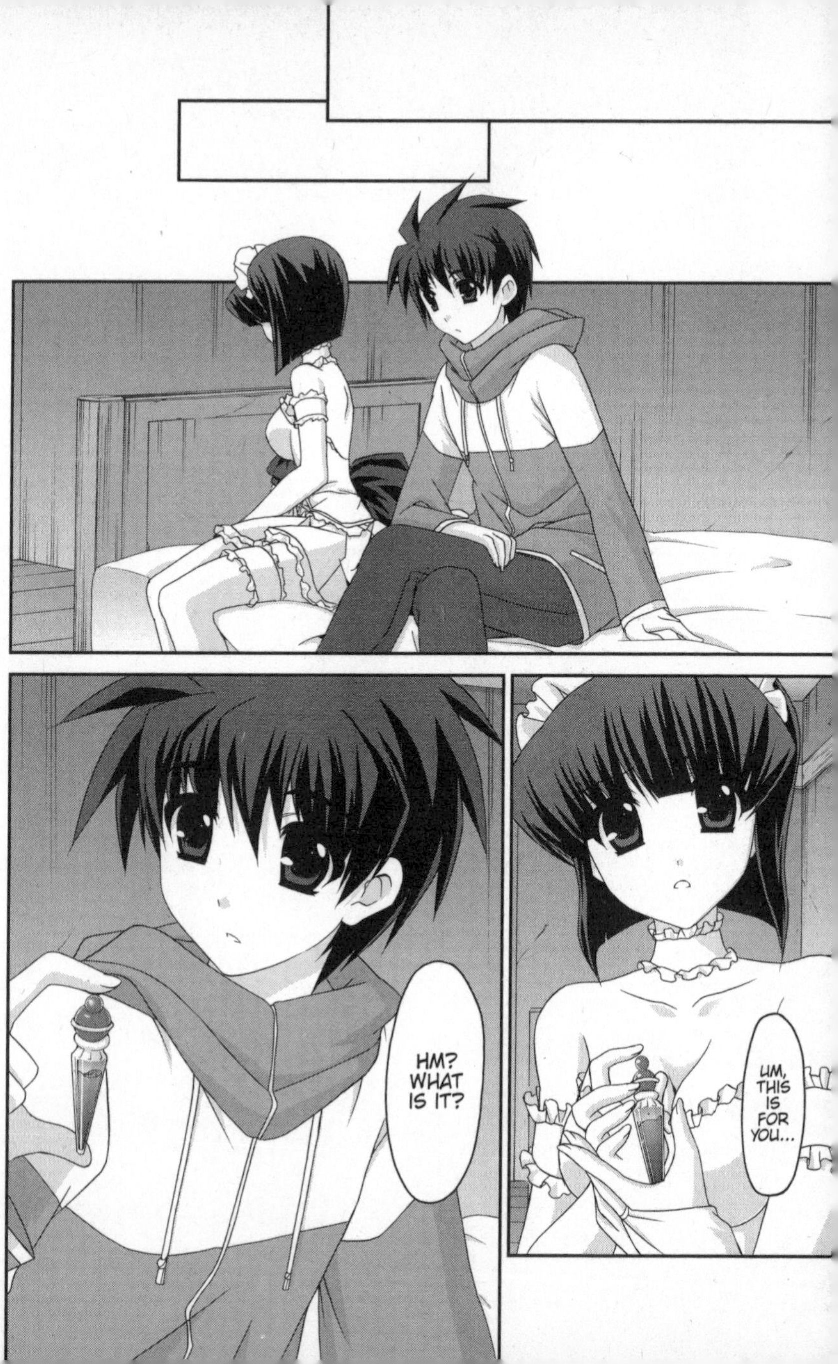
UM, THIS IS FOR YOU...
HM? WHAT IS IT?

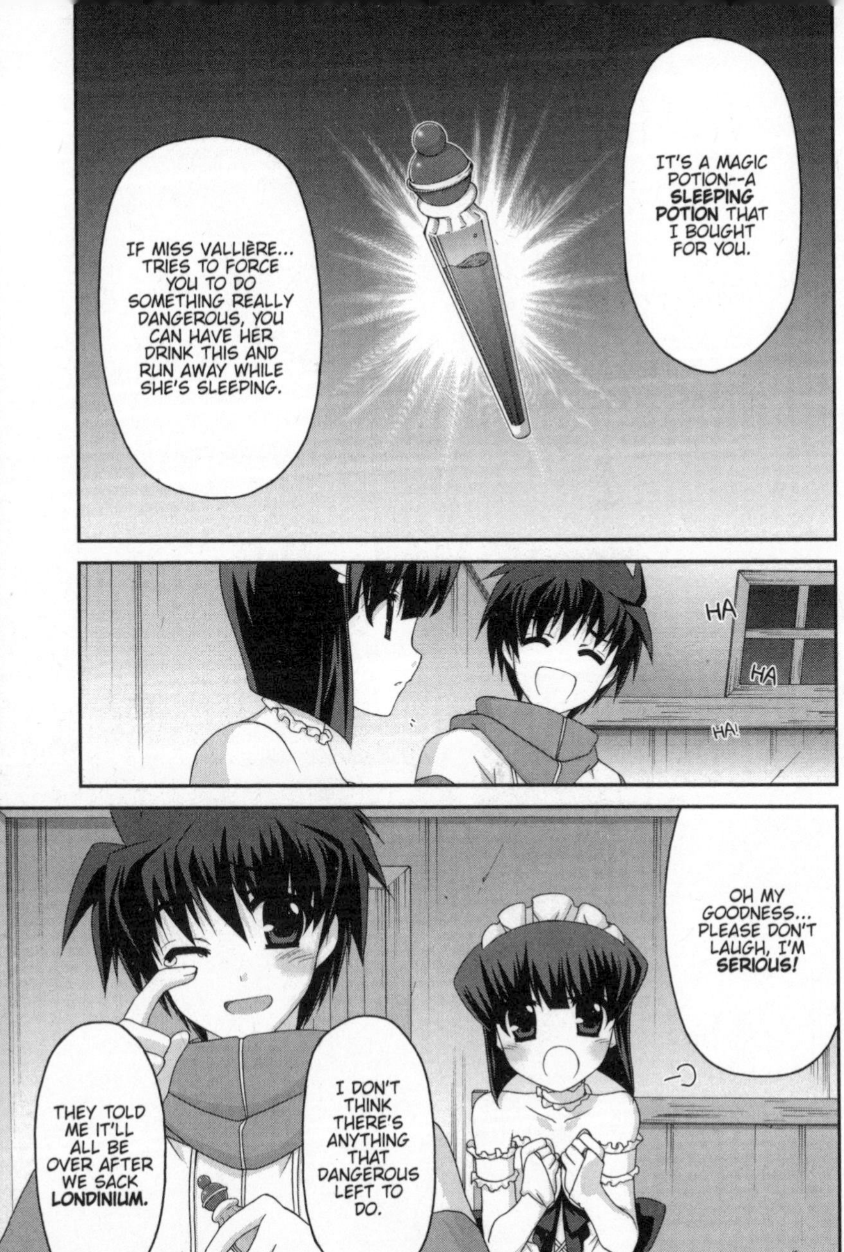
IT'S A MAGIC POTION--A **SLEEPING POTION** THAT I BOUGHT FOR YOU.
IF MISS VALLIÈRE... TRIES TO FORCE YOU TO DO SOMETHING REALLY DANGEROUS, YOU CAN HAVE HER DRINK THIS AND RUN AWAY WHILE SHE'S SLEEPING.
HA
HA
HA!
OH MY GOODNESS... PLEASE DON'T LAUGH, I'M **SERIOUS!**
I DON'T THINK THERE'S ANYTHING THAT DANGEROUS LEFT TO DO.
THEY TOLD ME IT'LL ALL BE OVER AFTER WE SACK **LONDINIUM.**

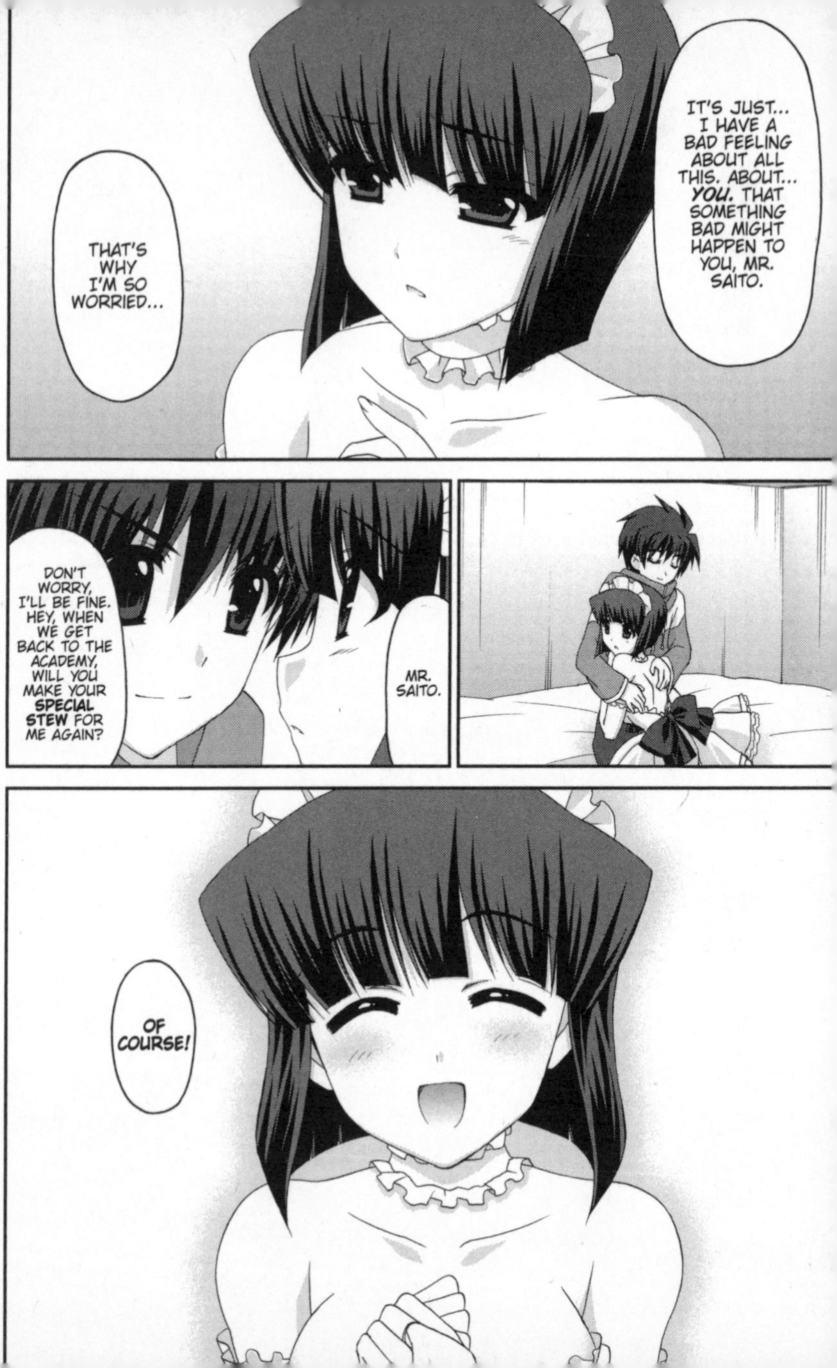
IT'S JUST... I HAVE A BAD FEELING ABOUT ALL THIS. ABOUT... YOU. THAT SOMETHING BAD MIGHT HAPPEN TO YOU, MR. SAITO.
THAT'S WHY I'M SO WORRIED...
MR. SAITO.
DON'T WORRY, I'LL BE FINE. HEY, WHEN WE GET BACK TO THE ACADEMY, WILL YOU MAKE YOUR SPECIAL STEW FOR ME AGAIN?
OF COURSE!

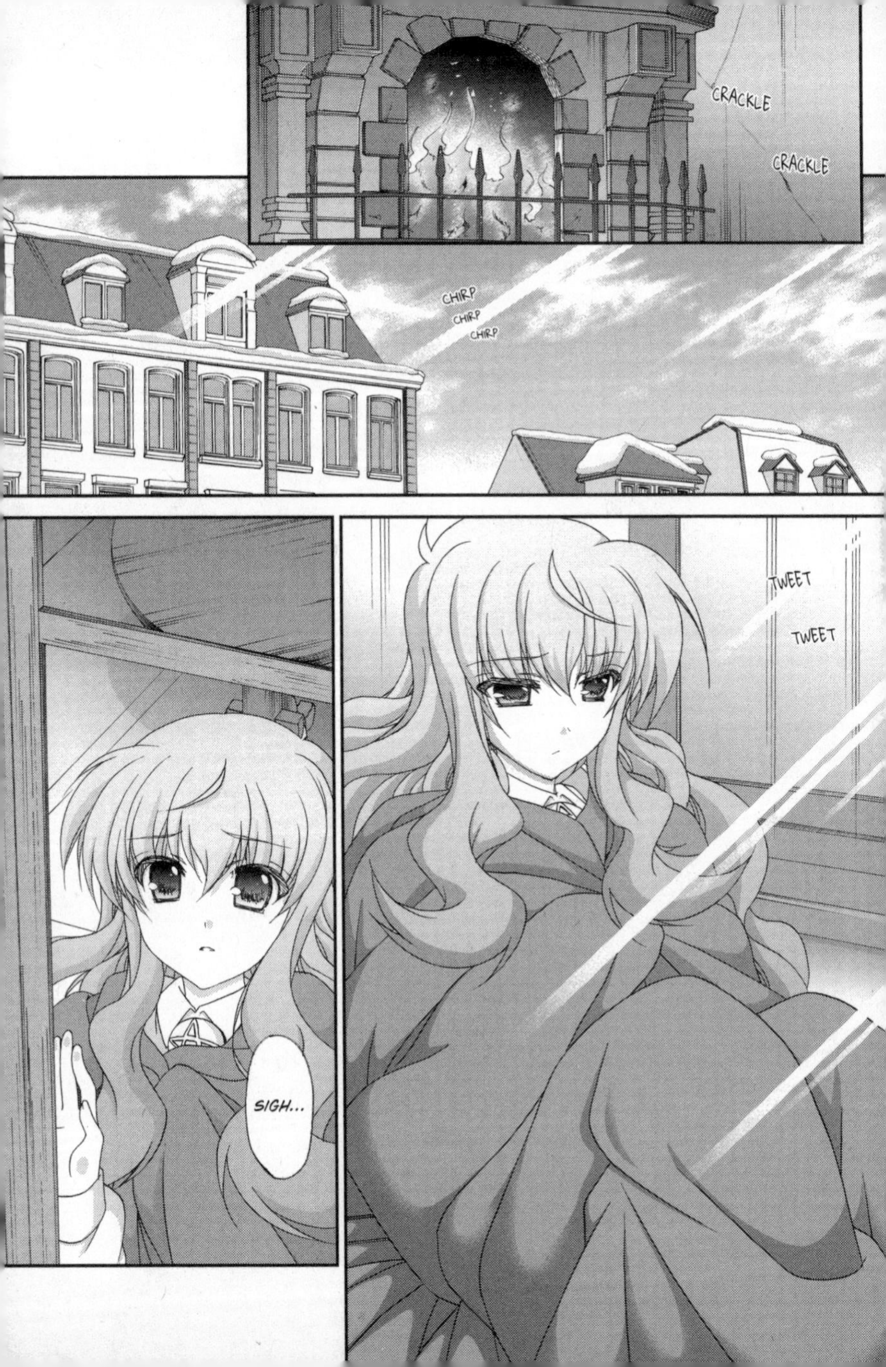
CRACKLE
CRACKLE
CHIRP
CHIRP
CHIRP
TWEET
TWEET
SIGH...

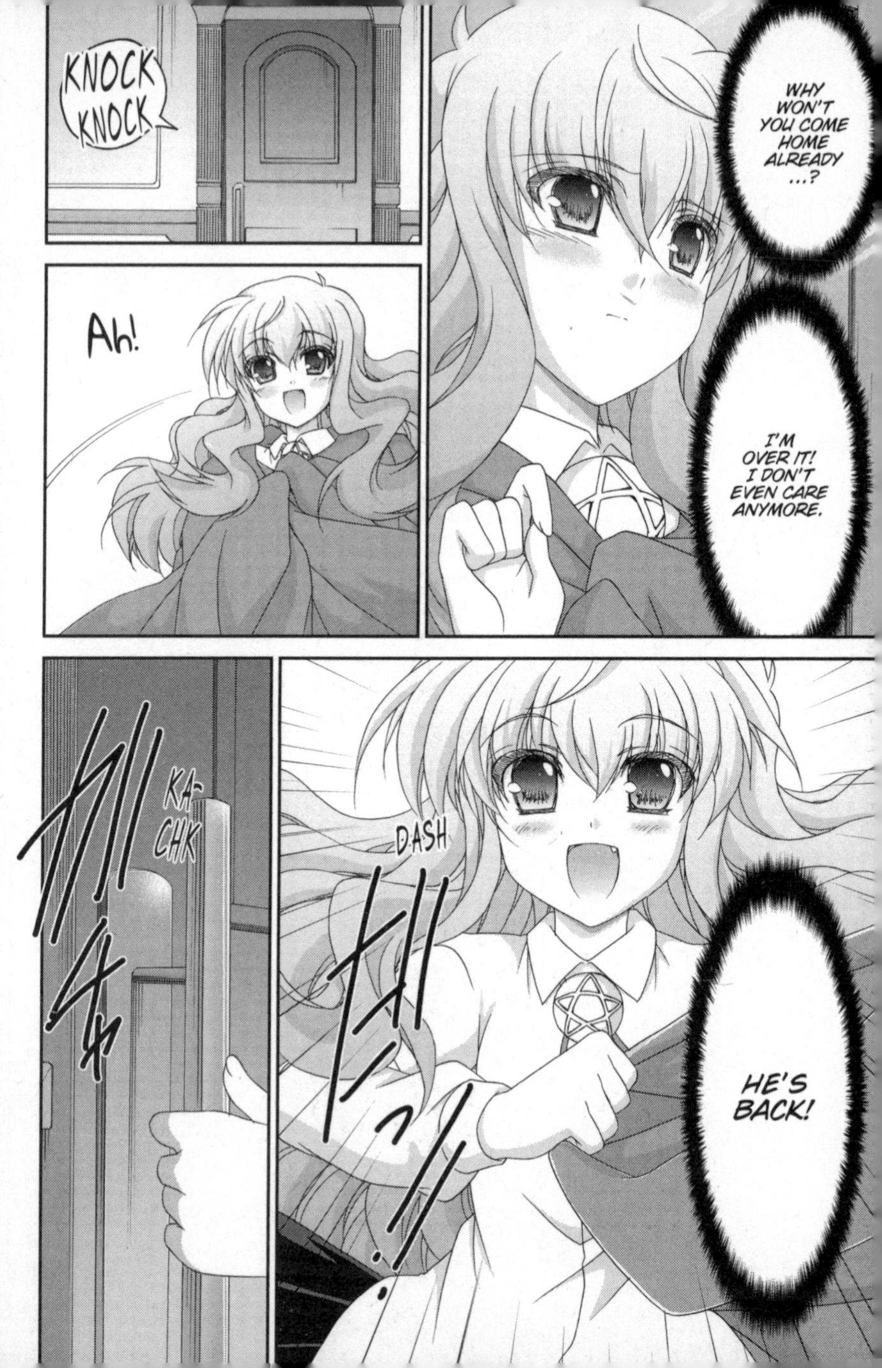
WHY WON'T YOU COME HOME ALREADY ...?
I'M OVER IT! I DON'T EVEN CARE ANYMORE.
KNOCK KNOCK
Ah!
DASH
HE'S BACK!
KA-CHK

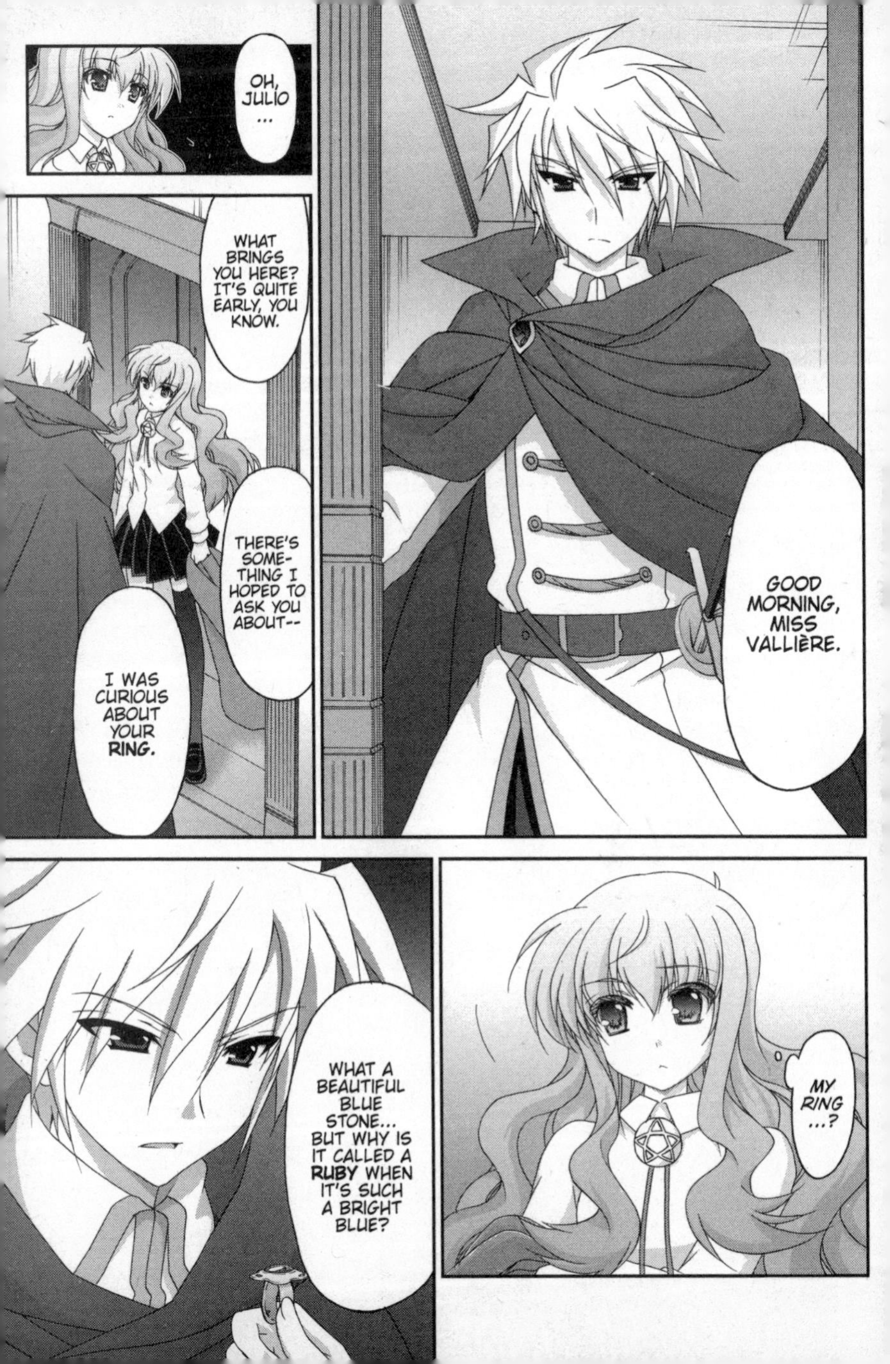
GOOD MORNING, MISS VALLIÈRE.
OH, JULIO ...
WHAT BRINGS YOU HERE? IT'S QUITE EARLY, YOU KNOW.
THERE'S SOME-THING I HOPED TO ASK YOU ABOUT--
I WAS CURIOUS ABOUT YOUR **RING**.
MY RING ...?
WHAT A BEAUTIFUL BLUE STONE... BUT WHY IS IT CALLED A **RUBY** WHEN IT'S SUCH A BRIGHT BLUE?

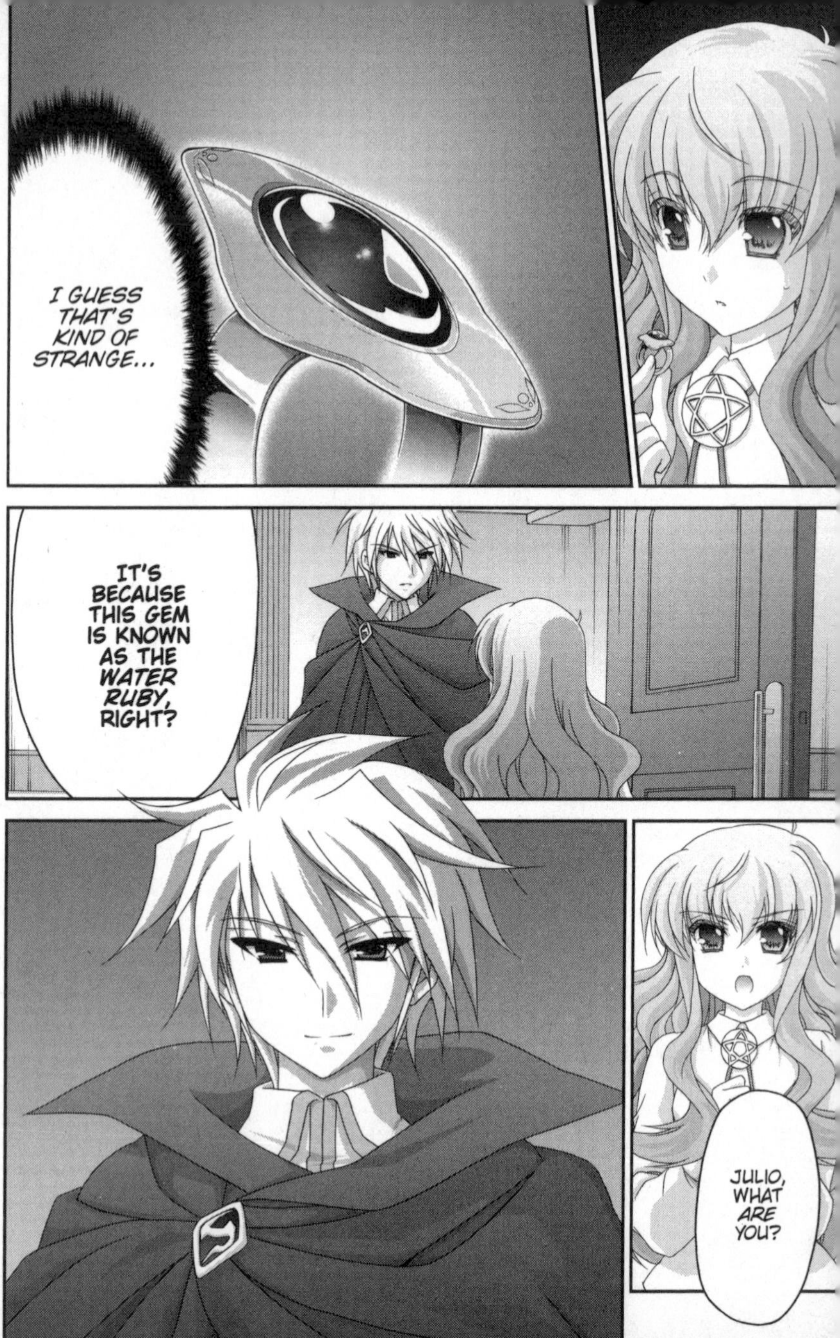
I GUESS THAT'S KIND OF STRANGE...
IT'S BECAUSE THIS GEM IS KNOWN AS THE WATER RUBY, RIGHT?
JULIO, WHAT ARE YOU?

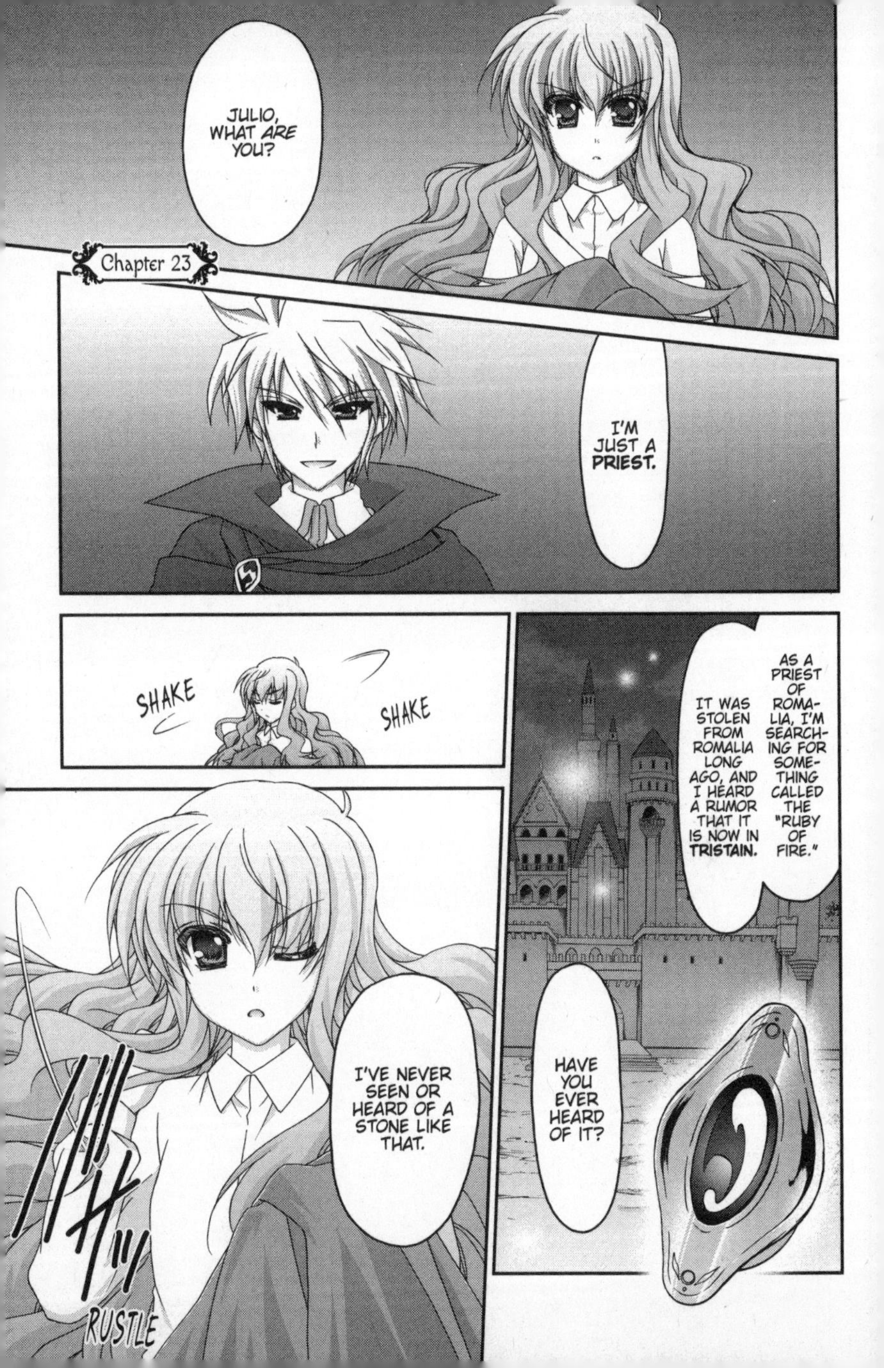
Chapter 23
JULIO, WHAT ARE YOU?
I'M JUST A PRIEST.
AS A PRIEST OF ROMALIA, I'M SEARCHING FOR SOMETHING CALLED THE "RUBY OF FIRE."
IT WAS STOLEN FROM ROMALIA LONG AGO, AND I HEARD A RUMOR THAT IT IS NOW IN TRISTAIN.
HAVE YOU EVER HEARD OF IT?
SHAKE
SHAKE
I'VE NEVER SEEN OR HEARD OF A STONE LIKE THAT.
RUSTLE

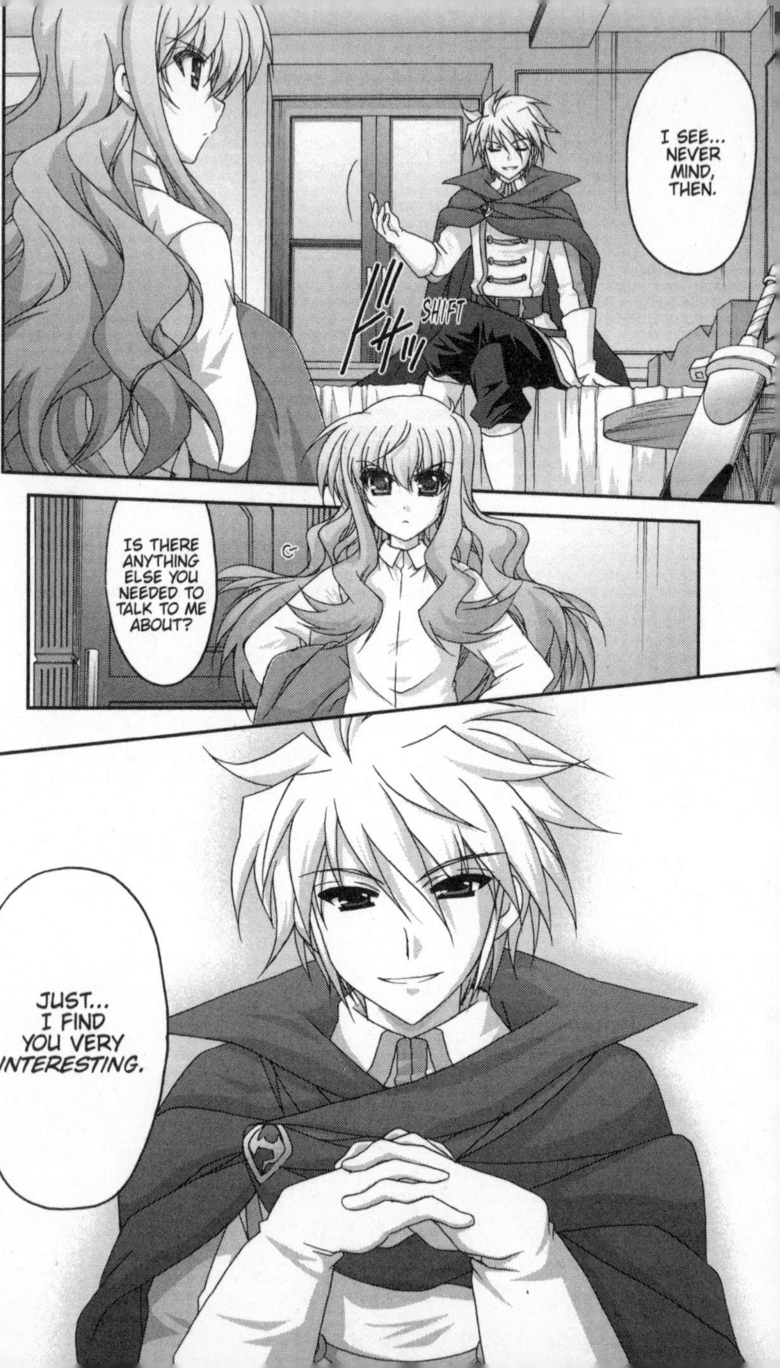
I SEE... NEVER MIND, THEN.
SHIFT
IS THERE ANYTHING ELSE YOU NEEDED TO TALK TO ME ABOUT?
JUST... I FIND YOU VERY INTERESTING.

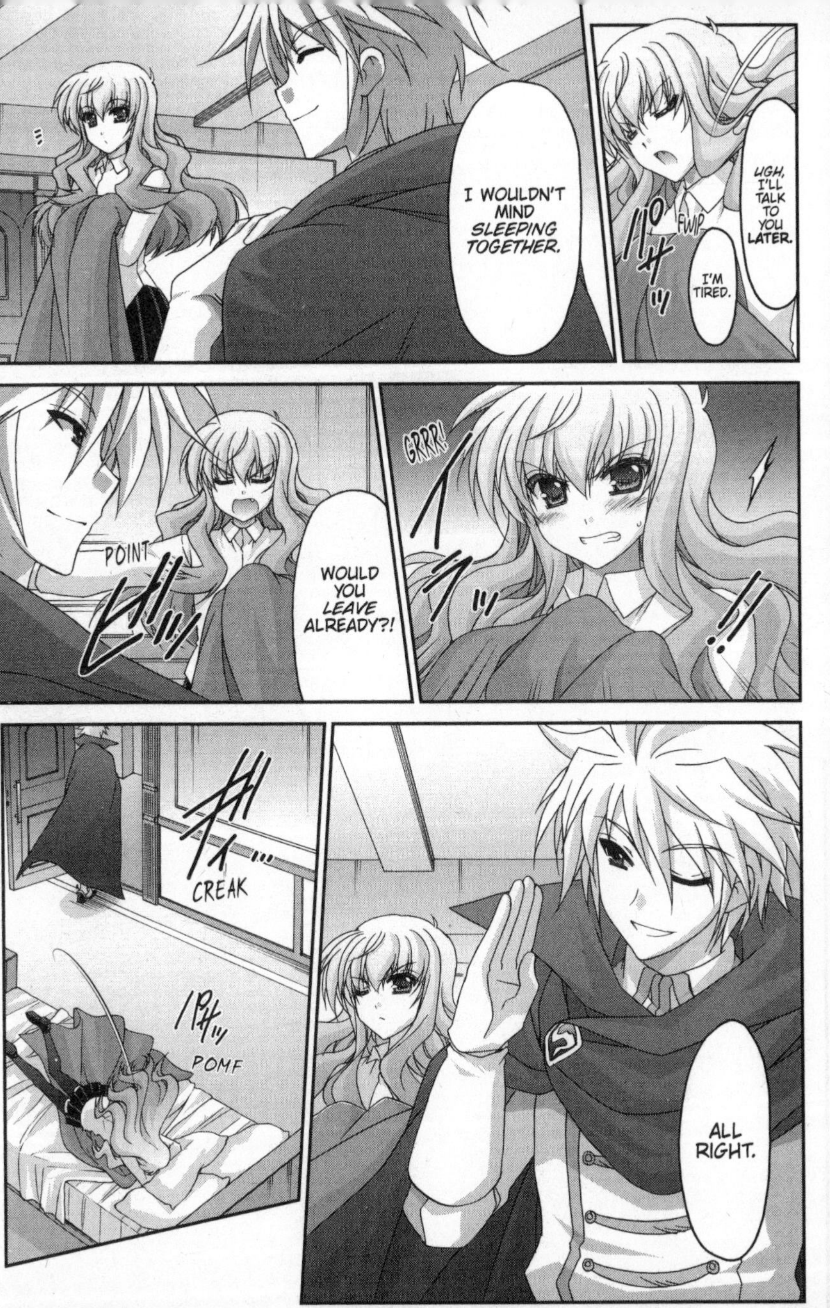
UGH, I'LL TALK TO YOU LATER.
FWIP
I'M TIRED.
I WOULDN'T MIND SLEEPING TOGETHER.
GRRR!
WOULD YOU LEAVE ALREADY?!
POINT
ALL RIGHT.
CREAK
POMF

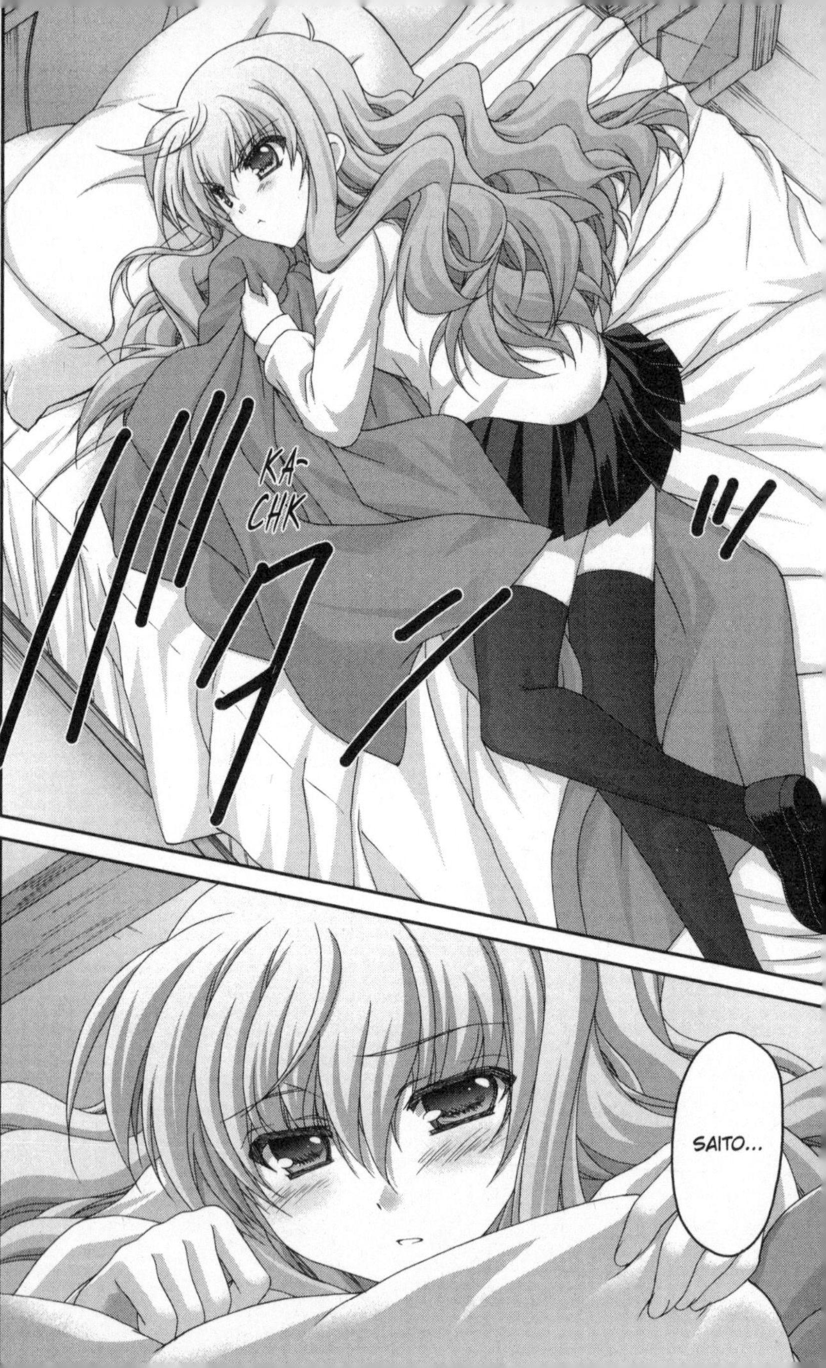
KA-CHK
SAITO...

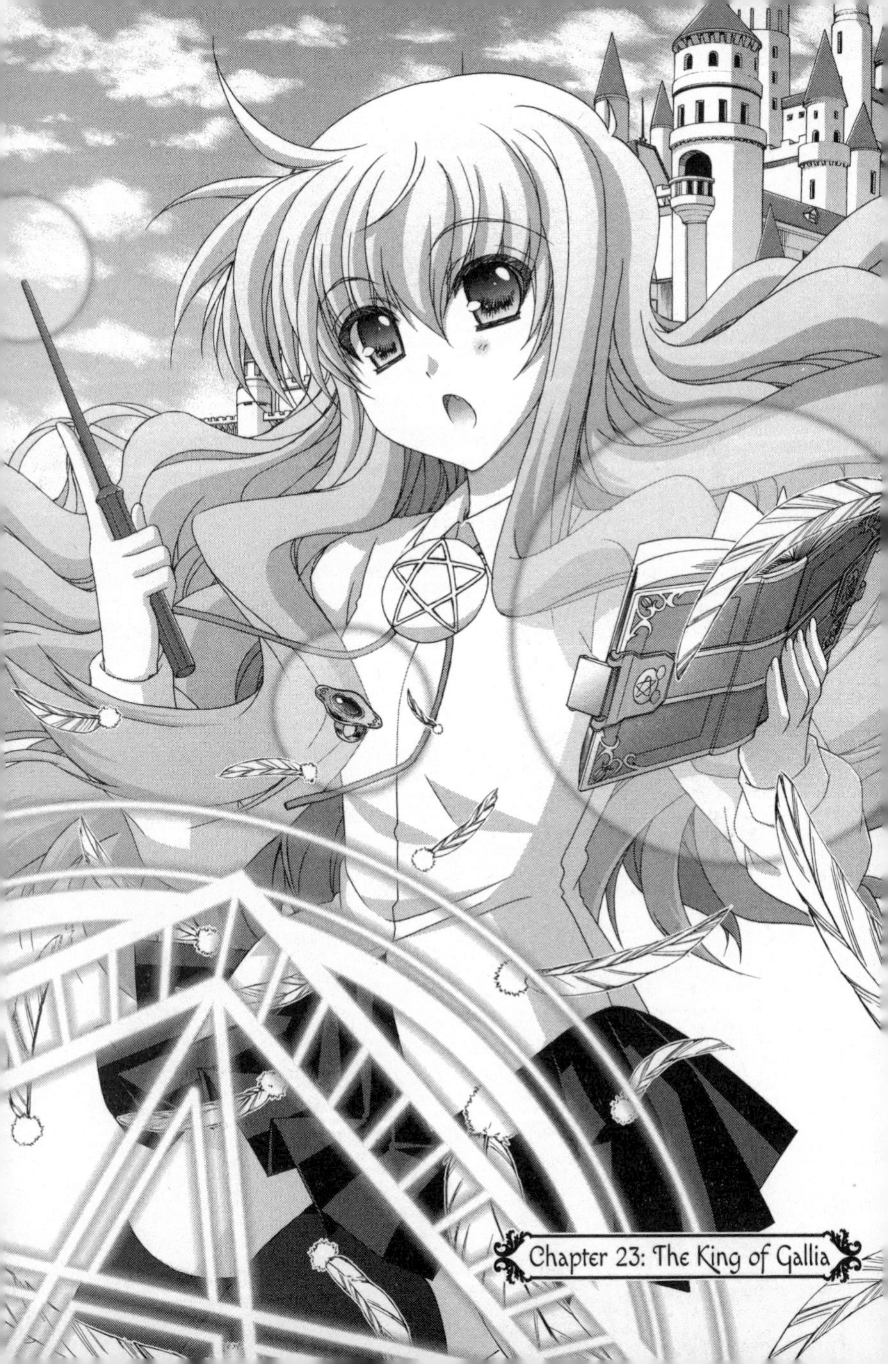
Chapter 23: The King of Gallia

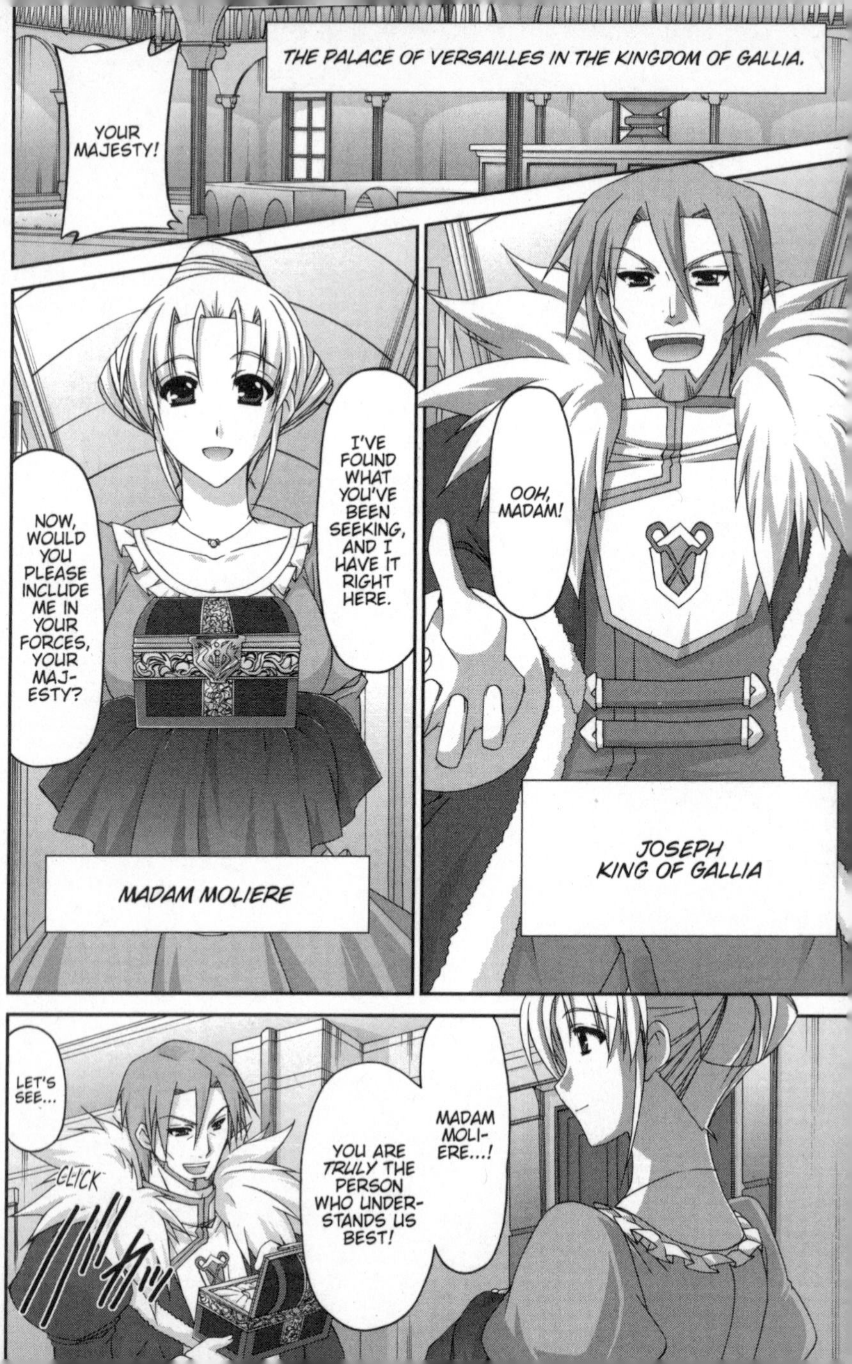
THE PALACE OF VERSAILLES IN THE KINGDOM OF GALLIA.
YOUR MAJESTY!
OOH, MADAM!
JOSEPH KING OF GALLIA
I'VE FOUND WHAT YOU'VE BEEN SEEKING, AND I HAVE IT RIGHT HERE.
NOW, WOULD YOU PLEASE INCLUDE ME IN YOUR FORCES, YOUR MAJ-ESTY?
MADAM MOLIERE
MADAM MOLI-ERE...!
YOU ARE *TRULY* THE PERSON WHO UNDER-STANDS US BEST!
LET'S SEE...
CLICK

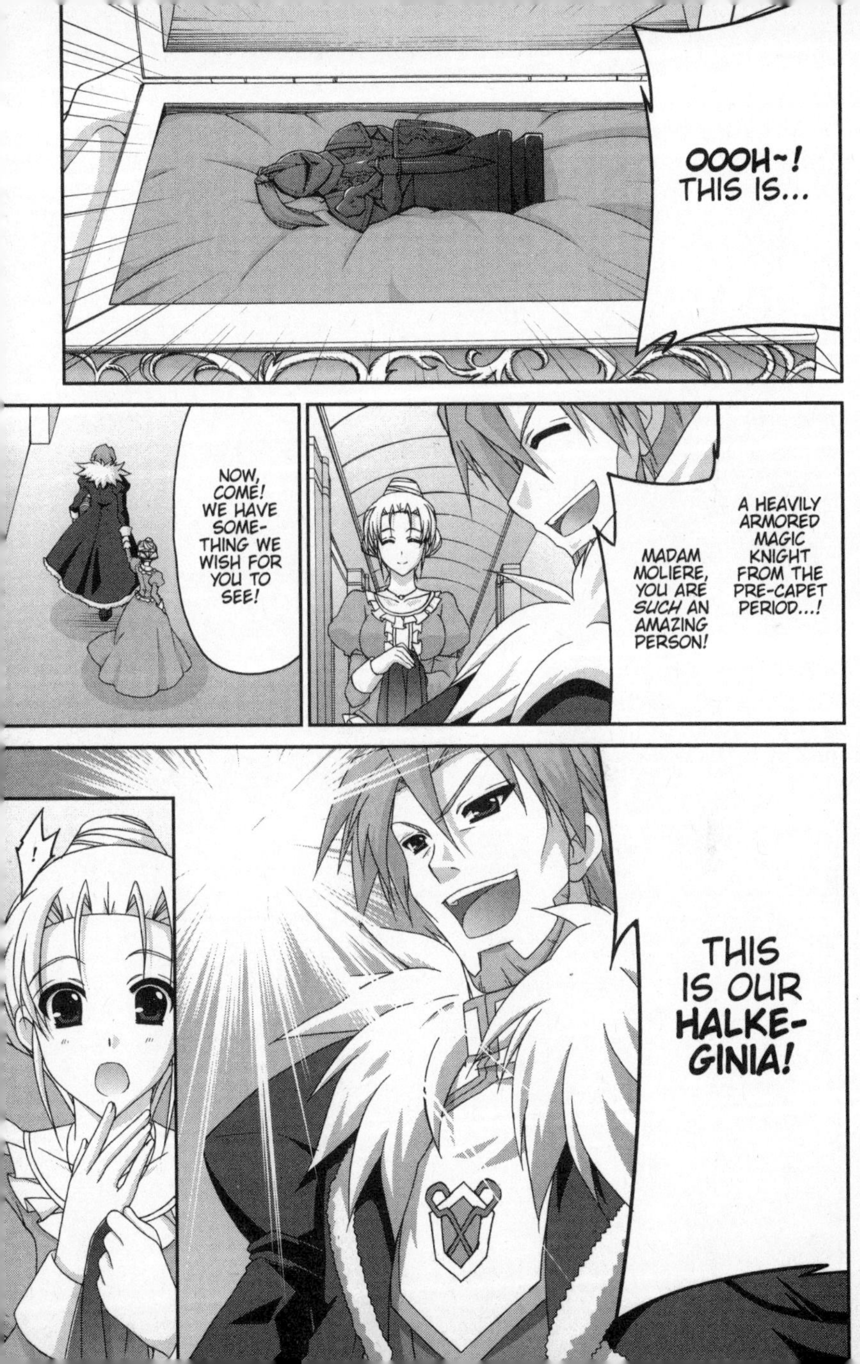
OOOH~! THIS IS...
A HEAVILY ARMORED MAGIC KNIGHT FROM THE PRE-CAPET PERIOD...!
MADAM MOLIERE, YOU ARE SUCH AN AMAZING PERSON!
NOW, COME! WE HAVE SOMETHING WE WISH FOR YOU TO SEE!
THIS IS OUR HALKEGINIA!
!

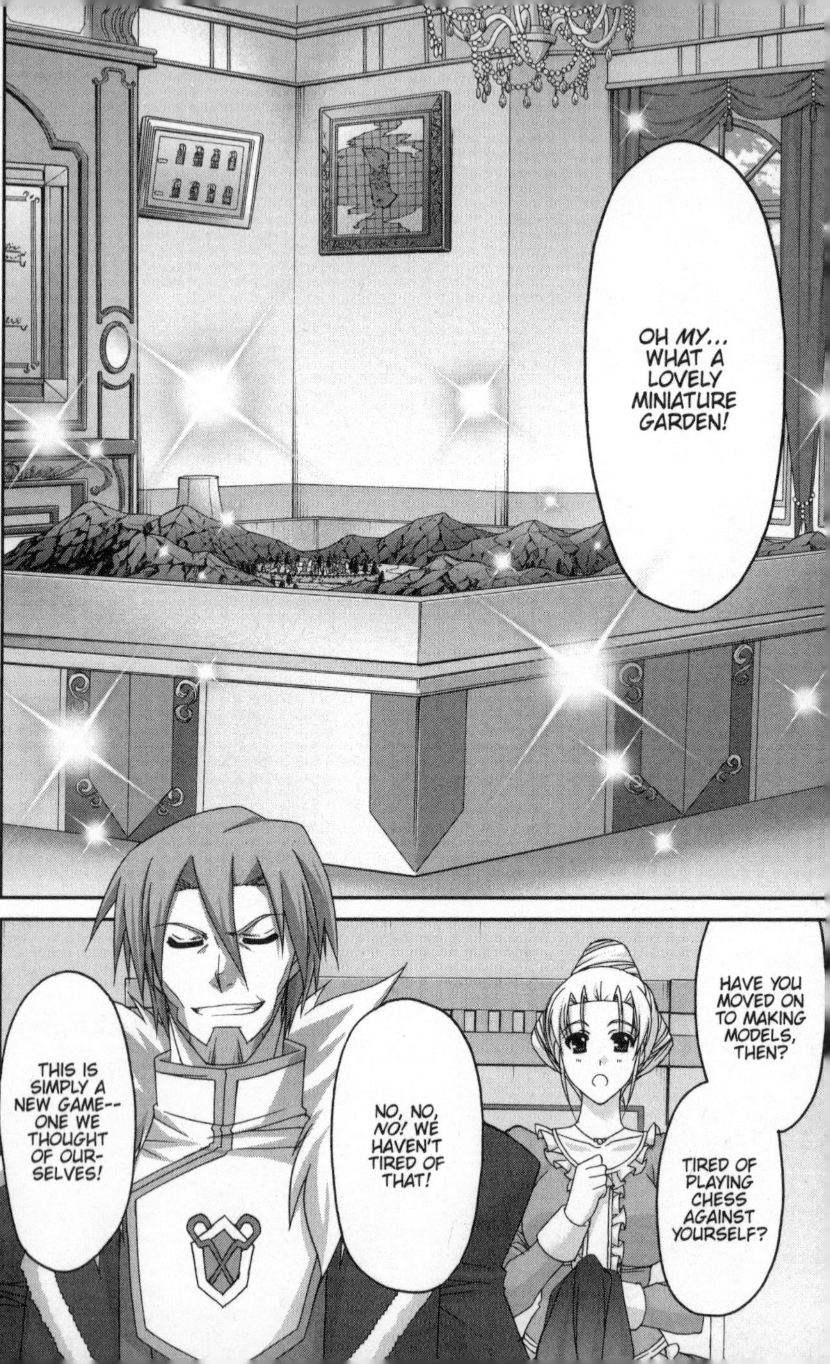
OH *MY*... WHAT A LOVELY MINIATURE GARDEN!
HAVE YOU MOVED ON TO MAKING MODELS, THEN?
TIRED OF PLAYING CHESS AGAINST YOURSELF?
NO, NO, *NO!* WE HAVEN'T TIRED OF THAT!
THIS IS SIMPLY A NEW GAME--ONE WE THOUGHT OF OUR-SELVES!

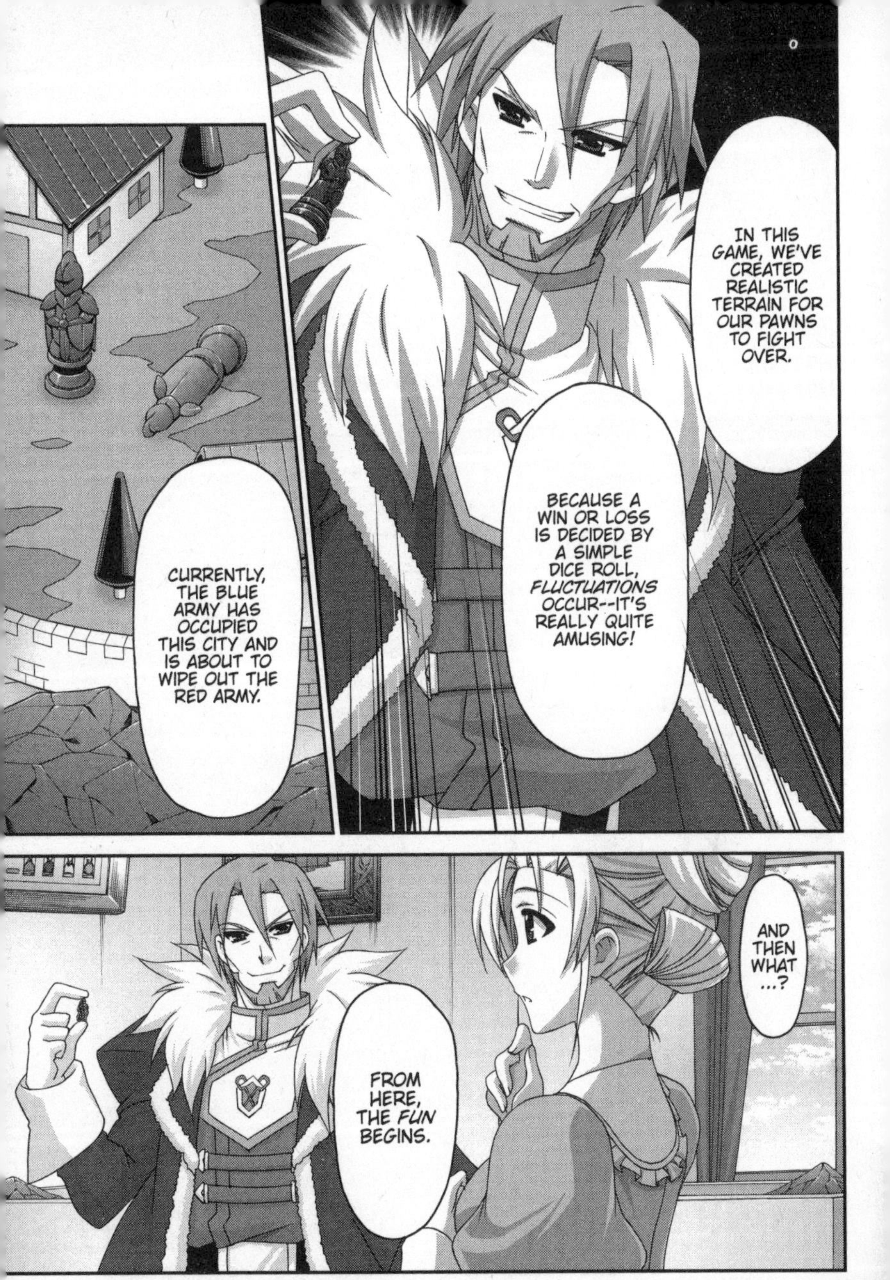
IN THIS GAME, WE'VE CREATED REALISTIC TERRAIN FOR OUR PAWNS TO FIGHT OVER.
BECAUSE A WIN OR LOSS IS DECIDED BY A SIMPLE DICE ROLL, *FLUCTUATIONS* OCCUR--IT'S REALLY QUITE AMUSING!
CURRENTLY, THE BLUE ARMY HAS OCCUPIED THIS CITY AND IS ABOUT TO WIPE OUT THE RED ARMY.
AND THEN WHAT ...?
FROM HERE, THE *FUN* BEGINS.

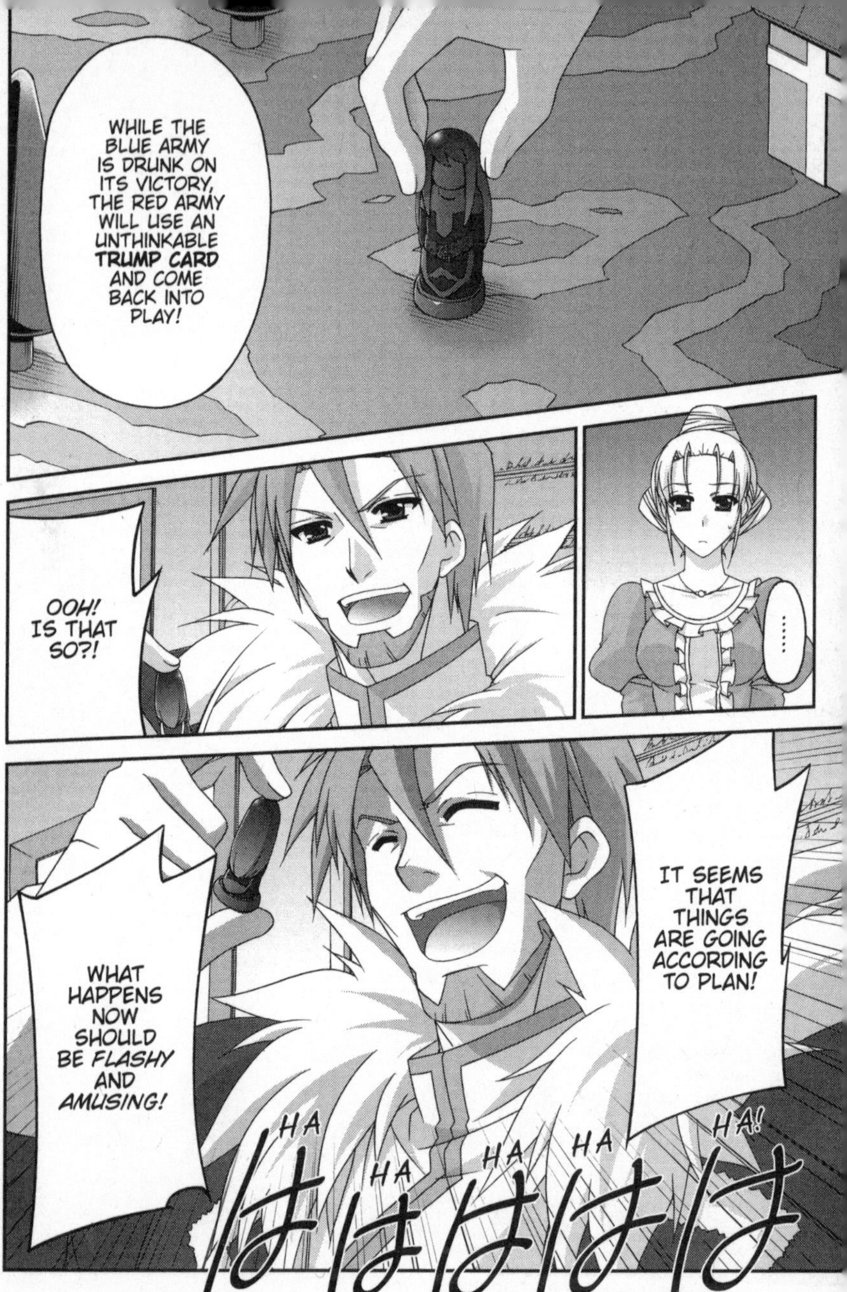
WHILE THE BLUE ARMY IS DRUNK ON ITS VICTORY, THE RED ARMY WILL USE AN UNTHINKABLE **TRUMP CARD** AND COME BACK INTO PLAY!
......
OOH! IS THAT SO?!
IT SEEMS THAT THINGS ARE GOING ACCORDING TO PLAN!
WHAT HAPPENS NOW SHOULD BE *FLASHY* AND *AMUSING!*
HA HA HA HA HA!
ははははは

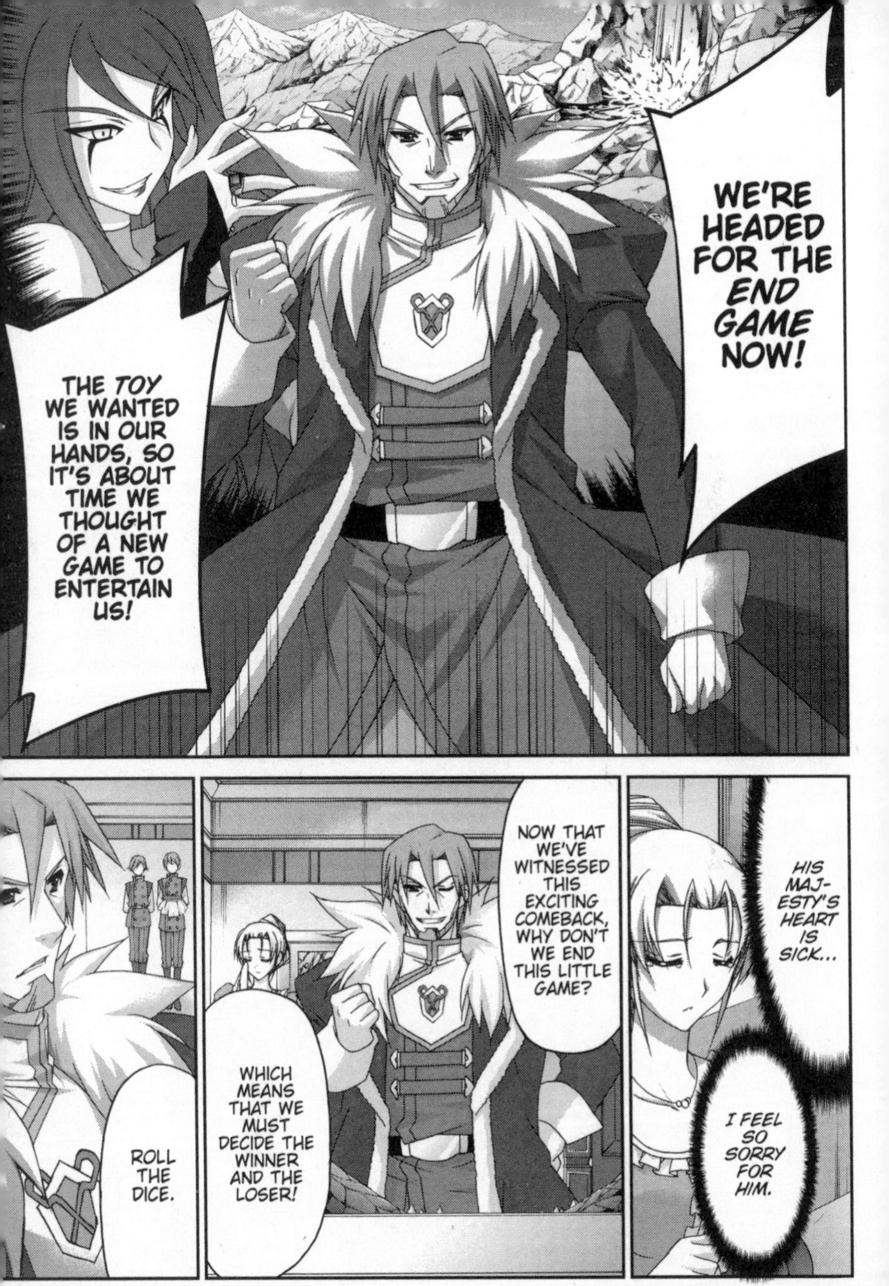
WE'RE HEADED FOR THE *END GAME* NOW!
THE *TOY* WE WANTED IS IN OUR HANDS, SO IT'S ABOUT TIME WE THOUGHT OF A NEW GAME TO ENTERTAIN US!
HIS MAJ-ESTY'S HEART IS SICK...
I FEEL SO SORRY FOR HIM.
NOW THAT WE'VE WITNESSED THIS EXCITING COMEBACK, WHY DON'T WE END THIS LITTLE GAME?
WHICH MEANS THAT WE MUST DECIDE THE WINNER AND THE LOSER!
ROLL THE DICE.

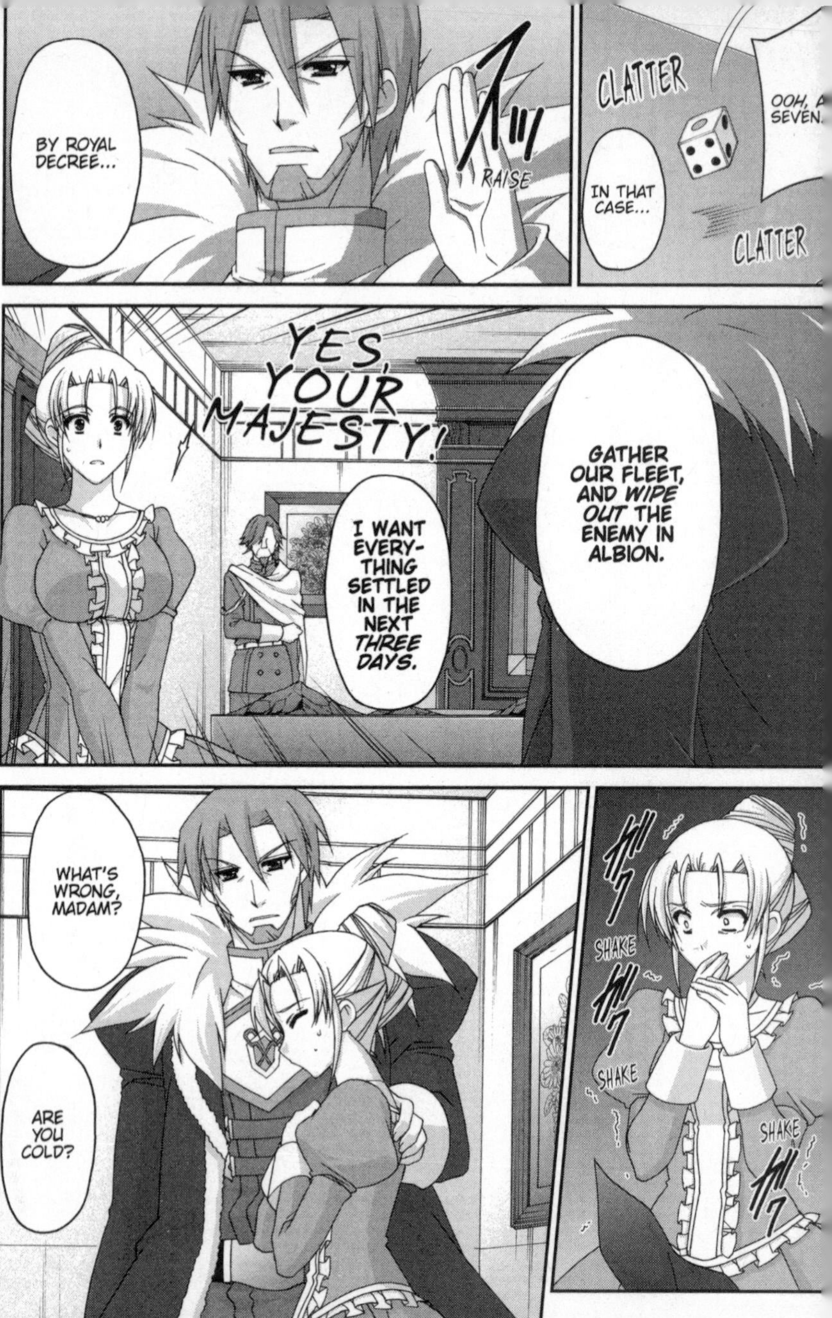
OOH, A SEVEN.
CLATTER
IN THAT CASE...
CLATTER
BY ROYAL DECREE...
RAISE
GATHER OUR FLEET, AND *WIPE OUT* THE ENEMY IN ALBION.
I WANT EVERYTHING SETTLED IN THE NEXT *THREE* DAYS.
YES, YOUR MAJESTY!
SHAKE
SHAKE
SHAKE
WHAT'S WRONG, MADAM?
ARE YOU COLD?

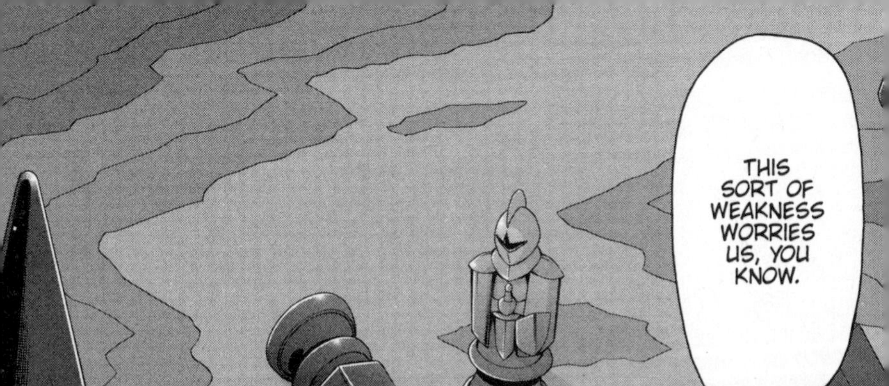
THIS SORT OF WEAKNESS WORRIES US, YOU KNOW.
THROW SOME MORE WOOD ON THE FIRE.

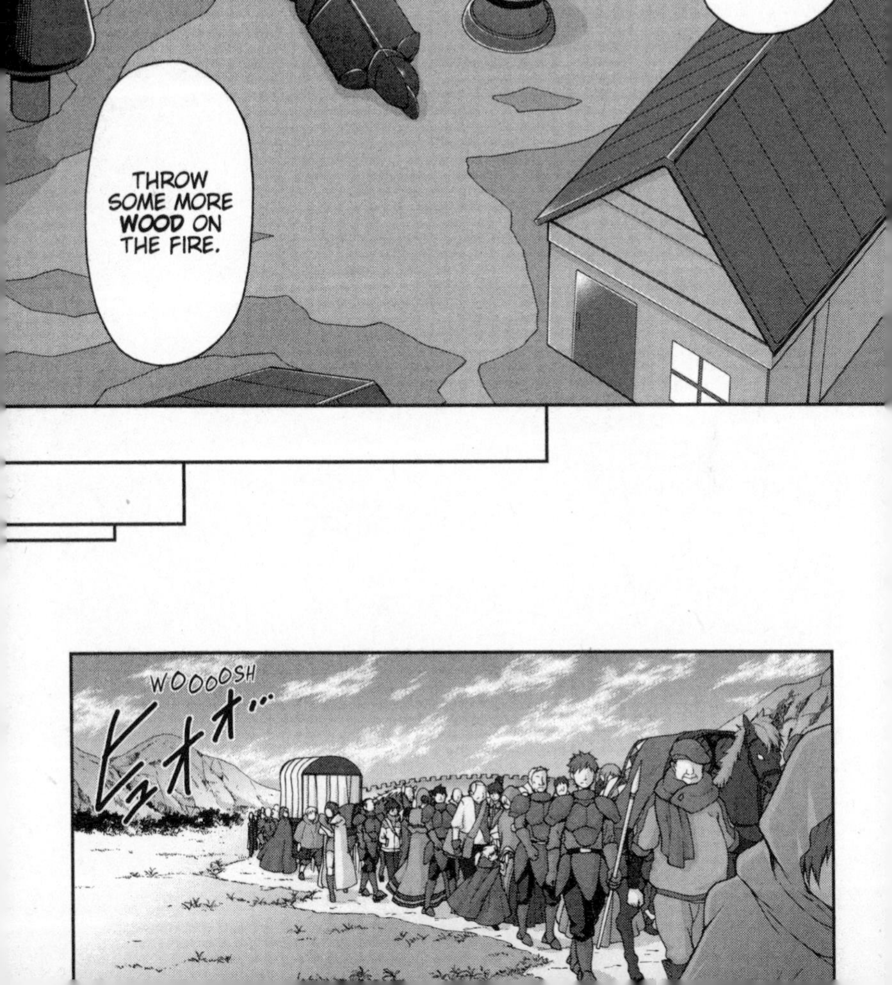
WOOOOSH
ヒュオオ…

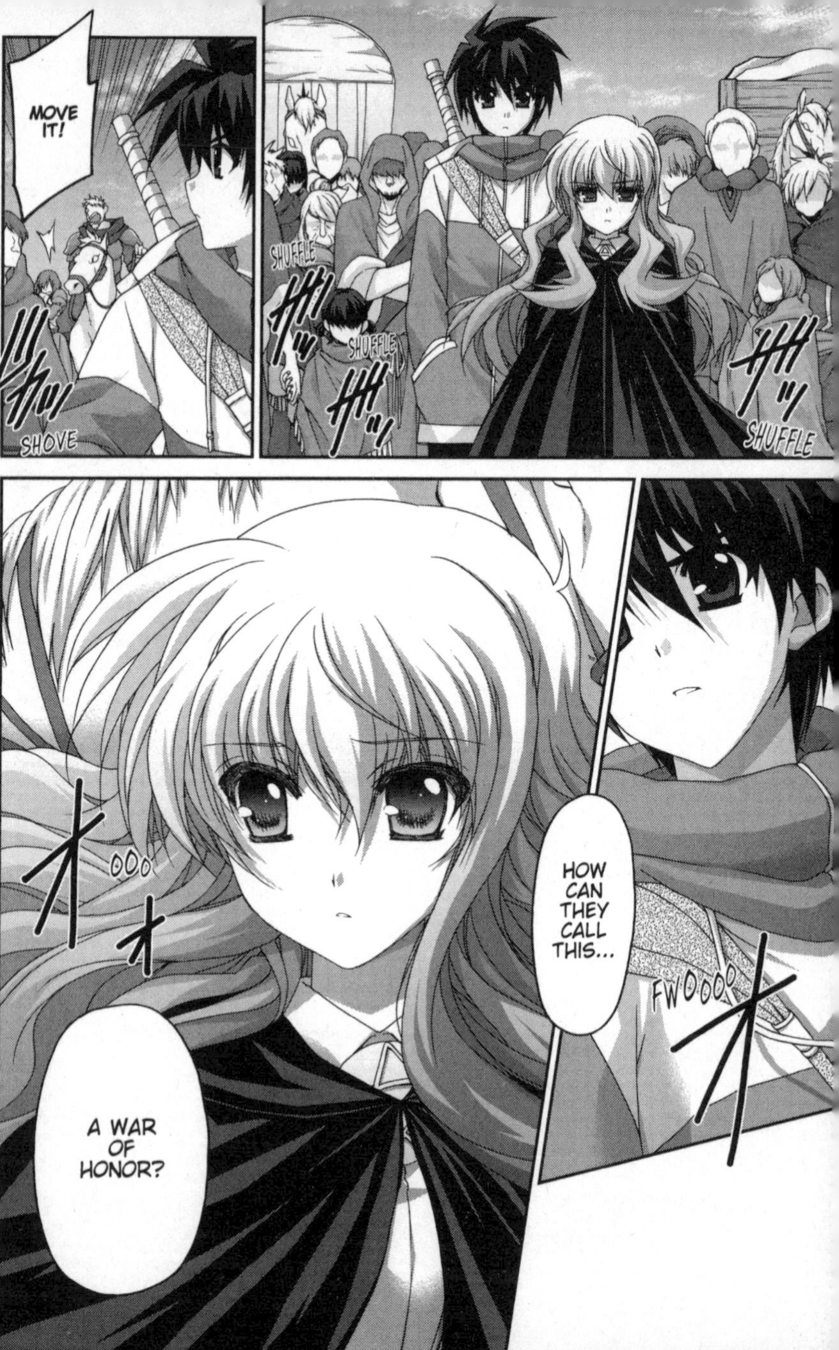
SHUFFLE
SHUFFLE
SHUFFLE
MOVE IT!
SHOVE
HOW CAN THEY CALL THIS...
FWOOO
OOO
A WAR OF HONOR?

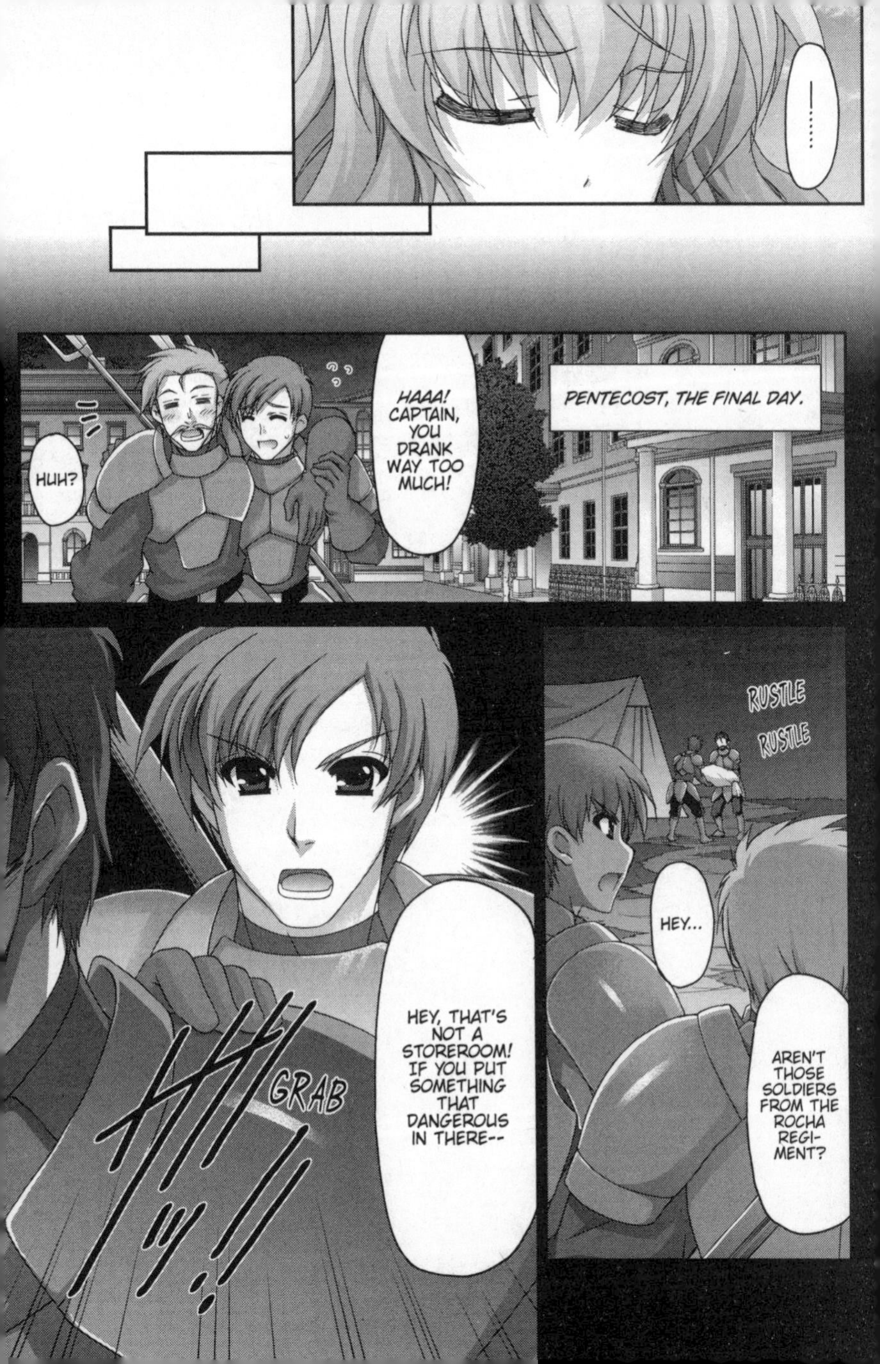
......!
PENTECOST, THE FINAL DAY.
HAAA! CAPTAIN, YOU DRANK WAY TOO MUCH!
HUH?
RUSTLE
RUSTLE
HEY...
AREN'T THOSE SOLDIERS FROM THE ROCHA REGIMENT?
HEY, THAT'S NOT A STOREROOM! IF YOU PUT SOMETHING THAT DANGEROUS IN THERE--
GRAB

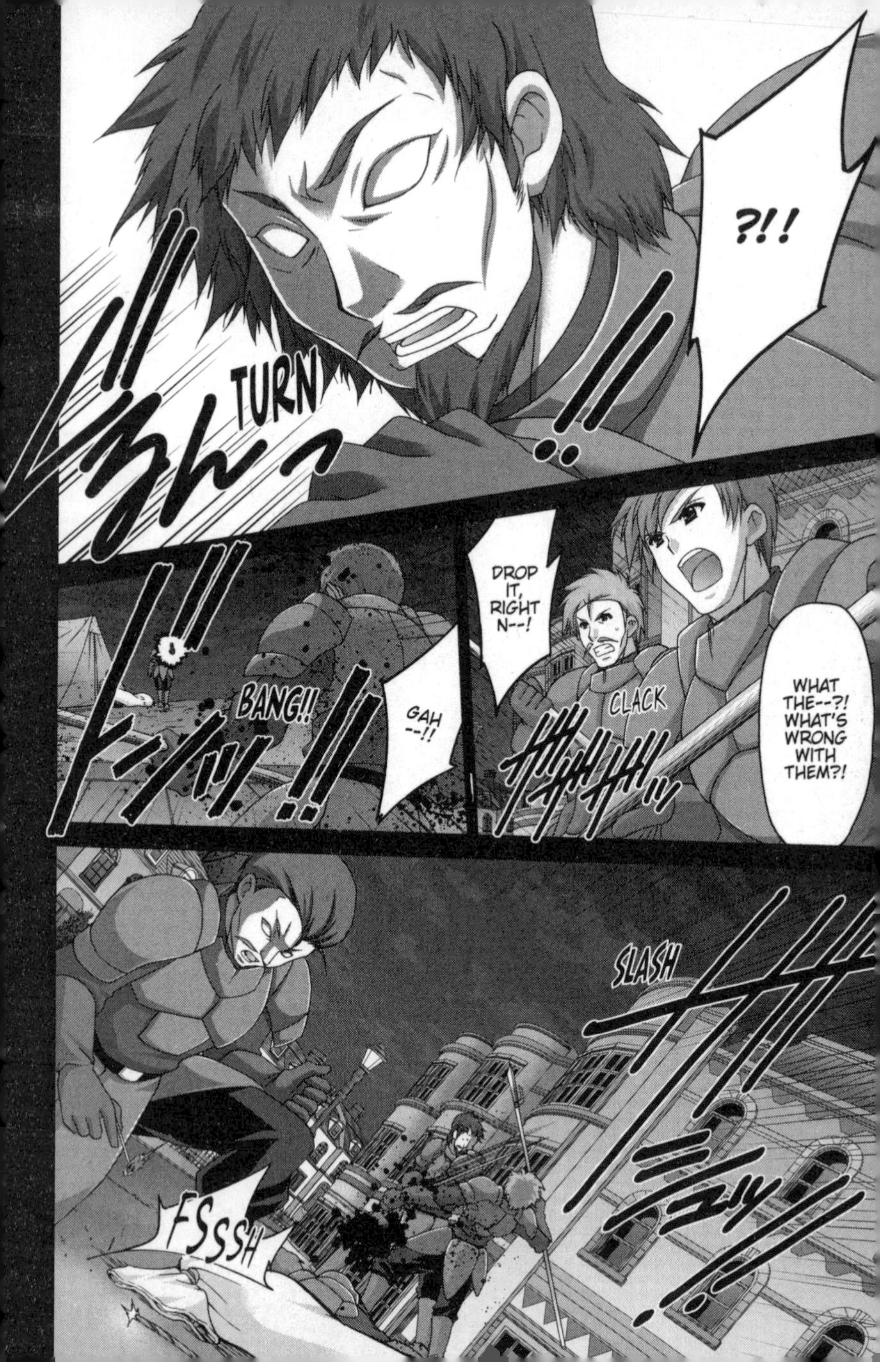
?!!
TURN
WHAT THE--?! WHAT'S WRONG WITH THEM?!
DROP IT, RIGHT N--!
CLACK
GAH--!!
BANG!!
SLASH
FSSSH

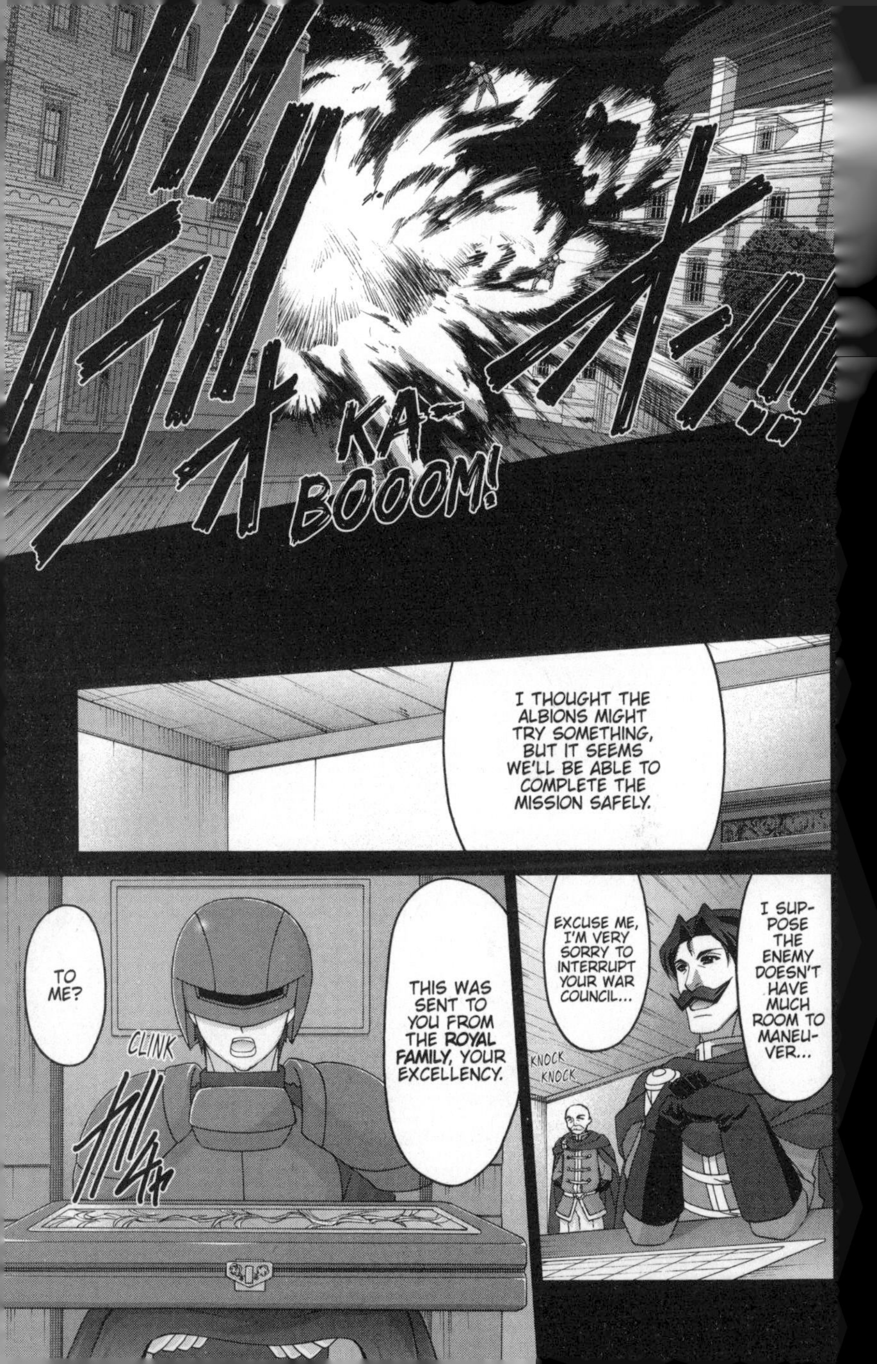
KA-BOOOM!
I THOUGHT THE ALBIONS MIGHT TRY SOMETHING, BUT IT SEEMS WE'LL BE ABLE TO COMPLETE THE MISSION SAFELY.
I SUP-POSE THE ENEMY DOESN'T HAVE MUCH ROOM TO MANEU-VER...
KNOCK KNOCK
EXCUSE ME, I'M VERY SORRY TO INTERRUPT YOUR WAR COUNCIL...
THIS WAS SENT TO YOU FROM THE ROYAL FAMILY, YOUR EXCELLENCY.
TO ME?
CLINK

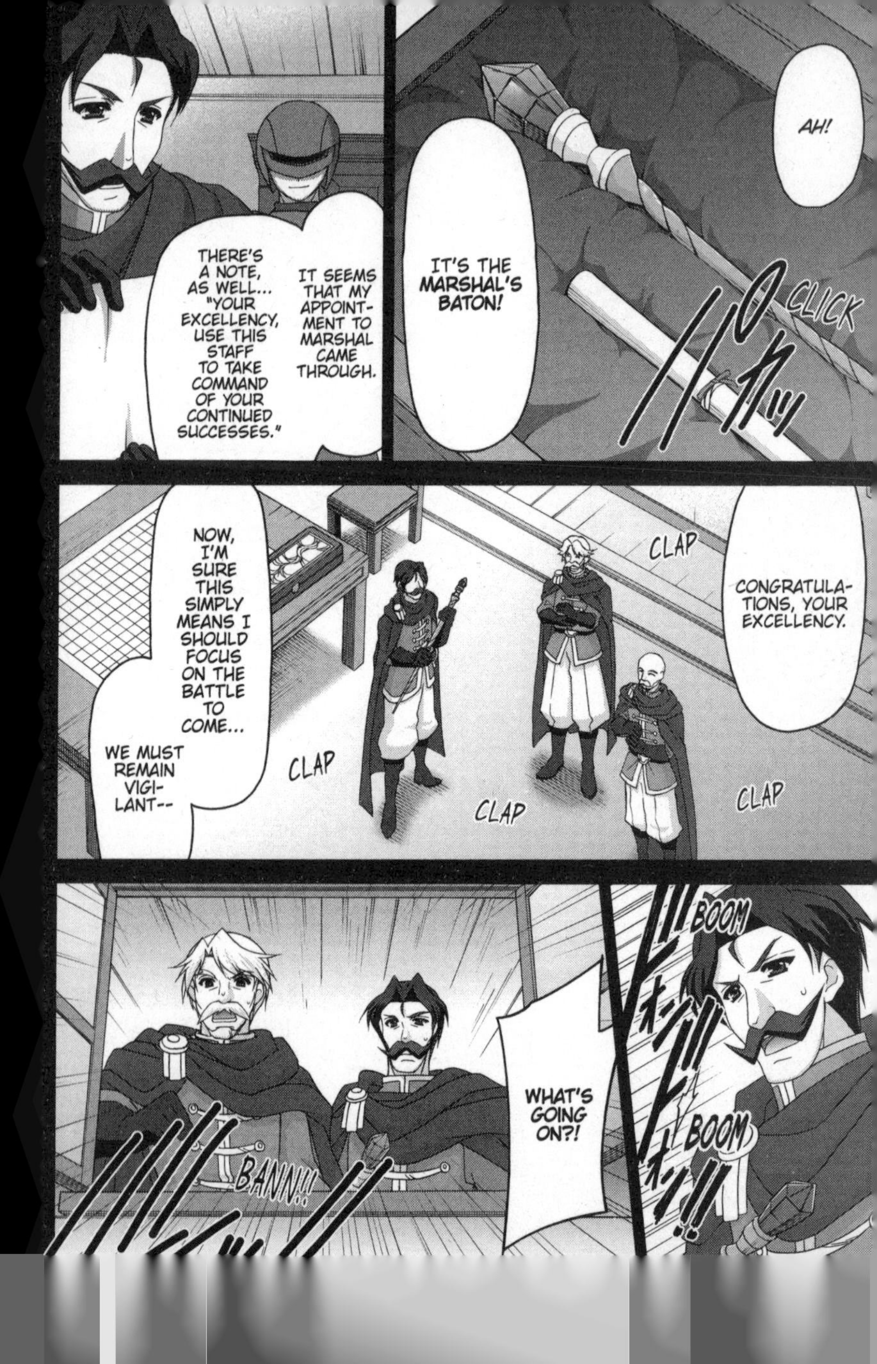
AH!
IT'S THE MARSHAL'S BATON!
CLICK
IT SEEMS THAT MY APPOINTMENT TO MARSHAL CAME THROUGH.
THERE'S A NOTE, AS WELL... "YOUR EXCELLENCY, USE THIS STAFF TO TAKE COMMAND OF YOUR CONTINUED SUCCESSES."
CONGRATULATIONS, YOUR EXCELLENCY.
CLAP
NOW, I'M SURE THIS SIMPLY MEANS I SHOULD FOCUS ON THE BATTLE TO COME...
WE MUST REMAIN VIGILANT--
CLAP
CLAP
CLAP
BOOM
BOOM
WHAT'S GOING ON?!
BANN!!

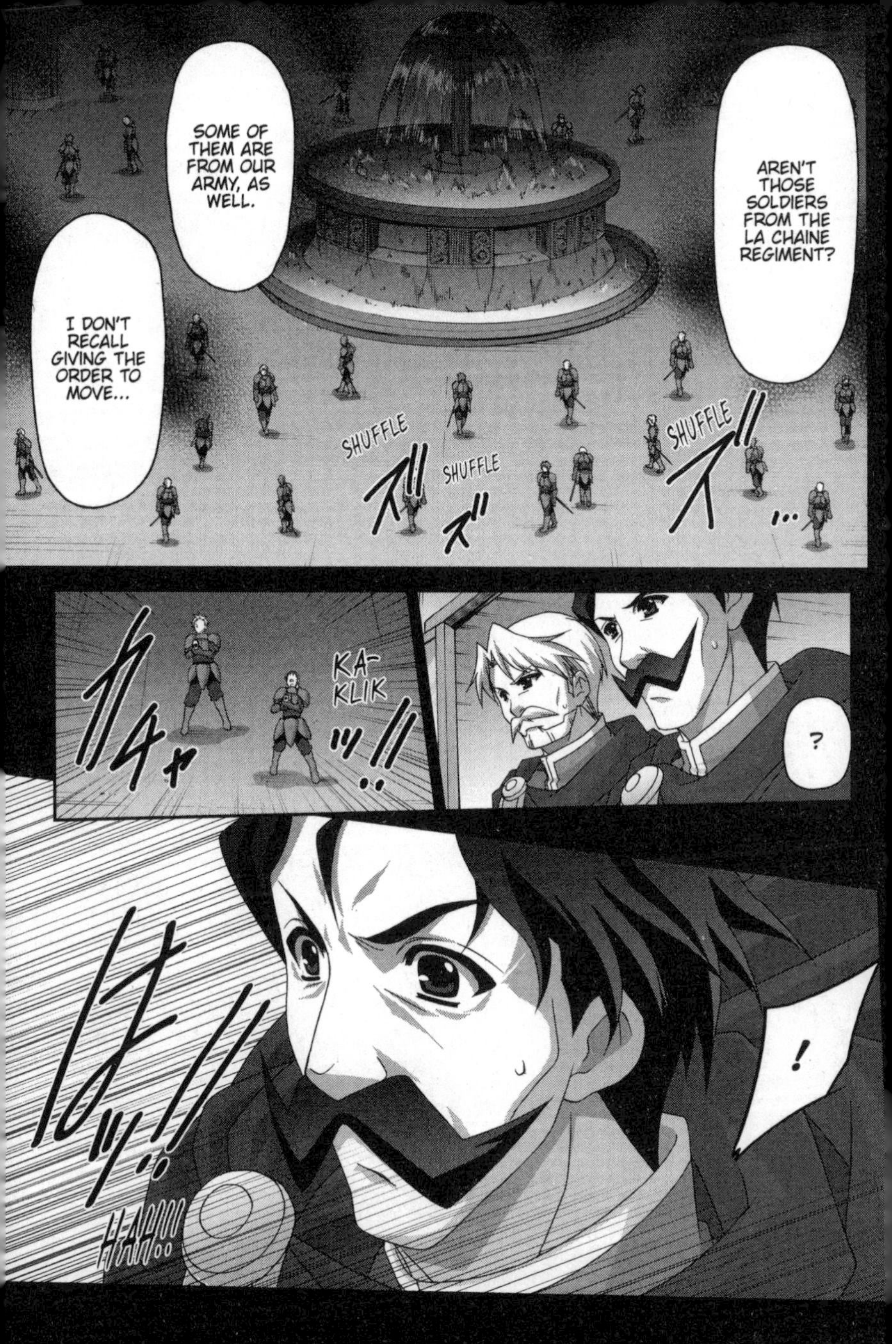
AREN'T THOSE SOLDIERS FROM THE LA CHAINE REGIMENT?
SOME OF THEM ARE FROM OUR ARMY, AS WELL.
I DON'T RECALL GIVING THE ORDER TO MOVE...
SHUFFLE
...
SHUFFLE
SHUFFLE
?
KA-KLIK
!
HAH!!

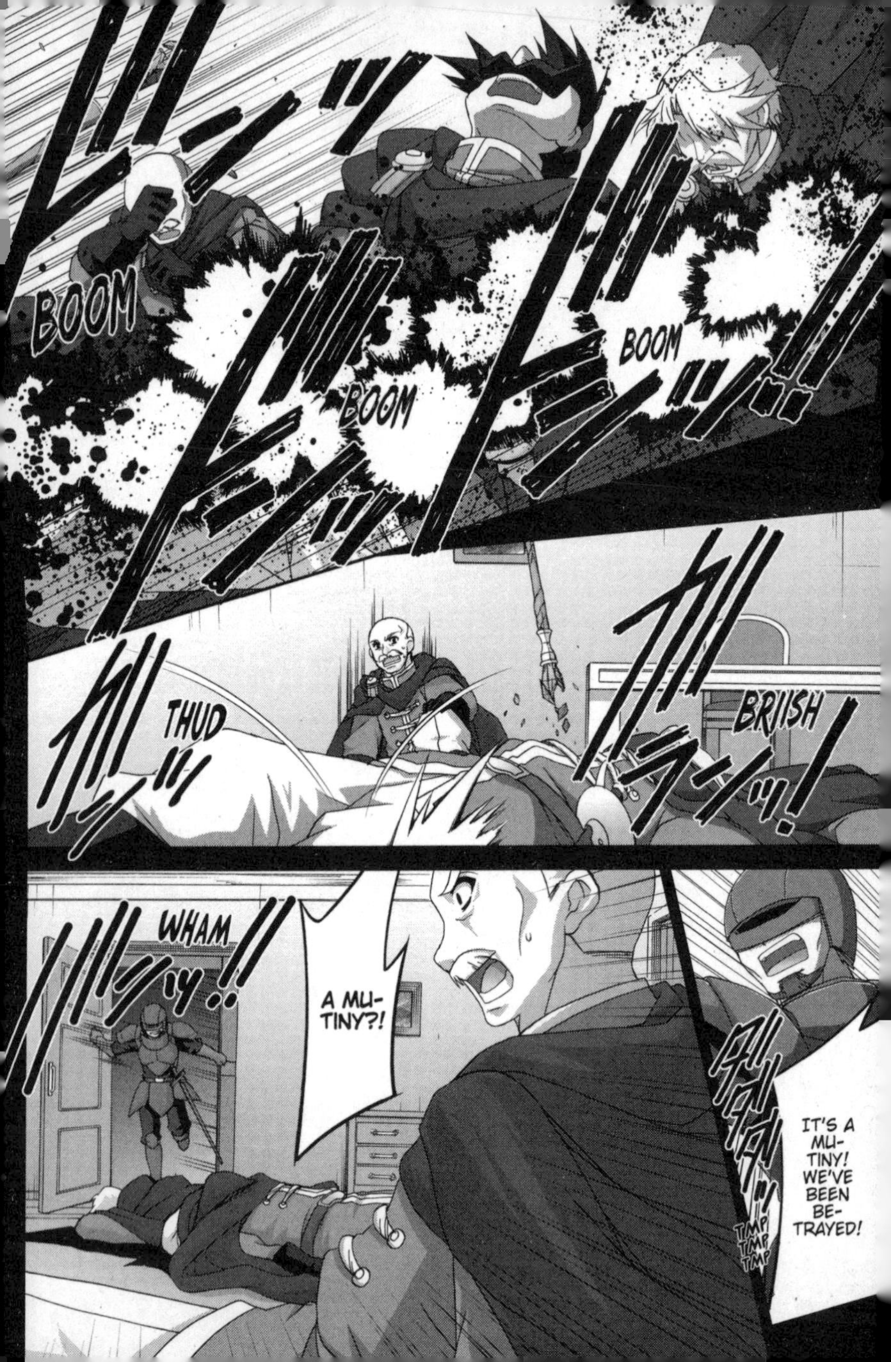
BOOM
BOOM
BOOM
BRIISH
THUD
IT'S A MU-TINY! WE'VE BEEN BE-TRAYED!
TMP TMP TMP
WHAM
A MU-TINY?!

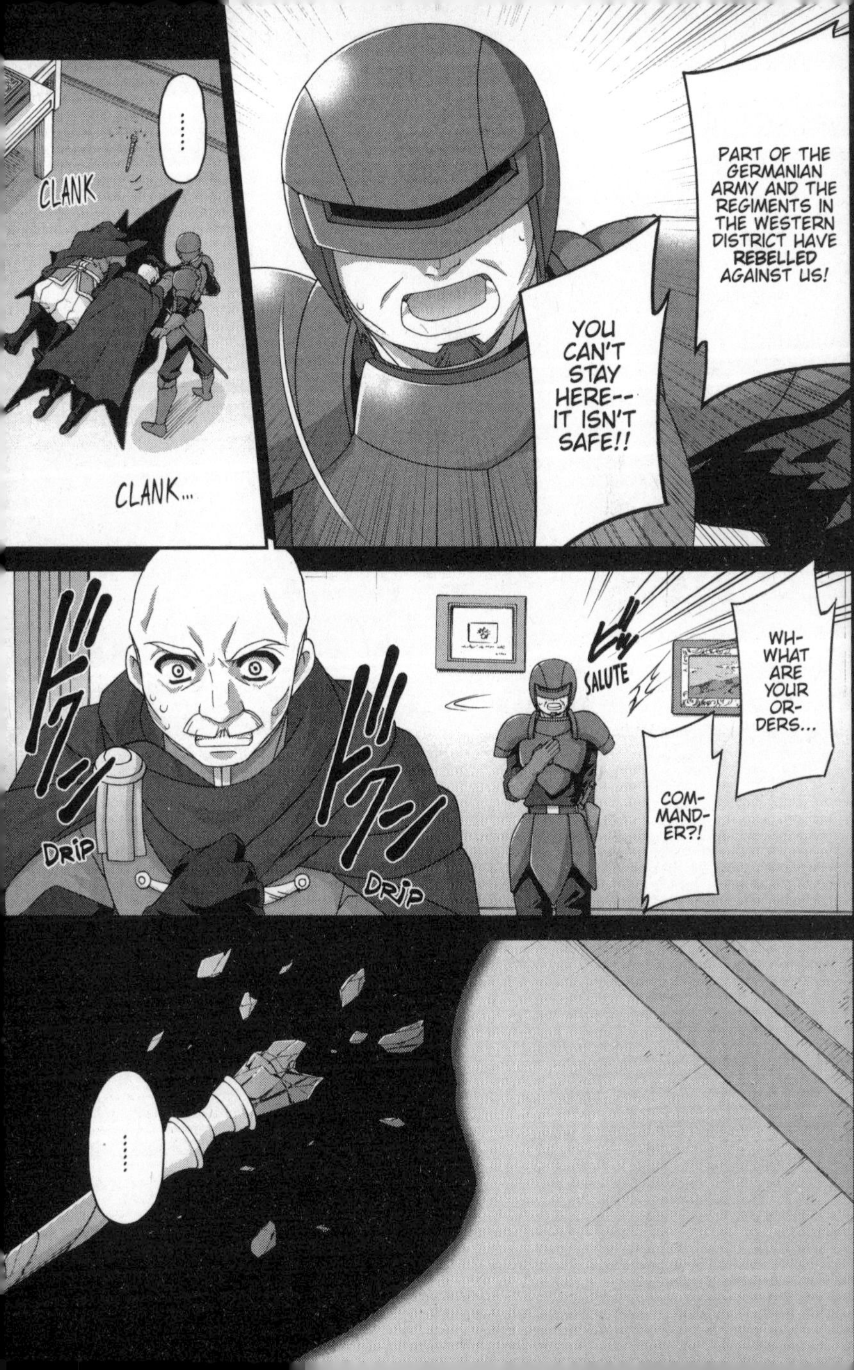
PART OF THE GERMANIAN ARMY AND THE REGIMENTS IN THE WESTERN DISTRICT HAVE REBELLED AGAINST US!
YOU CAN'T STAY HERE-- IT ISN'T SAFE!!
......
CLANK
CLANK...
WH-WHAT ARE YOUR OR-DERS...
COM-MAND-ER?!
SALUTE
DRIP
DRIP
......

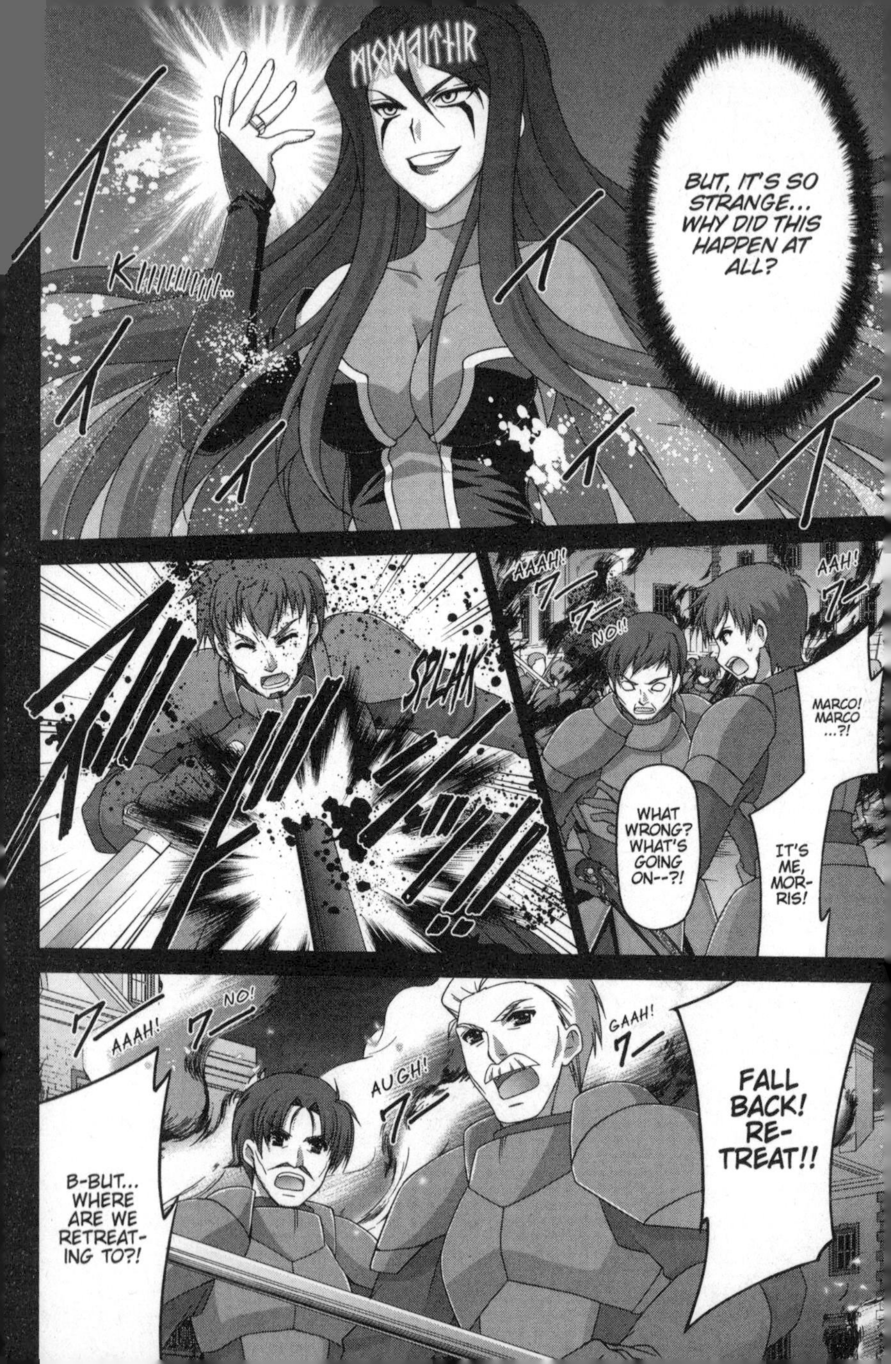
BUT, IT'S SO STRANGE... WHY DID THIS HAPPEN AT ALL?
Kiiiiiiiiii...
AAH!
MARCO! MARCO ...?!
AAAH!
NO!!
IT'S ME, MOR-RIS!
WHAT WRONG? WHAT'S GOING ON--?!
SPLAK
FALL BACK! RE-TREAT!!
GAAH!
NO!
AUGH!
AAAH!
B-BUT... WHERE ARE WE RETREAT-ING TO?!

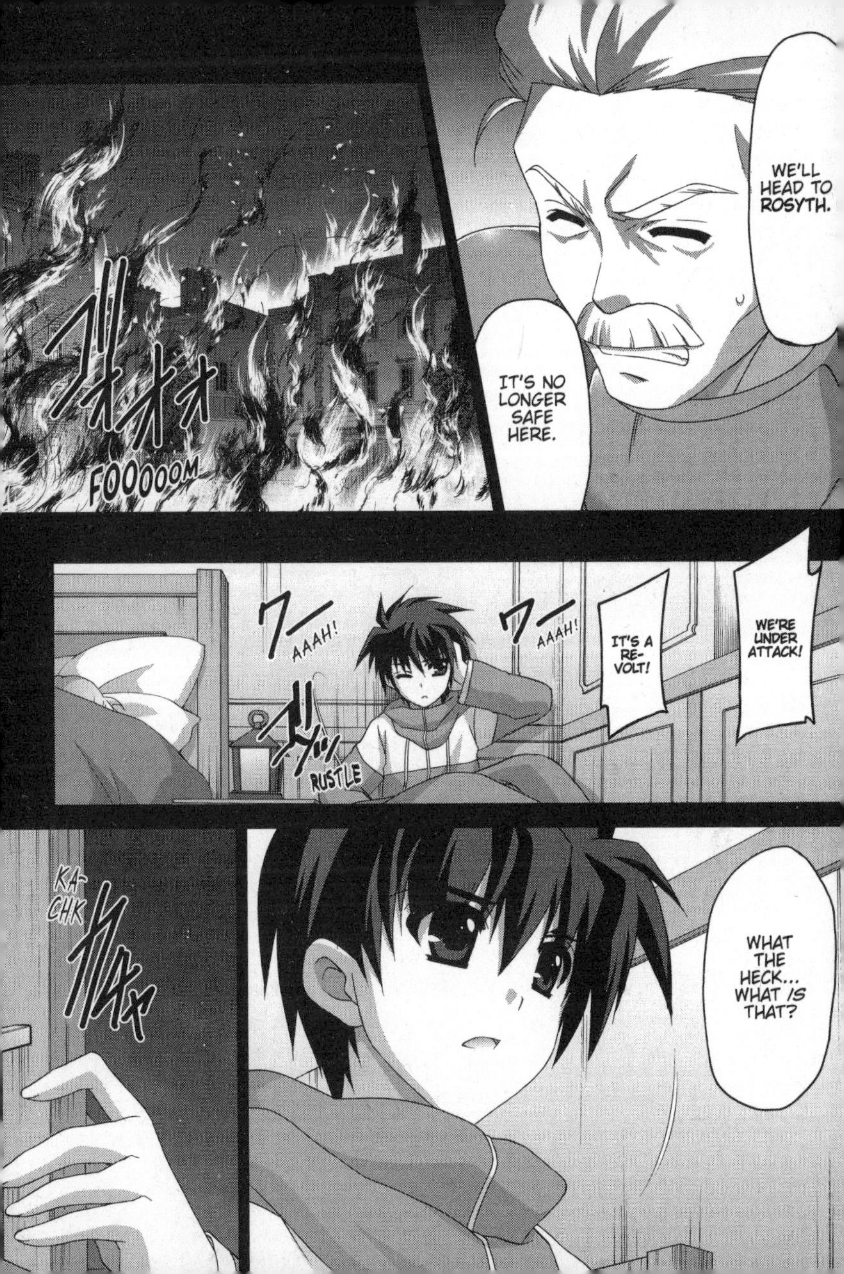
WE'LL HEAD TO ROSYTH.
IT'S NO LONGER SAFE HERE.
FOOOOOM
WE'RE UNDER ATTACK!
IT'S A RE-VOLT!
AAAH!
AAAH!
RUSTLE
WHAT THE HECK... WHAT *IS* THAT?
KA-CHK

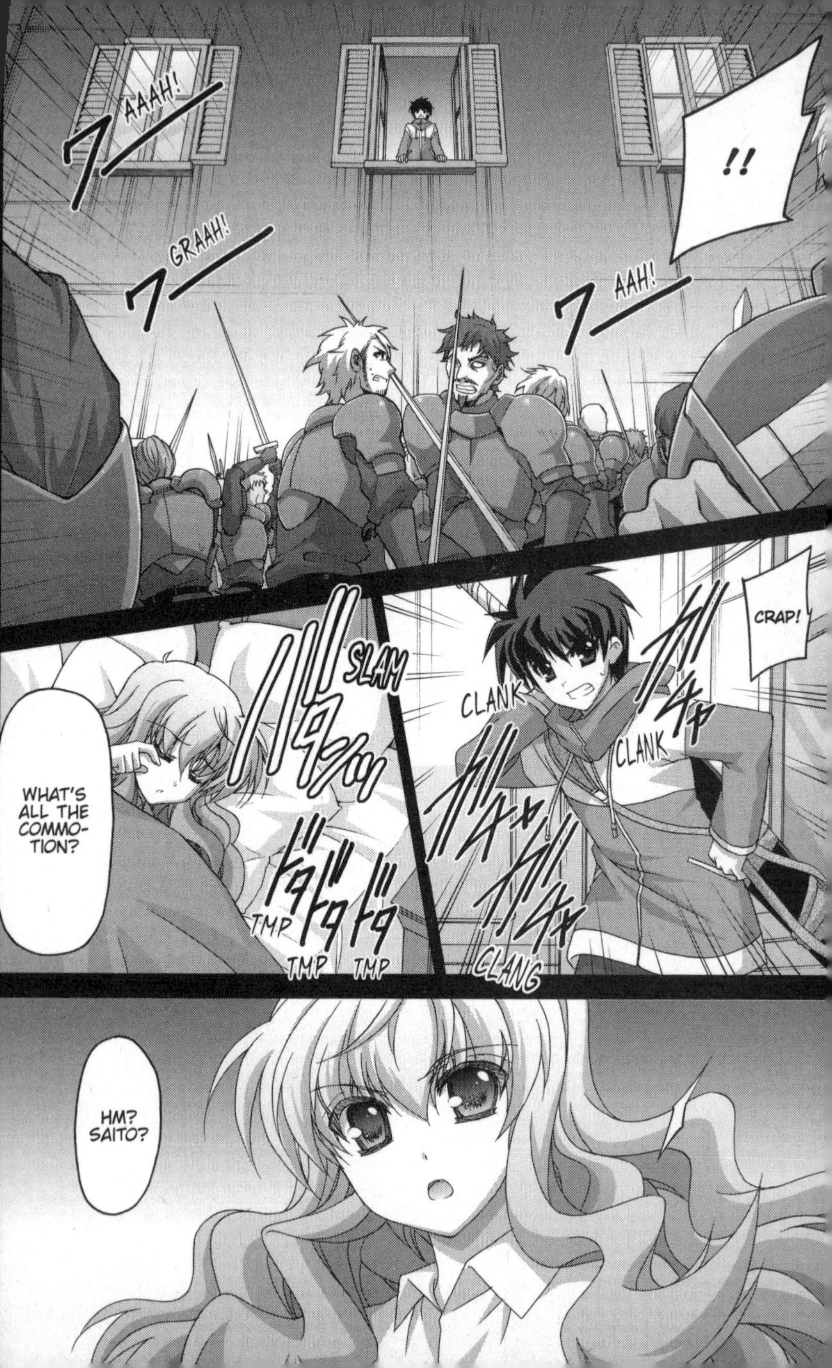
!!
AAH!
GRAAH!
AAAH!
CRAP!
CLANK
CLANK
CLANG
SLAM
WHAT'S ALL THE COMMO-TION?
TMP
TMP
TMP
HM? SAITO?

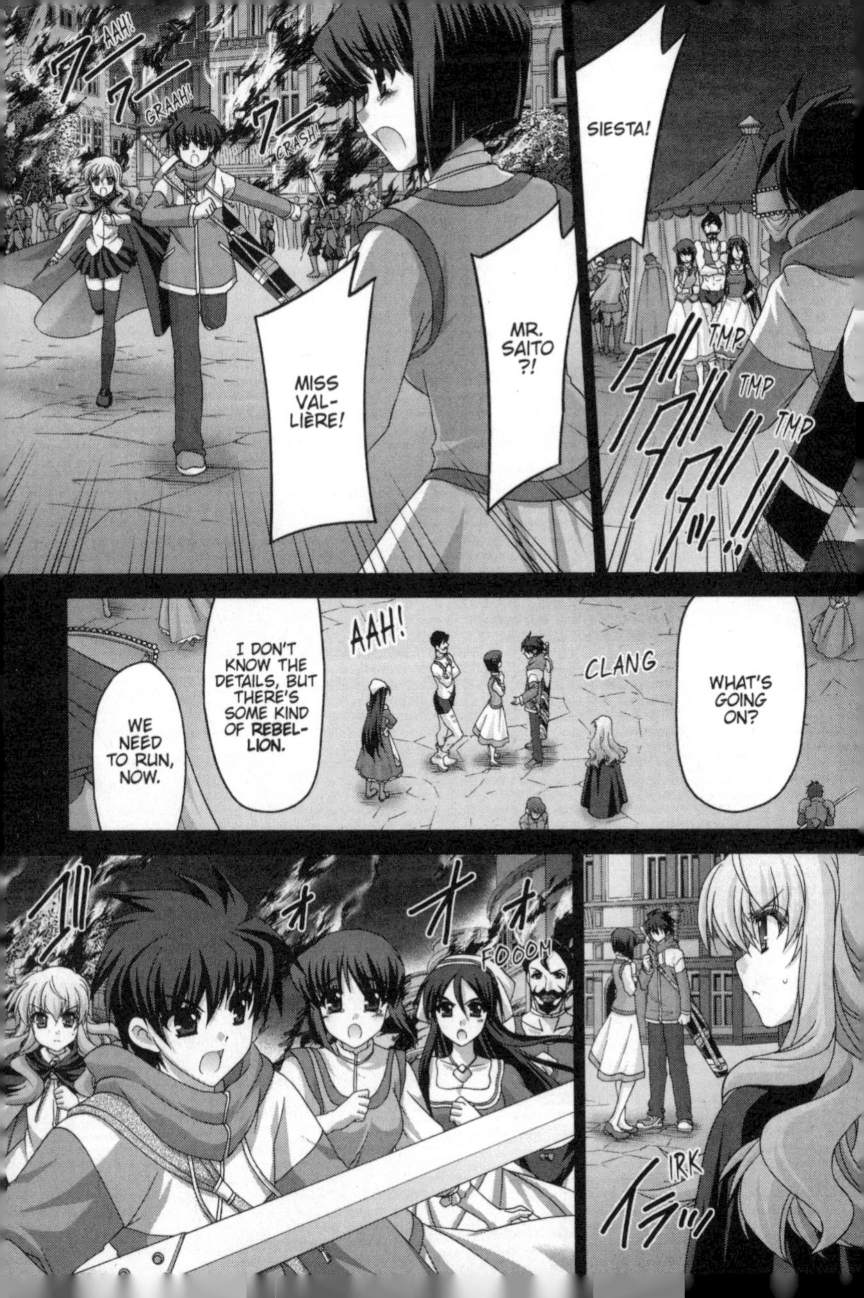
SIESTA!
TMP
TMP
TMP
CRASH!
GRAAH!
AAH!
MR. SAITO ?!
MISS VAL-LIÈRE!
WHAT'S GOING ON?
CLANG
AAH!
I DON'T KNOW THE DETAILS, BUT THERE'S SOME KIND OF REBEL-LION.
WE NEED TO RUN, NOW.
IRK
FOOOM

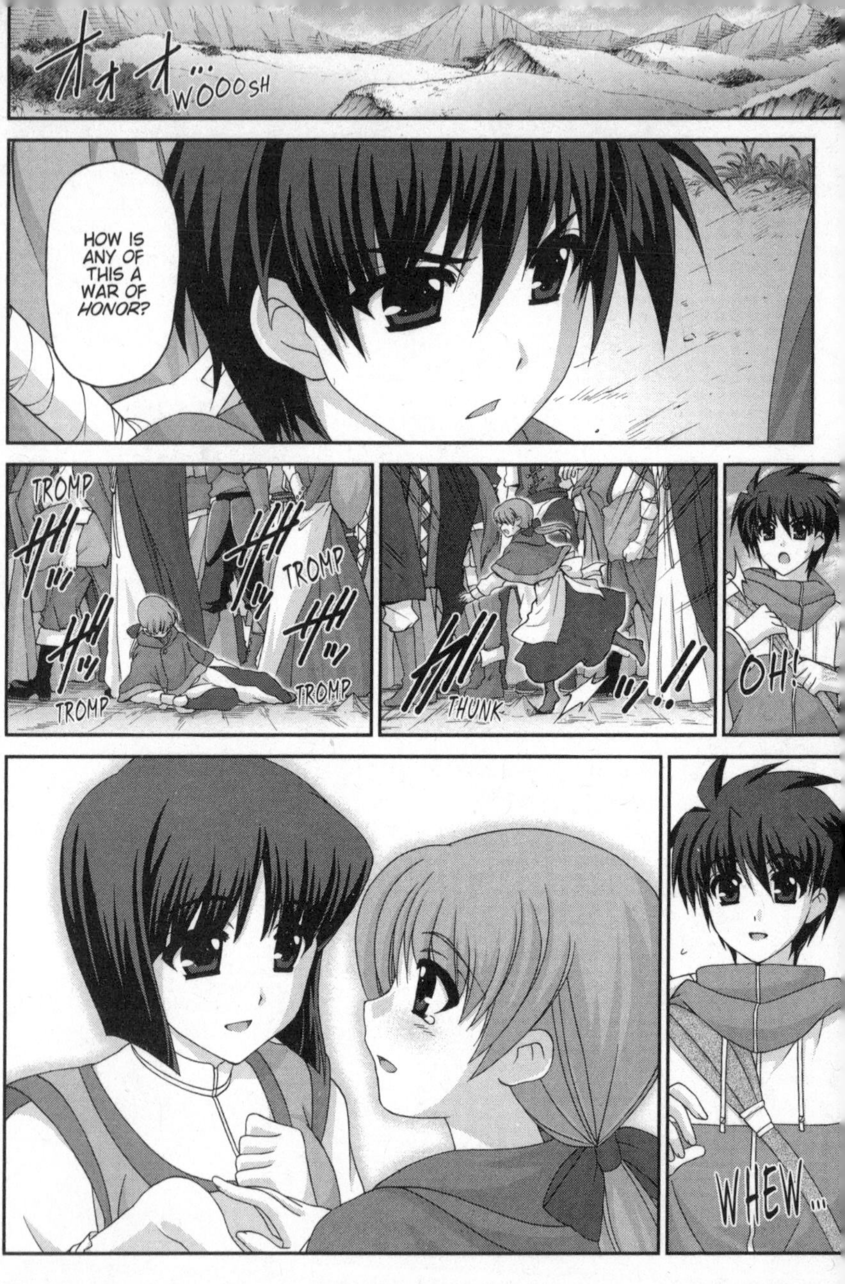

WOOOSH
HOW IS ANY OF THIS A WAR OF *HONOR?*
OH!
THUNK
TROMP
TROMP
TROMP
TROMP
WHEW...

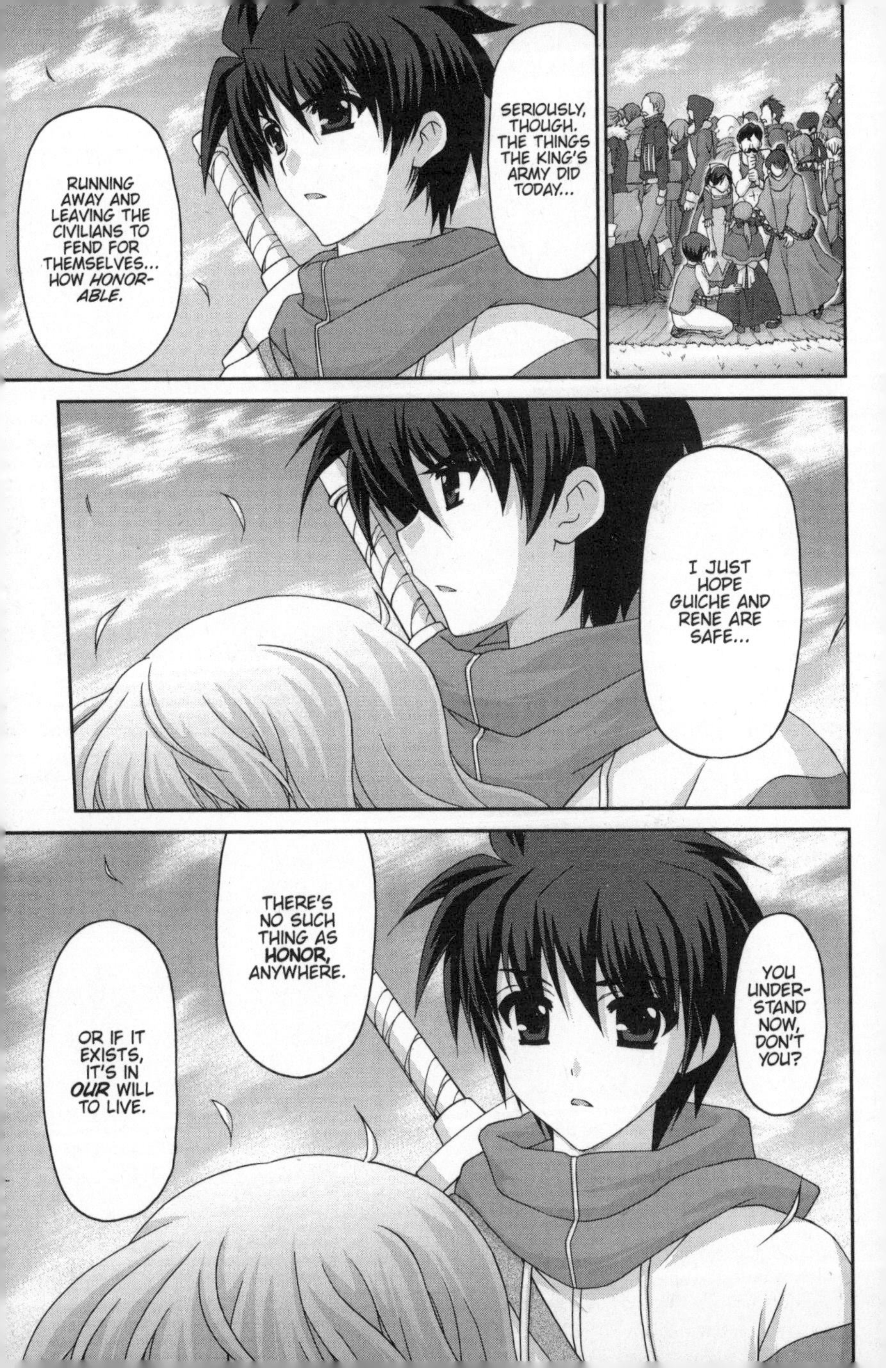
SERIOUSLY, THOUGH. THE THINGS THE KING'S ARMY DID TODAY...
RUNNING AWAY AND LEAVING THE CIVILIANS TO FEND FOR THEMSELVES... HOW *HONORABLE*.
I JUST HOPE GUICHE AND RENE ARE SAFE...
YOU UNDERSTAND NOW, DON'T YOU?
THERE'S NO SUCH THING AS **HONOR**, ANYWHERE.
OR IF IT EXISTS, IT'S IN **OUR** WILL TO LIVE.

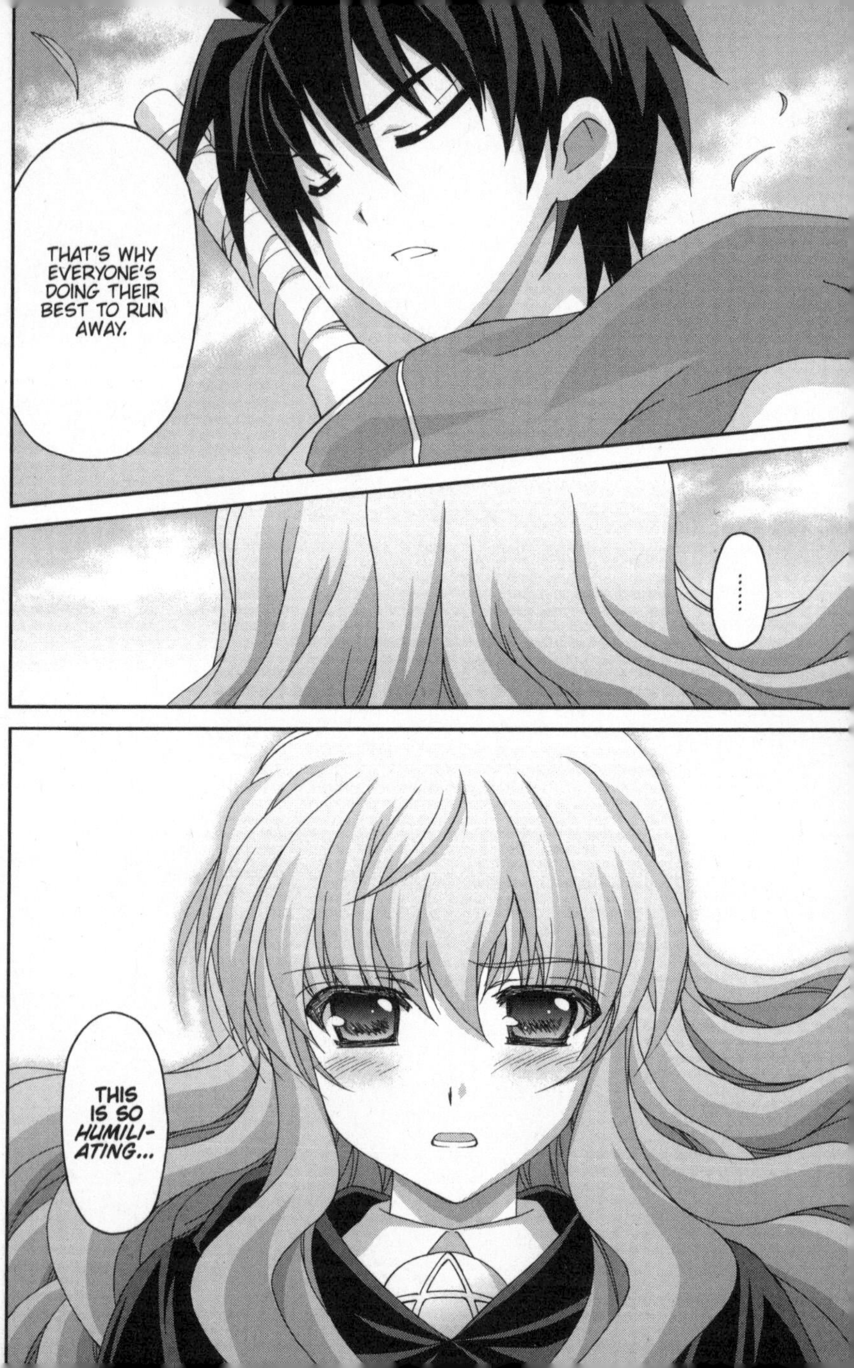
THAT'S WHY EVERYONE'S DOING THEIR BEST TO RUN AWAY.
......
THIS IS SO *HUMILI-ATING...*

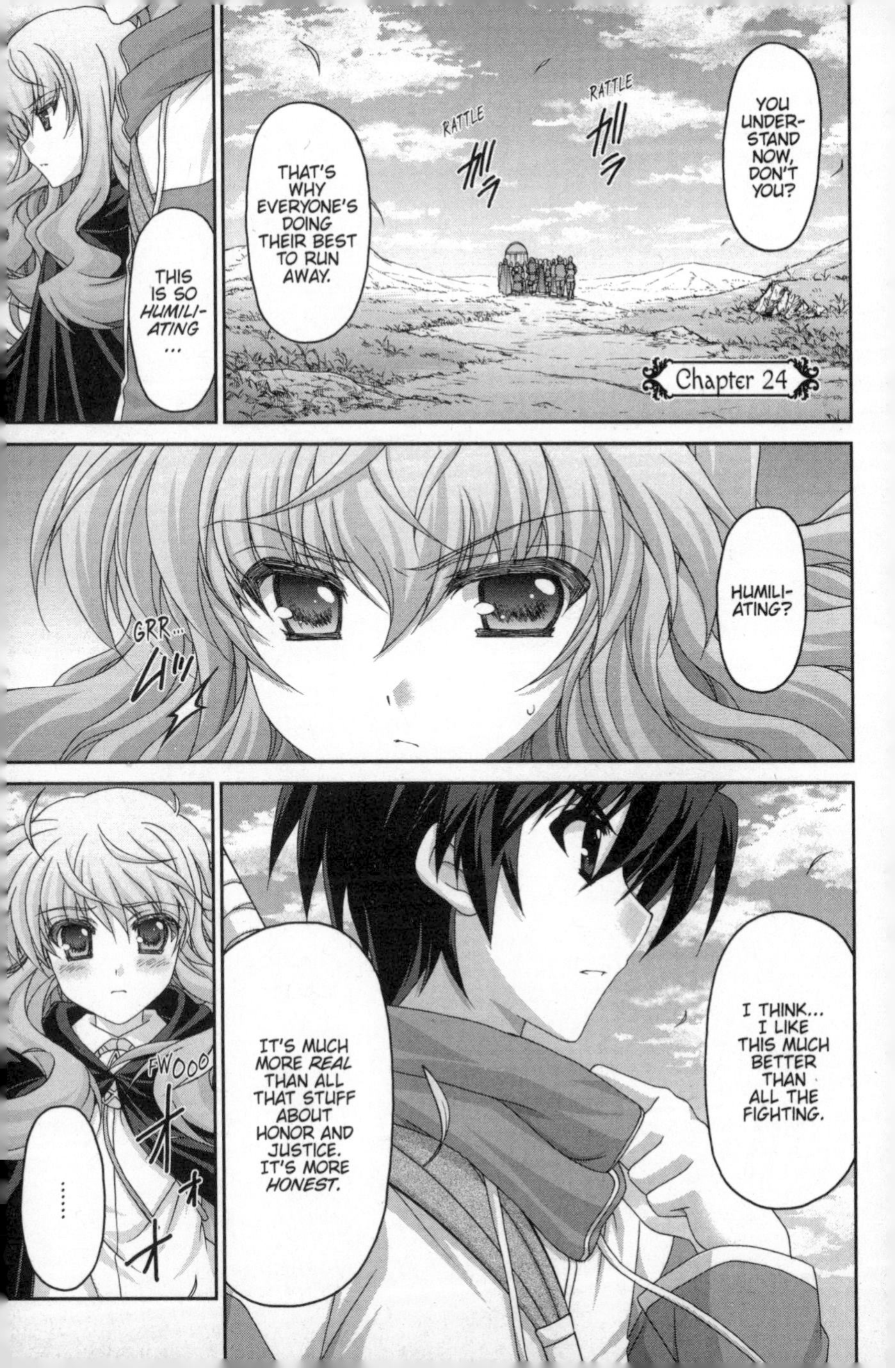
YOU UNDERSTAND NOW, DON'T YOU?
RATTLE
RATTLE
THAT'S WHY EVERYONE'S DOING THEIR BEST TO RUN AWAY.
Chapter 24
THIS IS SO *HUMILIATING* ...
HUMILIATING?
GRR...
I THINK... I LIKE THIS MUCH BETTER THAN ALL THE FIGHTING.
IT'S MUCH MORE *REAL* THAN ALL THAT STUFF ABOUT HONOR AND JUSTICE. IT'S MORE *HONEST*.
FWOOO
......

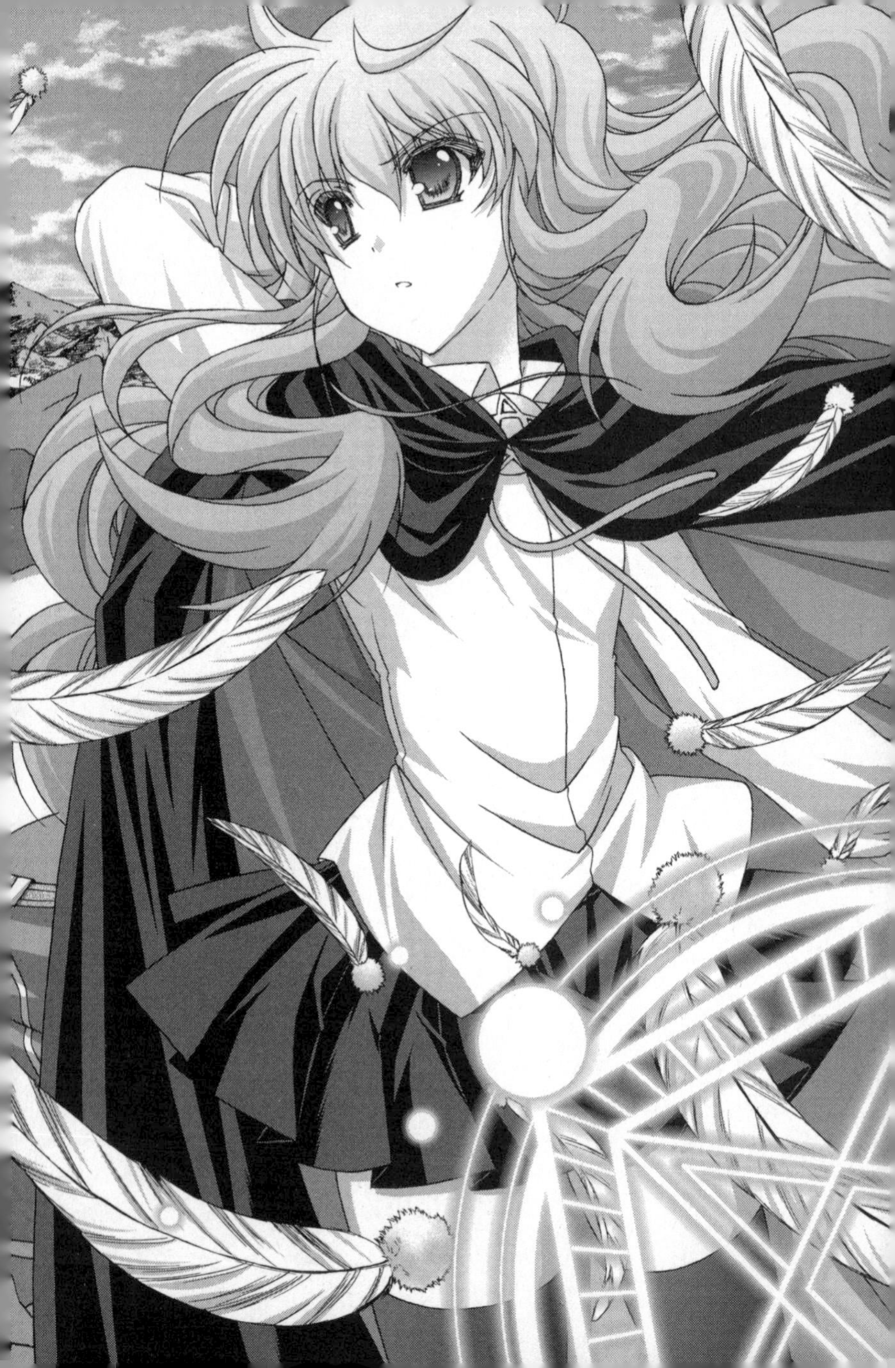

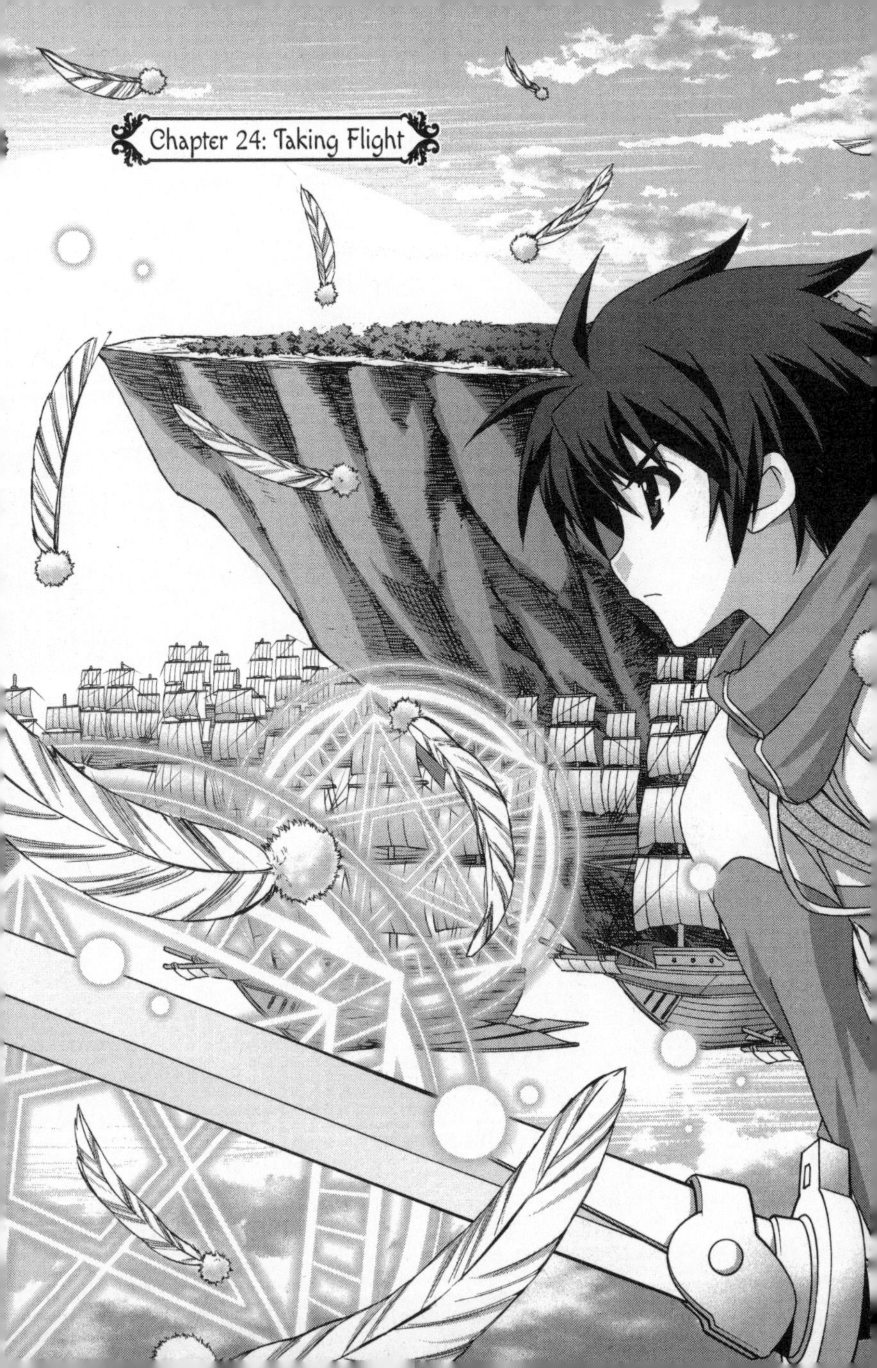
Chapter 24: Taking Flight

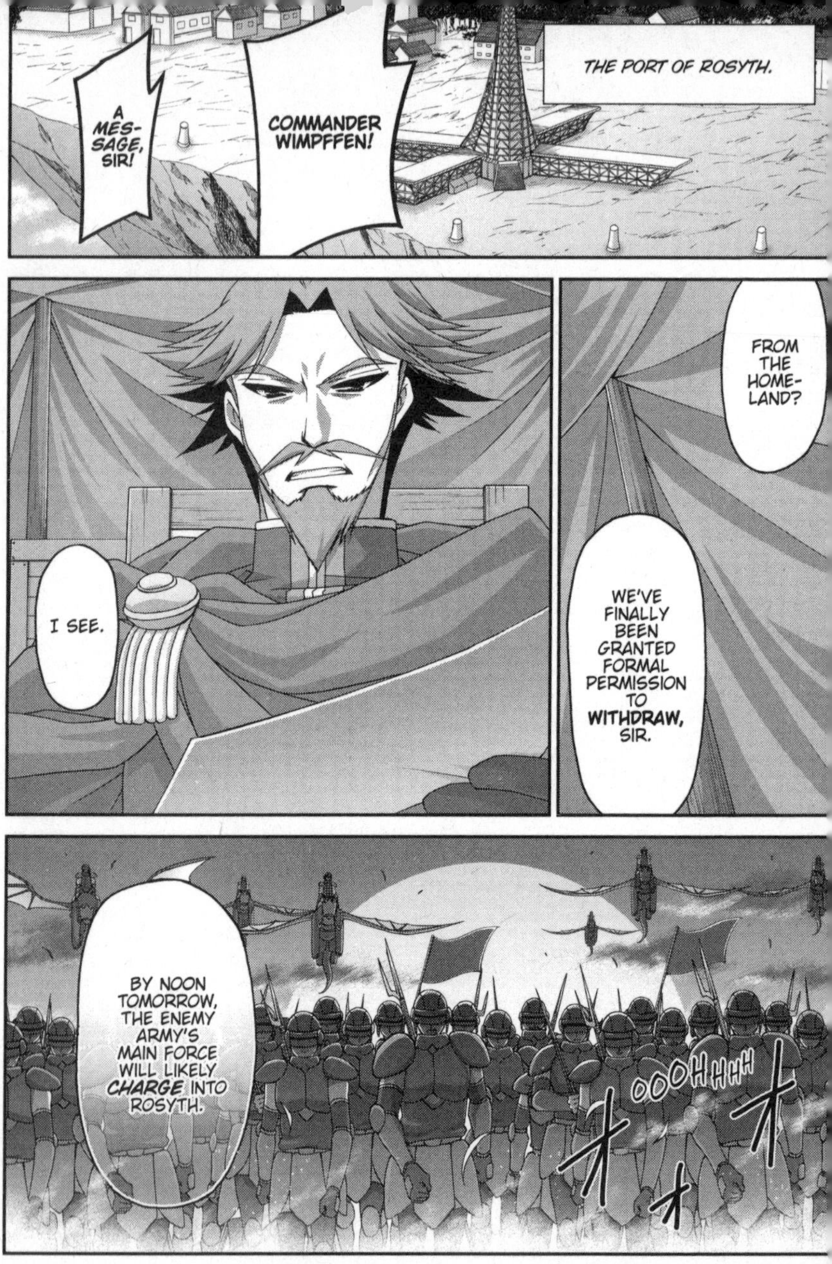
THE PORT OF ROSYTH.
COMMANDER WIMPFFEN!
A MES-SAGE, SIR!
FROM THE HOME-LAND?
WE'VE FINALLY BEEN GRANTED FORMAL PERMISSION TO WITHDRAW, SIR.
I SEE.
OOOHHHH
BY NOON TOMORROW, THE ENEMY ARMY'S MAIN FORCE WILL LIKELY CHARGE INTO ROSYTH.

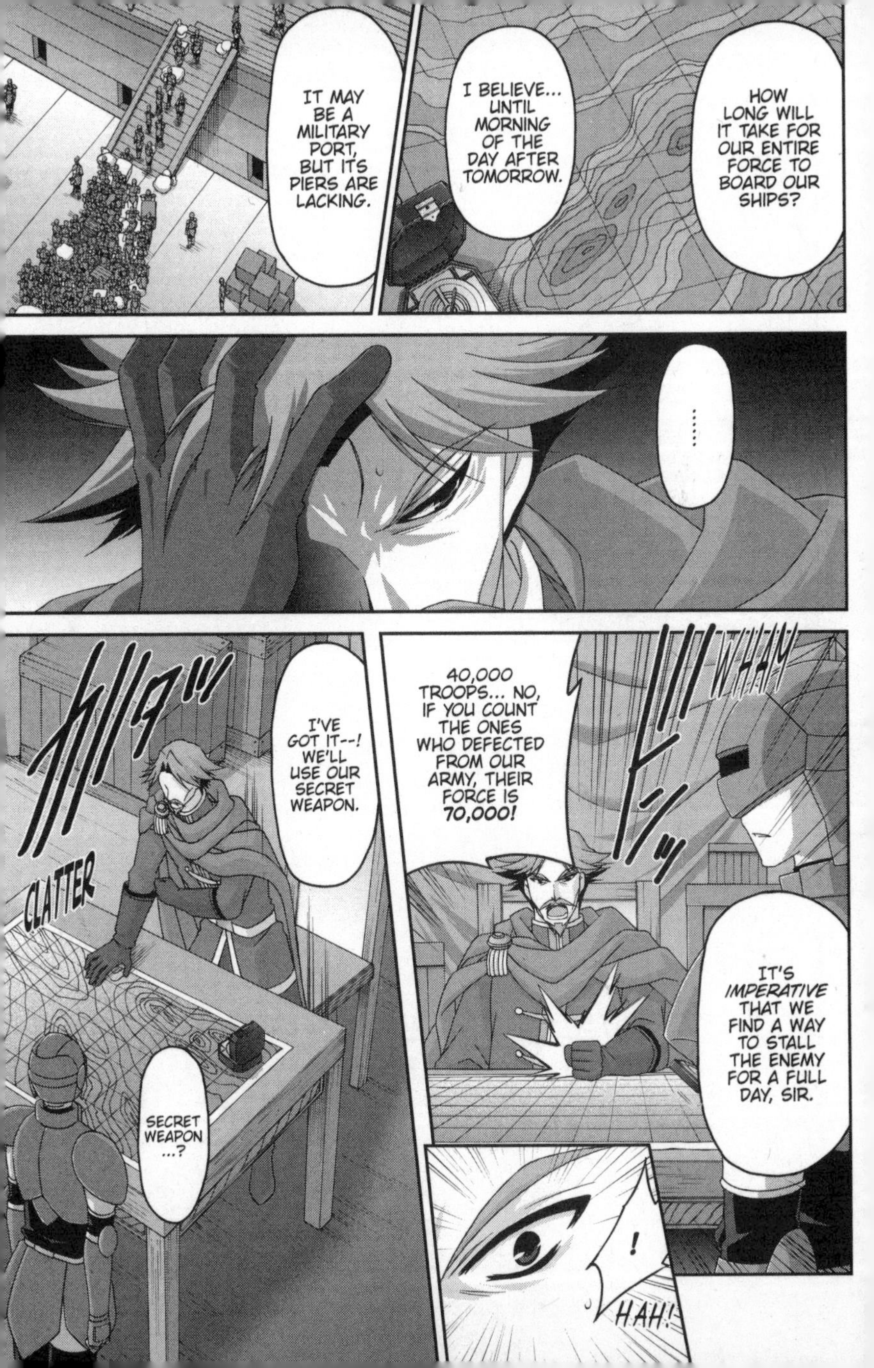
HOW LONG WILL IT TAKE FOR OUR ENTIRE FORCE TO BOARD OUR SHIPS?
I BELIEVE... UNTIL MORNING OF THE DAY AFTER TOMORROW.
IT MAY BE A MILITARY PORT, BUT ITS PIERS ARE LACKING.
......
WHAM
40,000 TROOPS... NO, IF YOU COUNT THE ONES WHO DEFECTED FROM OUR ARMY, THEIR FORCE IS **70,000!**
IT'S *IMPERATIVE* THAT WE FIND A WAY TO STALL THE ENEMY FOR A FULL DAY, SIR.
!
HAH!
I'VE GOT IT--! WE'LL USE OUR SECRET WEAPON.
CLATTER
SECRET WEAPON ...?

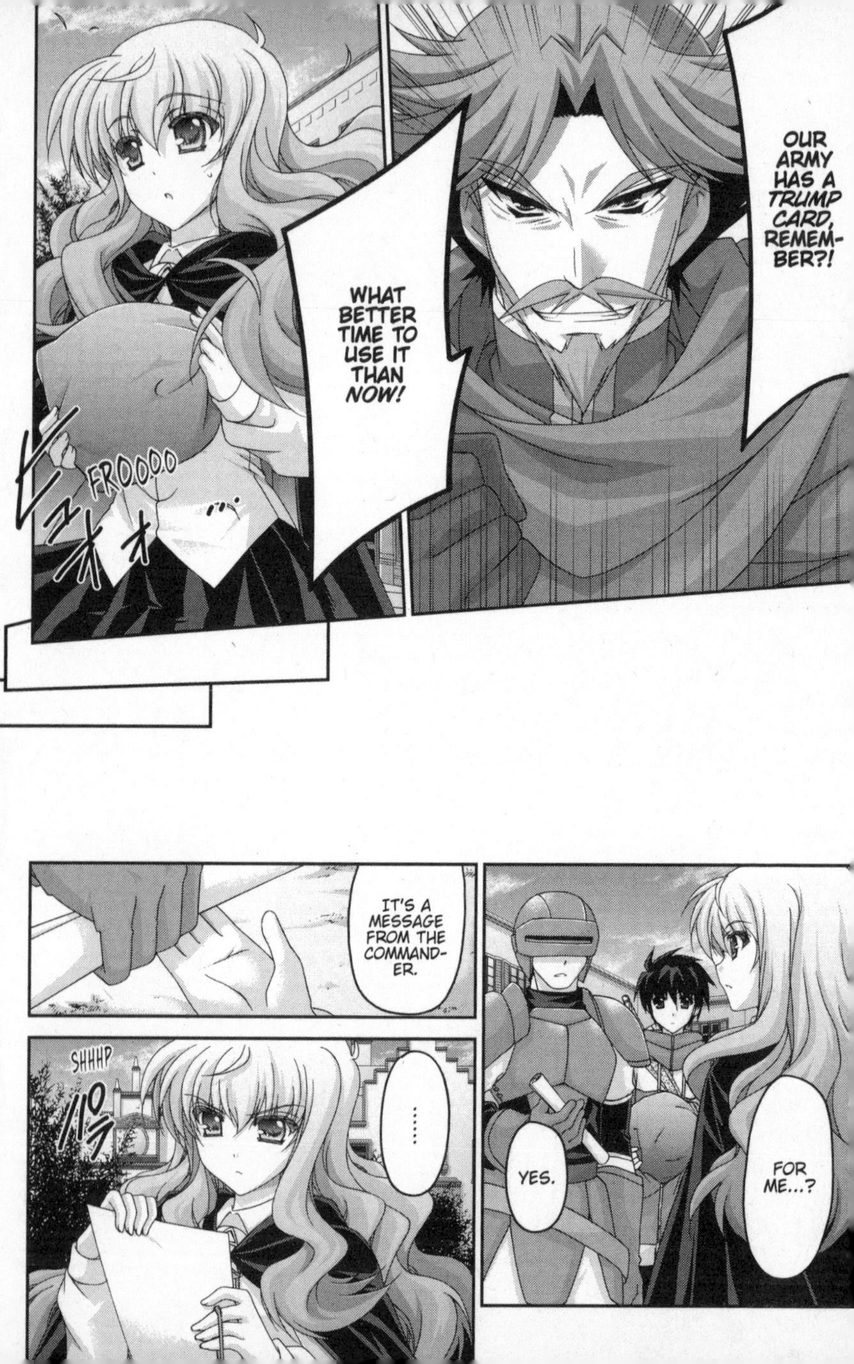
OUR ARMY HAS A TRUMP CARD, REMEMBER?!
WHAT BETTER TIME TO USE IT THAN NOW!
ヒュオオ
FROOOO
FOR ME...?
YES.
IT'S A MESSAGE FROM THE COMMANDER.
SHHHP
パラ
......

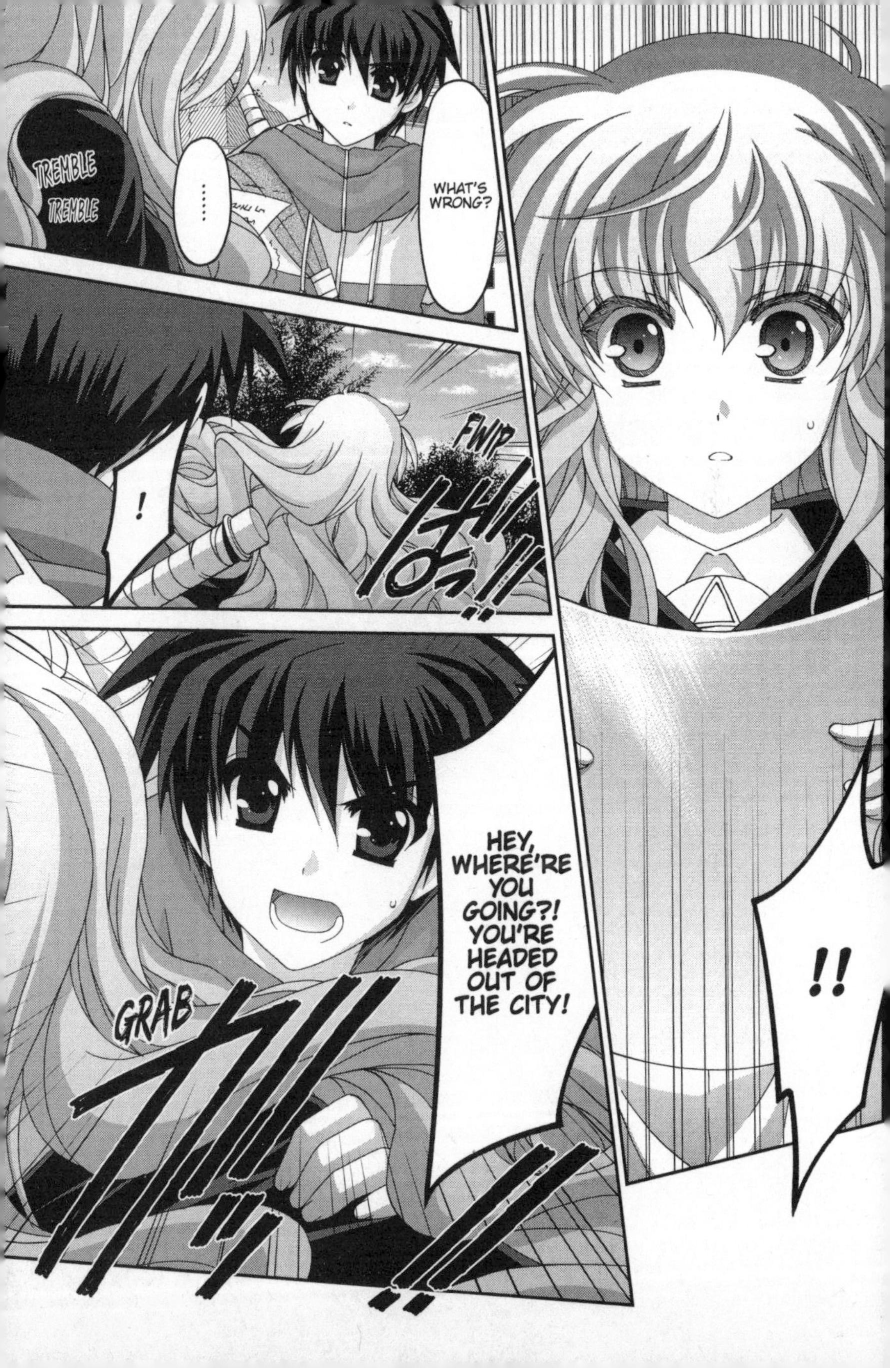

WHAT'S WRONG?
......
TREMBLE
TREMBLE
FWIP
!
!!
HEY, WHERE'RE YOU GOING?! YOU'RE HEADED OUT OF THE CITY!
GRAB

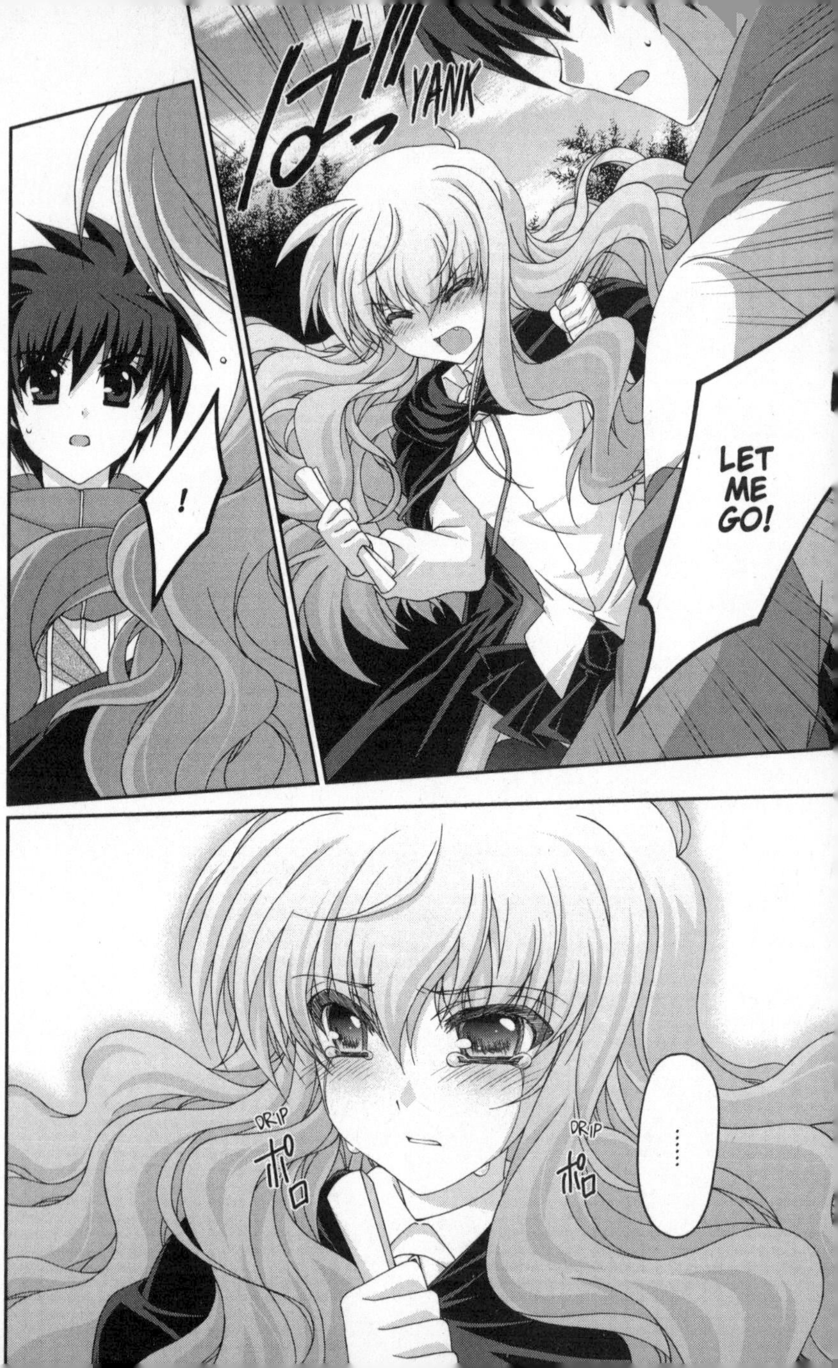
はっ
YANK
LET ME GO!
!
……
DRIP
ポロ
DRIP
ポロ

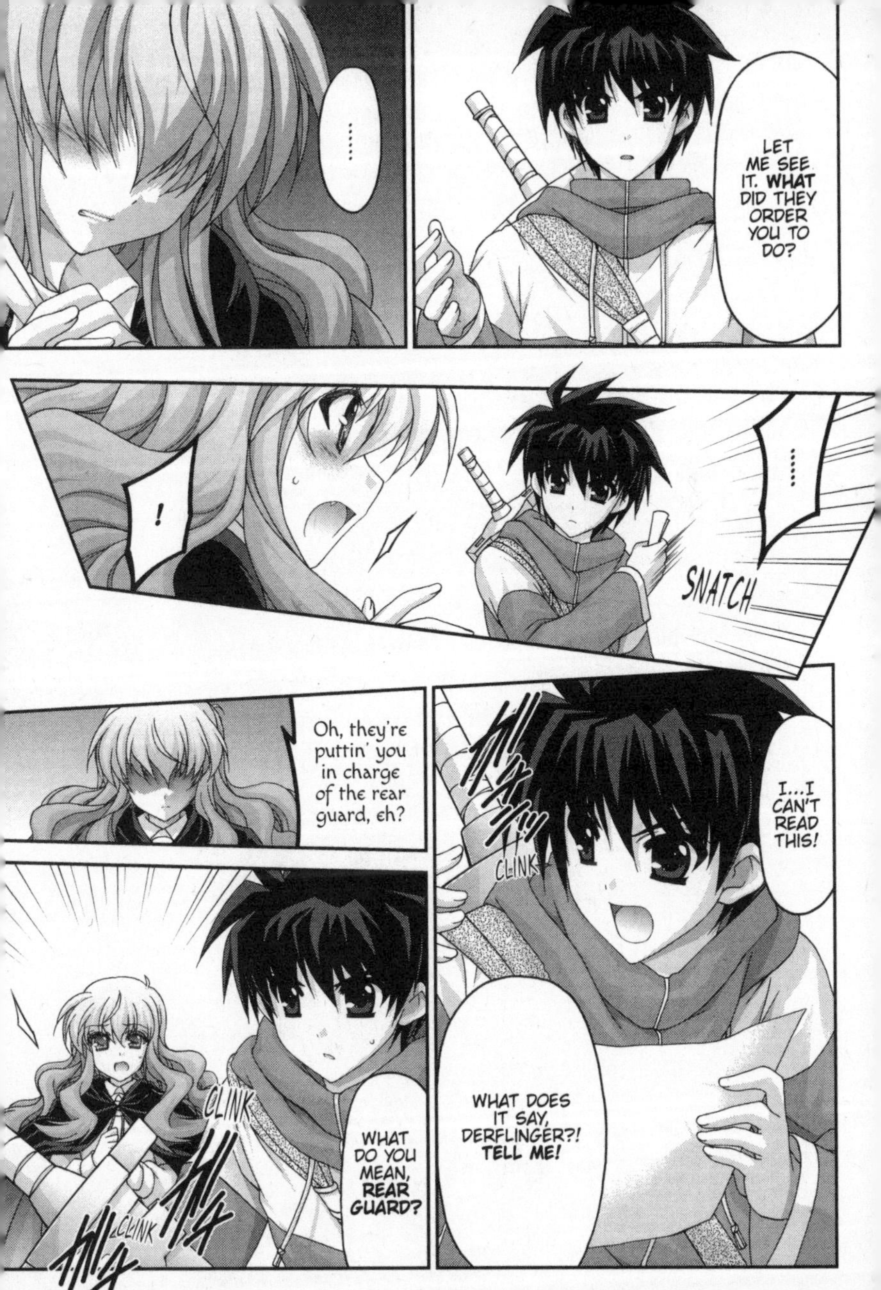
LET ME SEE IT. WHAT DID THEY ORDER YOU TO DO?
......
......
SNATCH
!
I...I CAN'T READ THIS!
CLINK
WHAT DOES IT SAY, DERFLINGER?! TELL ME!
Oh, they're puttin' you in charge of the rear guard, eh?
WHAT DO YOU MEAN, REAR GUARD?
CLINK
CLINK

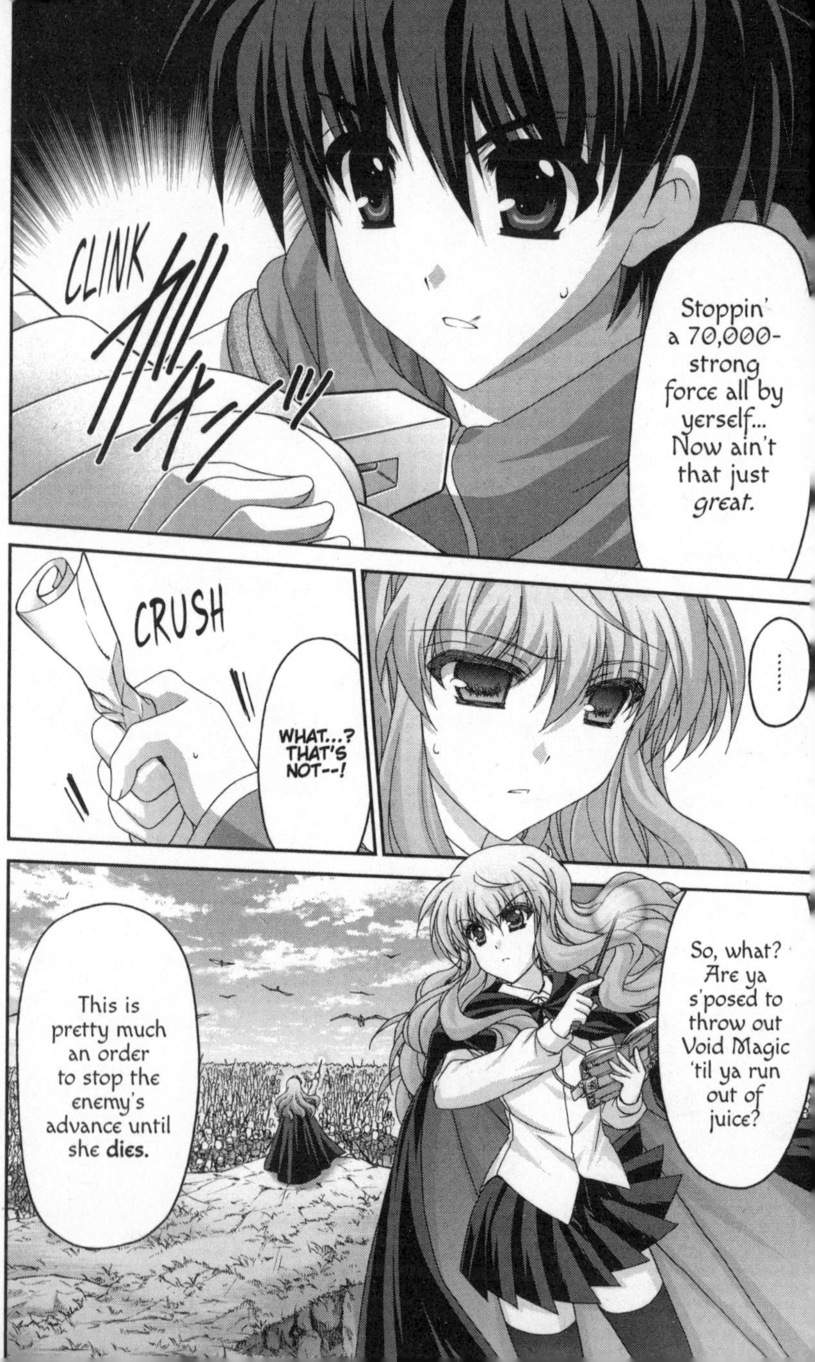
CLINK
Stoppin' a 70,000-strong force all by yerself... Now ain't that just *great.*
......
CRUSH
WHAT...? THAT'S NOT--!
So, what? Are ya s'posed to throw out Void Magic 'til ya run out of juice?
This is pretty much an order to stop the enemy's advance until she **dies.**

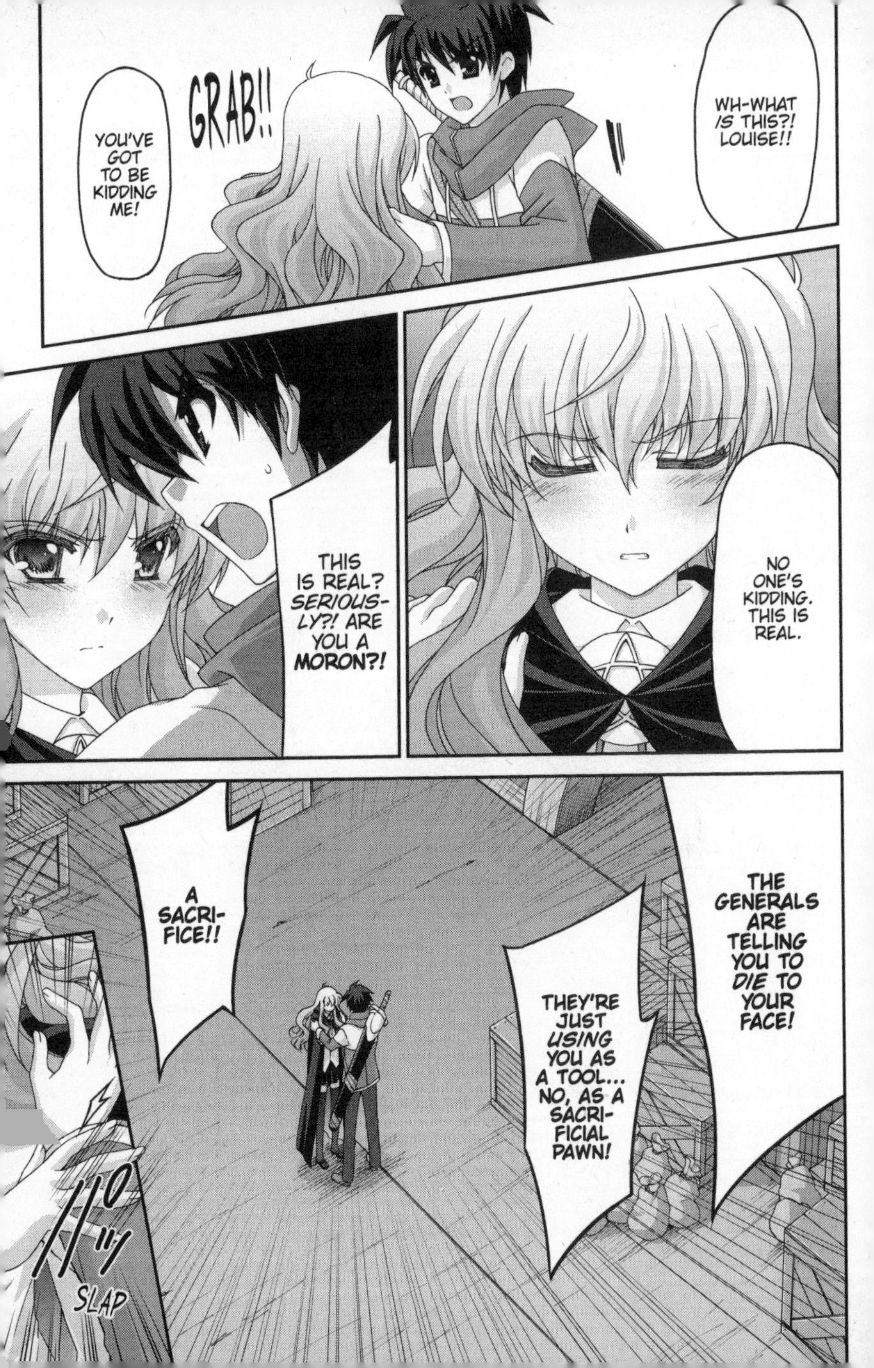
WH-WHAT IS THIS?! LOUISE!!
GRAB!!
YOU'VE GOT TO BE KIDDING ME!
NO ONE'S KIDDING. THIS IS REAL.
THIS IS REAL? SERIOUSLY?! ARE YOU A MORON?!
THE GENERALS ARE TELLING YOU TO DIE TO YOUR FACE!
THEY'RE JUST USING YOU AS A TOOL... NO, AS A SACRIFICIAL PAWN!
A SACRIFICE!!
SLAP

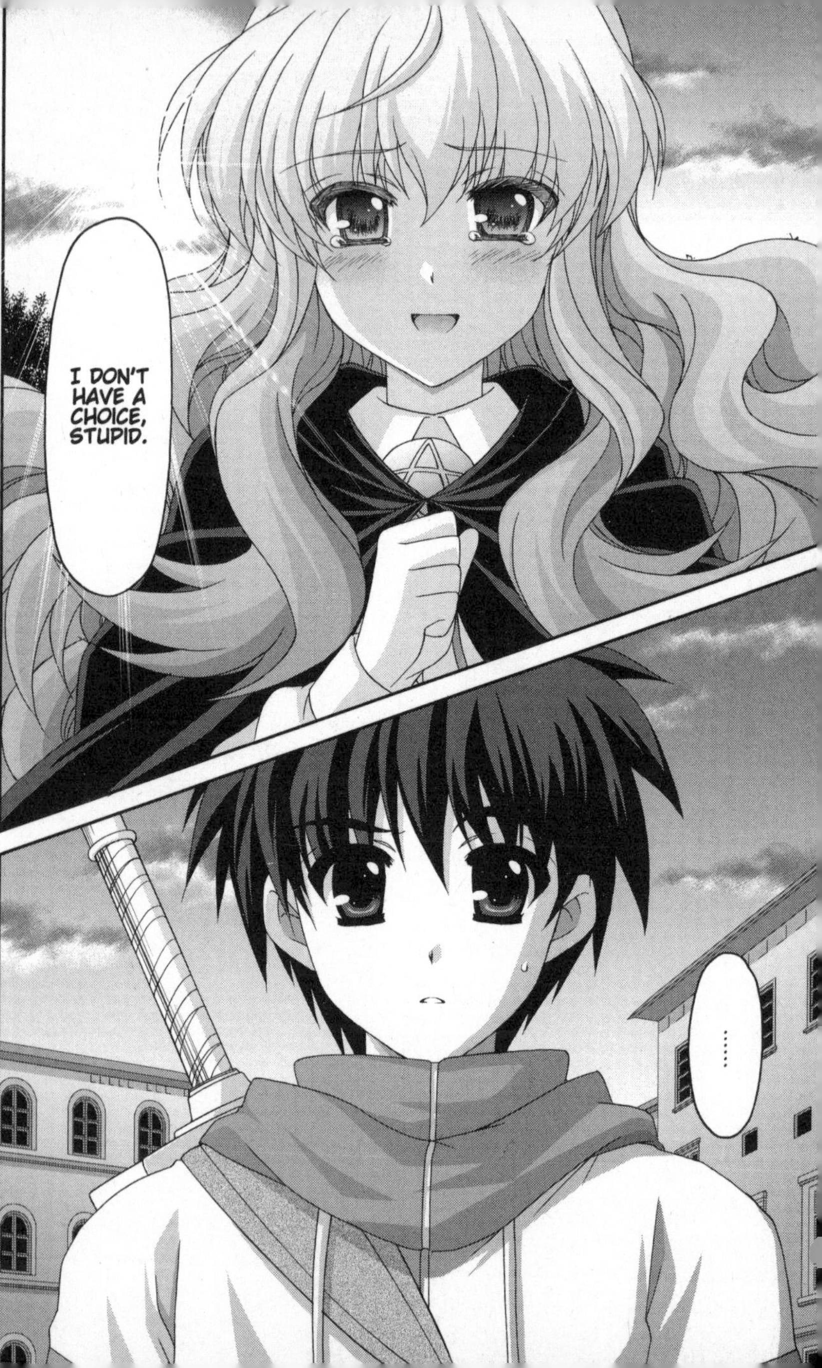
I DON'T HAVE A CHOICE, STUPID.
......

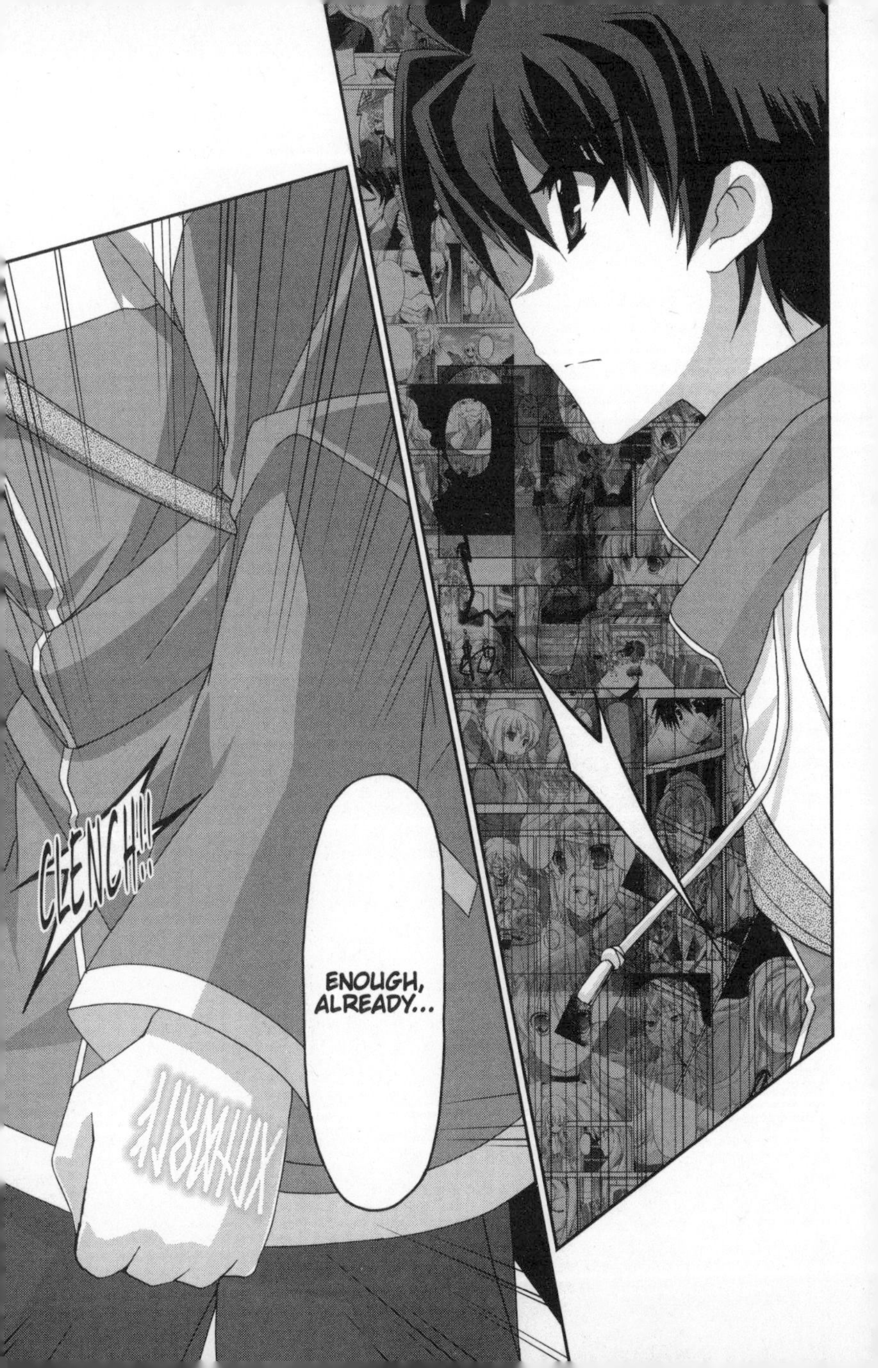
ENOUGH, ALREADY...
CLENCH!!

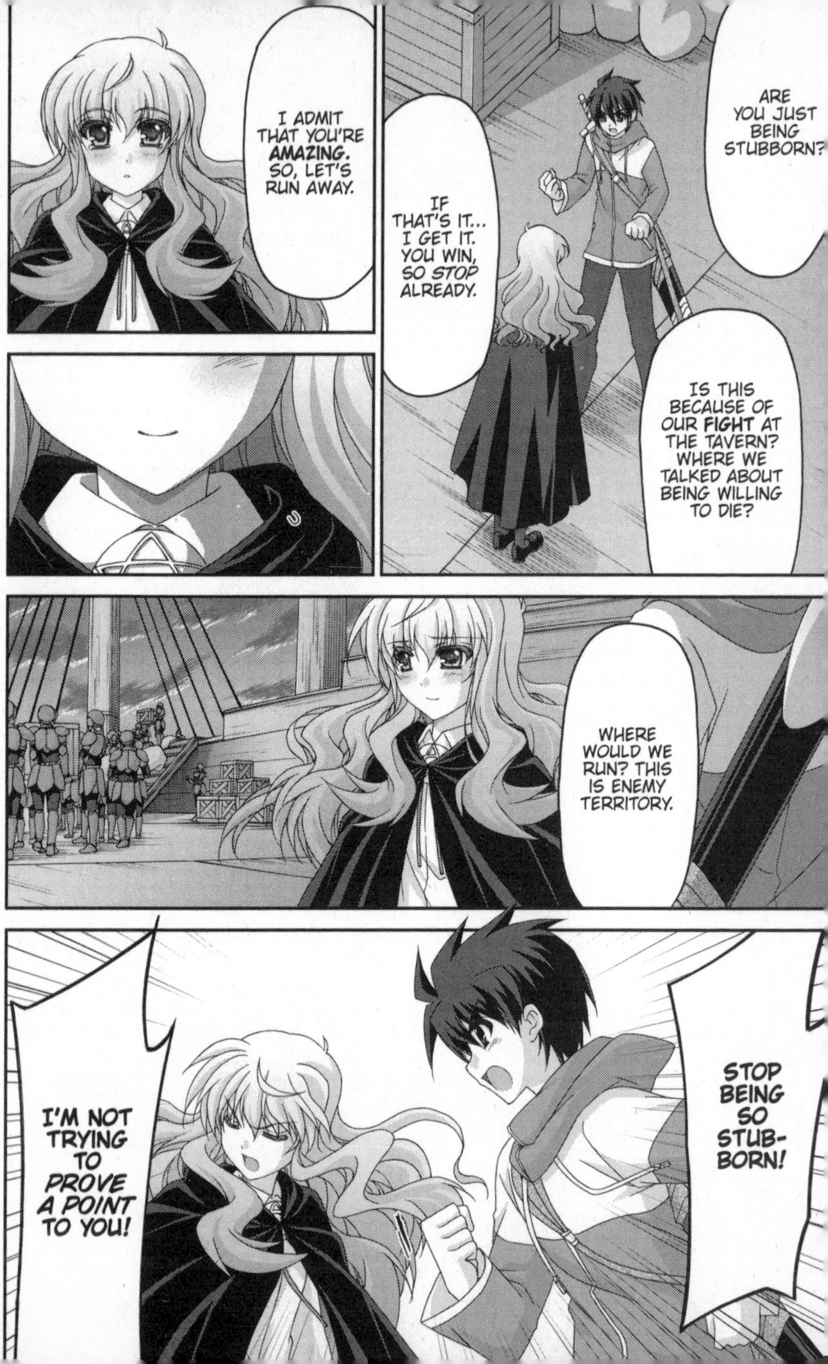
ARE YOU JUST BEING STUBBORN?
IS THIS BECAUSE OF OUR **FIGHT** AT THE TAVERN? WHERE WE TALKED ABOUT BEING WILLING TO DIE?
IF THAT'S IT... I GET IT. YOU WIN, SO *STOP* ALREADY.
I ADMIT THAT YOU'RE **AMAZING.** SO, LET'S RUN AWAY.
WHERE WOULD WE RUN? THIS IS ENEMY TERRITORY.
STOP BEING SO STUB-BORN!
I'M NOT TRYING TO *PROVE* A POINT TO YOU!

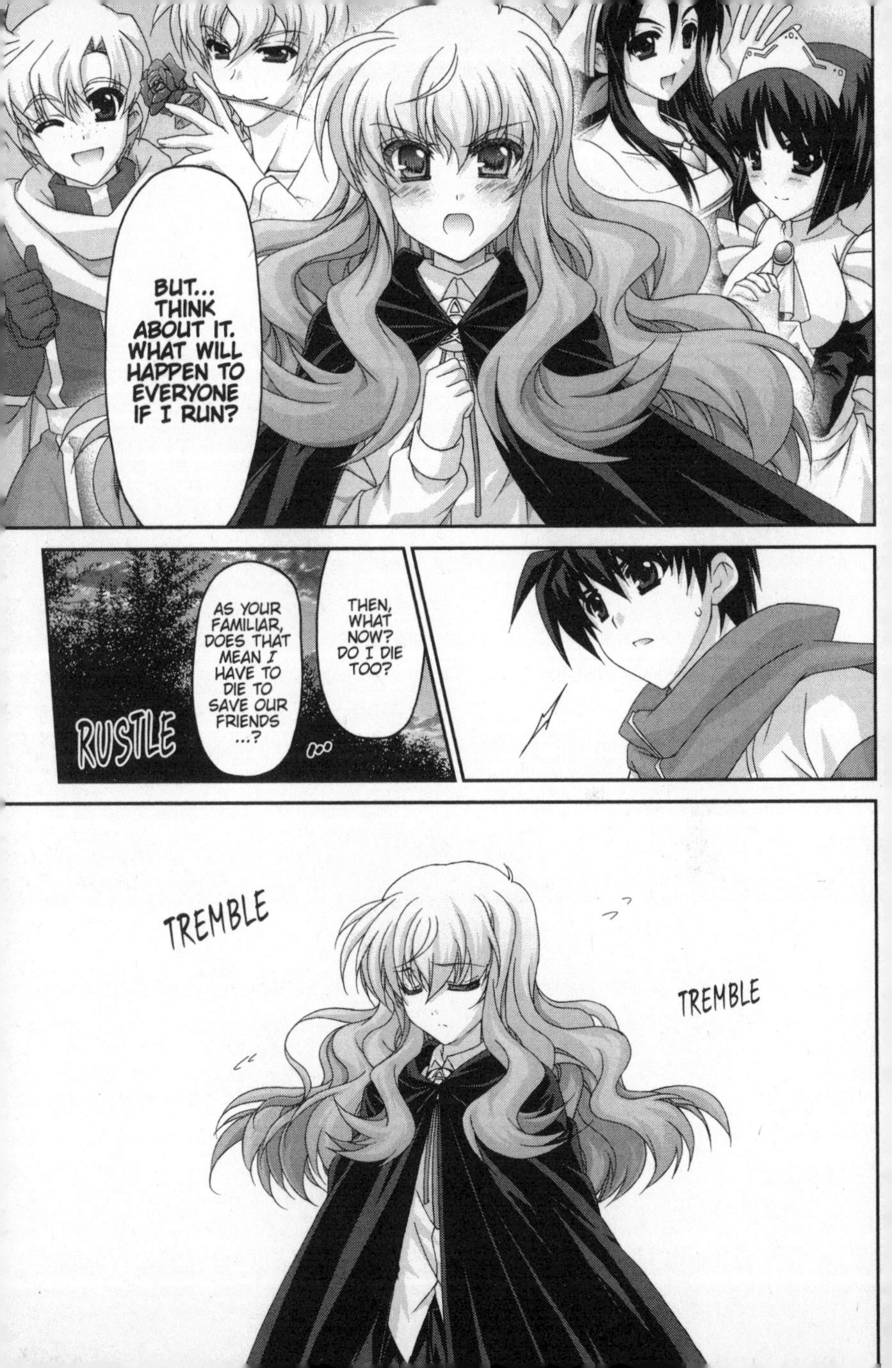
BUT... THINK ABOUT IT. WHAT WILL HAPPEN TO EVERYONE IF I RUN?
THEN, WHAT NOW? DO I DIE TOO?
AS YOUR FAMILIAR, DOES THAT MEAN *I* HAVE TO DIE TO SAVE OUR FRIENDS ...?
RUSTLE
...
TREMBLE
TREMBLE

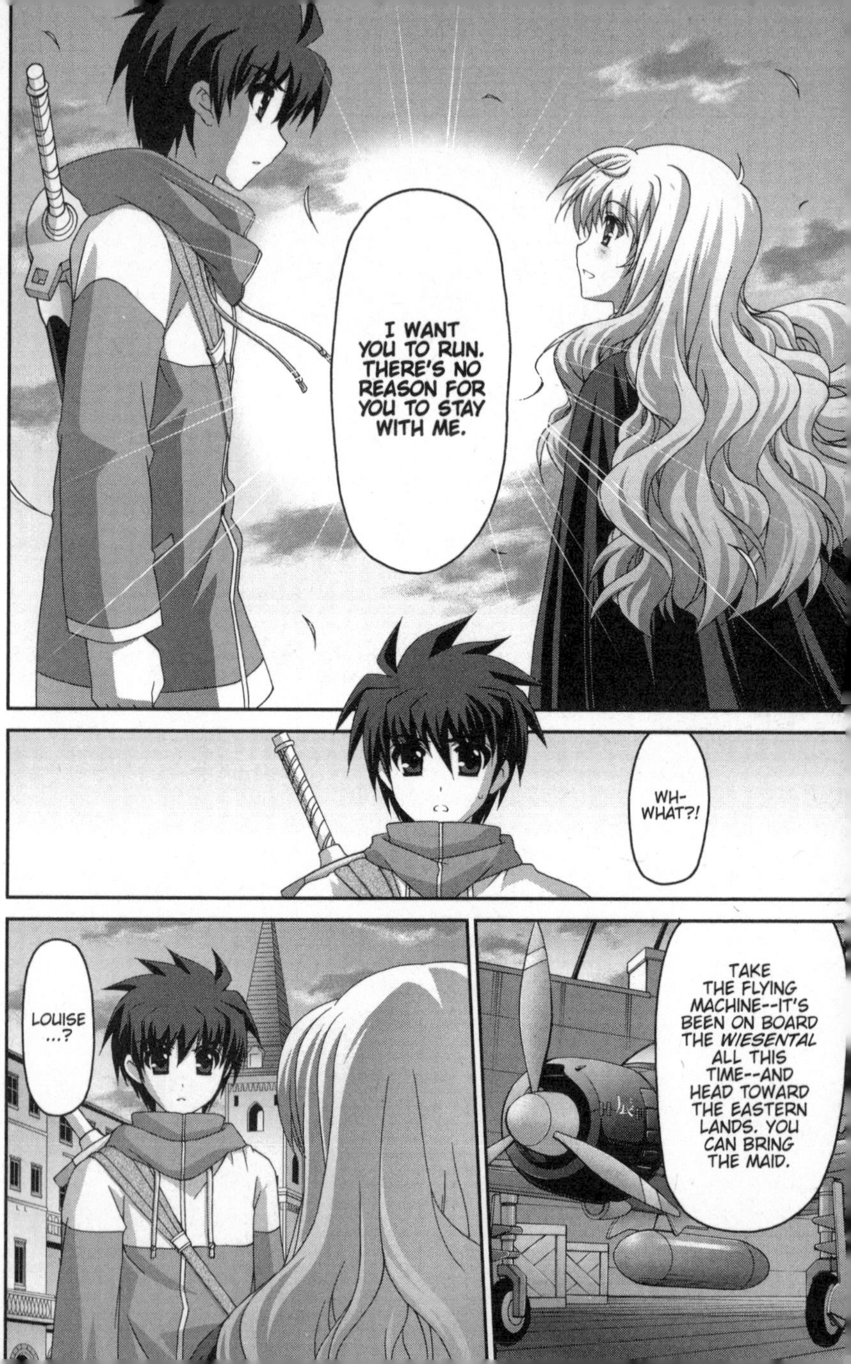
I WANT YOU TO RUN. THERE'S NO REASON FOR YOU TO STAY WITH ME.
WH- WHAT?!
TAKE THE FLYING MACHINE--IT'S BEEN ON BOARD THE *WIESENTAL* ALL THIS TIME--AND HEAD TOWARD THE EASTERN LANDS. YOU CAN BRING THE MAID.
LOUISE ...?

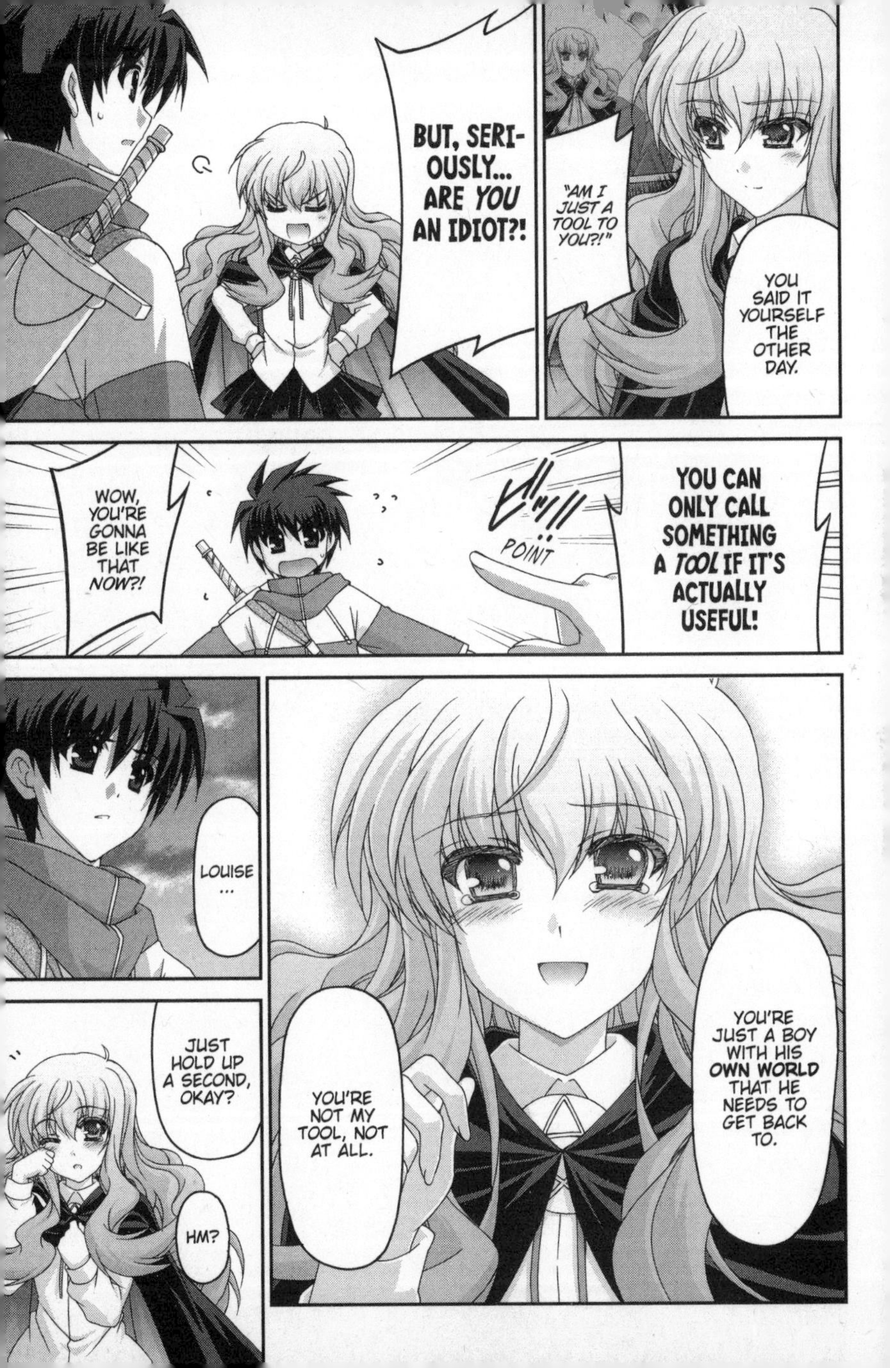
"AM I JUST A TOOL TO YOU?!"
YOU SAID IT YOURSELF THE OTHER DAY.
BUT, SERIOUSLY... ARE *YOU* AN IDIOT?!
YOU CAN ONLY CALL SOMETHING A *TOOL* IF IT'S ACTUALLY USEFUL!
POINT
WOW, YOU'RE GONNA BE LIKE THAT *NOW*?!
YOU'RE JUST A BOY WITH HIS **OWN WORLD** THAT HE NEEDS TO GET BACK TO.
YOU'RE NOT MY TOOL, NOT AT ALL.
LOUISE ...
JUST HOLD UP A SECOND, OKAY?
HM?

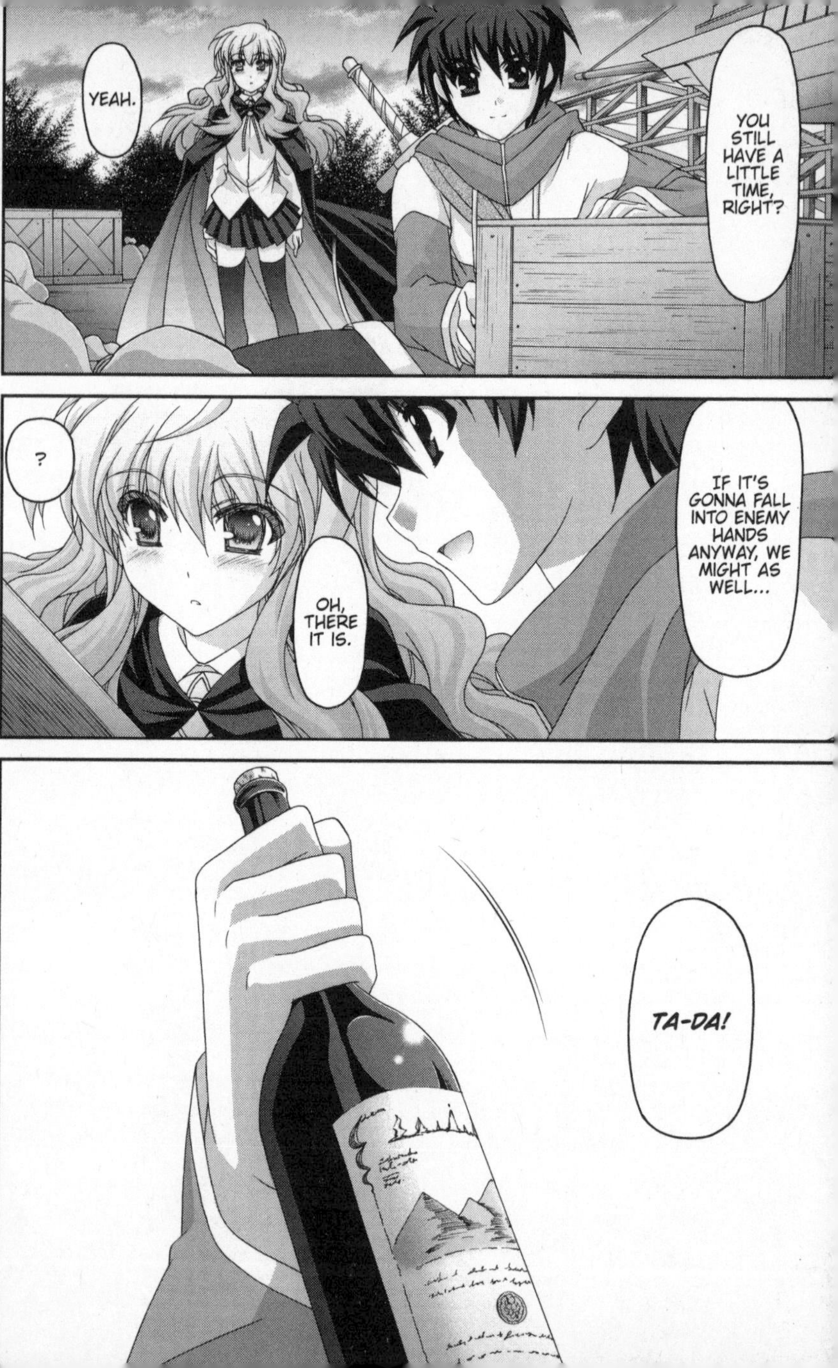
YOU STILL HAVE A LITTLE TIME, RIGHT?
YEAH.
IF IT'S GONNA FALL INTO ENEMY HANDS ANYWAY, WE MIGHT AS WELL...
OH, THERE IT IS.
?
TA-DA!

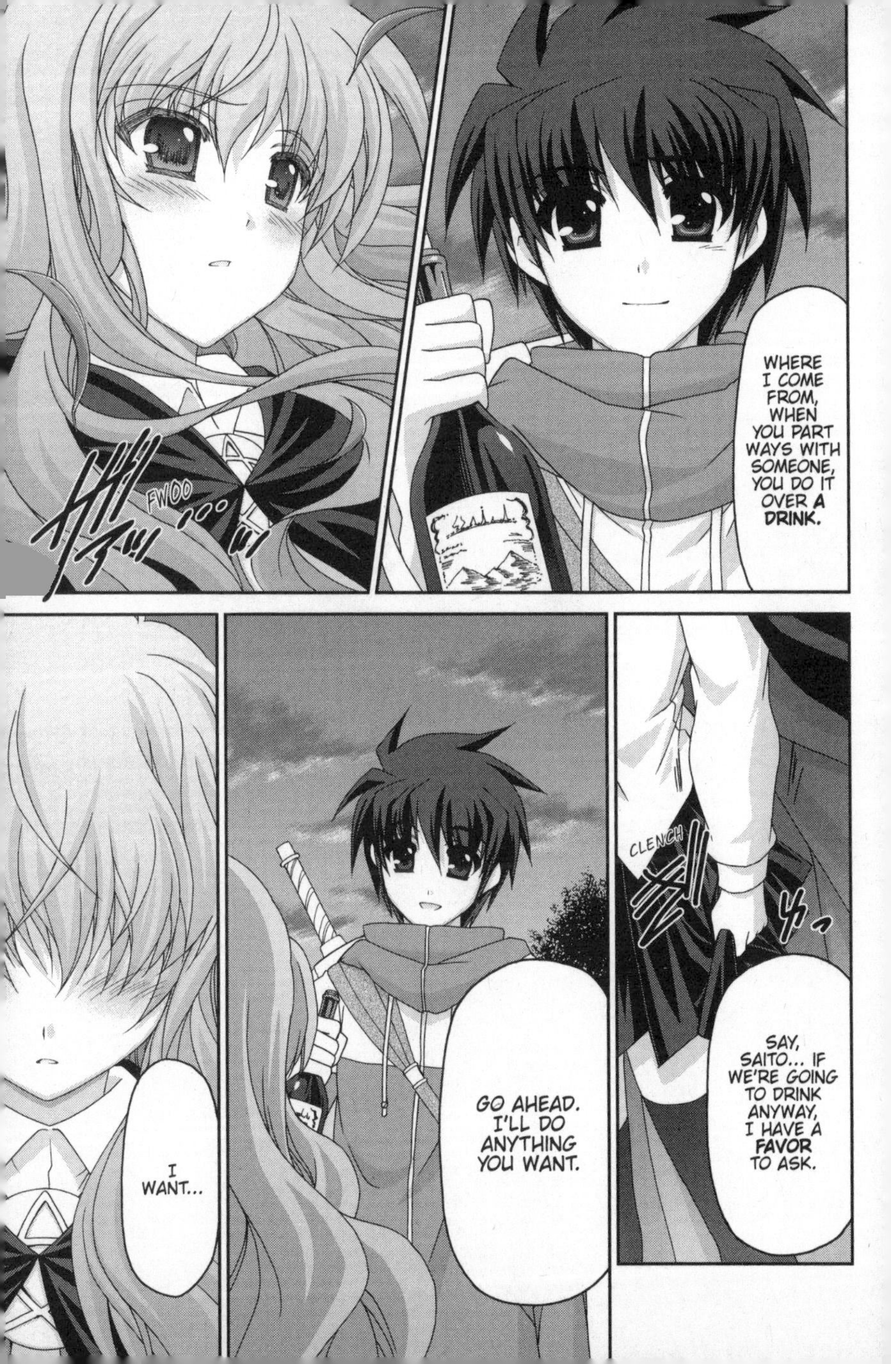
WHERE I COME FROM, WHEN YOU PART WAYS WITH SOMEONE, YOU DO IT OVER A DRINK.
FWOO
CLENCH
SAY, SAITO... IF WE'RE GOING TO DRINK ANYWAY, I HAVE A FAVOR TO ASK.
GO AHEAD. I'LL DO ANYTHING YOU WANT.
I WANT...

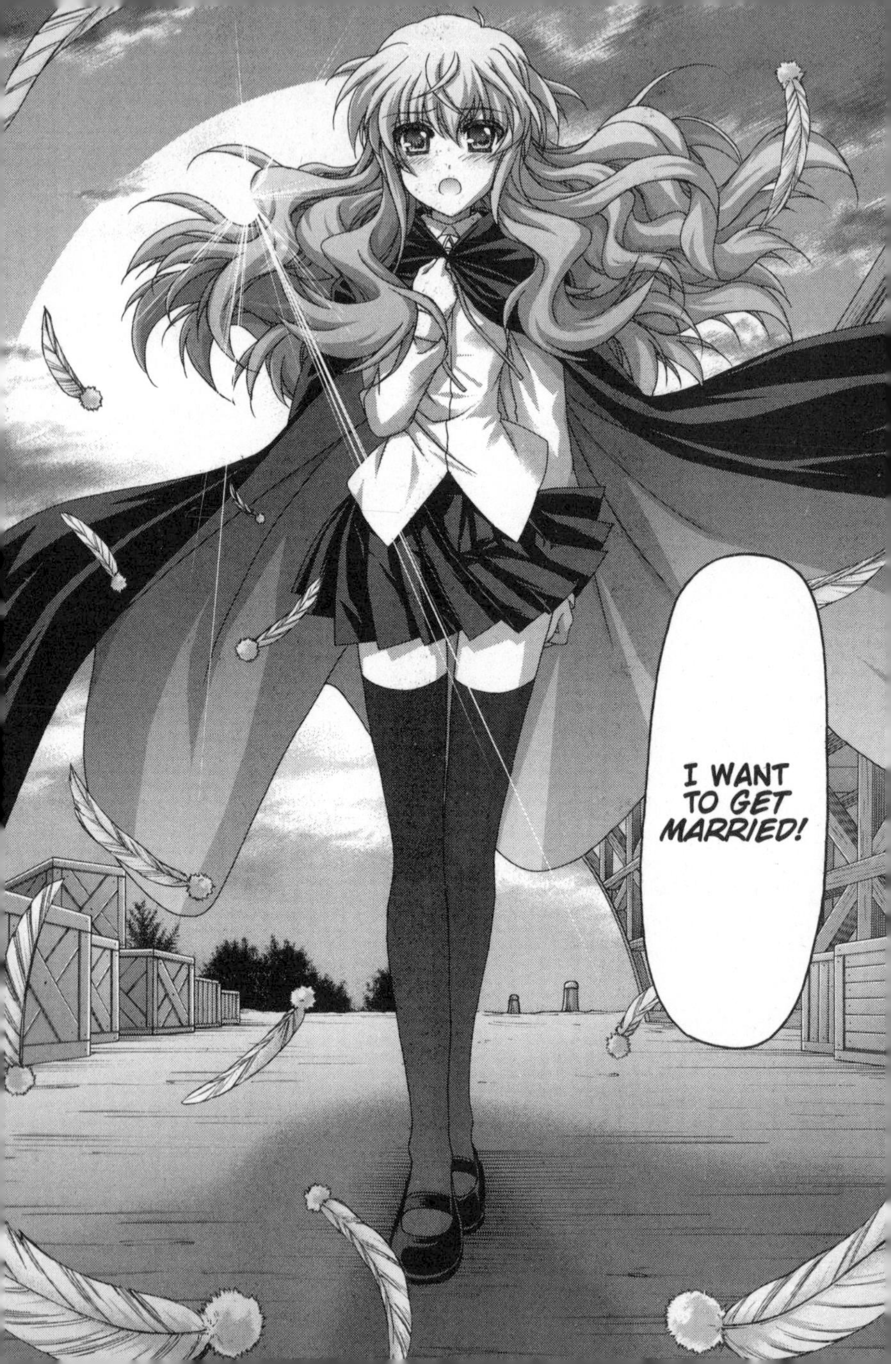
I WANT TO GET MARRIED!

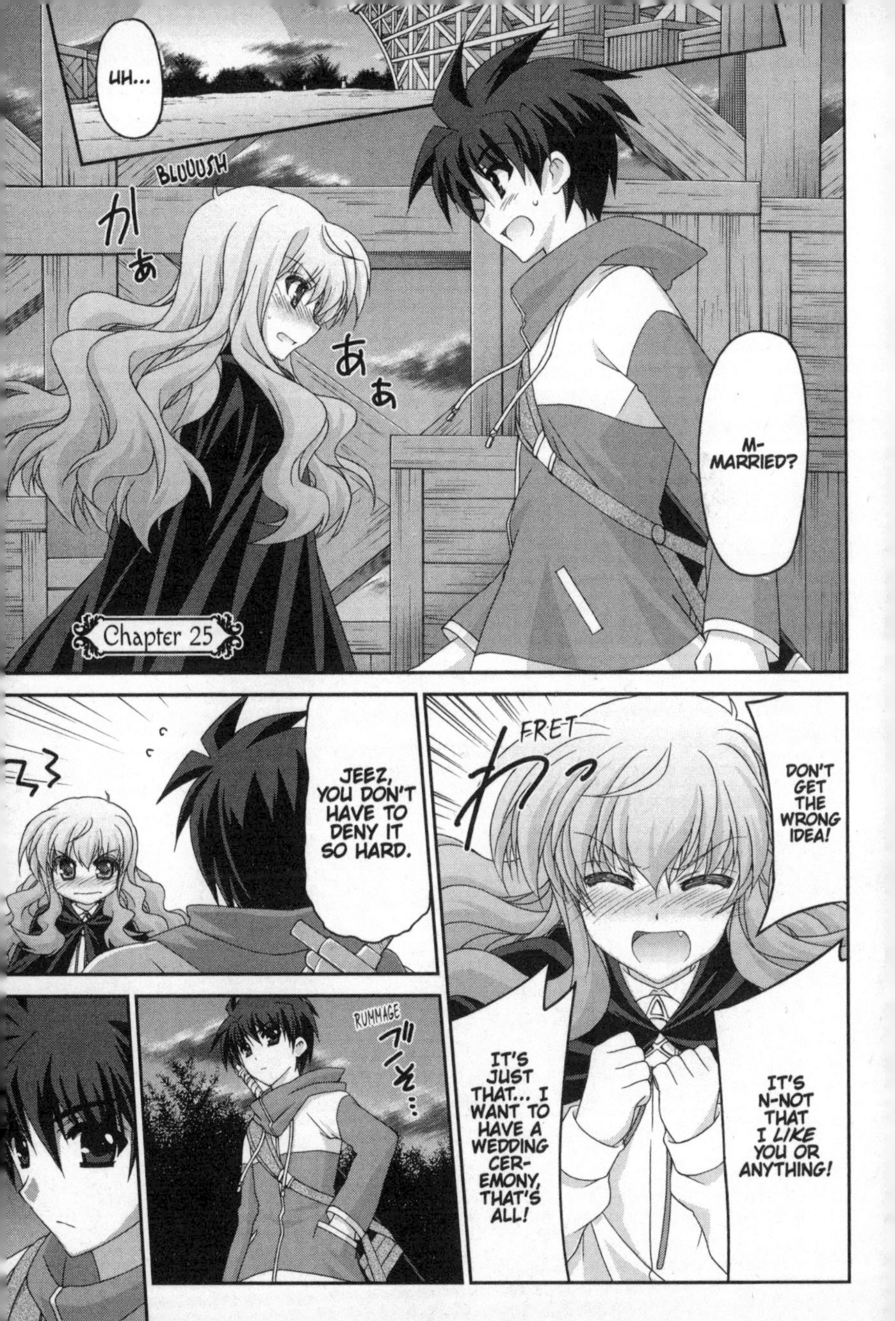
M-MARRIED?
UH...
BLUUUSH
かぁ
ああ
Chapter 25
FRET
わっ
DON'T GET THE WRONG IDEA!
IT'S N-NOT THAT I *LIKE* YOU OR ANYTHING!
IT'S JUST THAT... I WANT TO HAVE A WEDDING CER-EMONY, THAT'S ALL!
JEEZ, YOU DON'T HAVE TO DENY IT SO HARD.
RUMMAGE
ごそ…

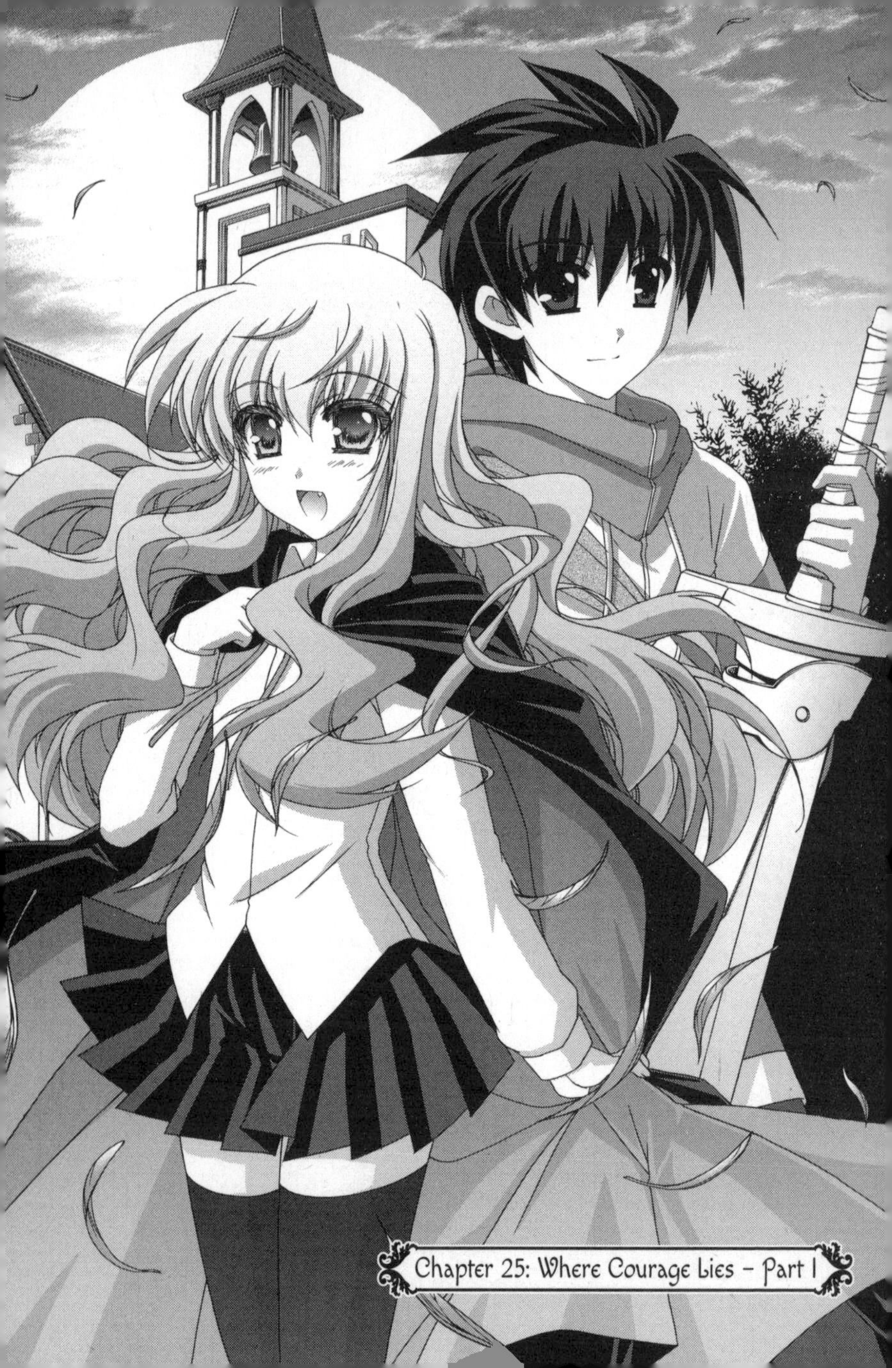

Chapter 25: Where Courage Lies – Part 1

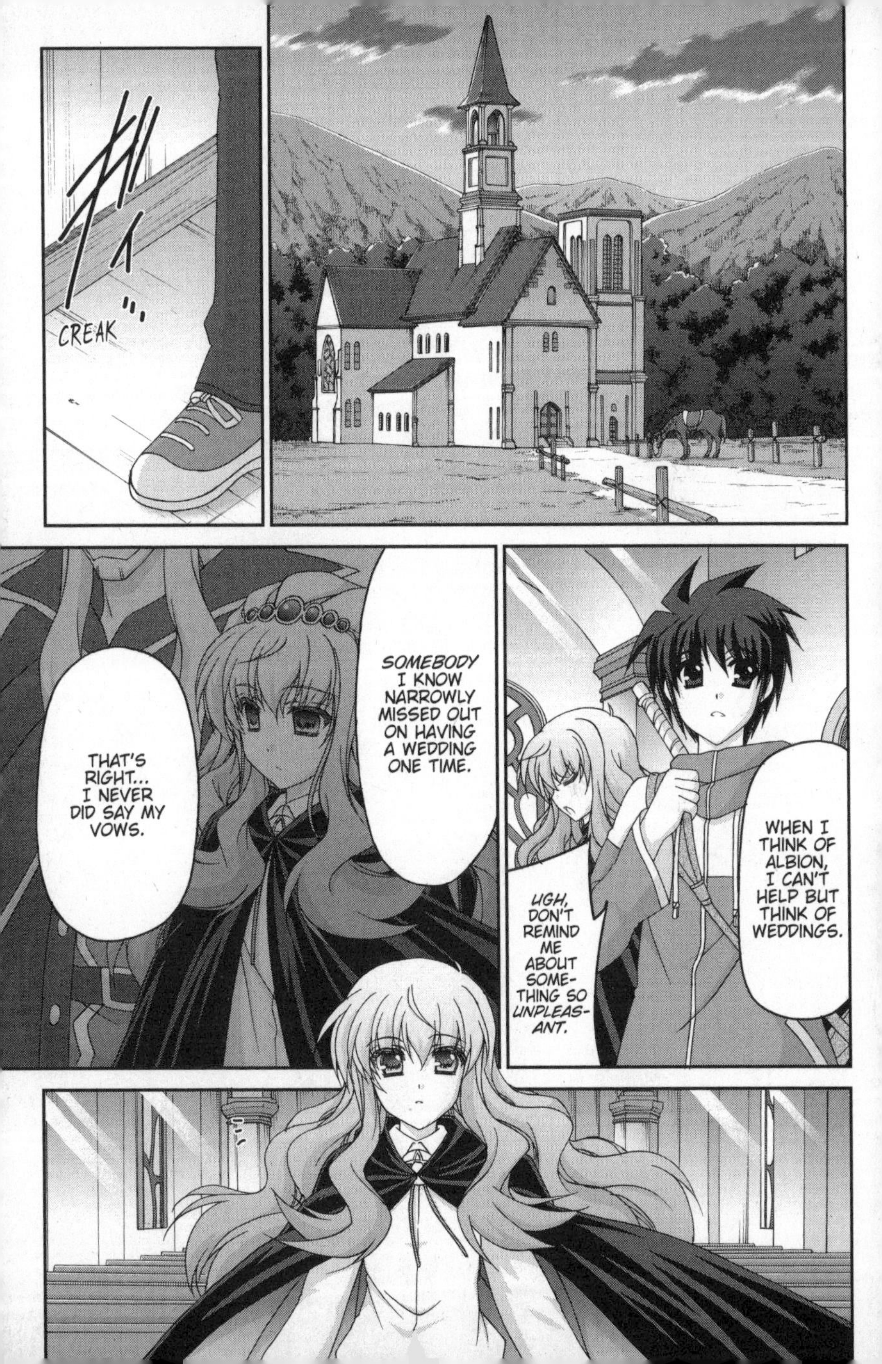
CREAK
WHEN I THINK OF ALBION, I CAN'T HELP BUT THINK OF WEDDINGS.
UGH, DON'T REMIND ME ABOUT SOME-THING SO UNPLEAS-ANT.
SOMEBODY I KNOW NARROWLY MISSED OUT ON HAVING A WEDDING ONE TIME.
THAT'S RIGHT... I NEVER DID SAY MY VOWS.

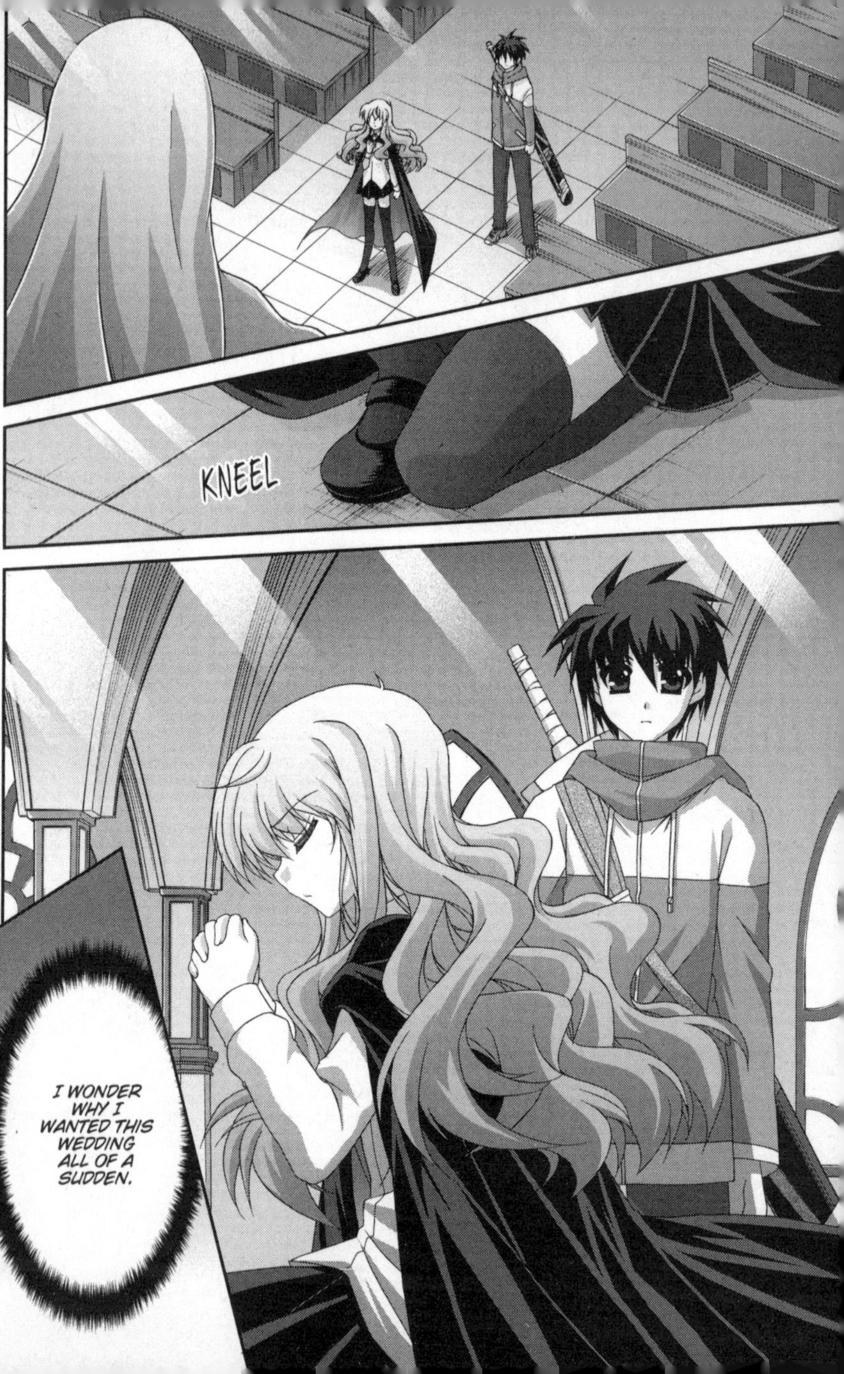
KNEEL
I WONDER WHY I WANTED THIS WEDDING ALL OF A SUDDEN.

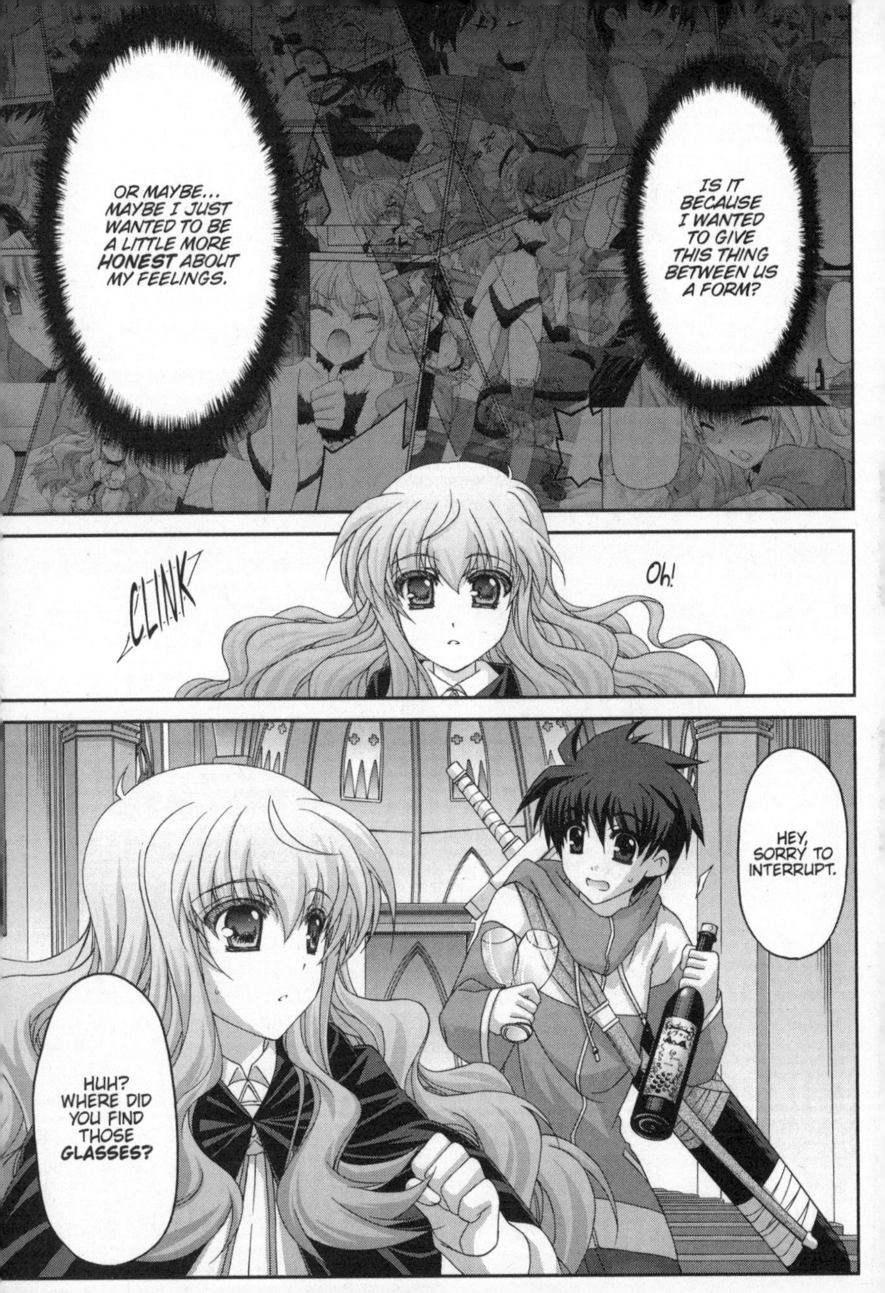
IS IT BECAUSE I WANTED TO GIVE THIS THING BETWEEN US A FORM?
OR MAYBE... MAYBE I JUST WANTED TO BE A LITTLE MORE HONEST ABOUT MY FEELINGS.
Oh!
CLINK
HEY, SORRY TO INTERRUPT.
HUH? WHERE DID YOU FIND THOSE GLASSES?

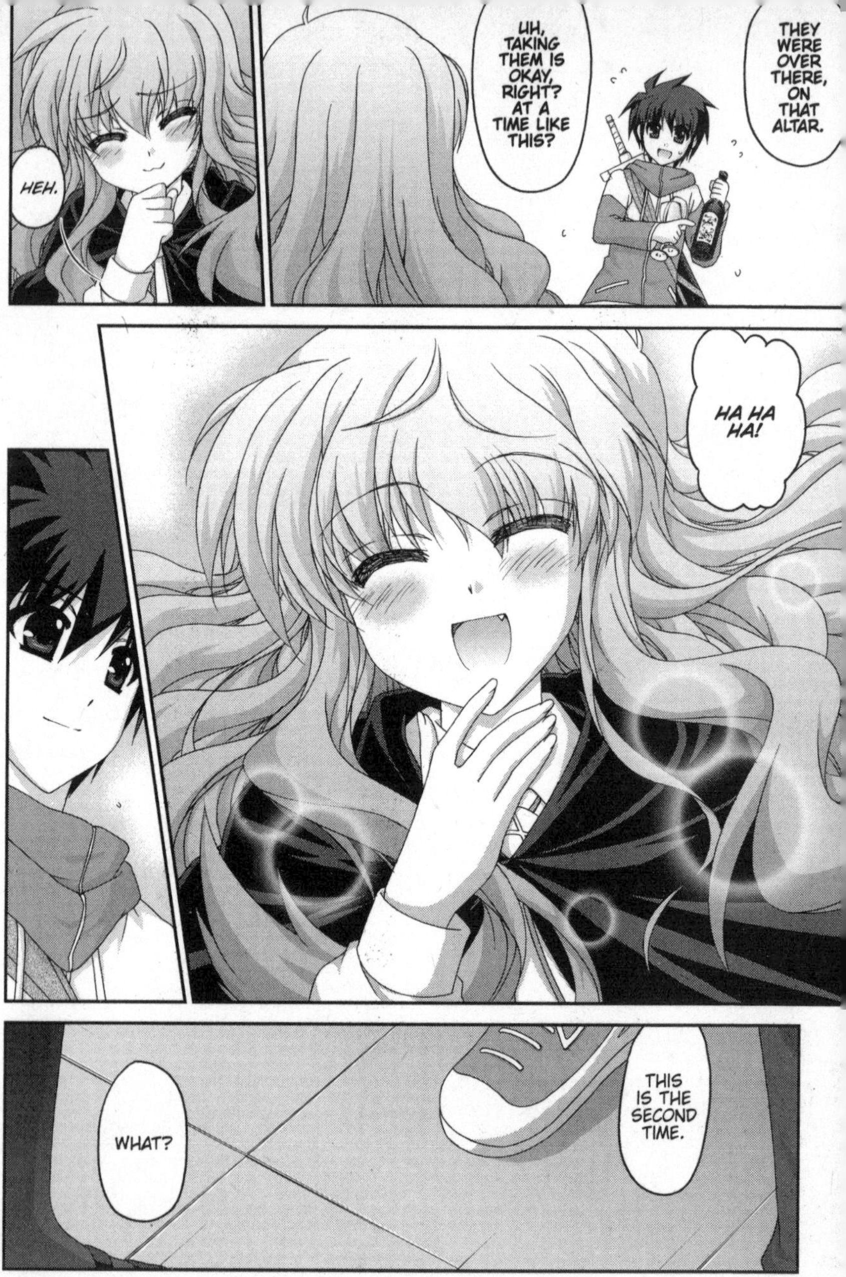
THEY WERE OVER THERE, ON THAT ALTAR.
UH, TAKING THEM IS OKAY, RIGHT? AT A TIME LIKE THIS?
HEH.
HA HA HA!
THIS IS THE SECOND TIME.
WHAT?

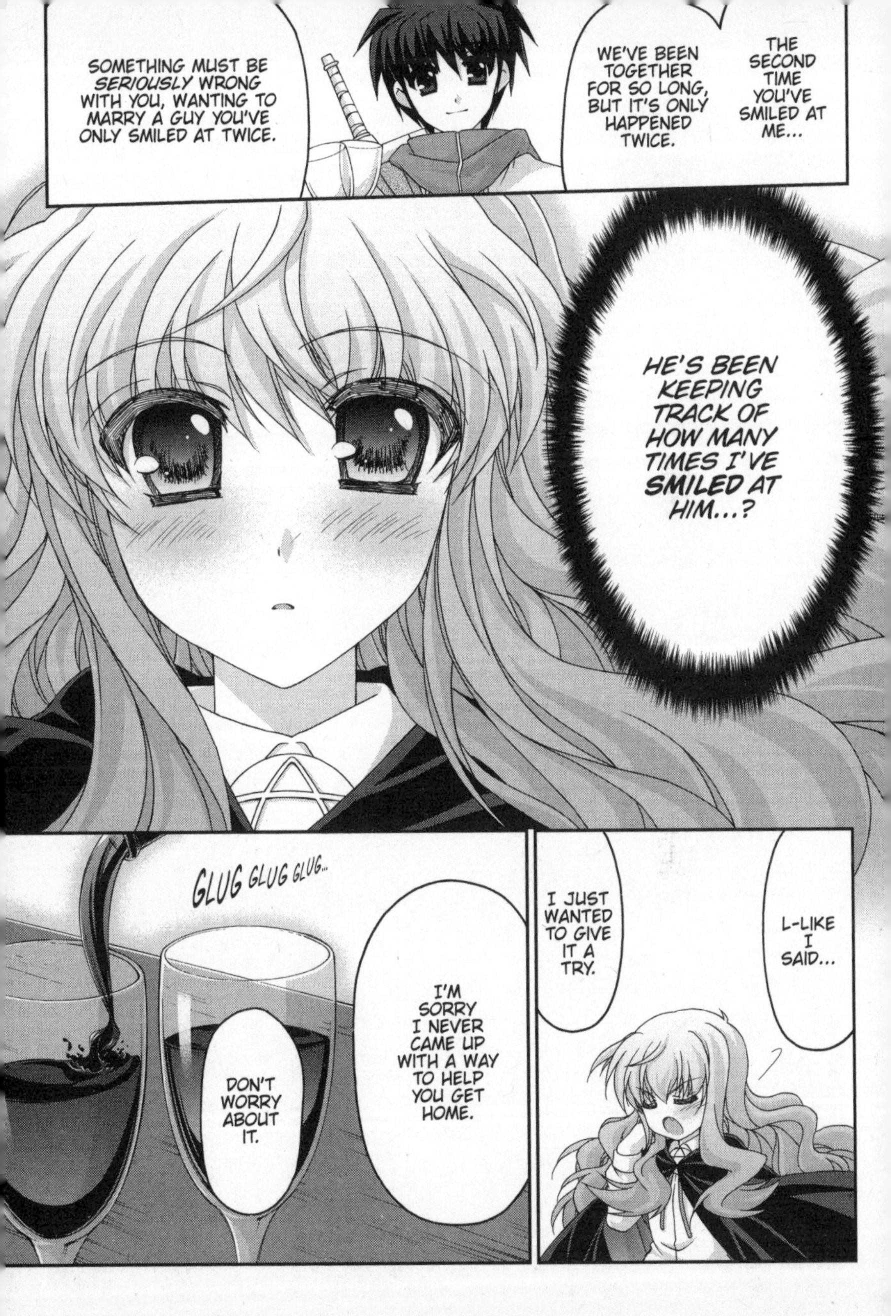
THE SECOND TIME YOU'VE SMILED AT ME...
WE'VE BEEN TOGETHER FOR SO LONG, BUT IT'S ONLY HAPPENED TWICE.
SOMETHING MUST BE *SERIOUSLY* WRONG WITH YOU, WANTING TO MARRY A GUY YOU'VE ONLY SMILED AT TWICE.
HE'S BEEN KEEPING TRACK OF HOW MANY TIMES I'VE **SMILED** AT HIM...?
L-LIKE I SAID...
I JUST WANTED TO GIVE IT A TRY.
I'M SORRY I NEVER CAME UP WITH A WAY TO HELP YOU GET HOME.
GLUG GLUG GLUG...
DON'T WORRY ABOUT IT.

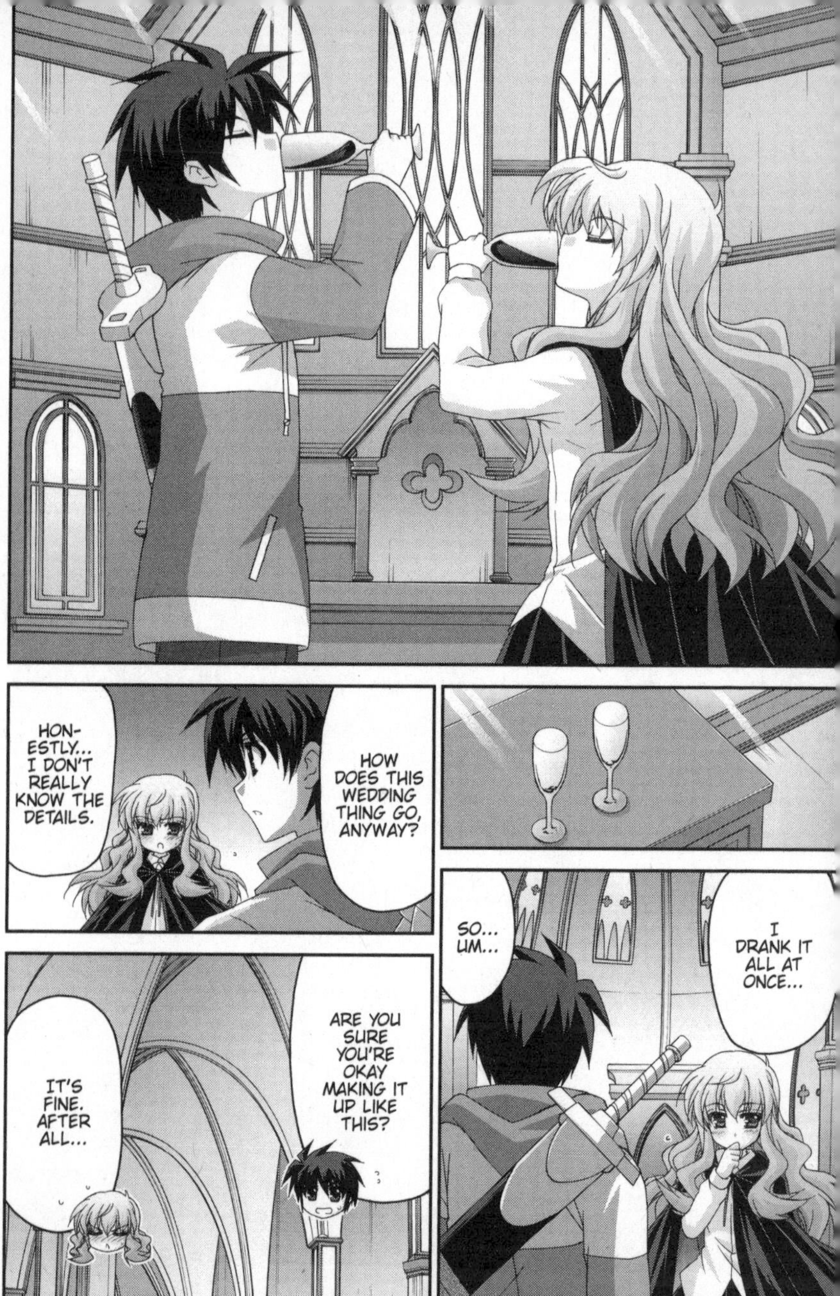

HOW DOES THIS WEDDING THING GO, ANYWAY?
HON-ESTLY... I DON'T REALLY KNOW THE DETAILS.
I DRANK IT ALL AT ONCE...
SO... UM...
ARE YOU SURE YOU'RE OKAY MAKING IT UP LIKE THIS?
IT'S FINE. AFTER ALL...

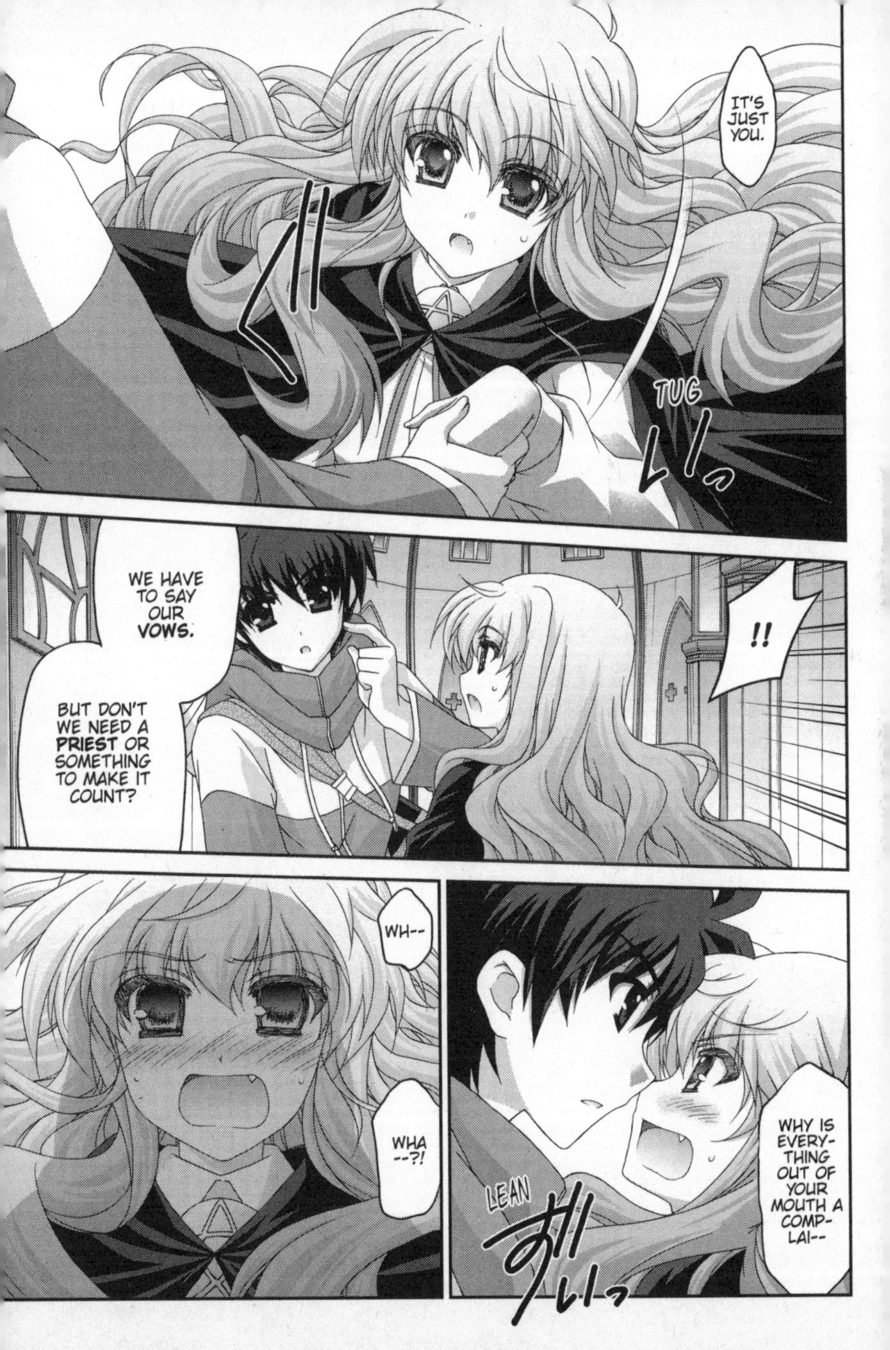
IT'S JUST YOU.
TUG
!!
WE HAVE TO SAY OUR VOWS.
BUT DON'T WE NEED A PRIEST OR SOMETHING TO MAKE IT COUNT?
WHY IS EVERY-THING OUT OF YOUR MOUTH A COMP-LAI--
LEAN
WH--
WHA --?!

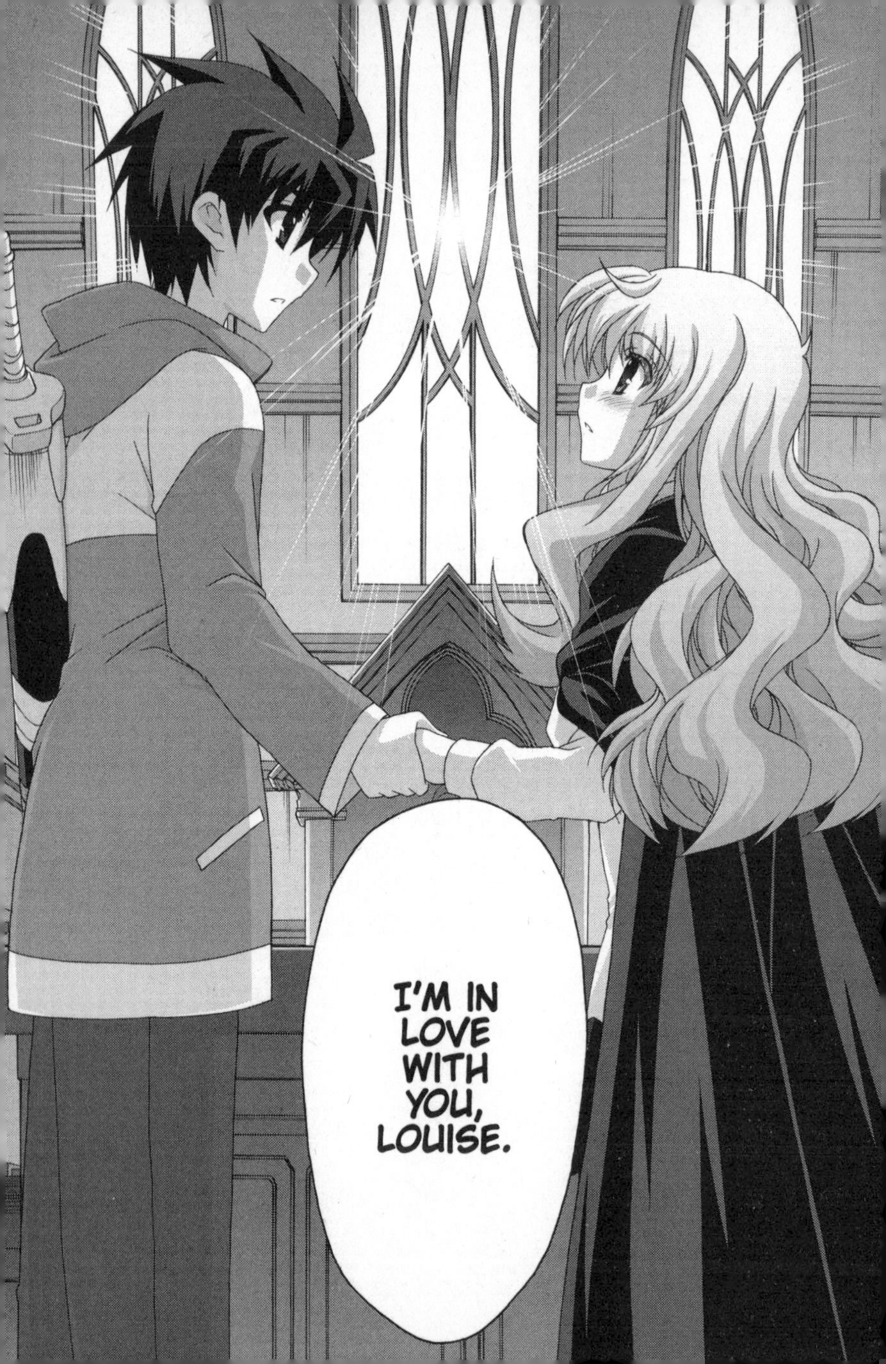
I'M IN LOVE WITH YOU, LOUISE.

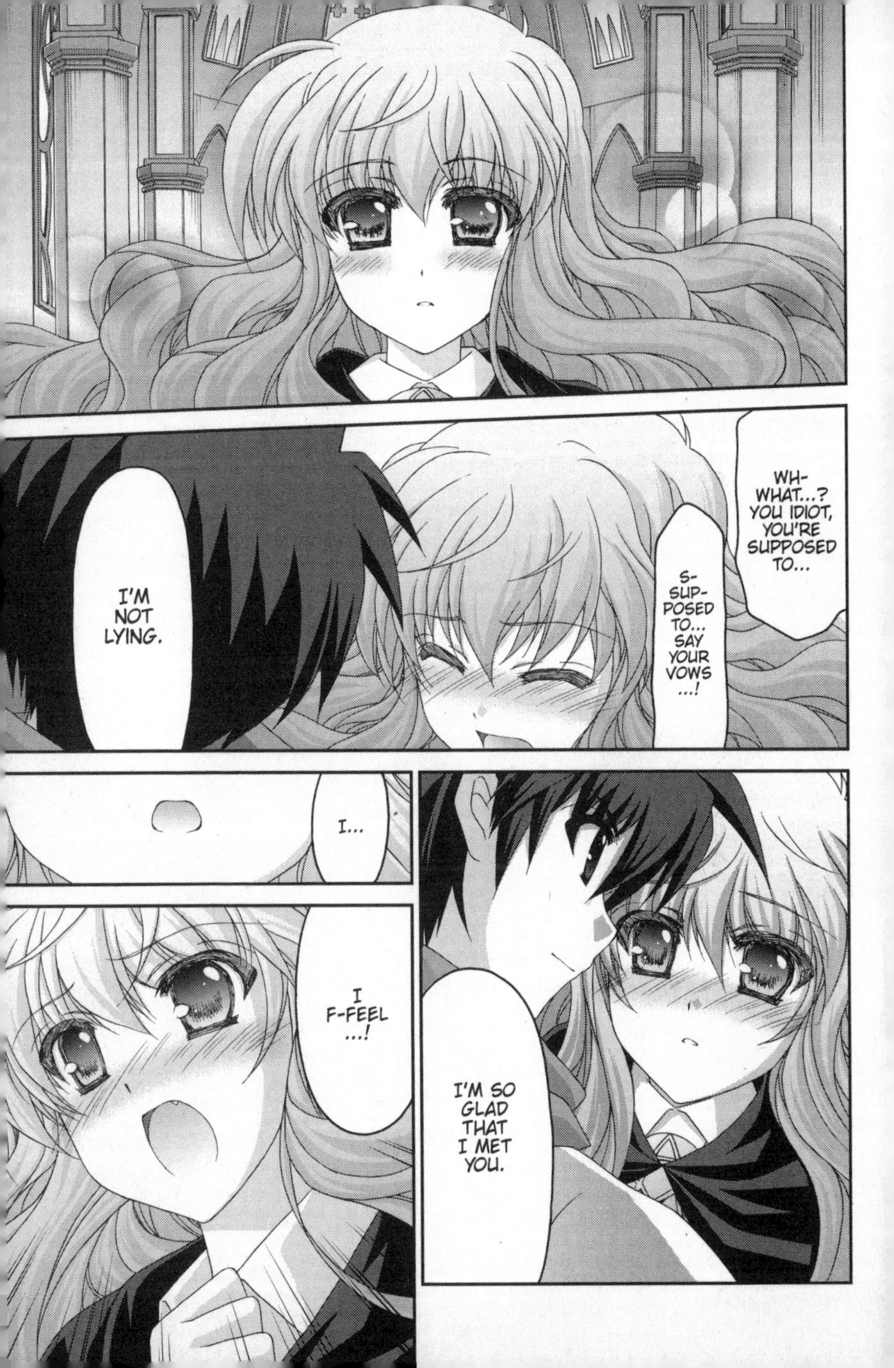
WH-WHAT...? YOU IDIOT, YOU'RE SUPPOSED TO...
S-SUPPOSED TO... SAY YOUR VOWS...!
I'M NOT LYING.
I'M SO GLAD THAT I MET YOU.
I...
I F-FEEL...!

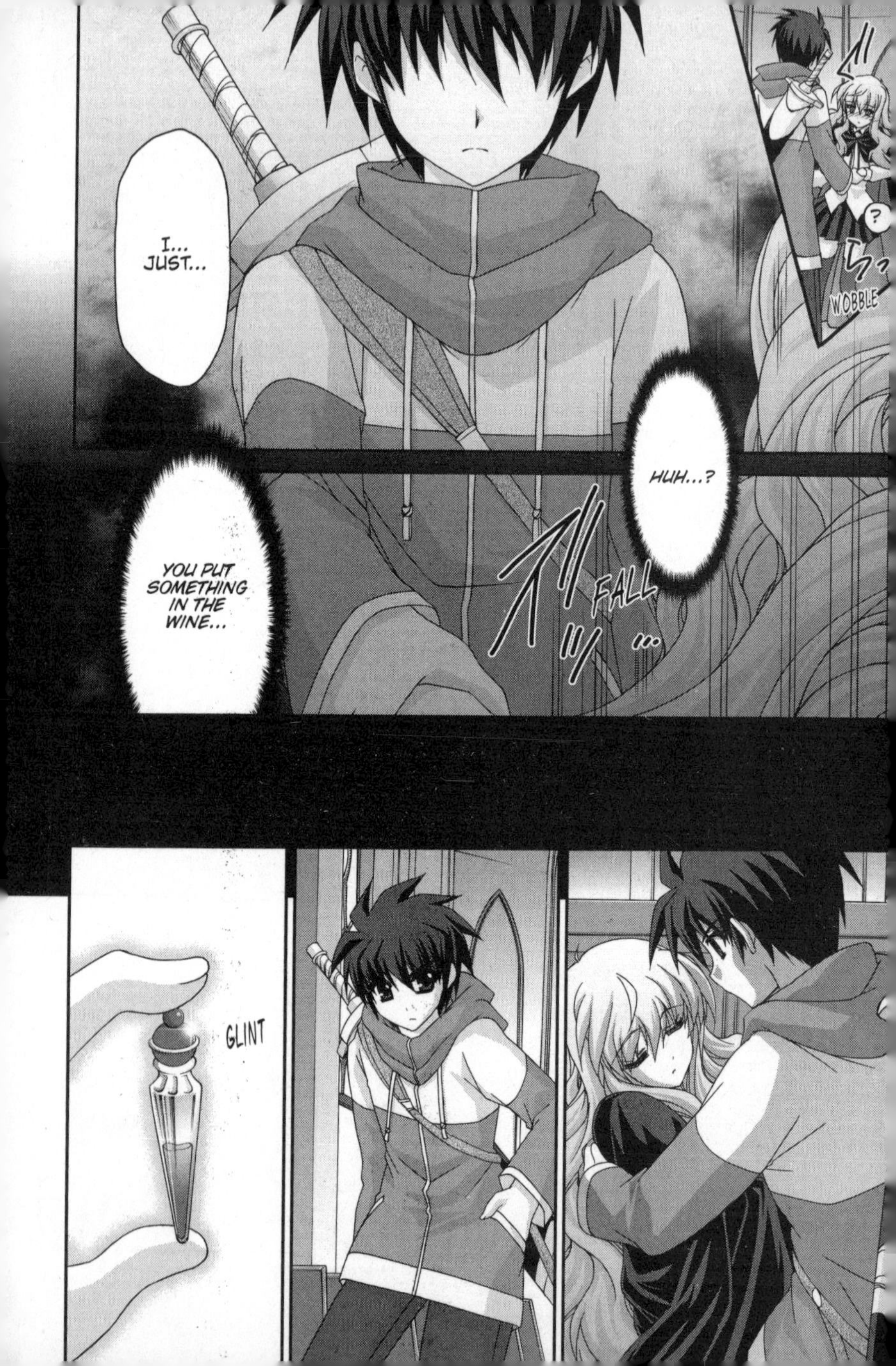
?
WOBBLE
I... JUST...
HUH...?
FALL
YOU PUT SOMETHING IN THE WINE...
GLINT

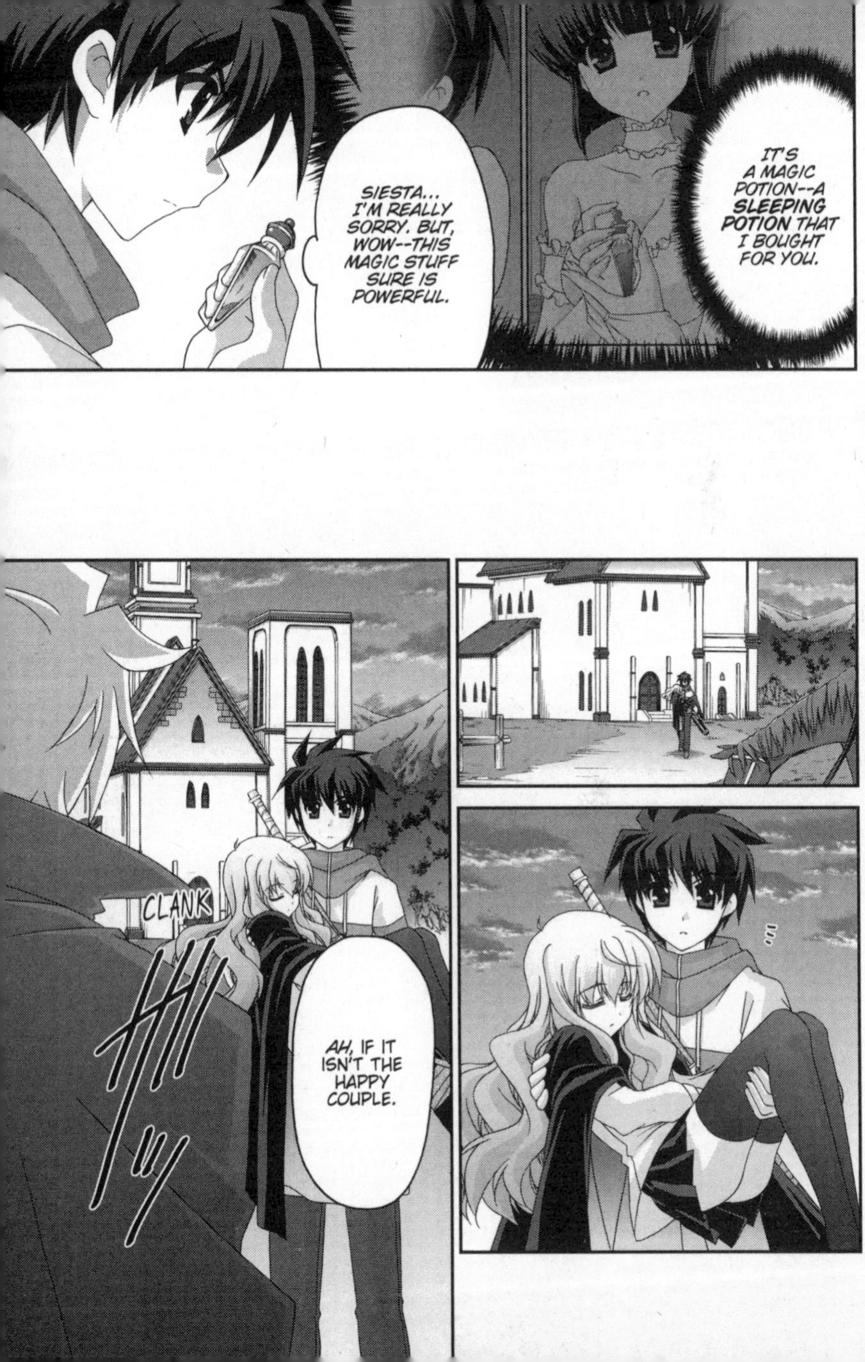
IT'S A MAGIC POTION--A **SLEEPING POTION** THAT I BOUGHT FOR YOU.
SIESTA... I'M REALLY SORRY. BUT, WOW--THIS MAGIC STUFF SURE IS POWERFUL.
CLANK
AH, IF IT ISN'T THE HAPPY COUPLE.

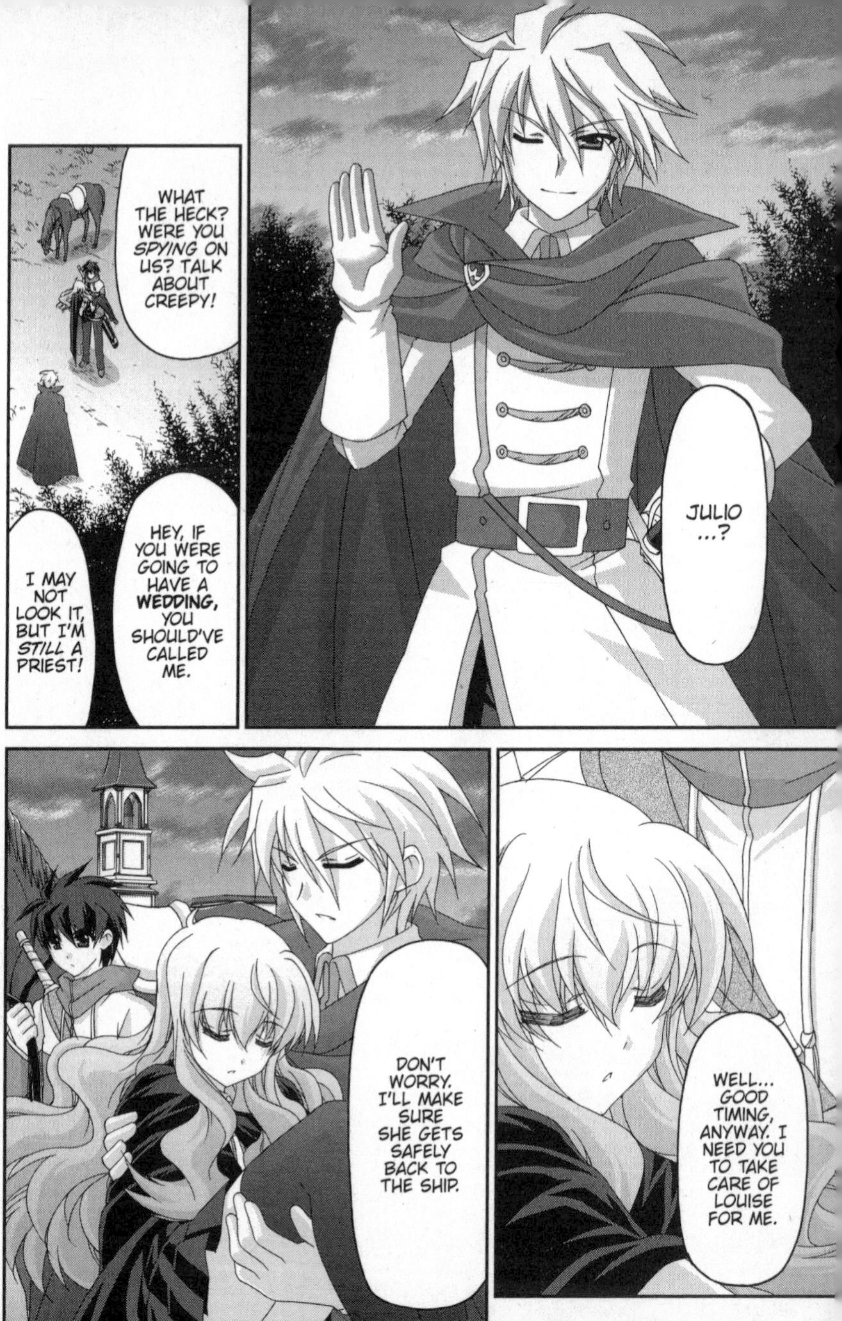
JULIO ...?
WHAT THE HECK? WERE YOU *SPYING* ON US? TALK ABOUT CREEPY!
HEY, IF YOU WERE GOING TO HAVE A **WEDDING,** YOU SHOULD'VE CALLED ME.
I MAY NOT LOOK IT, BUT I'M *STILL* A PRIEST!
WELL... GOOD TIMING, ANYWAY. I NEED YOU TO TAKE CARE OF LOUISE FOR ME.
DON'T WORRY. I'LL MAKE SURE SHE GETS SAFELY BACK TO THE SHIP.

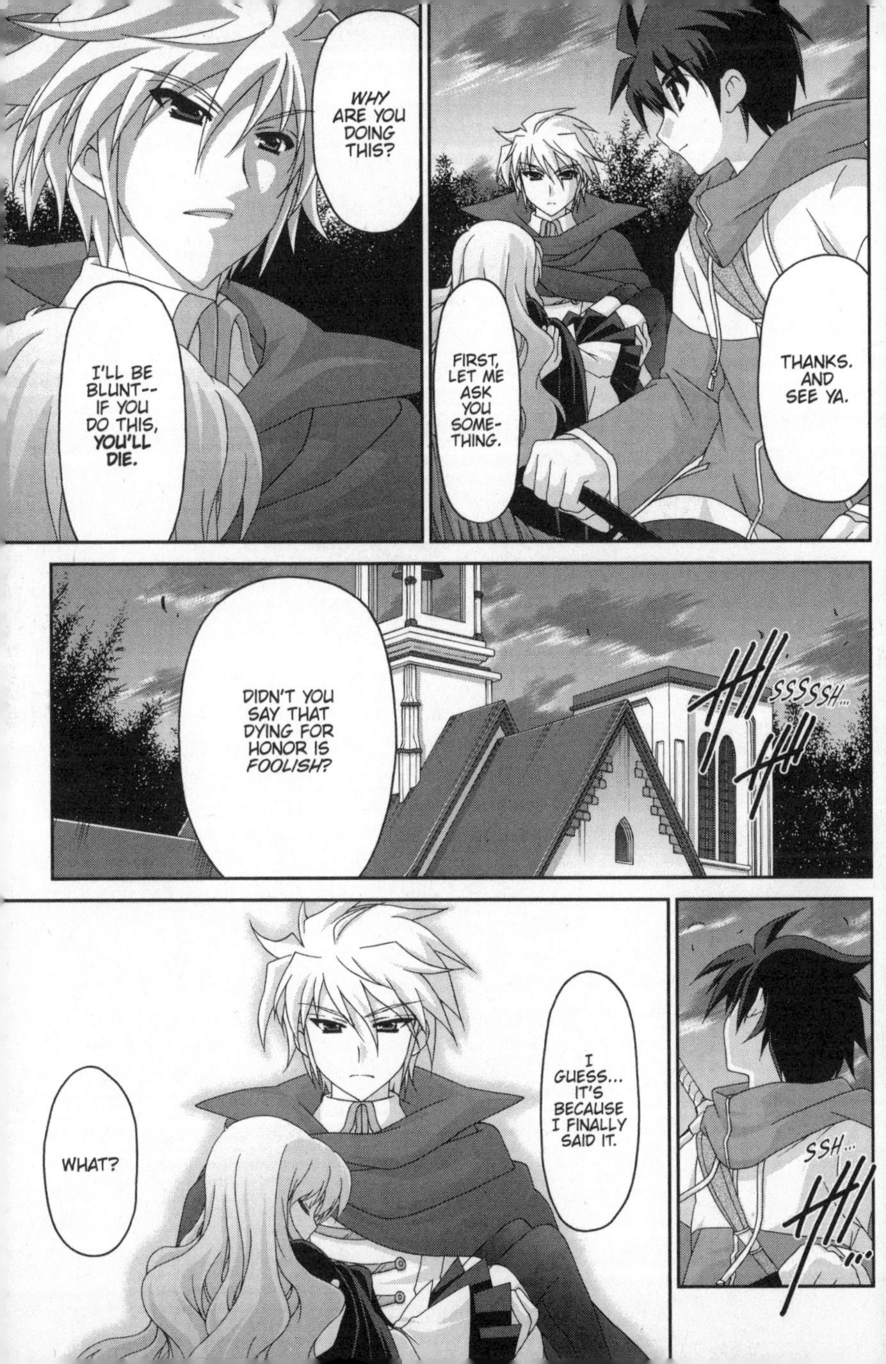
THANKS. AND SEE YA.
FIRST, LET ME ASK YOU SOMETHING.
WHY ARE YOU DOING THIS?
I'LL BE BLUNT-- IF YOU DO THIS, YOU'LL DIE.
SSSSSH...
DIDN'T YOU SAY THAT DYING FOR HONOR IS FOOLISH?
SSH...
I GUESS... IT'S BECAUSE I FINALLY SAID IT.
WHAT?

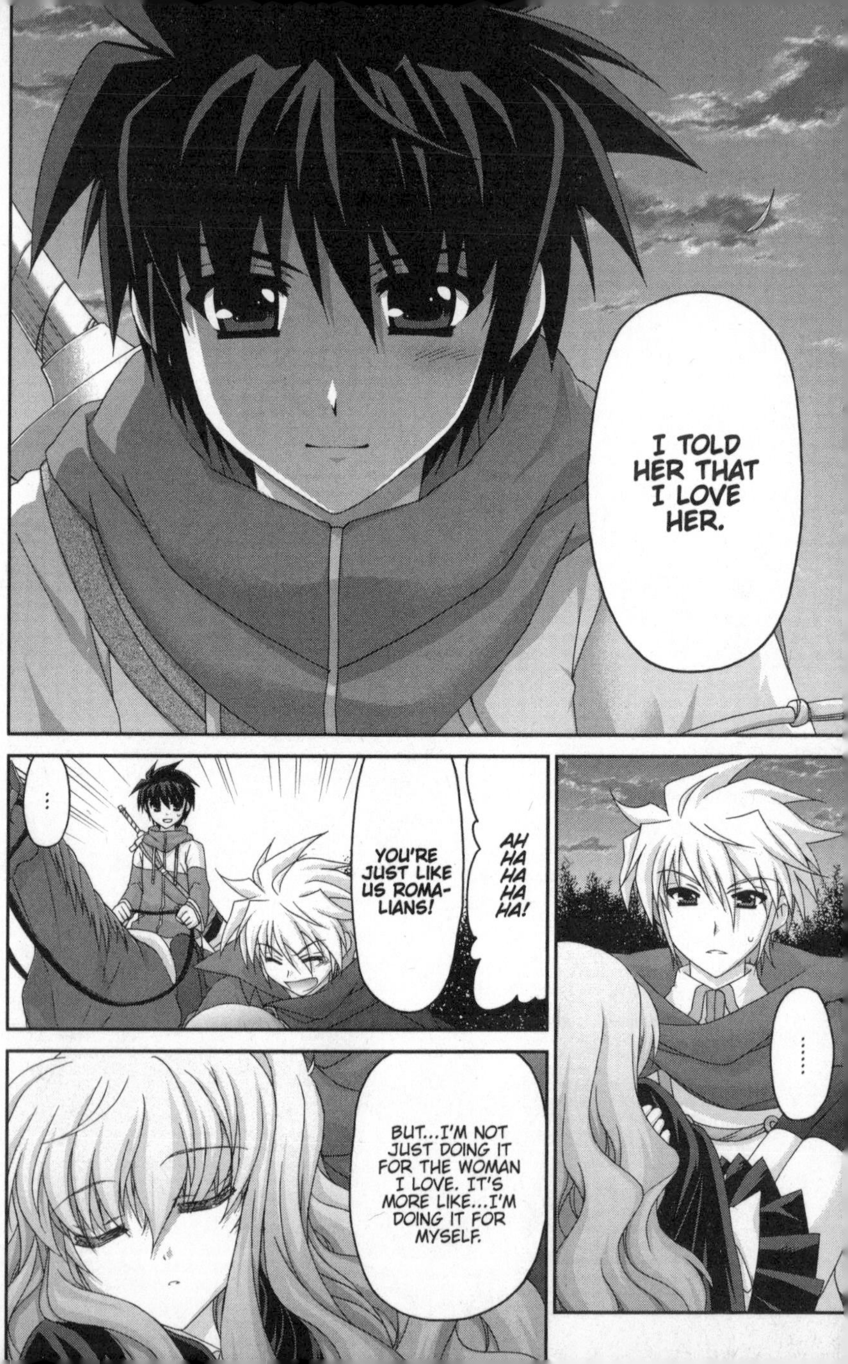

I TOLD HER THAT I LOVE HER.
AH HA HA HA HA HA!
YOU'RE JUST LIKE US ROMA-LIANS!
...
......
BUT...I'M NOT JUST DOING IT FOR THE WOMAN I LOVE. IT'S MORE LIKE...I'M DOING IT FOR MYSELF.

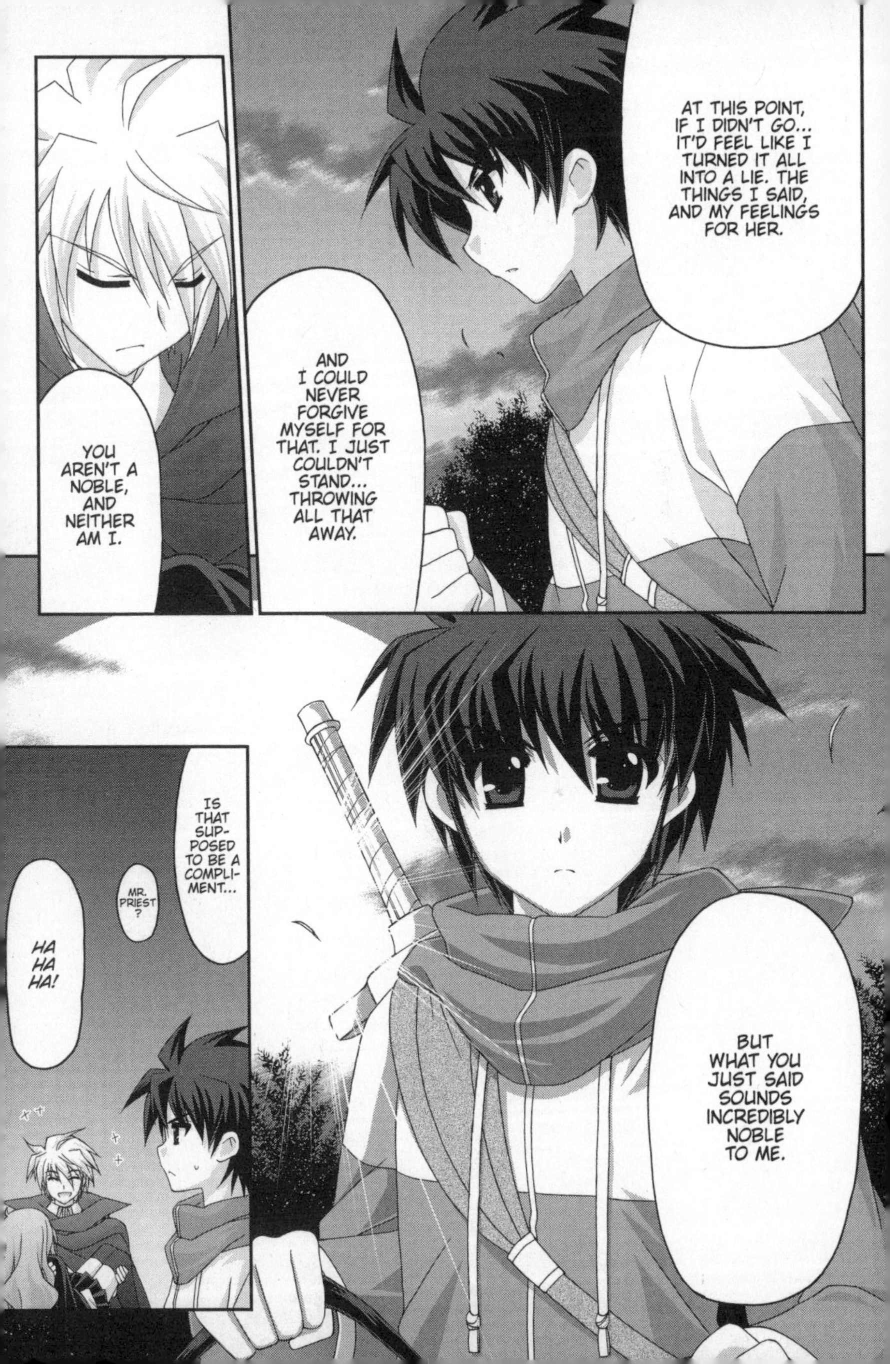
AT THIS POINT, IF I DIDN'T GO... IT'D FEEL LIKE I TURNED IT ALL INTO A LIE. THE THINGS I SAID, AND MY FEELINGS FOR HER.
AND I COULD NEVER FORGIVE MYSELF FOR THAT. I JUST COULDN'T STAND... THROWING ALL THAT AWAY.
YOU AREN'T A NOBLE, AND NEITHER AM I.
BUT WHAT YOU JUST SAID SOUNDS INCREDIBLY NOBLE TO ME.
IS THAT SUP-POSED TO BE A COMPLI-MENT...
MR. PRIEST?
HA HA HA!

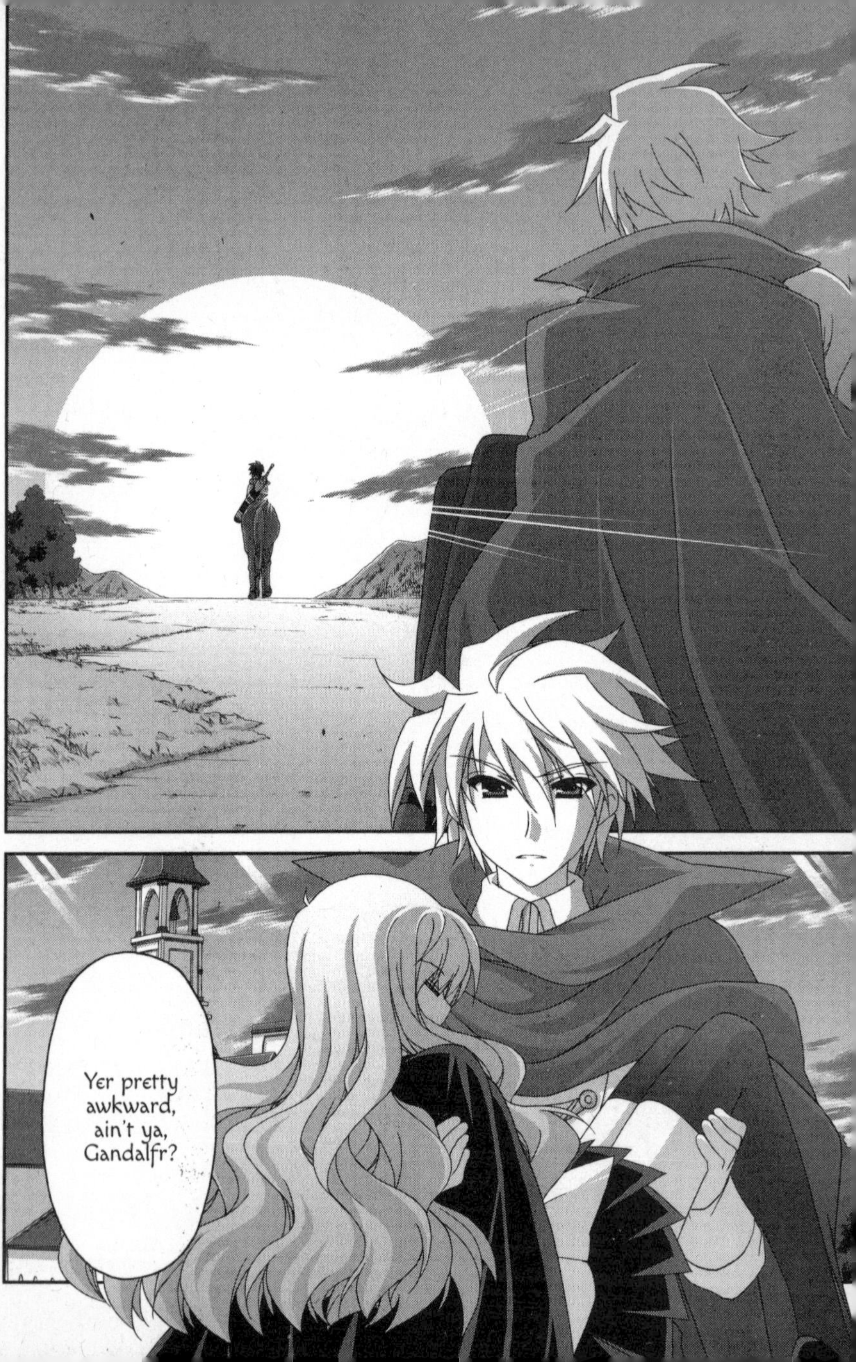
Yer pretty awkward, ain't ya, Gandalfr?

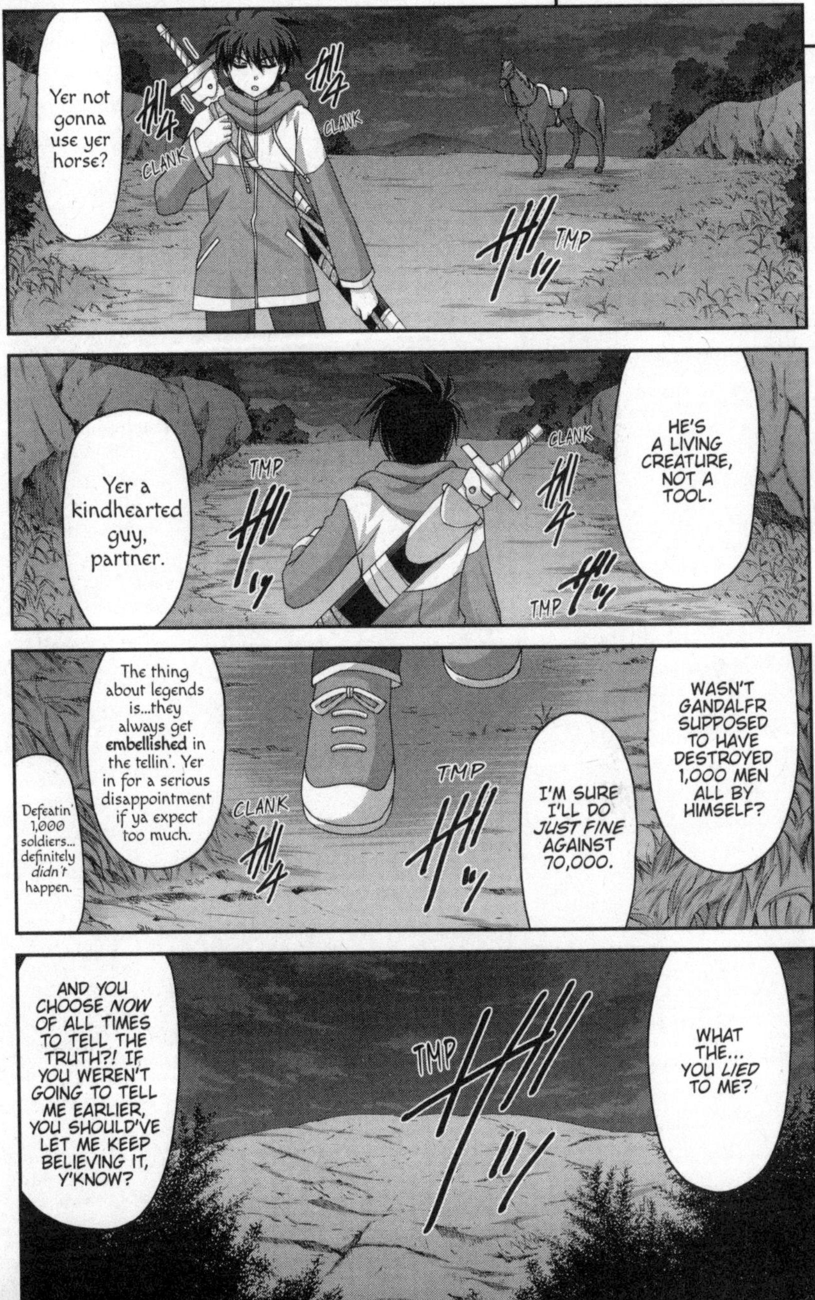
TMP
CLANK
CLANK
Yer not gonna use yer horse?
HE'S A LIVING CREATURE, NOT A TOOL.
CLANK
TMP
TMP
Yer a kindhearted guy, partner.
WASN'T GANDALFR SUPPOSED TO HAVE DESTROYED 1,000 MEN ALL BY HIMSELF?
I'M SURE I'LL DO *JUST FINE* AGAINST 70,000.
TMP
CLANK
The thing about legends is...they always get **embellished** in the tellin'. Yer in for a serious disappointment if ya expect too much.
Defeatin' 1,000 soldiers... definitely *didn't* happen.
WHAT THE... YOU *LIED* TO ME?
TMP
AND YOU CHOOSE *NOW* OF ALL TIMES TO TELL THE TRUTH?! IF YOU WEREN'T GOING TO TELL ME EARLIER, YOU SHOULD'VE LET ME KEEP BELIEVING IT, Y'KNOW?

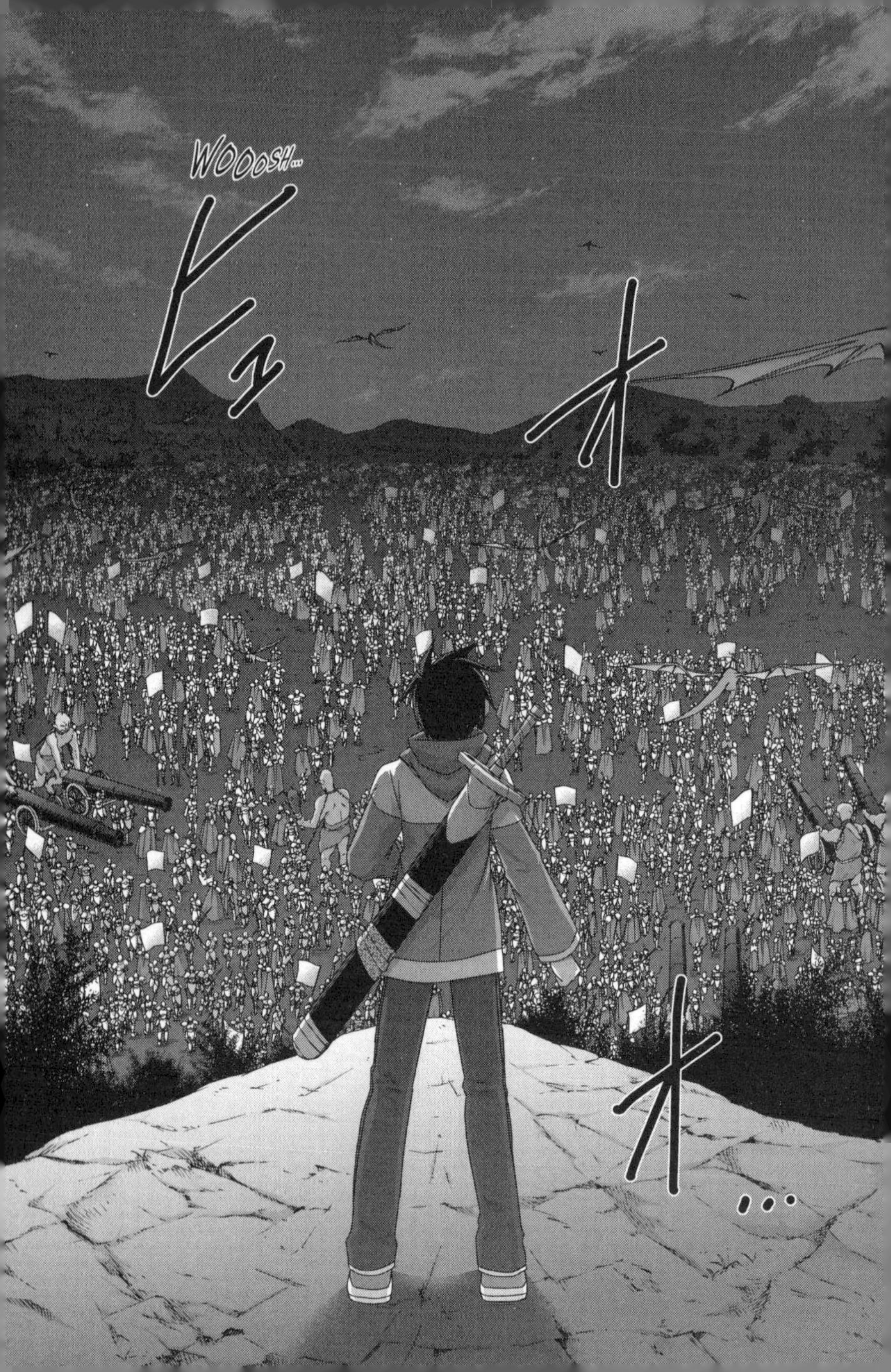
WOOOSH...
ヒュオオ…

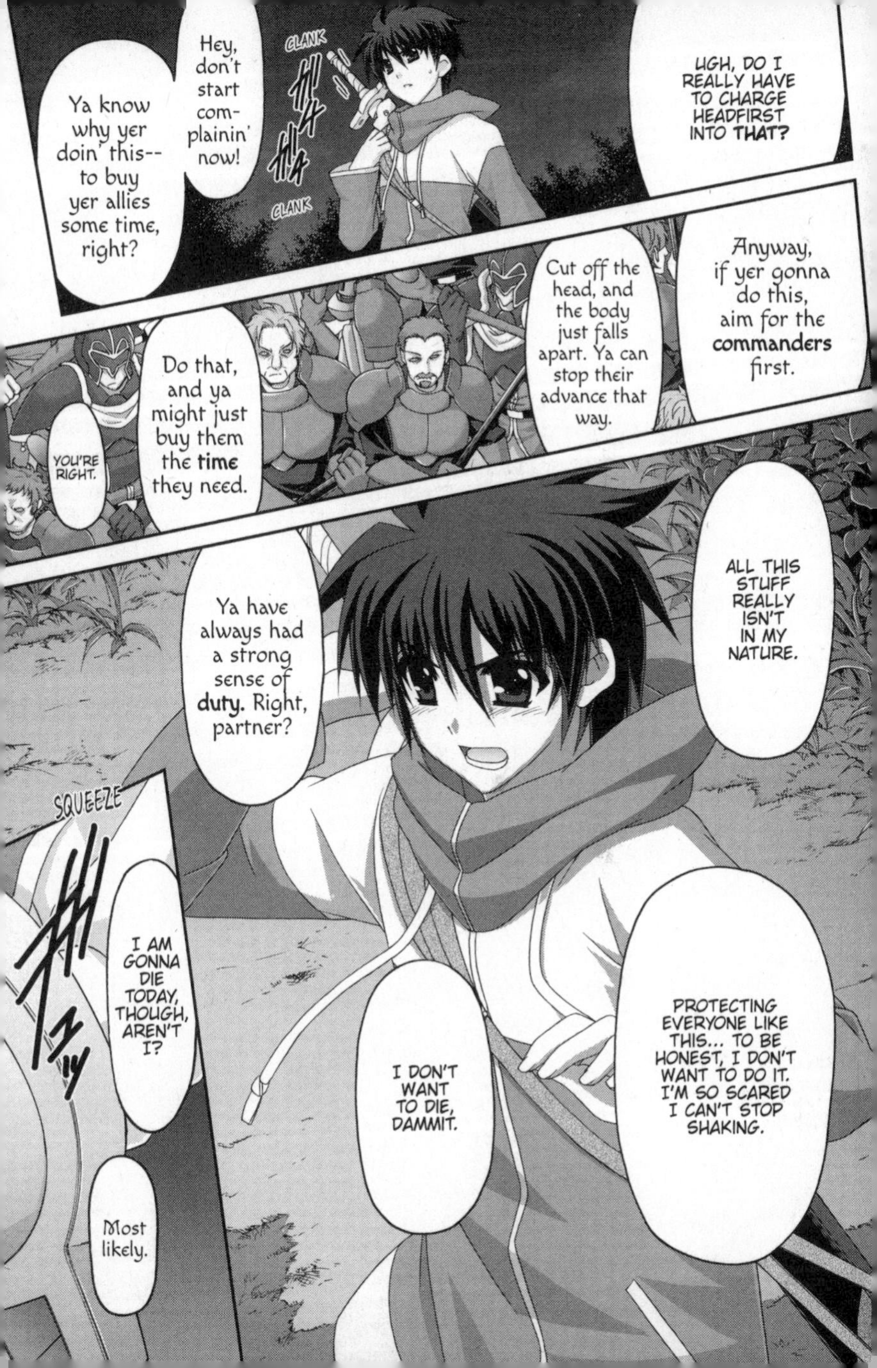
UGH, DO I REALLY HAVE TO CHARGE HEADFIRST INTO **THAT?**
CLANK
CLANK
Hey, don't start com-plainin' now!
Ya know why yer doin' this-- to buy yer allies some time, right?
Anyway, if yer gonna do this, aim for the **commanders** first.
Cut off the head, and the body just falls apart. Ya can stop their advance that way.
Do that, and ya might just buy them the **time** they need.
YOU'RE RIGHT.
ALL THIS STUFF REALLY ISN'T IN MY NATURE.
Ya have always had a strong sense of **duty.** Right, partner?
PROTECTING EVERYONE LIKE THIS... TO BE HONEST, I DON'T WANT TO DO IT. I'M SO SCARED I CAN'T STOP SHAKING.
I DON'T WANT TO DIE, DAMMIT.
I AM GONNA DIE TODAY, THOUGH, AREN'T I?
SQUEEZE
Most likely.

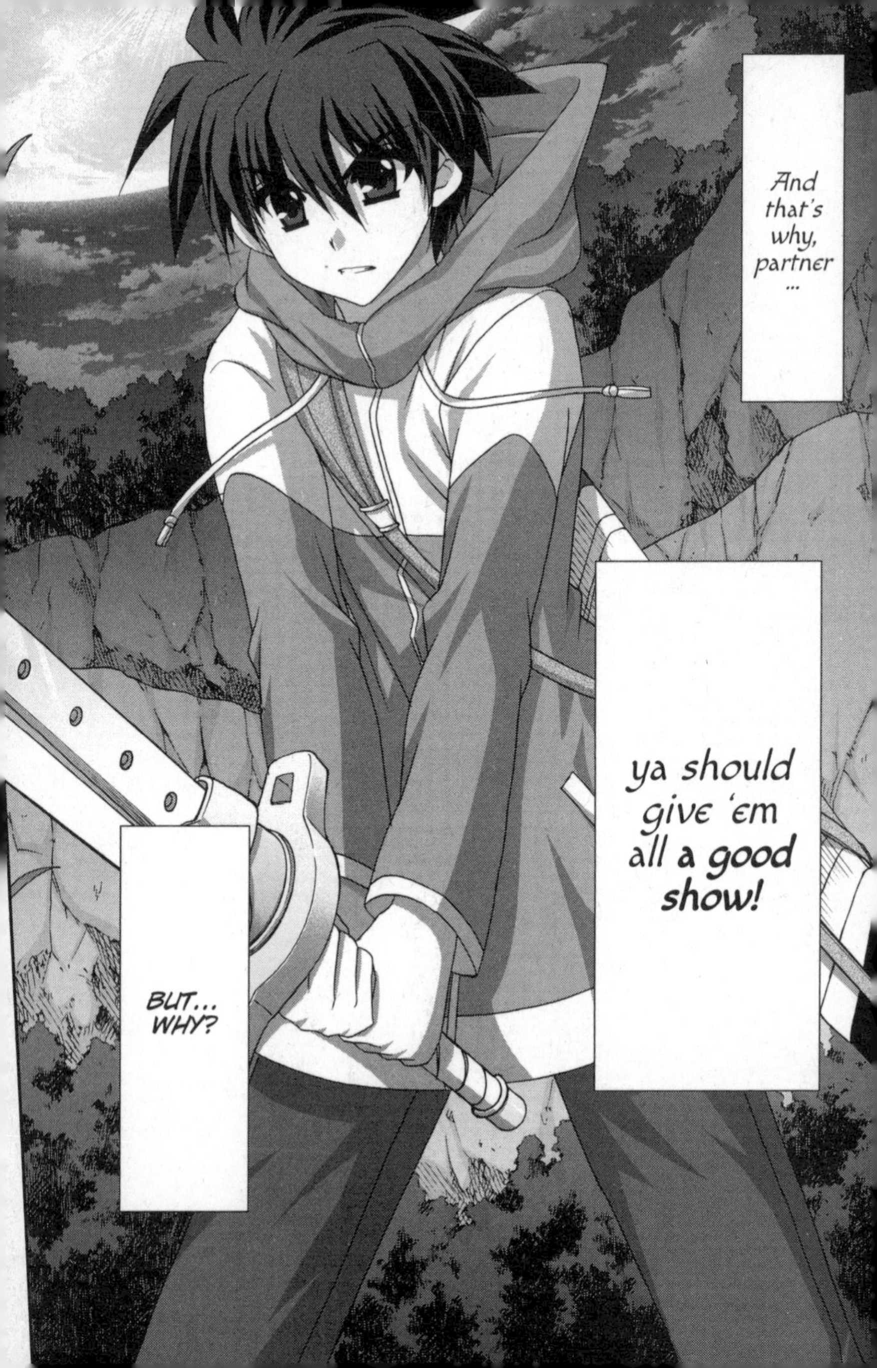
And that's why, partner ...
ya should give 'em all a good show!
BUT... WHY?

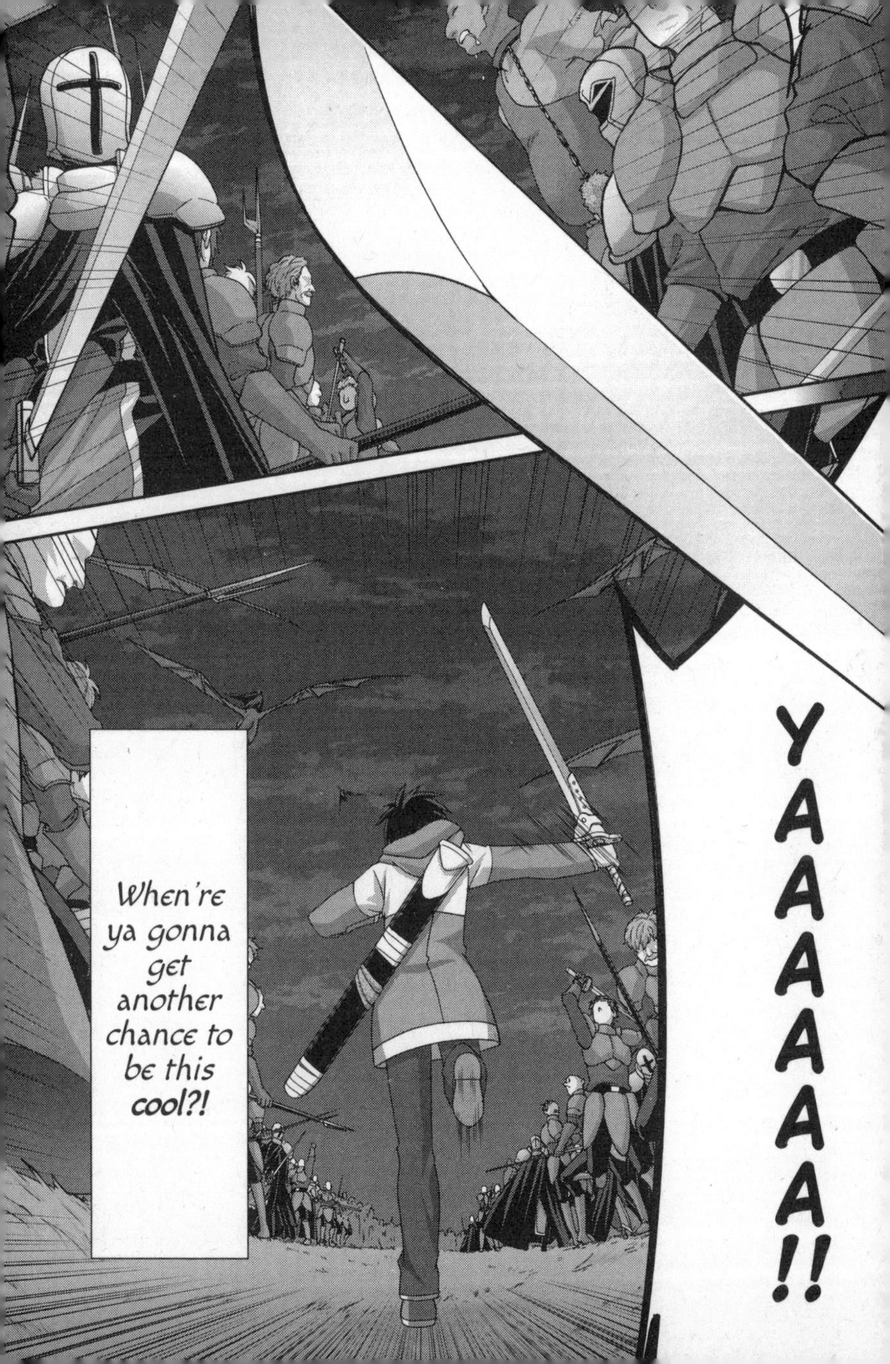
YAAAAAA!!
When're ya gonna get another chance to be this cool?!

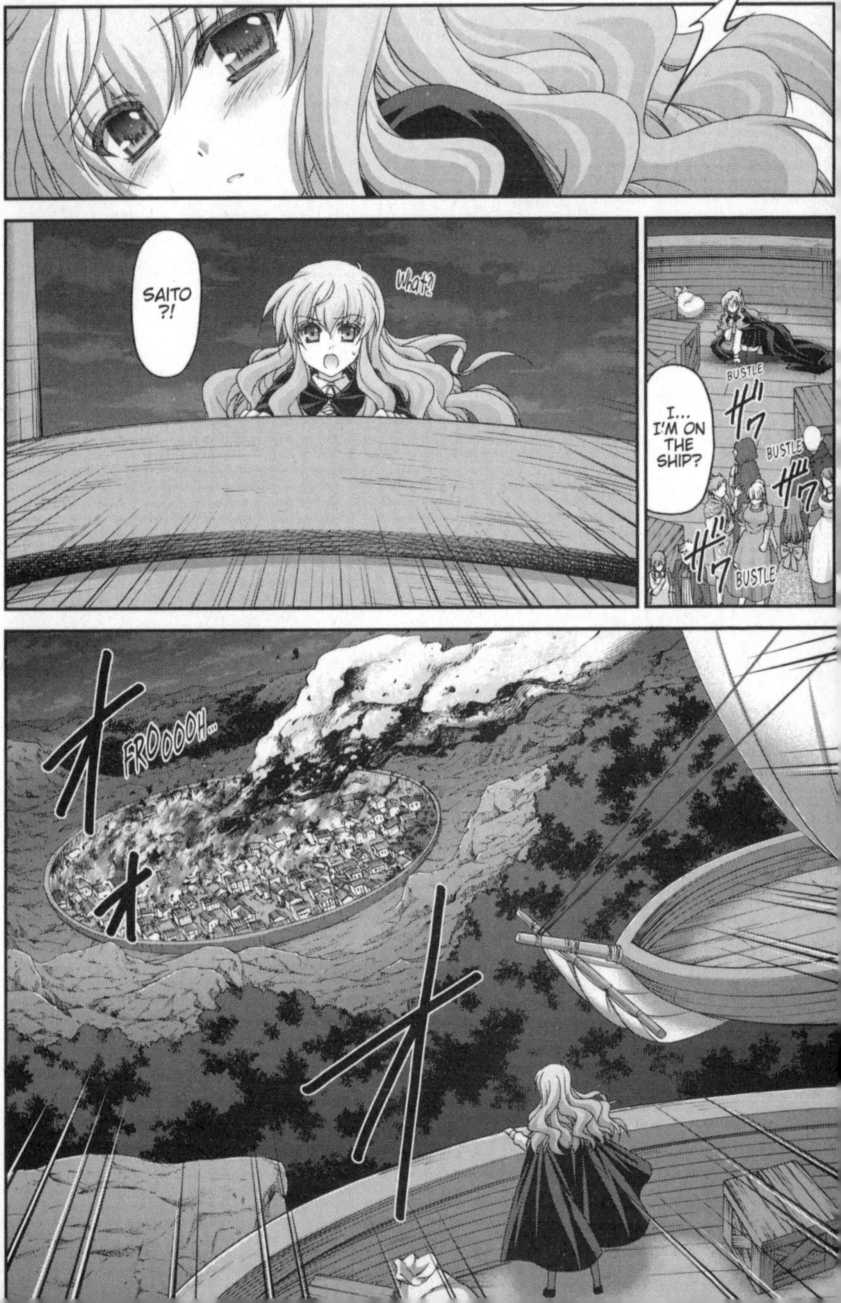
BUSTLE
I... I'M ON THE SHIP?
BUSTLE
BUSTLE
SAITO ?!
What?!
FROOOOH...

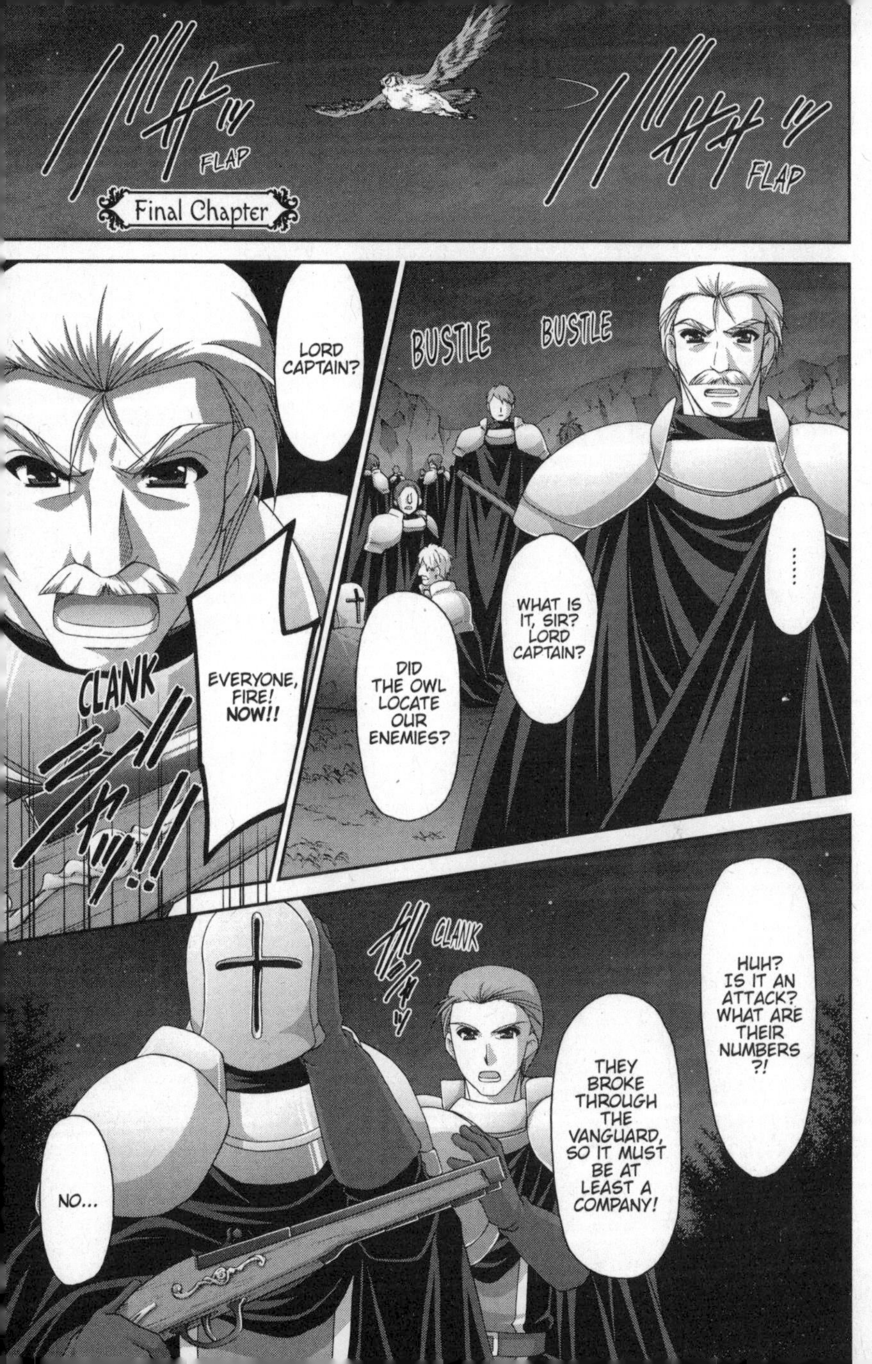
FLAP
FLAP
Final Chapter
BUSTLE
BUSTLE
......
WHAT IS IT, SIR? LORD CAPTAIN?
DID THE OWL LOCATE OUR ENEMIES?
LORD CAPTAIN?
EVERYONE, FIRE! NOW!!
CLANK
HUH? IS IT AN ATTACK? WHAT ARE THEIR NUMBERS?!
CLANK
THEY BROKE THROUGH THE VANGUARD, SO IT MUST BE AT LEAST A COMPANY!
NO...

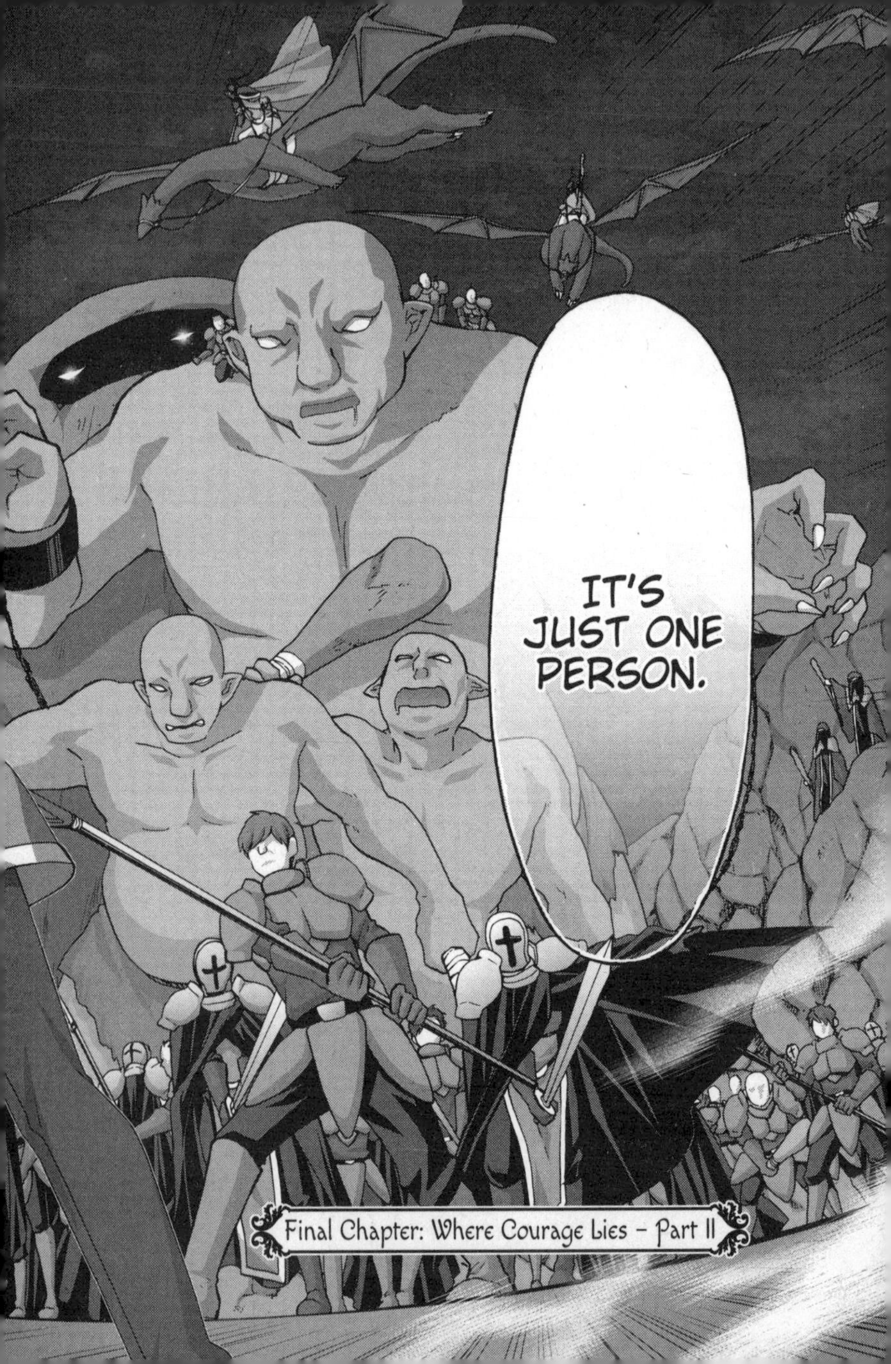
IT'S JUST ONE PERSON.
Final Chapter: Where Courage Lies – Part II

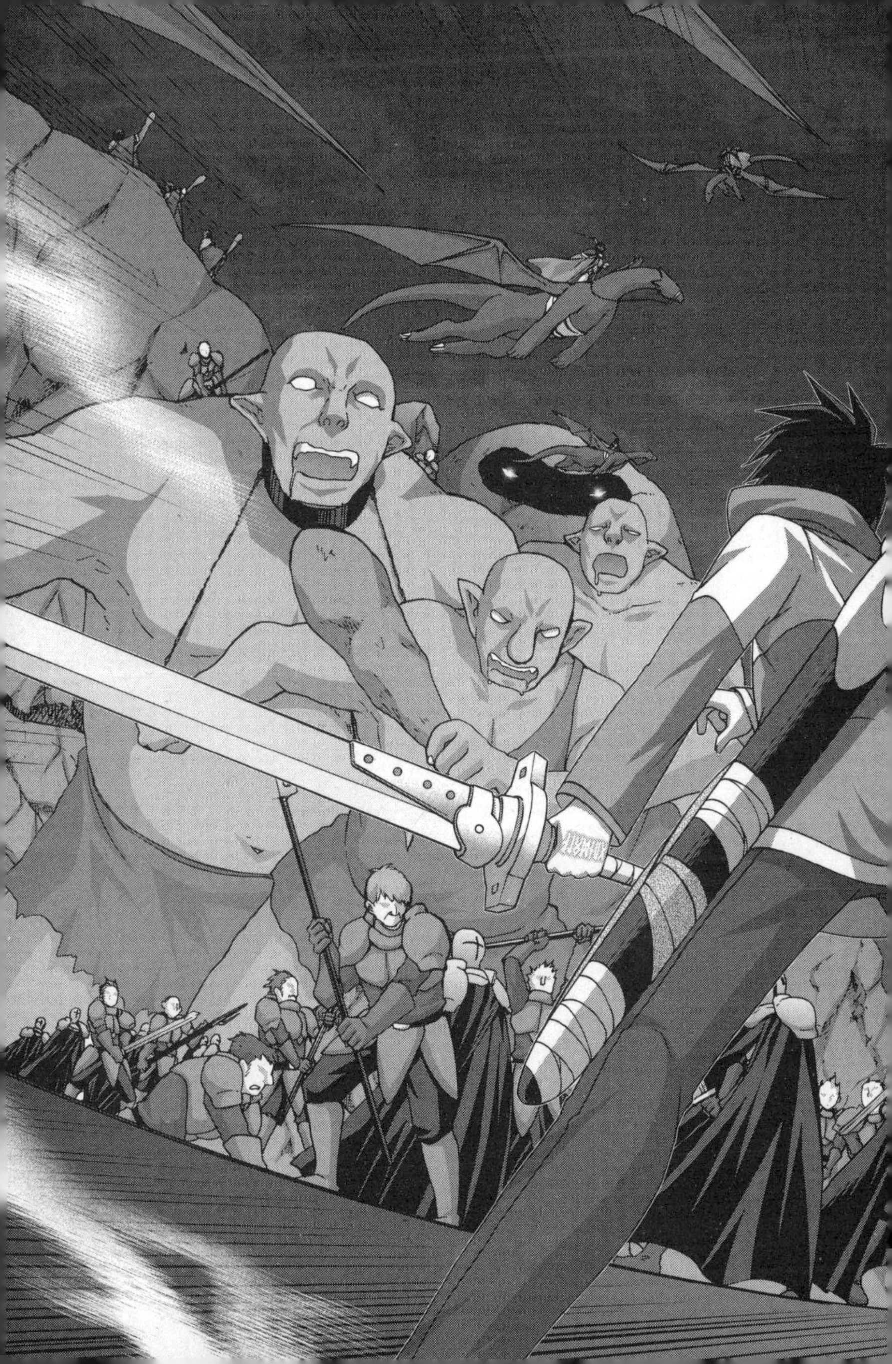

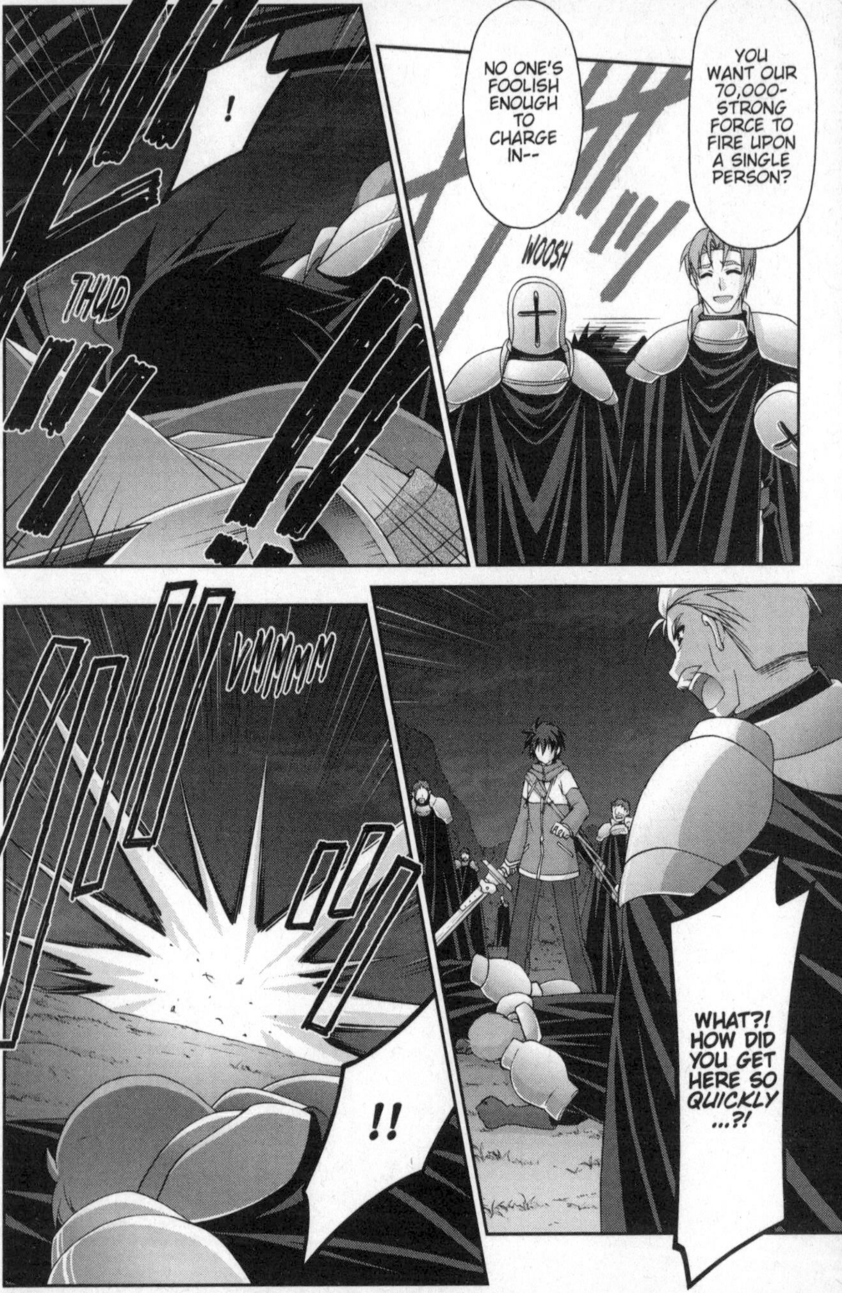
YOU WANT OUR 70,000-STRONG FORCE TO FIRE UPON A SINGLE PERSON?
NO ONE'S FOOLISH ENOUGH TO CHARGE IN--
WOOSH
!
THUD
WHAT?! HOW DID YOU GET HERE SO QUICKLY ...?!
VMMMMM
!!

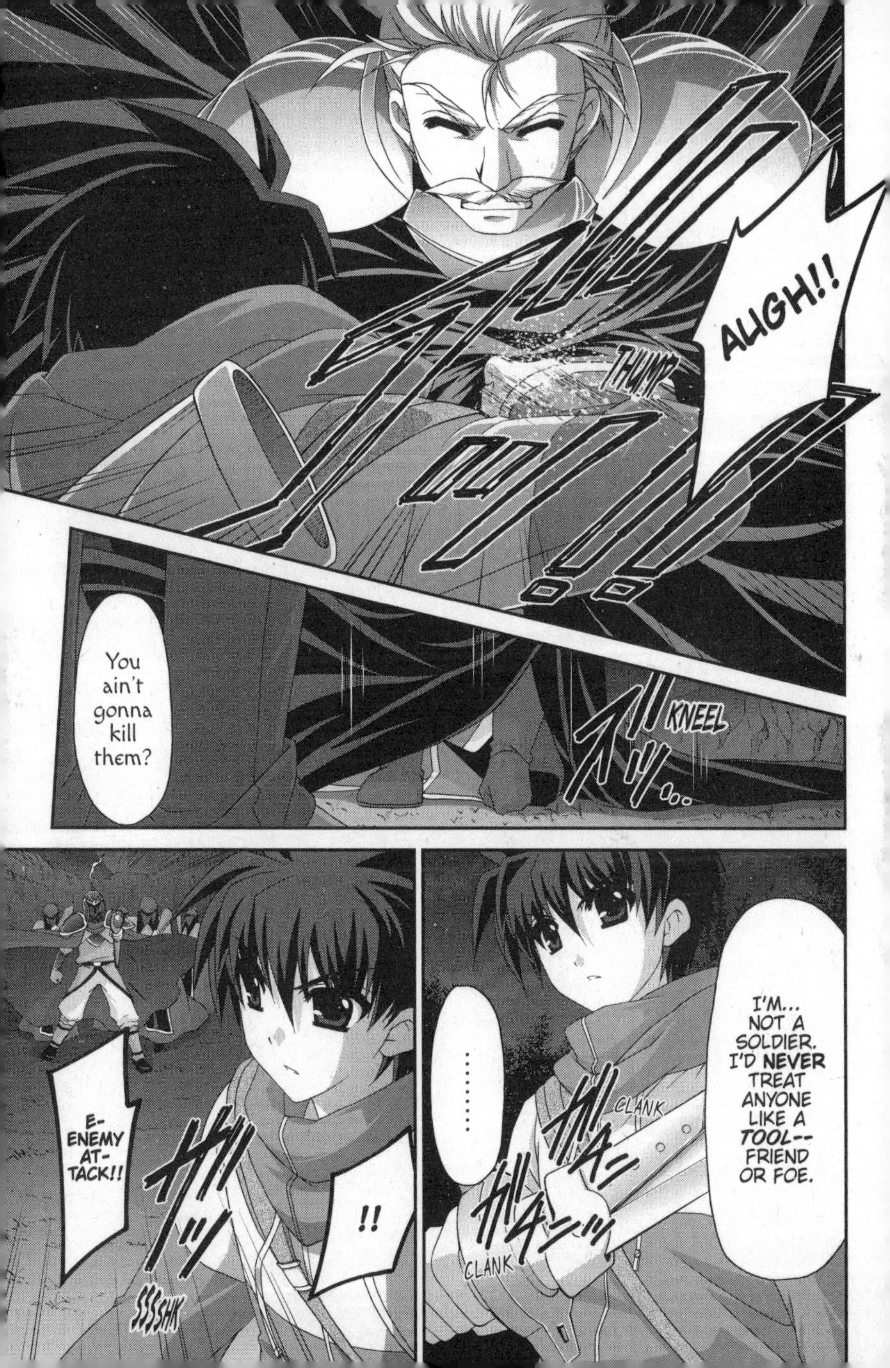
AUGH!!
THUMP
KNEEL
You ain't gonna kill them?
I'M... NOT A SOLDIER. I'D NEVER TREAT ANYONE LIKE A TOOL-- FRIEND OR FOE.
CLANK
CLANK
....
!!
E-ENEMY AT-TACK!!
SSSSHK

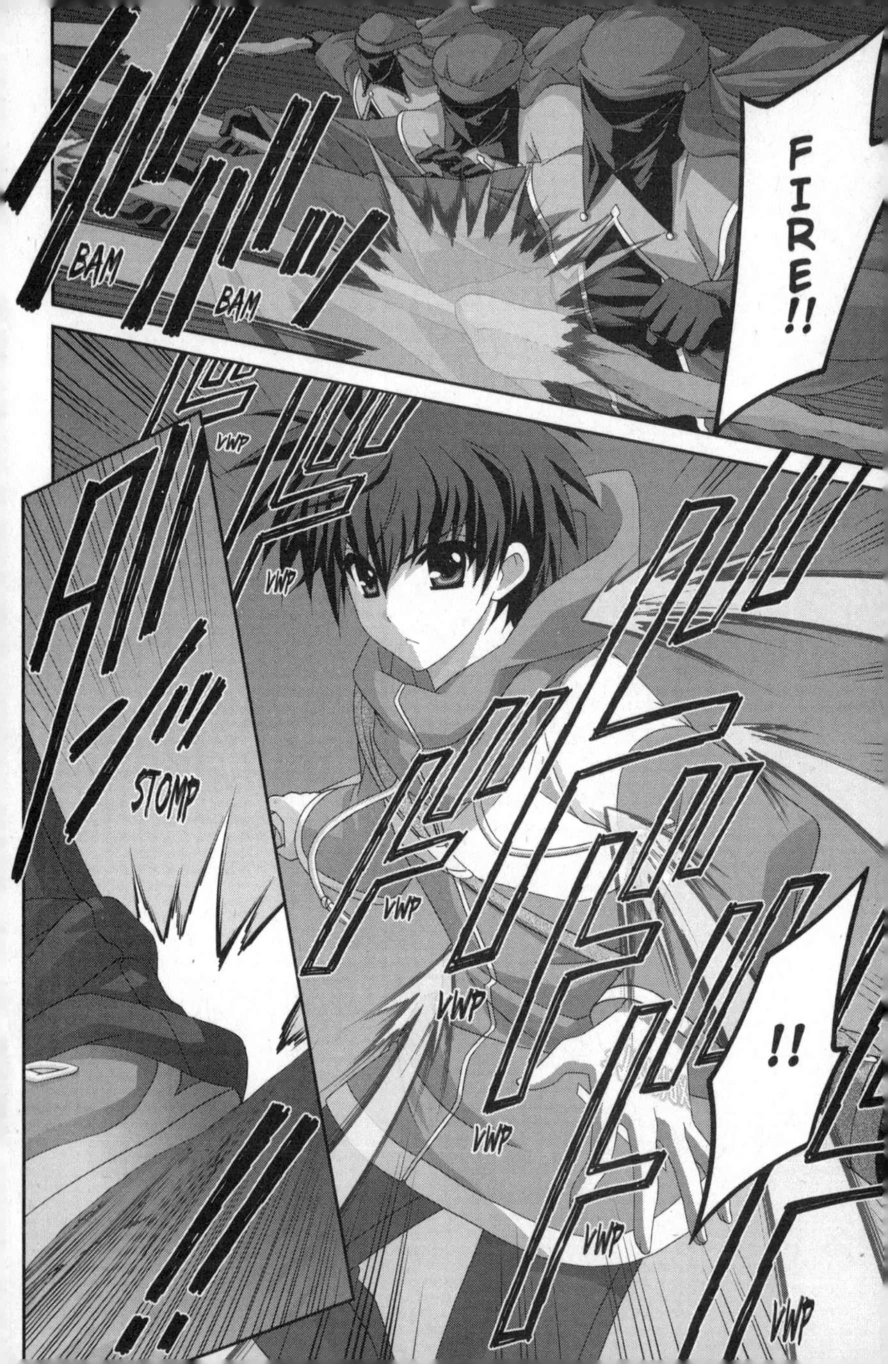
FIRE!!
BAM
BAM
VWP
VWP
!!
VWP
VWP
VWP
VWP
VWP
STOMP

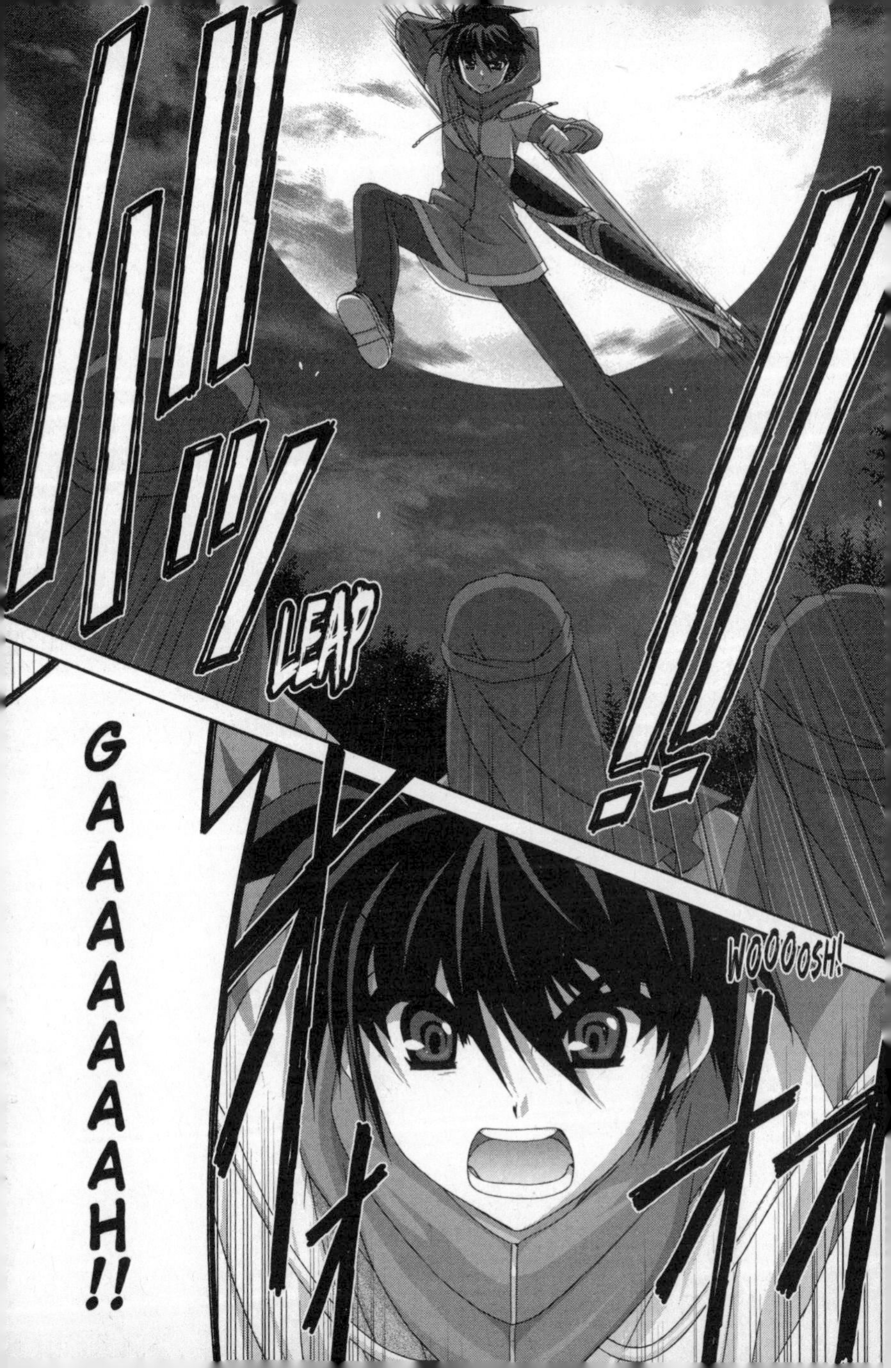
LEAP
WOOOOSH!
GAAAAAAAAAH!!

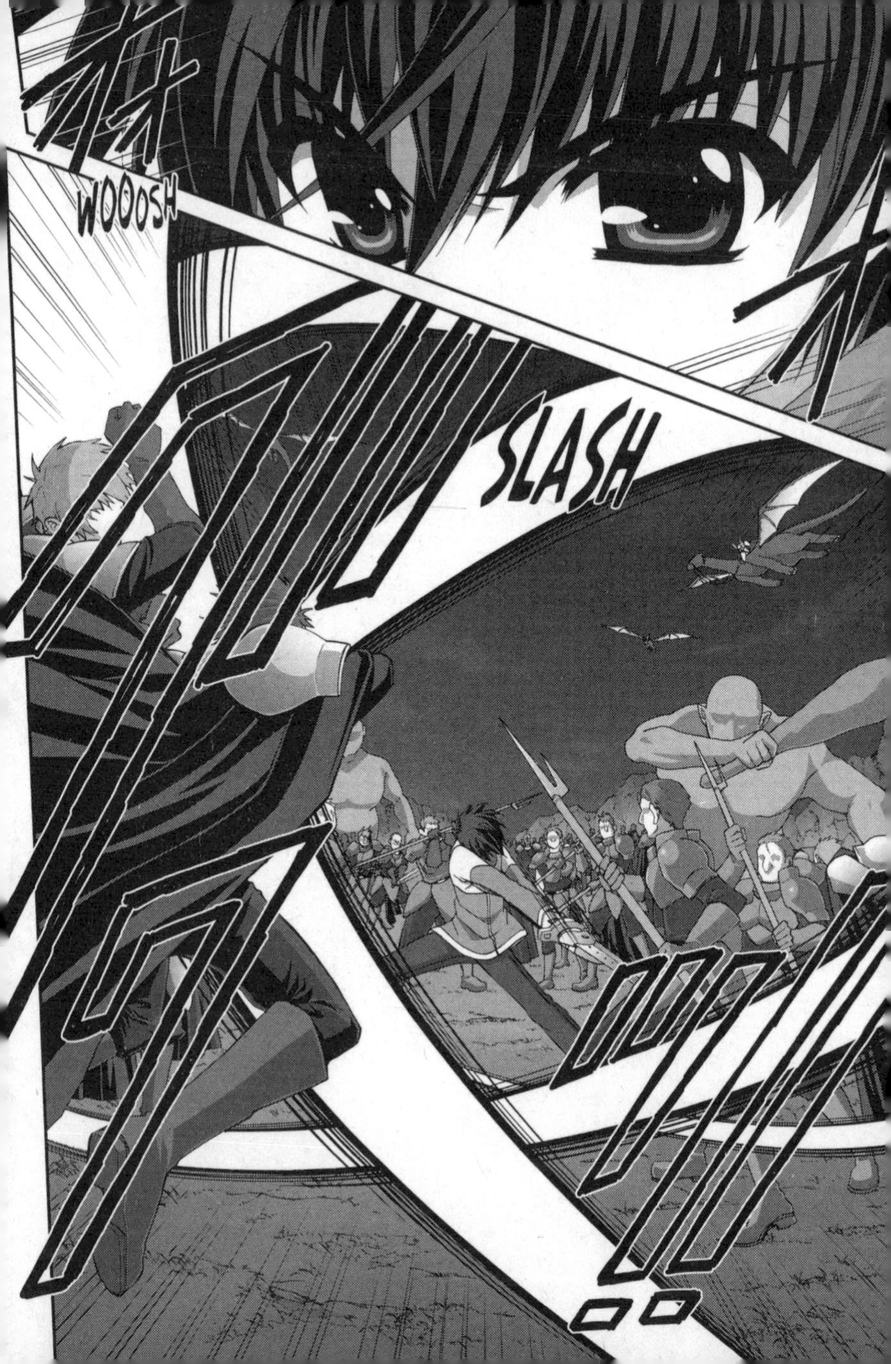
WOOSH
SLASH

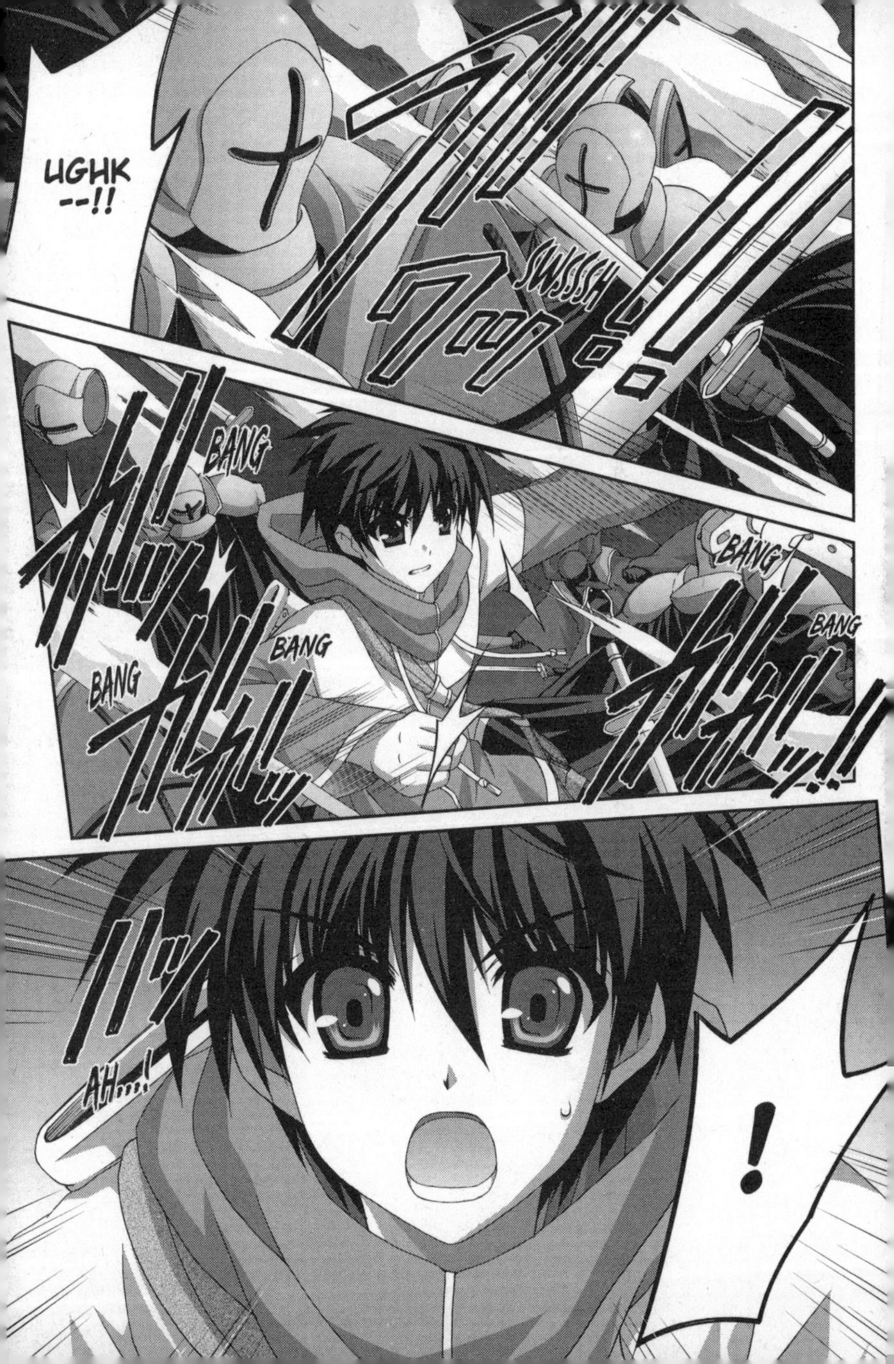
UGHK --!!
SWISSSH
BANG
BANG
BANG
BANG
BANG
!
AH...!

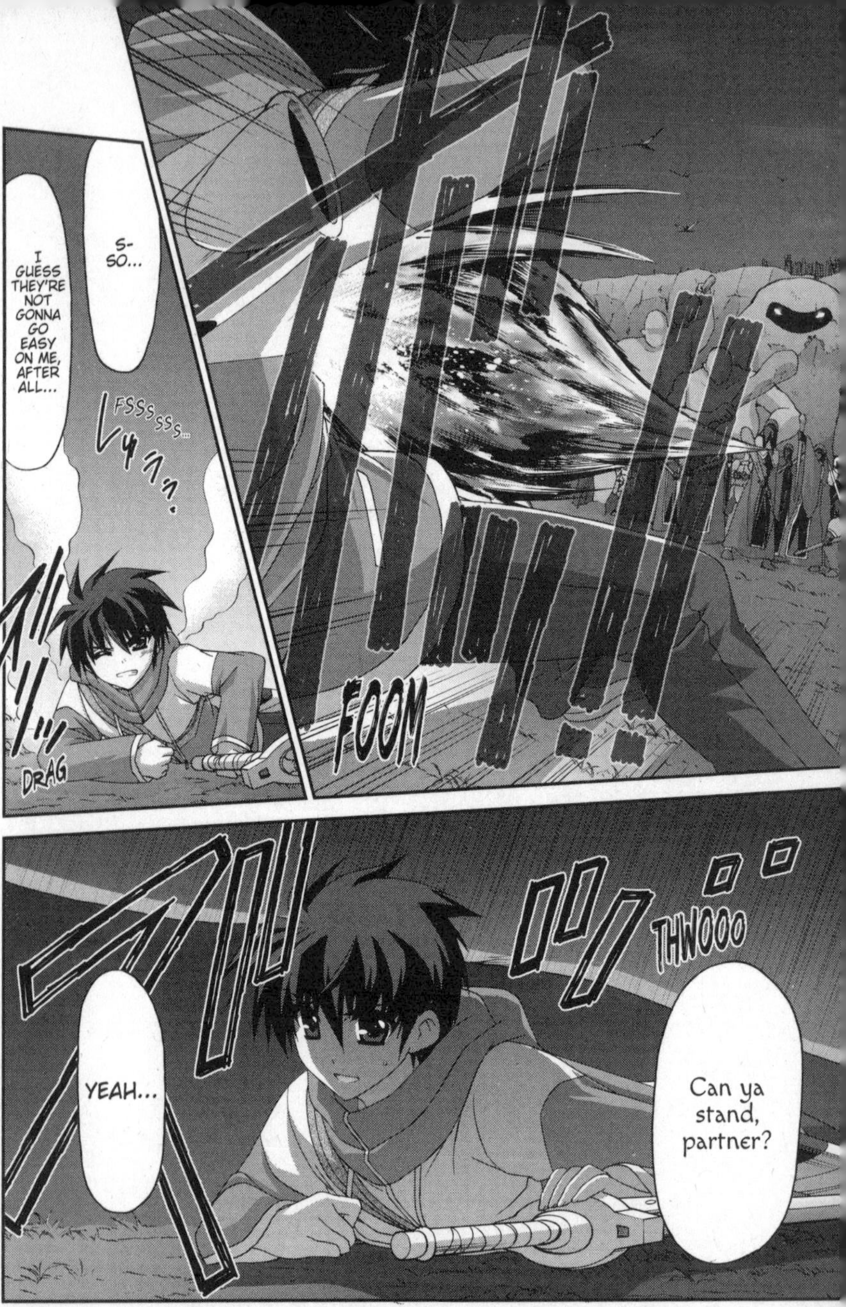
FOOM
S-SO...
I GUESS THEY'RE NOT GONNA GO EASY ON ME, AFTER ALL...
FSSSSSSS...
DRAG
THWOOO
Can ya stand, partner?
YEAH...

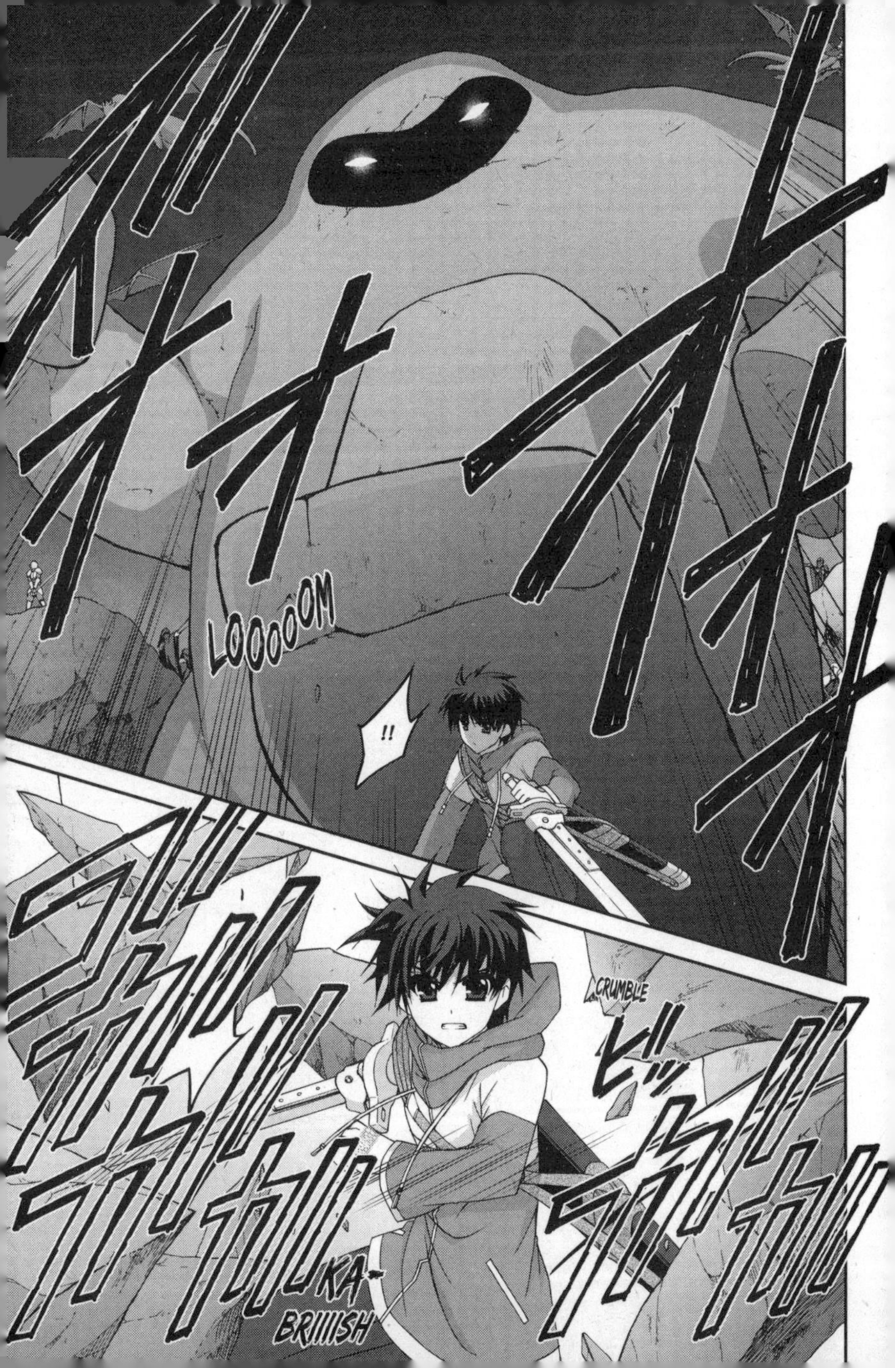
LOOOOOM
!!
CRUMBLE
KA-BRIIISH

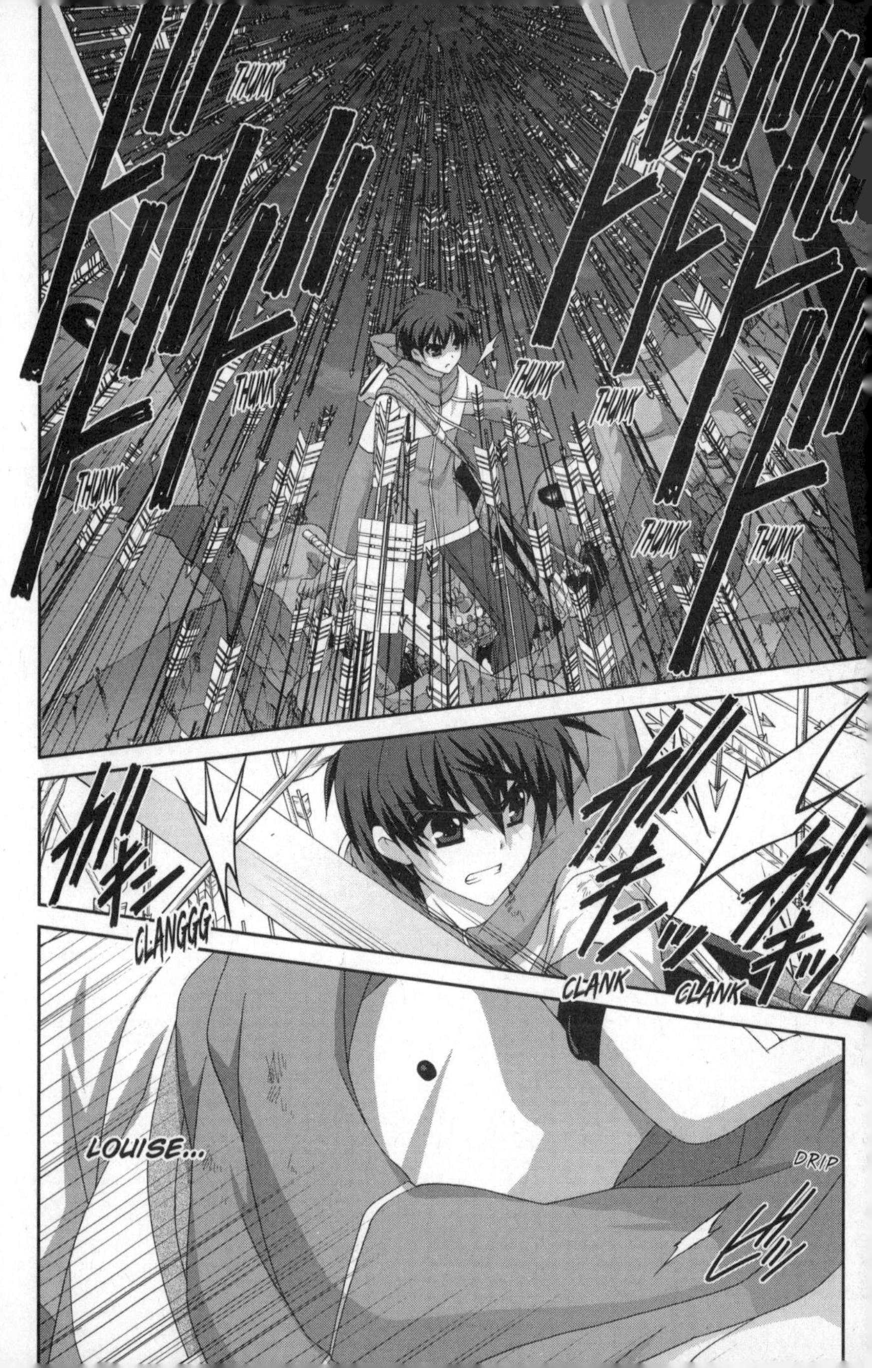
THUNK
THUNK
THUNK
THUNK
THUNK
THUNK
THUNK
CLANK
CLANK
CLANGGG
DRIP
LOUISE...

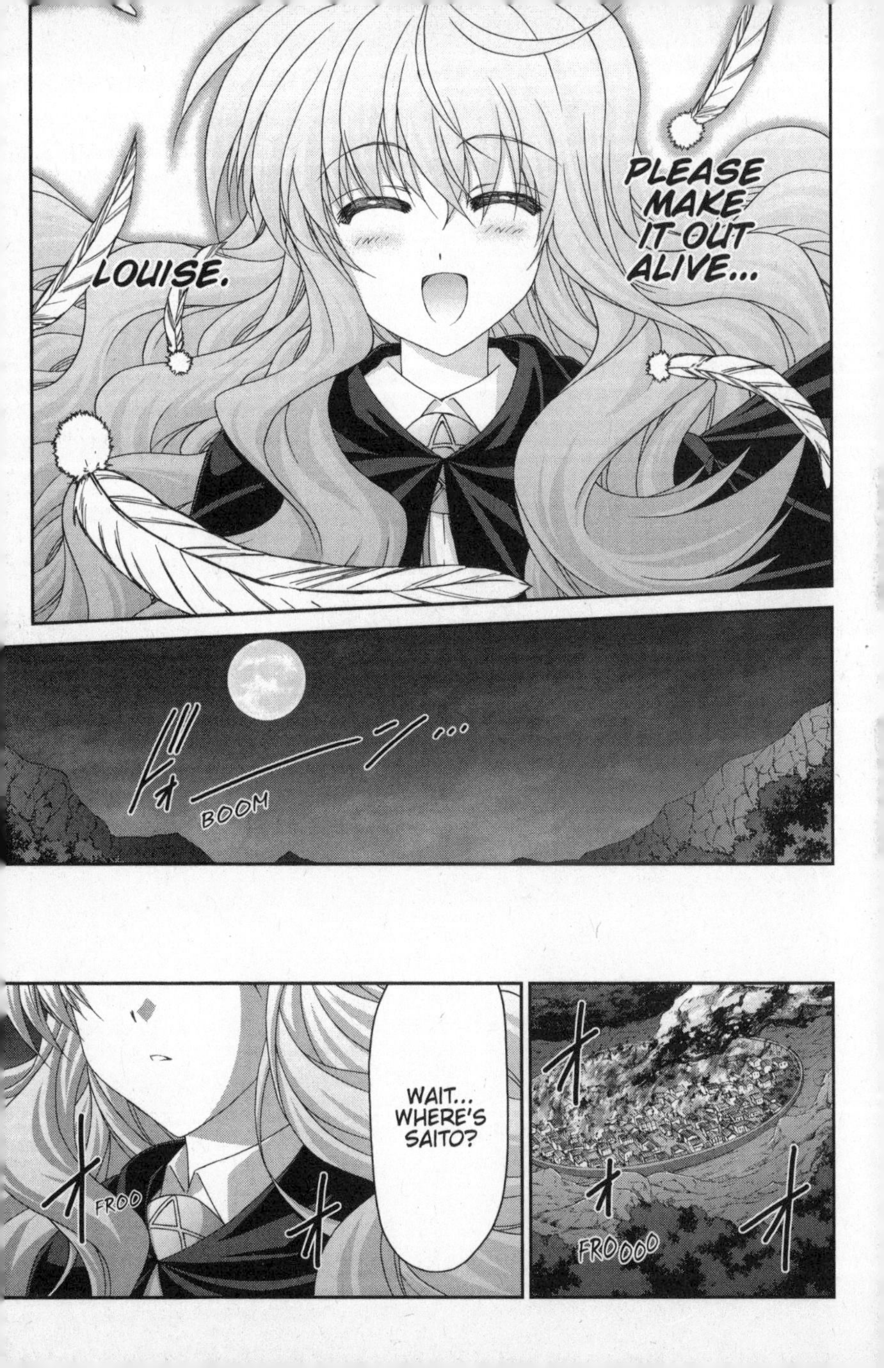
PLEASE MAKE IT OUT ALIVE...
LOUISE.
BOOM
FROOOO
WAIT... WHERE'S SAITO?
FROO

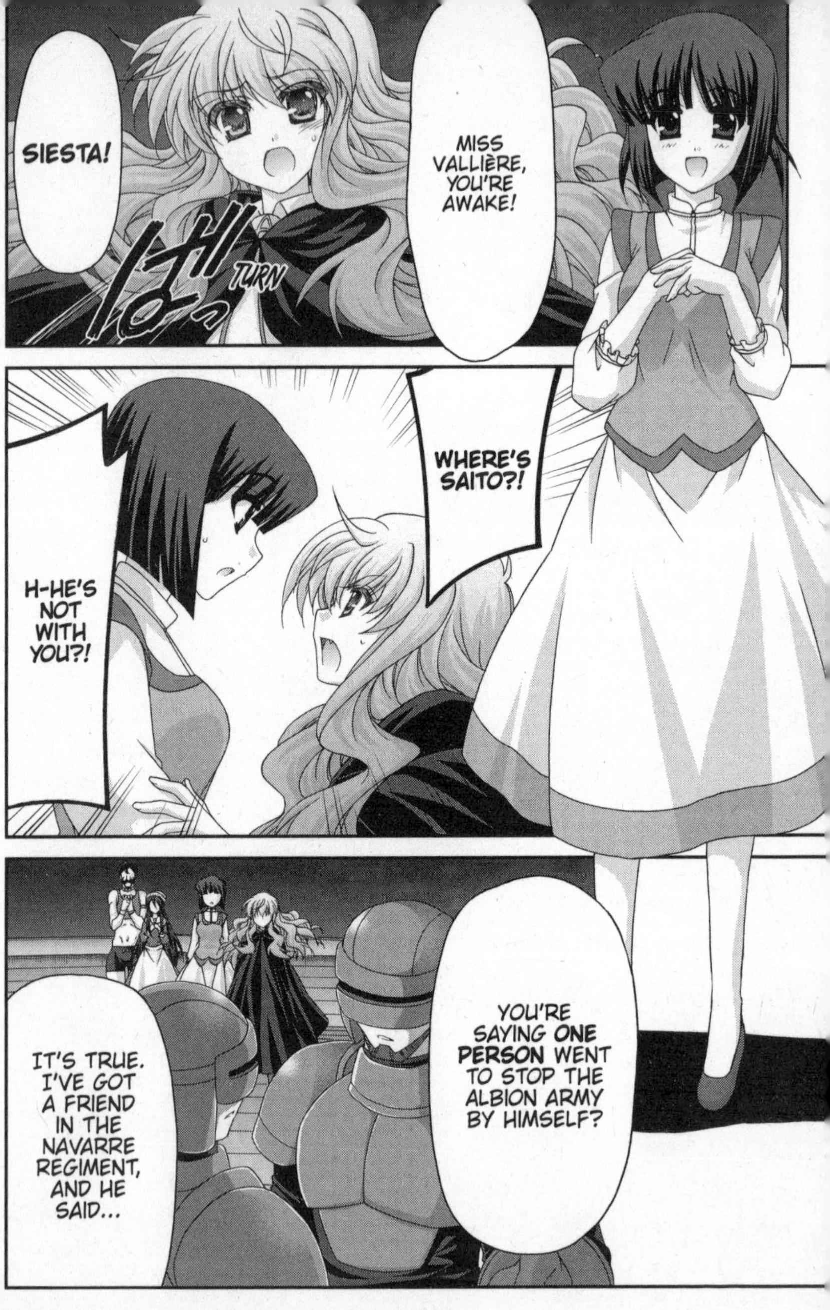
MISS VALLIÈRE, YOU'RE AWAKE!
SIESTA!
TURN
WHERE'S SAITO?!
H-HE'S NOT WITH YOU?!
YOU'RE SAYING ONE PERSON WENT TO STOP THE ALBION ARMY BY HIMSELF?
IT'S TRUE. I'VE GOT A FRIEND IN THE NAVARRE REGIMENT, AND HE SAID...

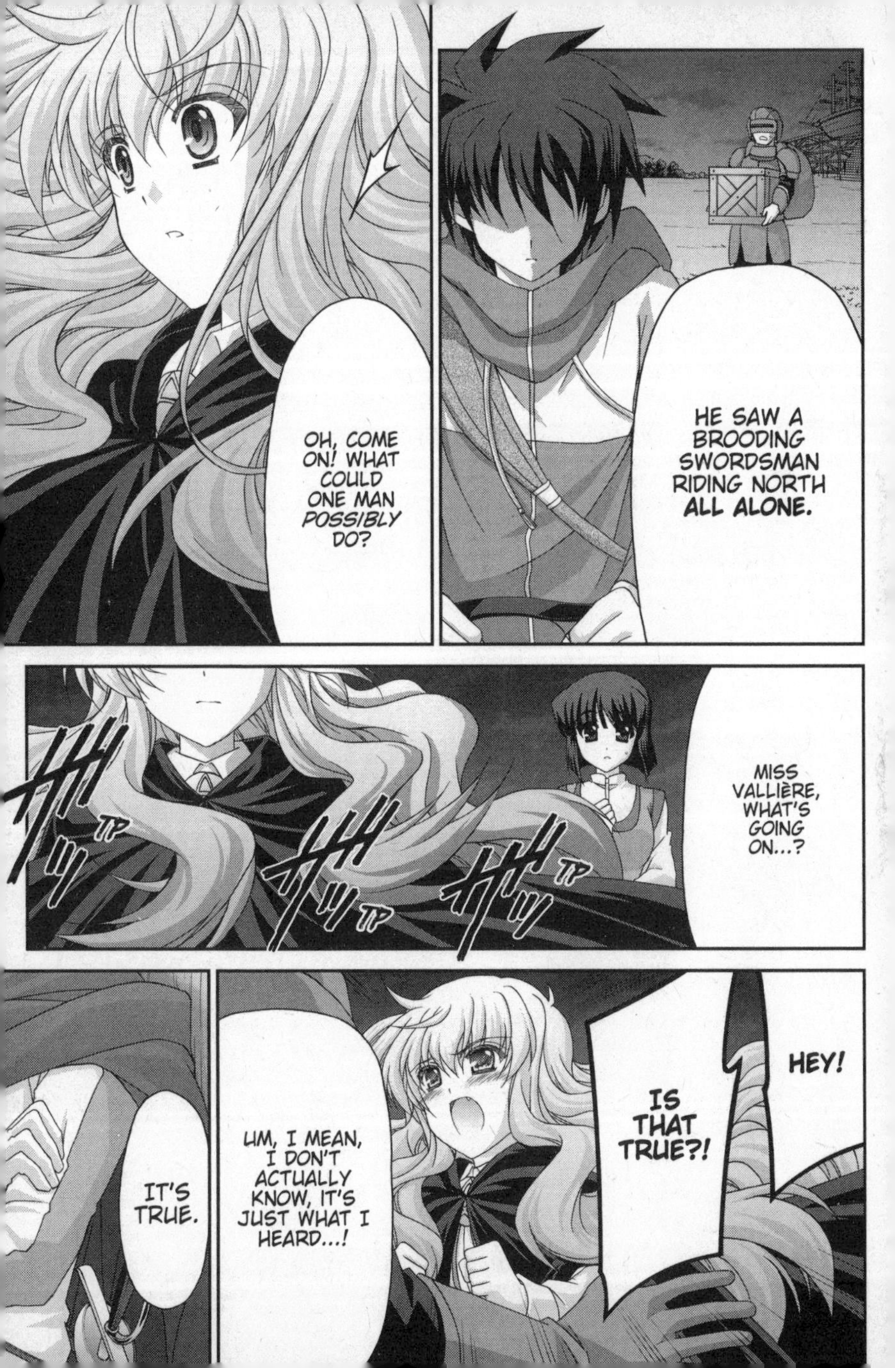
HE SAW A BROODING SWORDSMAN RIDING NORTH ALL ALONE.
OH, COME ON! WHAT COULD ONE MAN POSSIBLY DO?
MISS VALLIÈRE, WHAT'S GOING ON...?
TP
TP
TP
TP
HEY!
IS THAT TRUE?!
UM, I MEAN, I DON'T ACTUALLY KNOW, IT'S JUST WHAT I HEARD...!
IT'S TRUE.

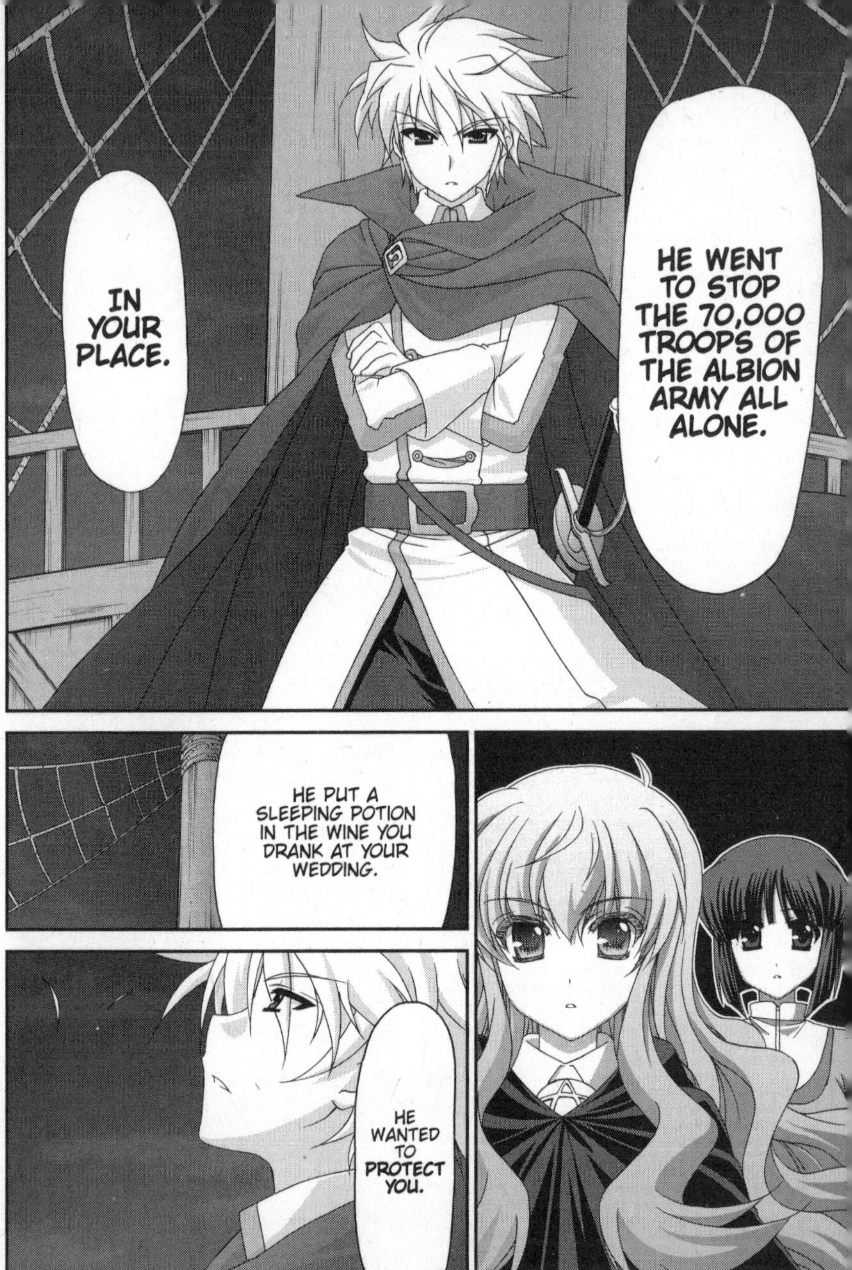
HE WENT TO STOP THE 70,000 TROOPS OF THE ALBION ARMY ALL ALONE.
IN YOUR PLACE.
HE PUT A SLEEPING POTION IN THE WINE YOU DRANK AT YOUR WEDDING.
HE WANTED TO PROTECT YOU.

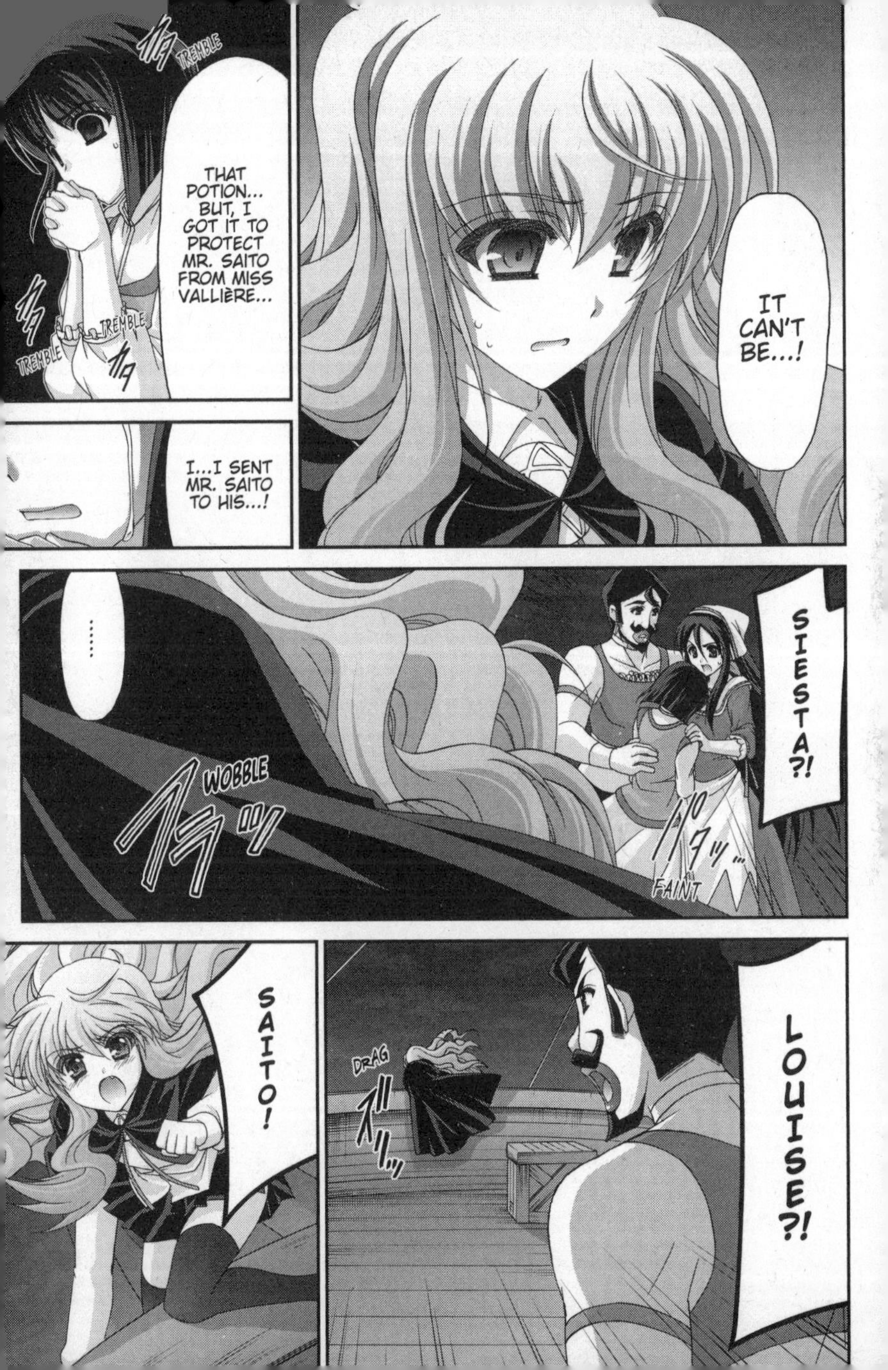
IT CAN'T BE...!
TREMBLE
THAT POTION... BUT, I GOT IT TO PROTECT MR. SAITO FROM MISS VALLIÈRE...
TREMBLE
TREMBLE
I...I SENT MR. SAITO TO HIS...!
SIESTA?!
FAINT
WOBBLE
......
LOUISE?!
DRAG
SAITO!

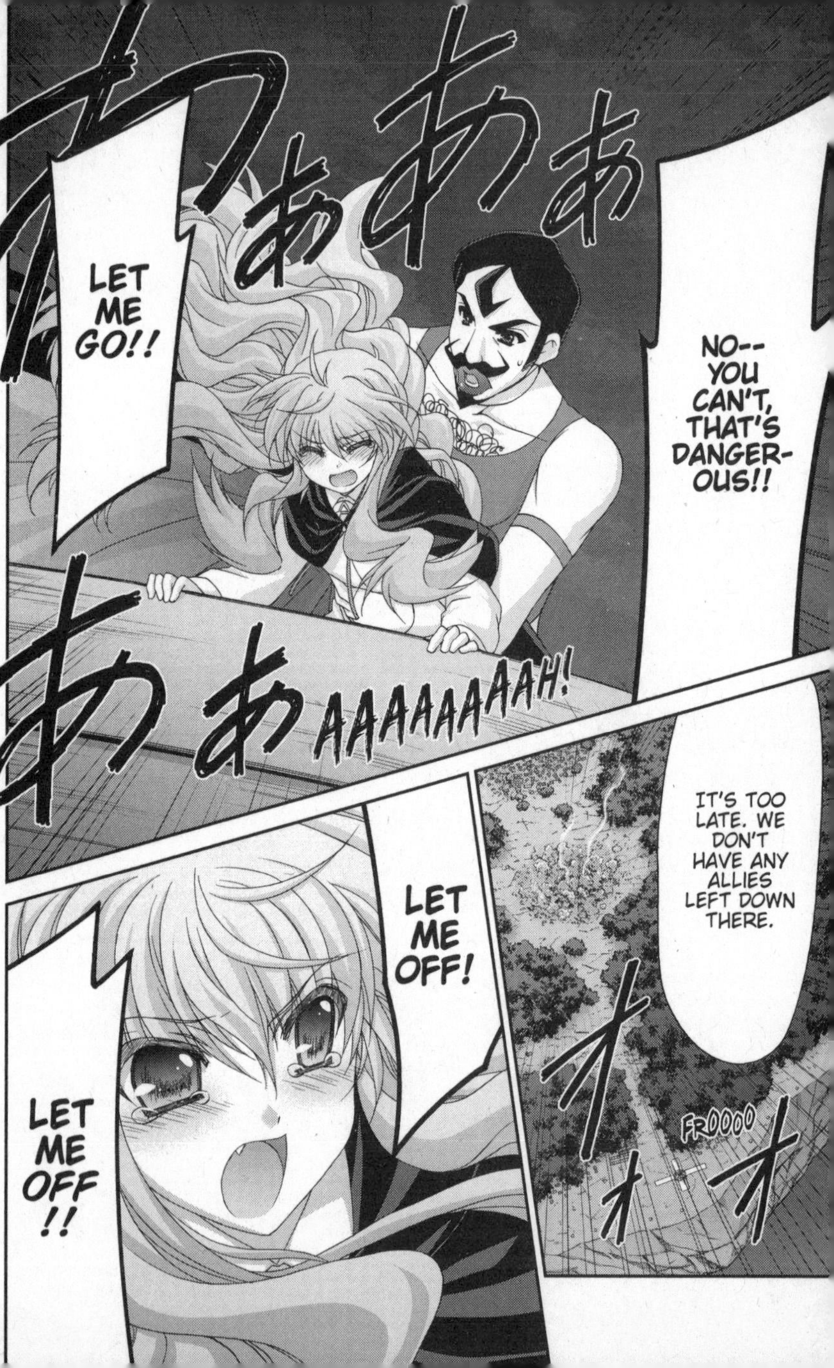
NO-- YOU CAN'T, THAT'S DANGER-OUS!!
LET ME GO!!
AAAAAAAAH!
IT'S TOO LATE. WE DON'T HAVE ANY ALLIES LEFT DOWN THERE.
FROOOO
LET ME OFF!
LET ME OFF!!

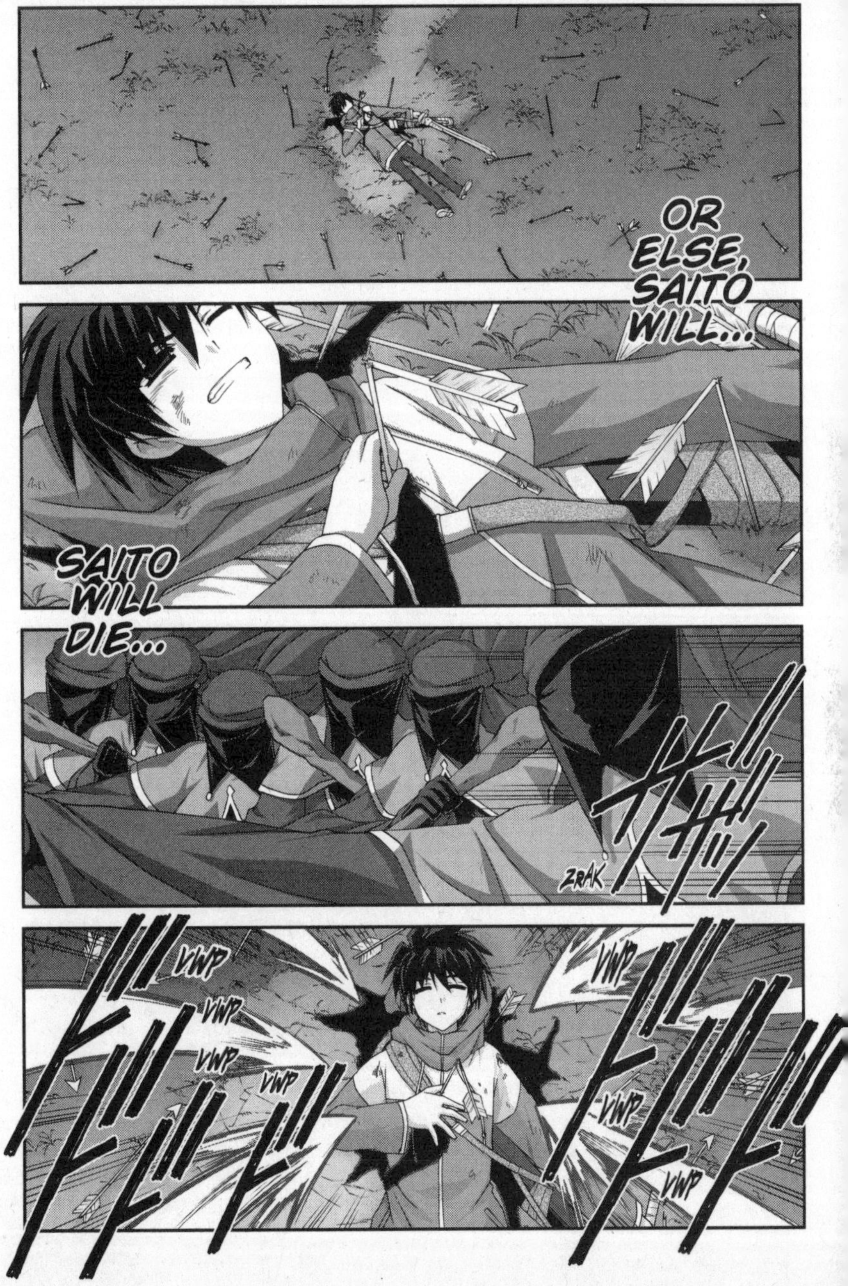
OR ELSE, SAITO WILL...
SAITO WILL DIE...
ZRAK
VWP
VWP
VWP
VWP
VWP
VWP
VWP

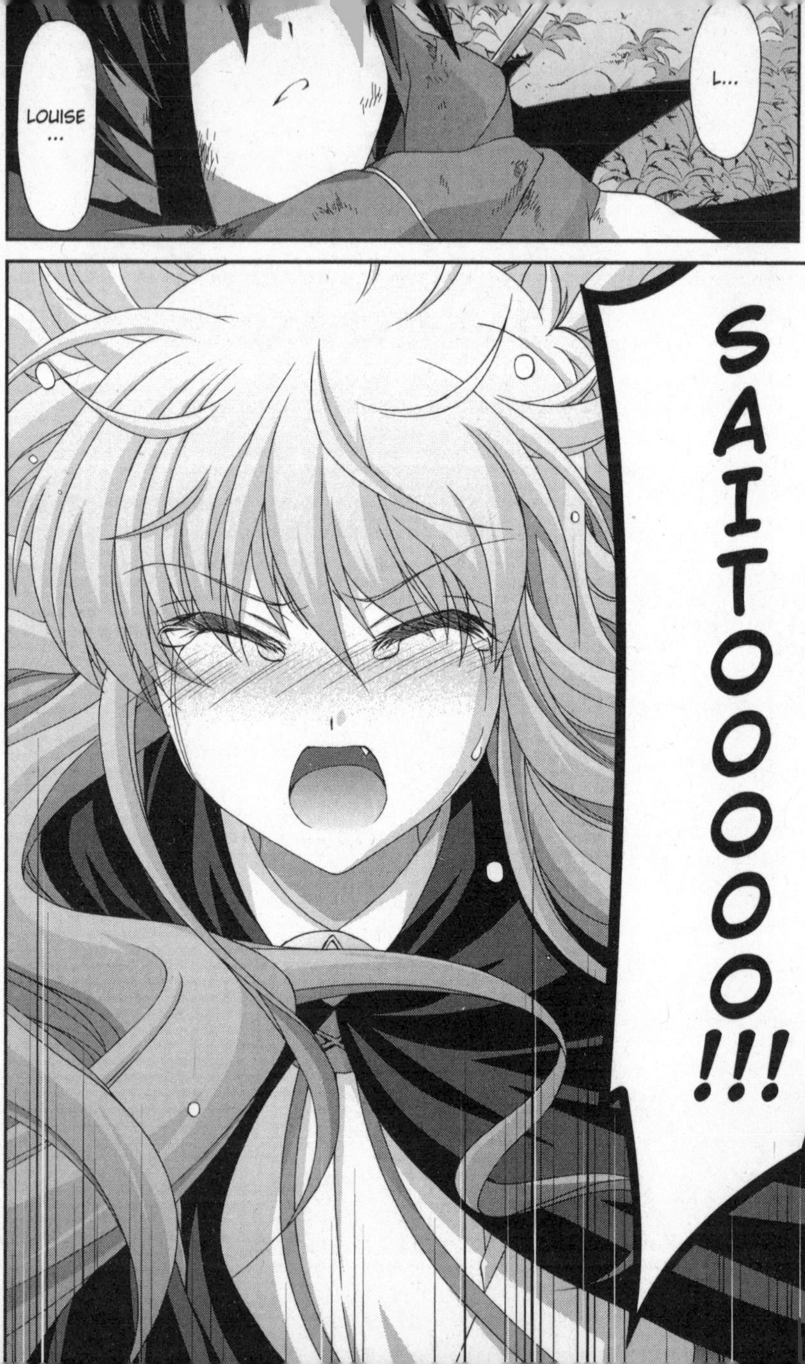
L...
LOUISE ...
SAITOOOOOO!!!

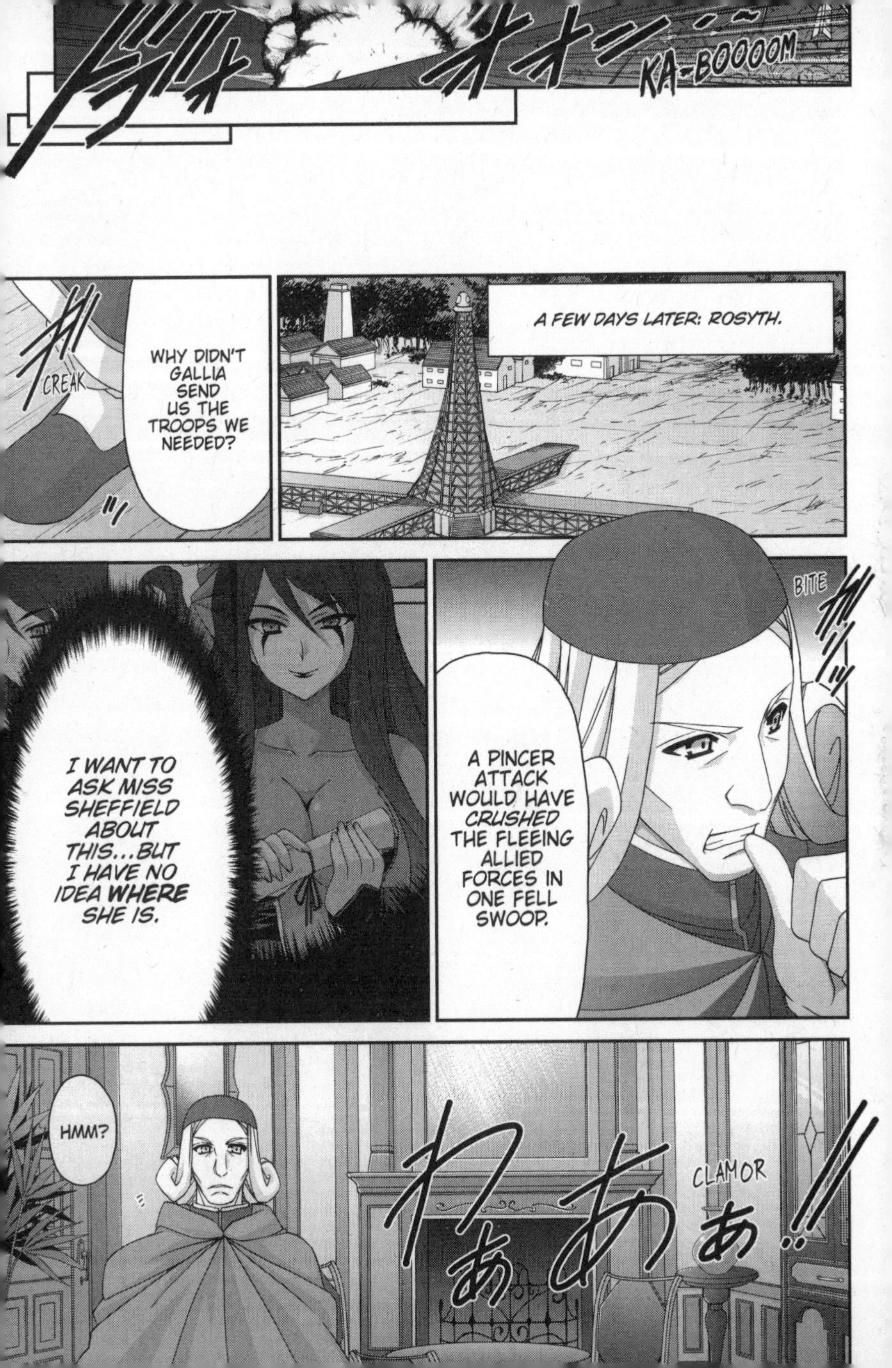
KA-BOOOOM
A FEW DAYS LATER: ROSYTH.
WHY DIDN'T GALLIA SEND US THE TROOPS WE NEEDED?
CREAK
BITE
A PINCER ATTACK WOULD HAVE CRUSHED THE FLEEING ALLIED FORCES IN ONE FELL SWOOP.
I WANT TO ASK MISS SHEFFIELD ABOUT THIS...BUT I HAVE NO IDEA WHERE SHE IS.
CLAMOR
HMM?

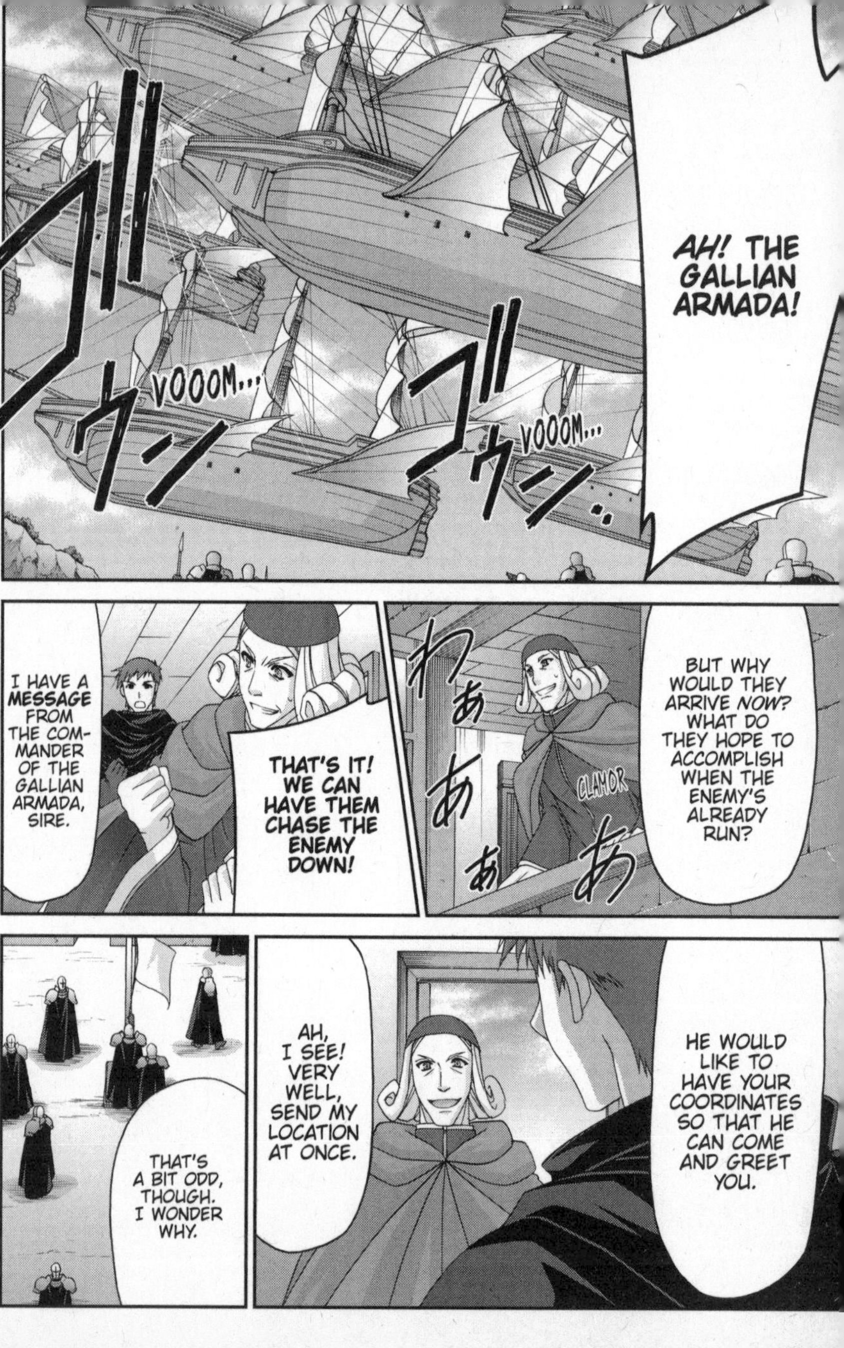
AH! THE GALLIAN ARMADA!
VOOOM...
VOOOM...
BUT WHY WOULD THEY ARRIVE NOW? WHAT DO THEY HOPE TO ACCOMPLISH WHEN THE ENEMY'S ALREADY RUN?
わああああ
CLAMOR
THAT'S IT! WE CAN HAVE THEM CHASE THE ENEMY DOWN!
I HAVE A MESSAGE FROM THE COMMANDER OF THE GALLIAN ARMADA, SIRE.
HE WOULD LIKE TO HAVE YOUR COORDINATES SO THAT HE CAN COME AND GREET YOU.
AH, I SEE! VERY WELL, SEND MY LOCATION AT ONCE.
THAT'S A BIT ODD, THOUGH. I WONDER WHY.

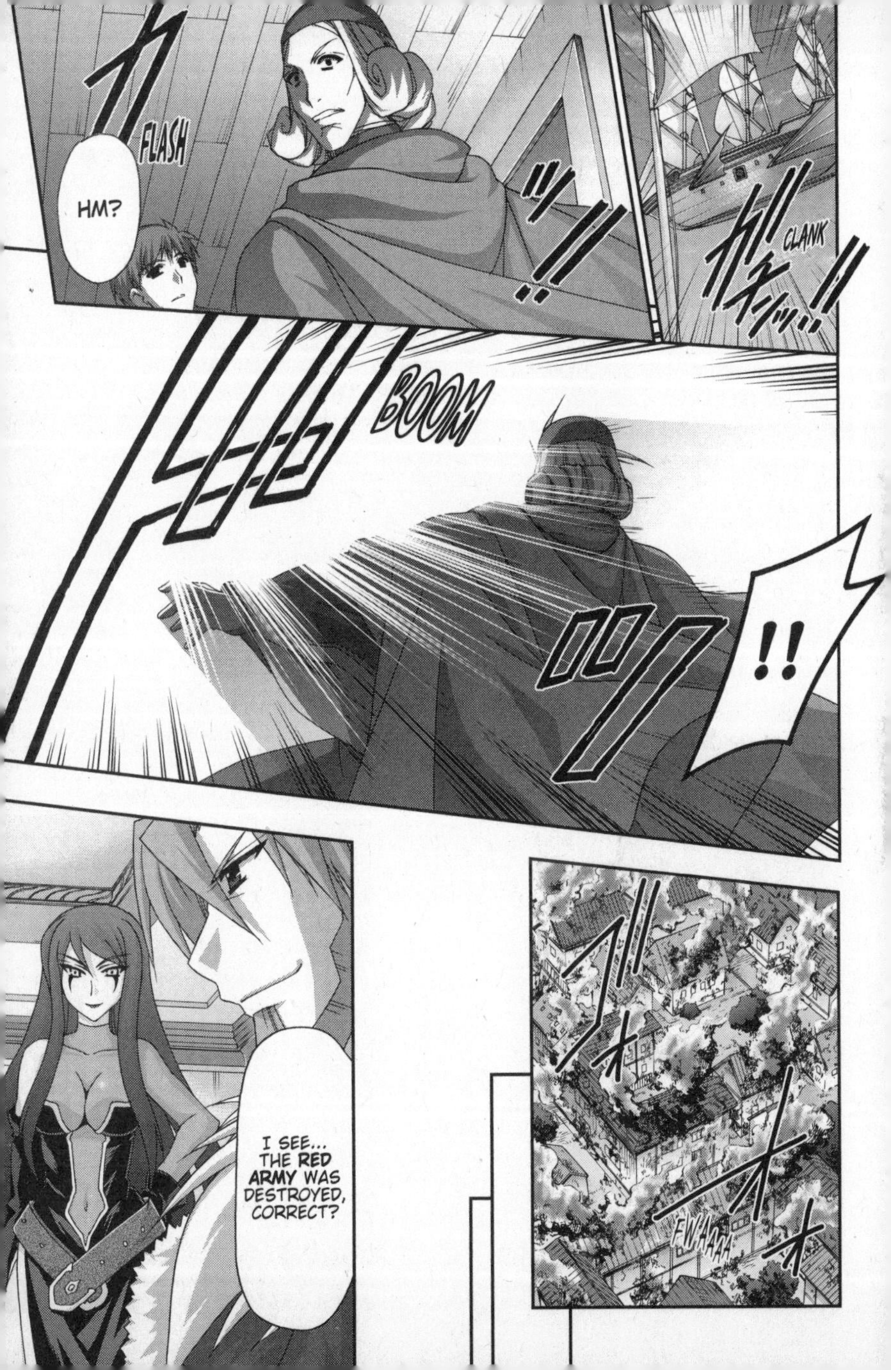
CLANK
FLASH
HM?
BOOM
!!
FWAAAA
I SEE... THE RED ARMY WAS DESTROYED, CORRECT?

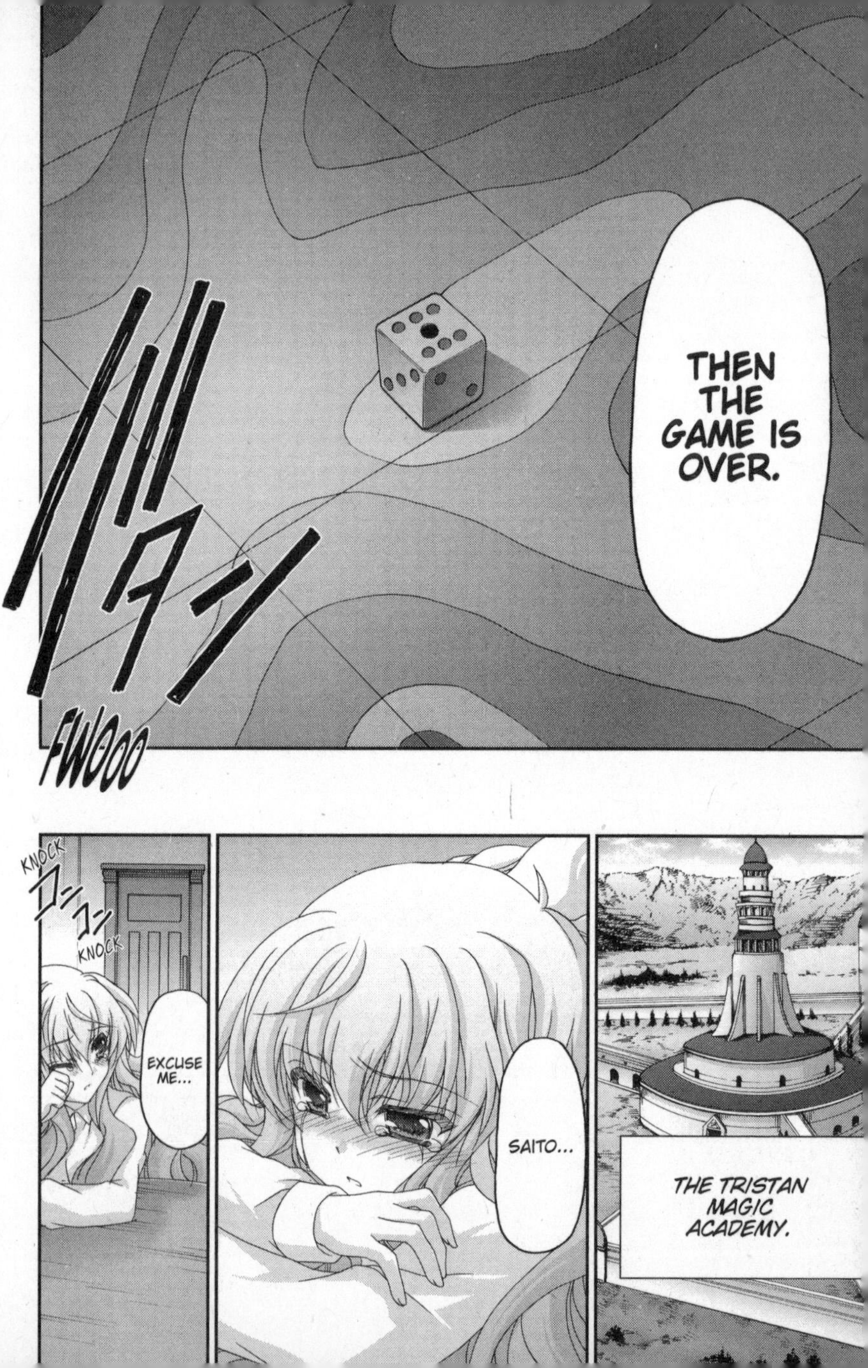

THEN THE GAME IS OVER.
FWOOO
THE TRISTAN MAGIC ACADEMY.
SAITO...
KNOCK
コン コン
KNOCK
EXCUSE ME...

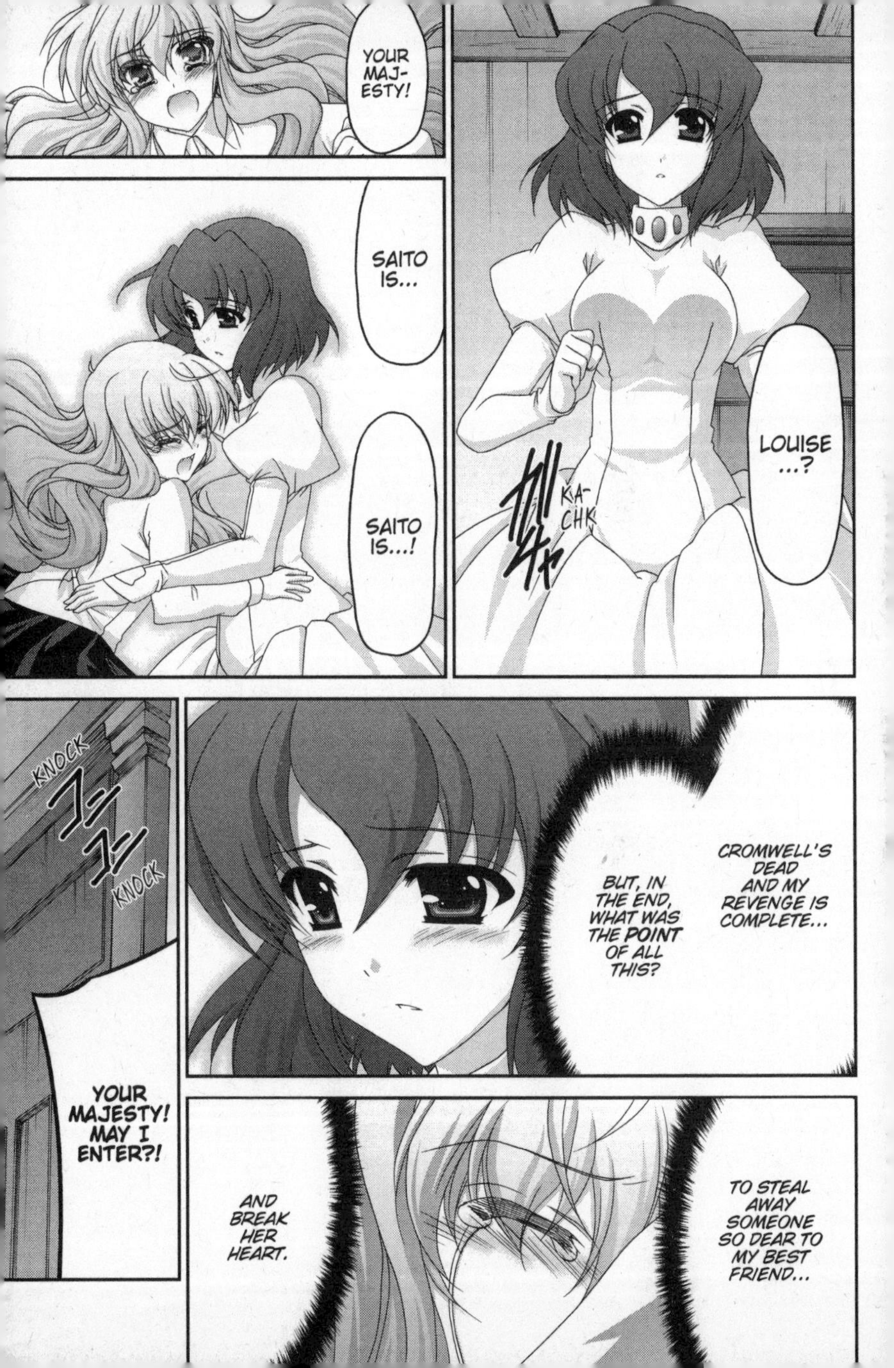
LOUISE...?
KA-CHK
YOUR MAJ-ESTY!
SAITO IS...
SAITO IS...!
CROMWELL'S DEAD AND MY REVENGE IS COMPLETE...
BUT, IN THE END, WHAT WAS THE POINT OF ALL THIS?
TO STEAL AWAY SOMEONE SO DEAR TO MY BEST FRIEND...
AND BREAK HER HEART.
KNOCK
KNOCK
YOUR MAJESTY! MAY I ENTER?!

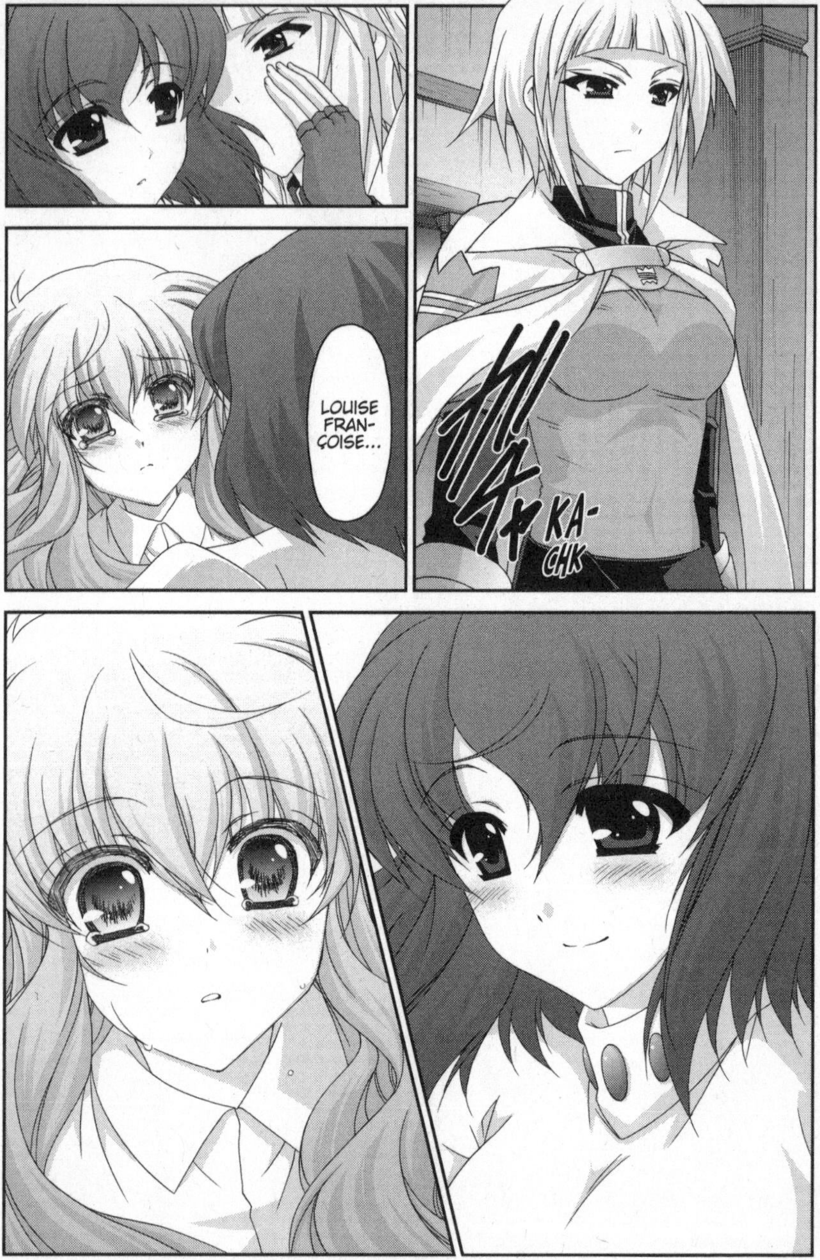

KA-CHK
LOUISE FRAN-ÇOISE...

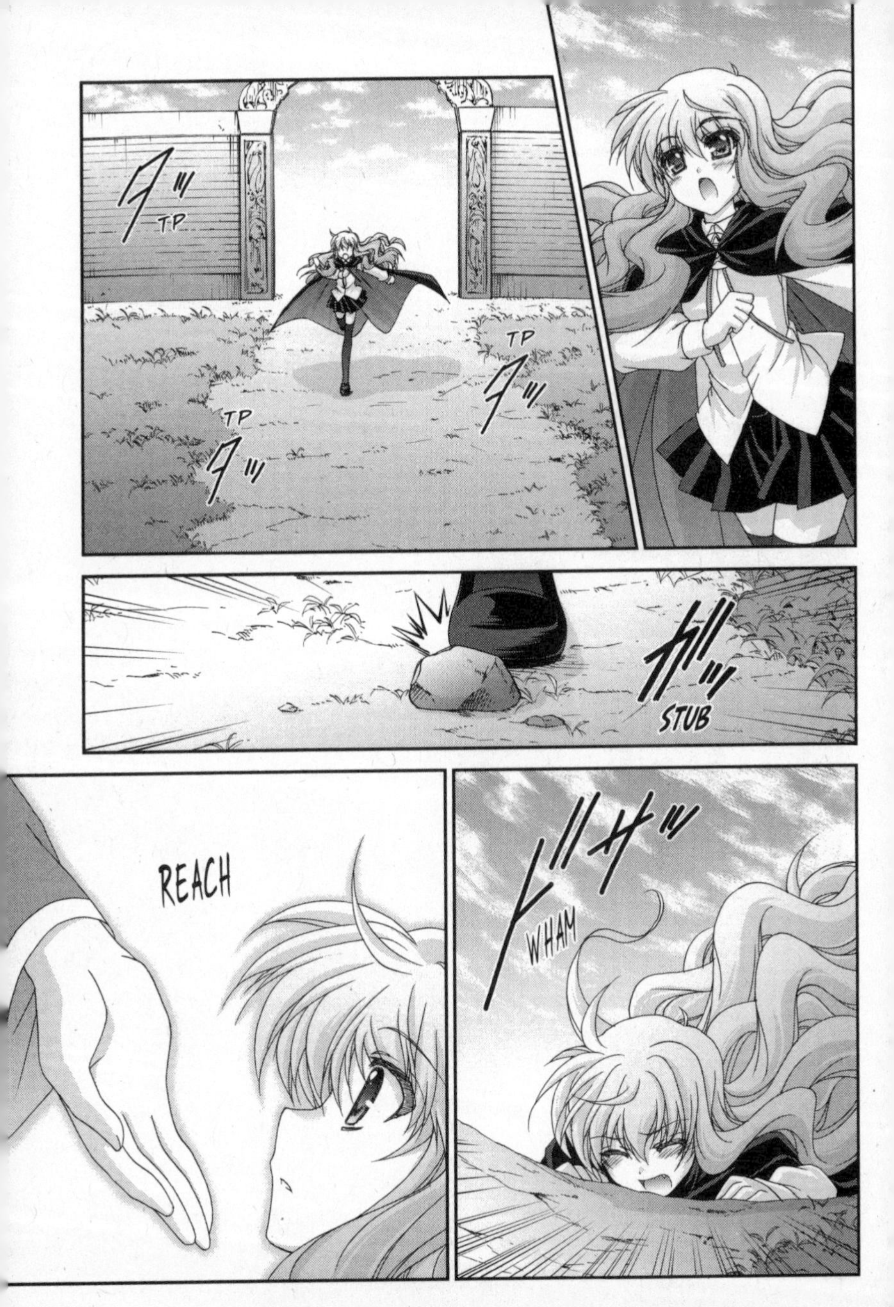
TP
TP
TP
STUB
WHAM
REACH

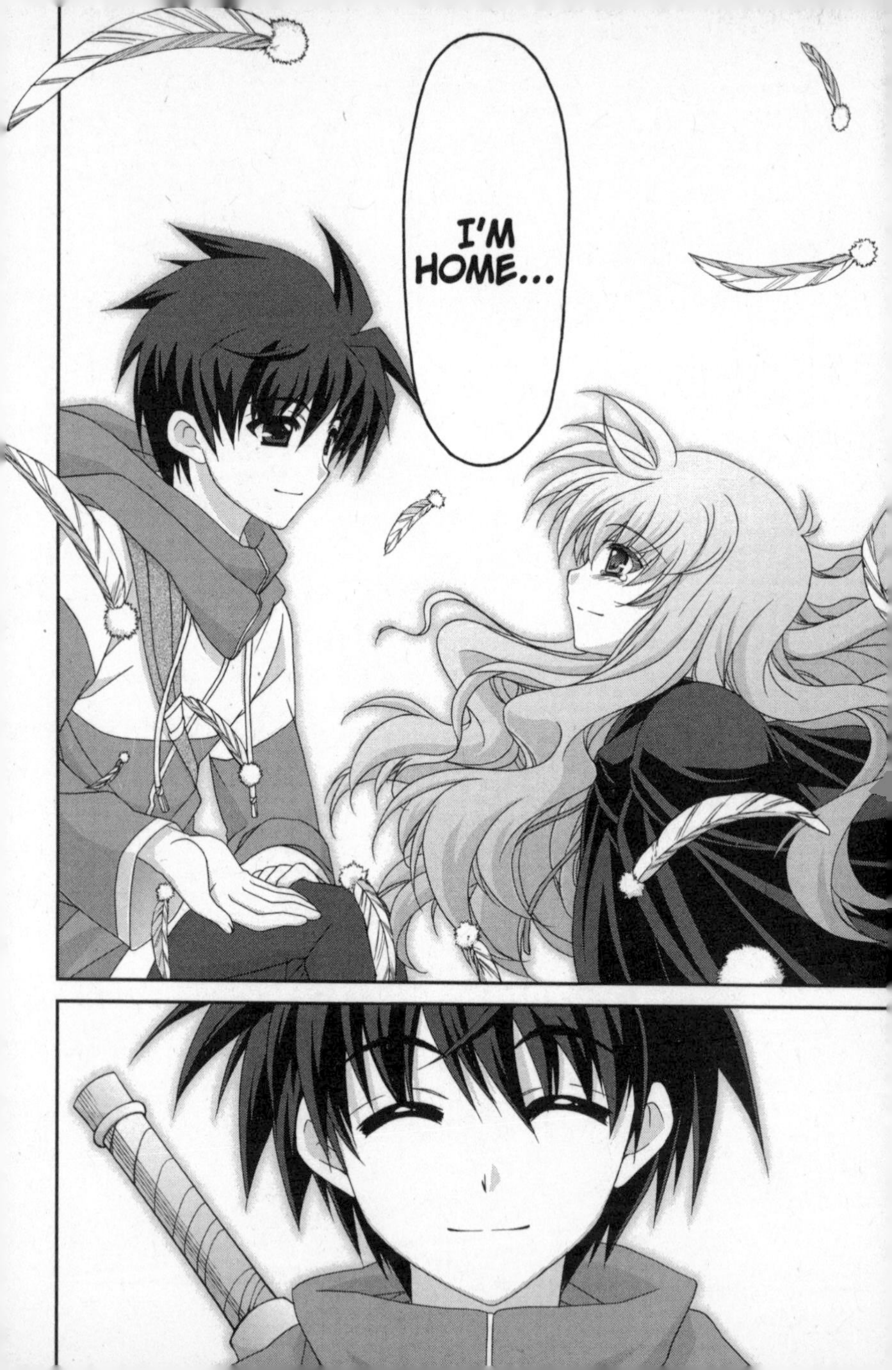
I'M HOME...

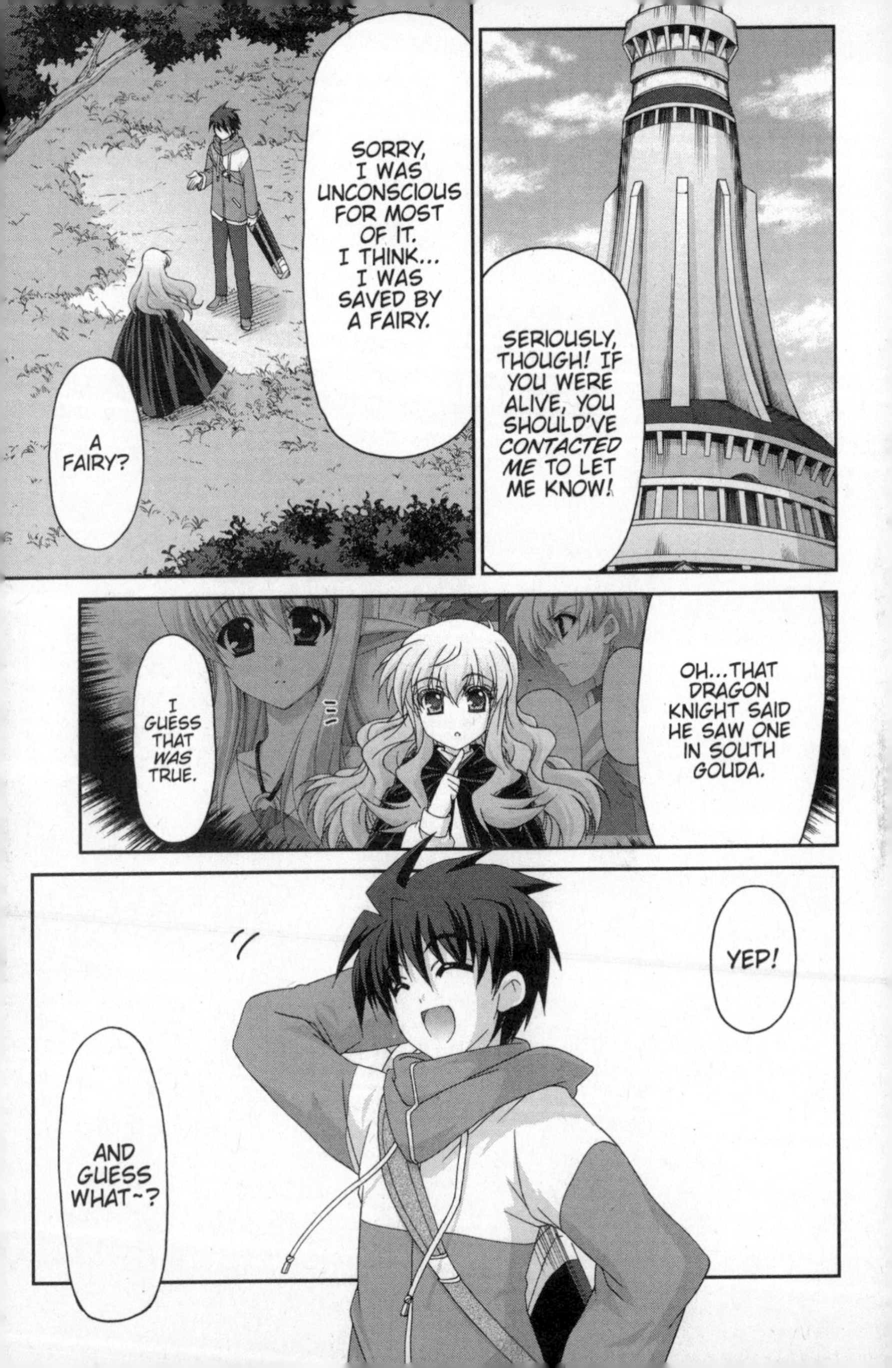
SERIOUSLY, THOUGH! IF YOU WERE ALIVE, YOU SHOULD'VE *CONTACTED ME* TO LET ME KNOW!
SORRY, I WAS UNCONSCIOUS FOR MOST OF IT. I THINK... I WAS SAVED BY A FAIRY.
A FAIRY?
OH...THAT DRAGON KNIGHT SAID HE SAW ONE IN SOUTH GOUDA.
I GUESS THAT *WAS* TRUE.
YEP!
AND GUESS WHAT~?

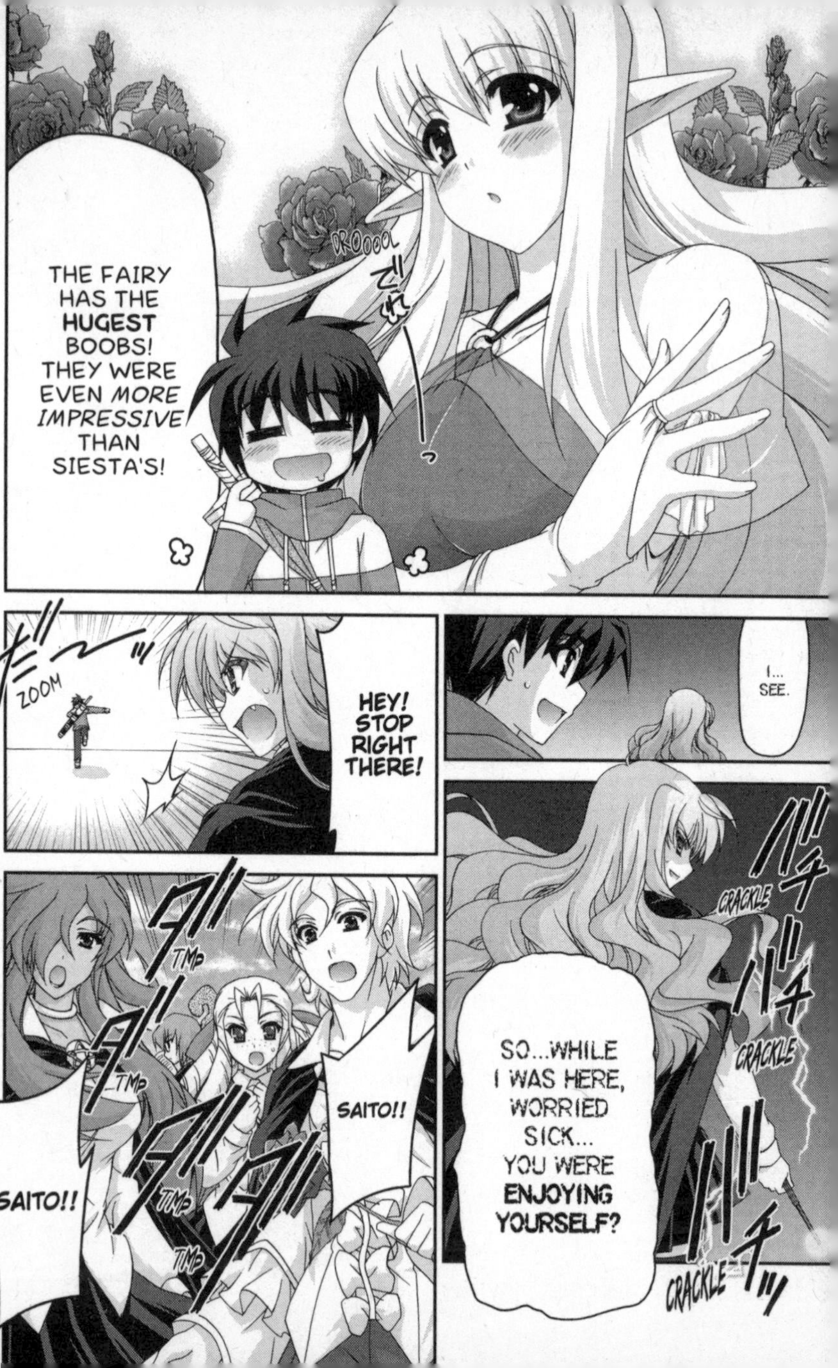
DROOOOL
でれ
THE FAIRY HAS THE HUGEST BOOBS! THEY WERE EVEN MORE IMPRESSIVE THAN SIESTA'S!
I... SEE.
CRACKLE
CRACKLE
CRACKLE
SO...WHILE I WAS HERE, WORRIED SICK... YOU WERE ENJOYING YOURSELF?
ZOOM
HEY! STOP RIGHT THERE!
TMP
TMP
TMP
TMP
SAITO!!
SAITO!!

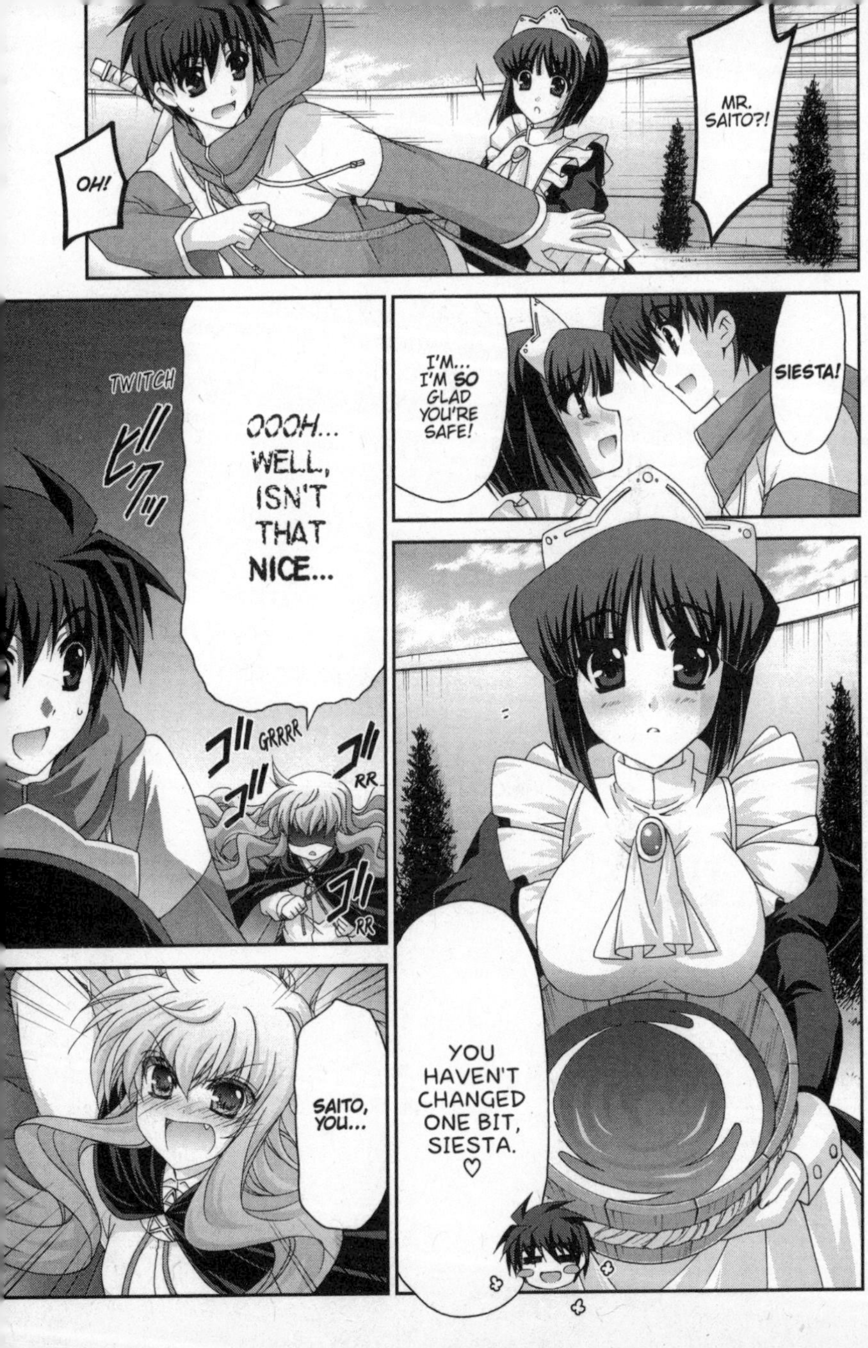
MR. SAITO?!
OH!
SIESTA!
I'M... I'M SO GLAD YOU'RE SAFE!
YOU HAVEN'T CHANGED ONE BIT, SIESTA. ♡
TWITCH
OOOH... WELL, ISN'T THAT NICE...
GRRRR
RR
RR
SAITO, YOU...

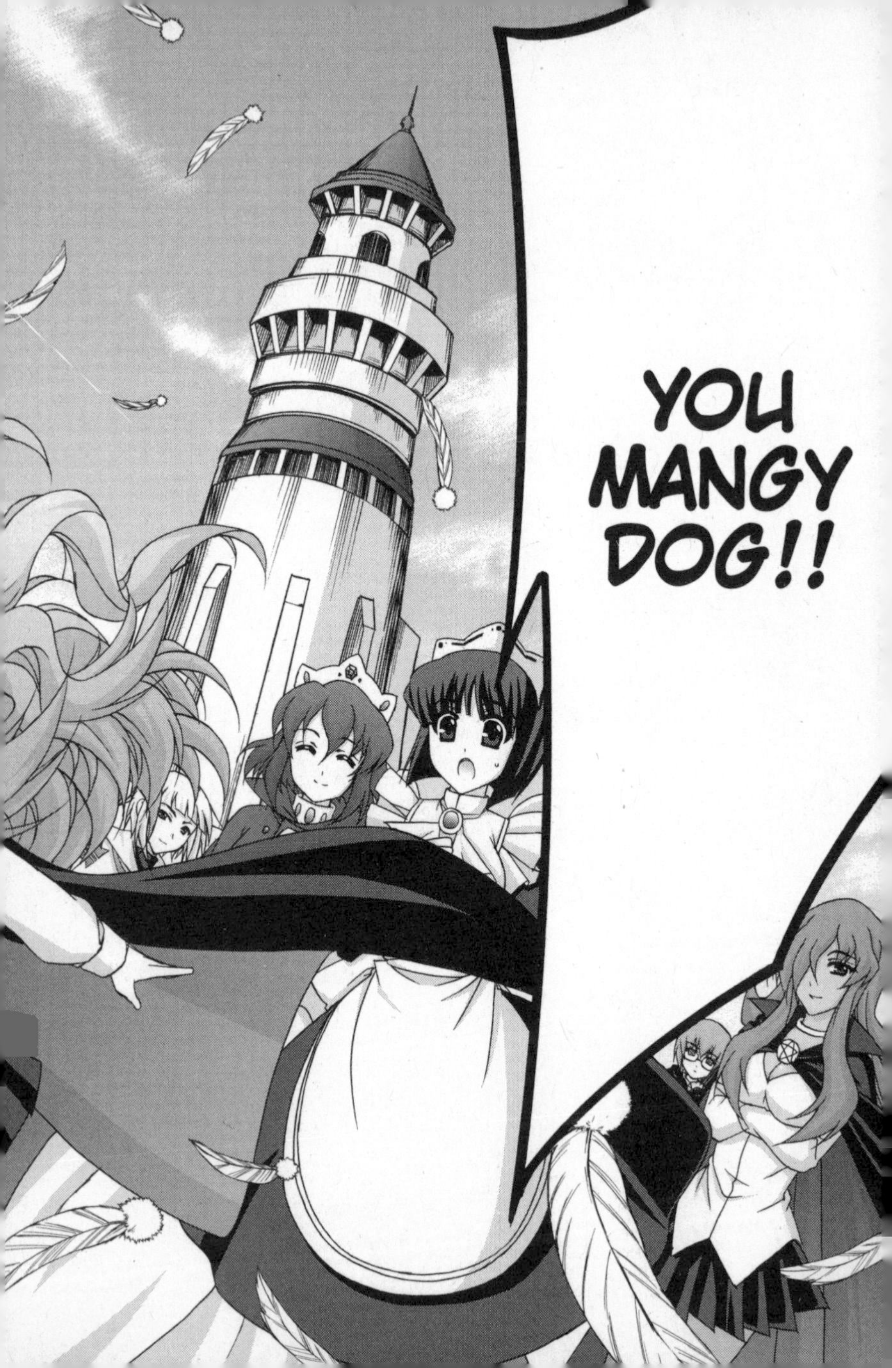
YOU MANGY DOG!!

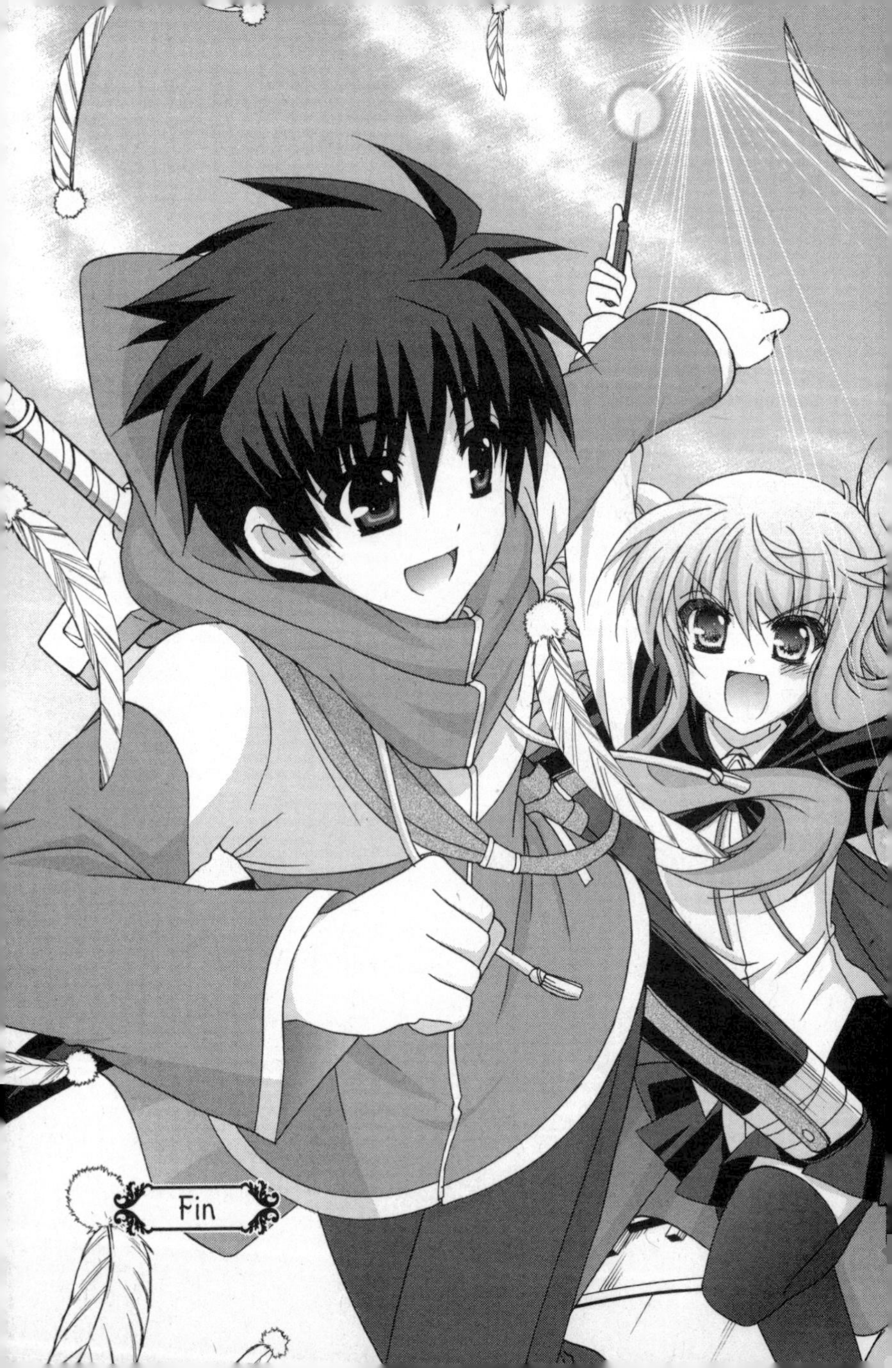
Fin

Hello! Or maybe it's "so nice to meet you"! My name is Yukari Higa.

Zero's Familiar: Chevalier has finally reached its last chapter!! Thank you so much to everyone who read it to the end...!!

The idea behind this piece was to "comic-ify" the sections of the original light novels that correspond to the second season of the anime. I was able to successfully draw and see this through to the end due to the warm support of Noboru Yamaguchi-sensei, who wrote the original novels; Eiji Usatsuki-sensei; all of my editors; and all you readers out there. Even in my own works, there haven't been many pieces I've drawn where the stars have aligned and things have gone this wonderfully. I'm so grateful that I was involved in this project. I'm so sad that it's over.

Now, although *Zero's Familiar: Chevalier* has come to a close, Saito and Louise's tale continues in the light novels, and the anime has had a third and fourth season as well. It would make me so happy if you continue to enjoy the world of *Zero's Familiar* through those media, too!

On that note, I hope to see you all again during my next project...!

Yukari Higa

Assistants
K.ishiduka
EIti YuU

RANKA

& Digital assistants

Highway star

Official site: http://pen.serio.jp/highwaystar
Blog: http://mekapen.blog116.fc2.com
Twitter: http://twitter.com/higayukari

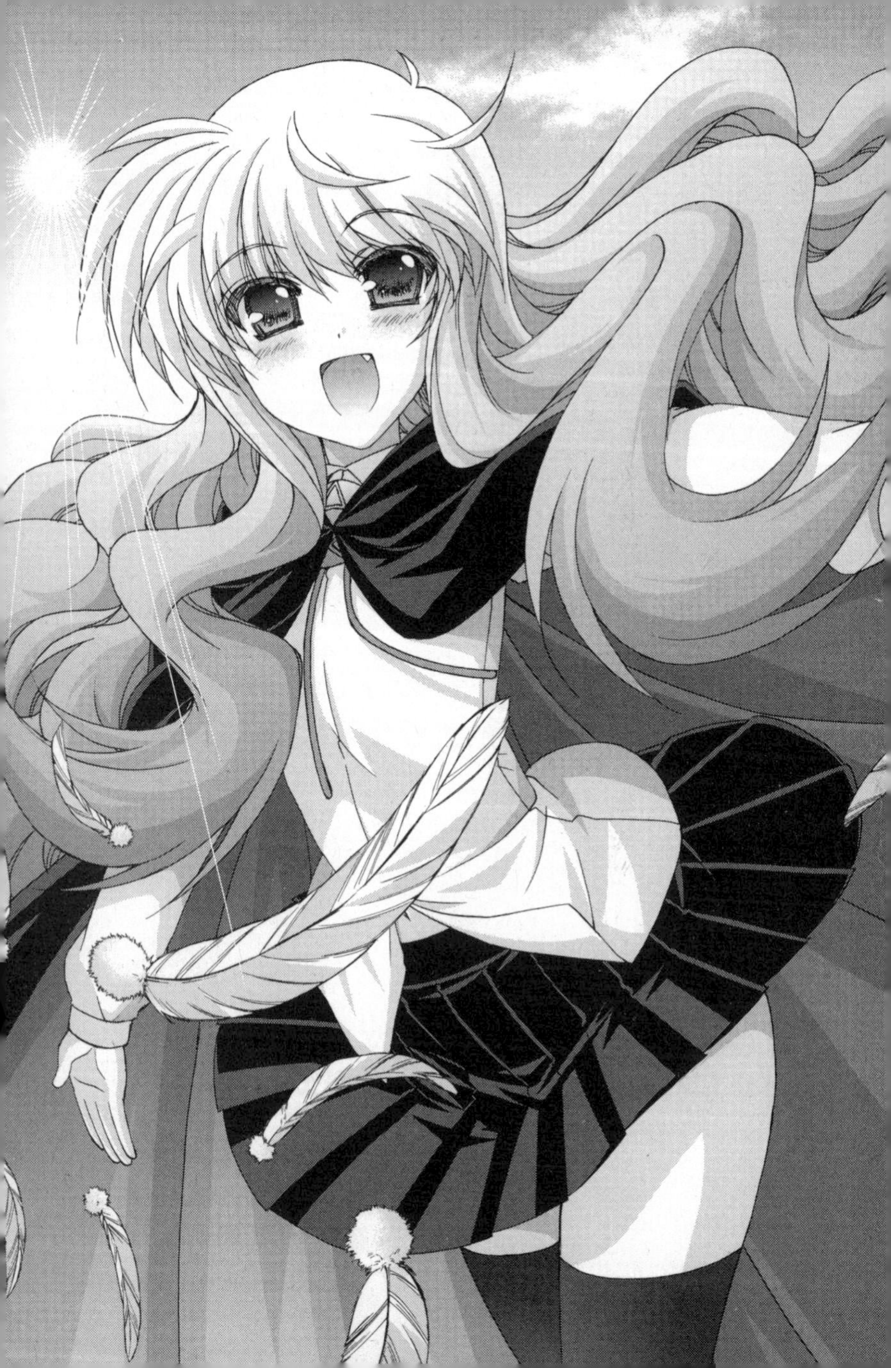

In Commemoration of the Release of Volume 4

A totes arbitrary

A Chevalier x Fwamiliar COLLABORATIVE 4 Koma!

with Masaya Takamura

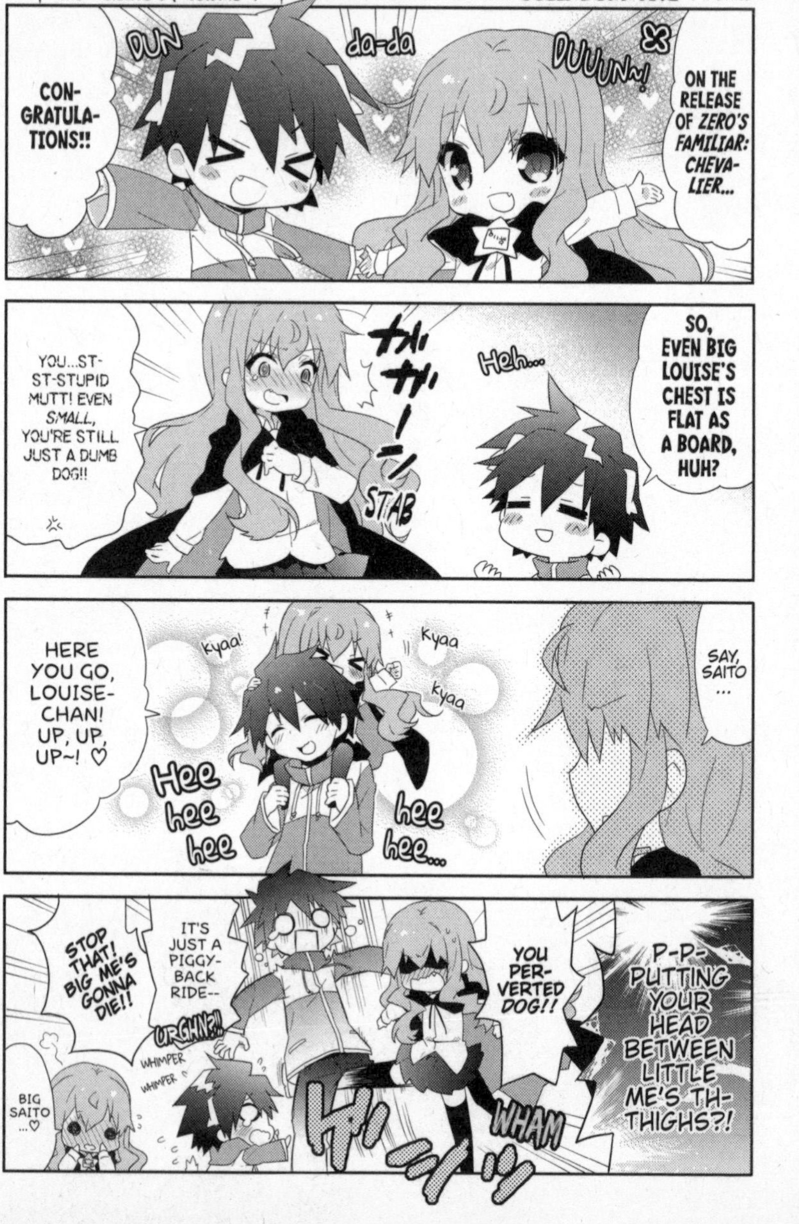
ON THE RELEASE OF ZERO'S FAMILIAR: CHEVALIER...
DUN
da-da
DUUUN~!
CONGRATULATIONS!!
SO, EVEN BIG LOUISE'S CHEST IS FLAT AS A BOARD, HUH?
Heh...
STAB
YOU...ST-ST-STUPID MUTT! EVEN SMALL, YOU'RE STILL JUST A DUMB DOG!!
SAY, SAITO ...
Kyaa
Kyaa!
Kyaa
hee hee...
Hee hee hee
HERE YOU GO, LOUISE-CHAN! UP, UP, UP~! ♡
P-P-PUTTING YOUR HEAD BETWEEN LITTLE ME'S TH-THIGHS?!
WHAM
YOU PERVERTED DOG!!
IT'S JUST A PIGGY-BACK RIDE--
URGHN?!
STOP THAT! BIG ME'S GONNA DIE!!
WHIMPER
WHIMPER
BIG SAITO ...♡

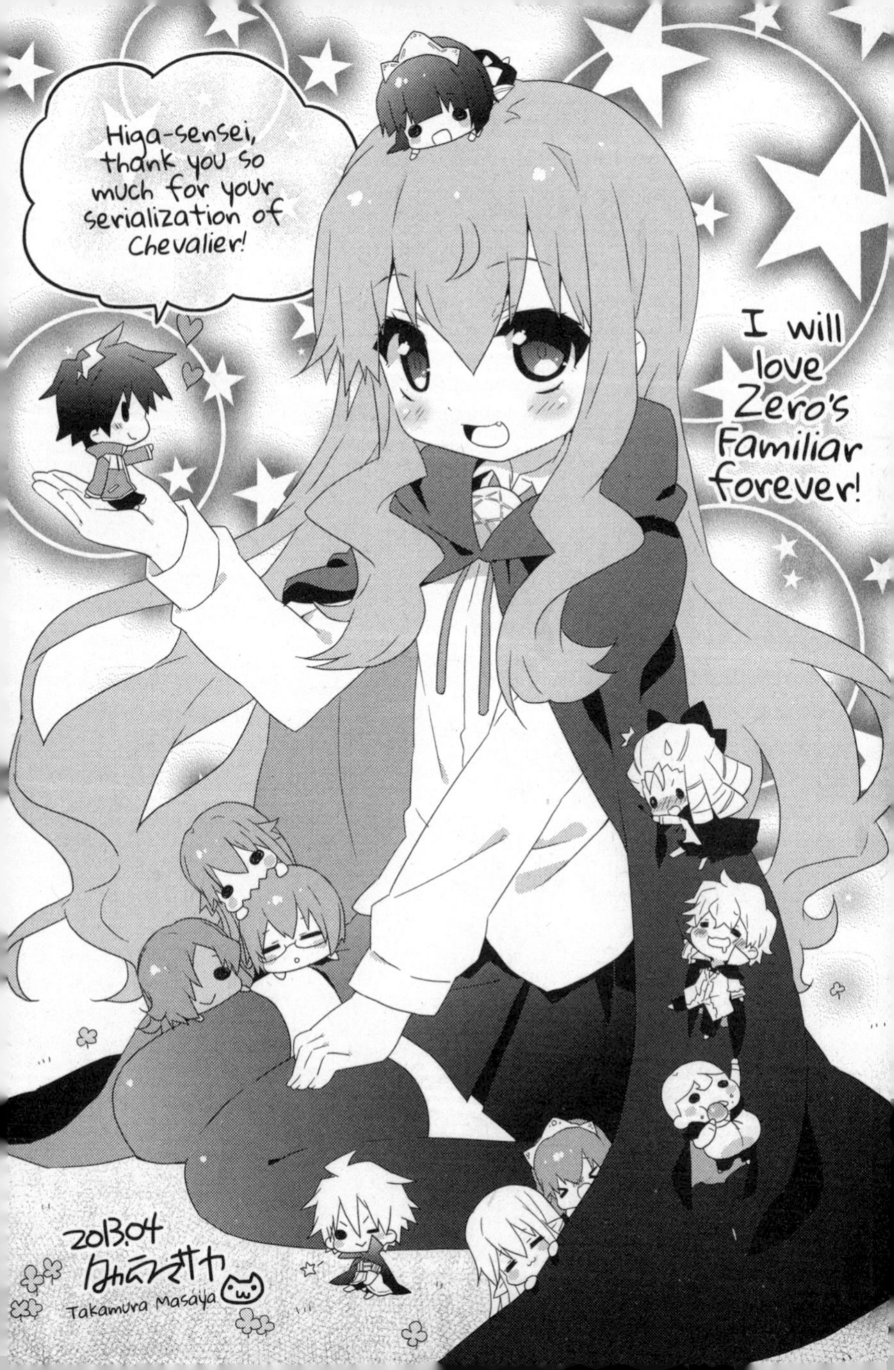
I will love Zero's Familiar forever!
Higa-sensei, thank you so much for your serialization of Chevalier!
2013.04
Takamura Masaya

Le Familier de Zero Chevalier

ZERO'S
FAMILIAR
Chevalier

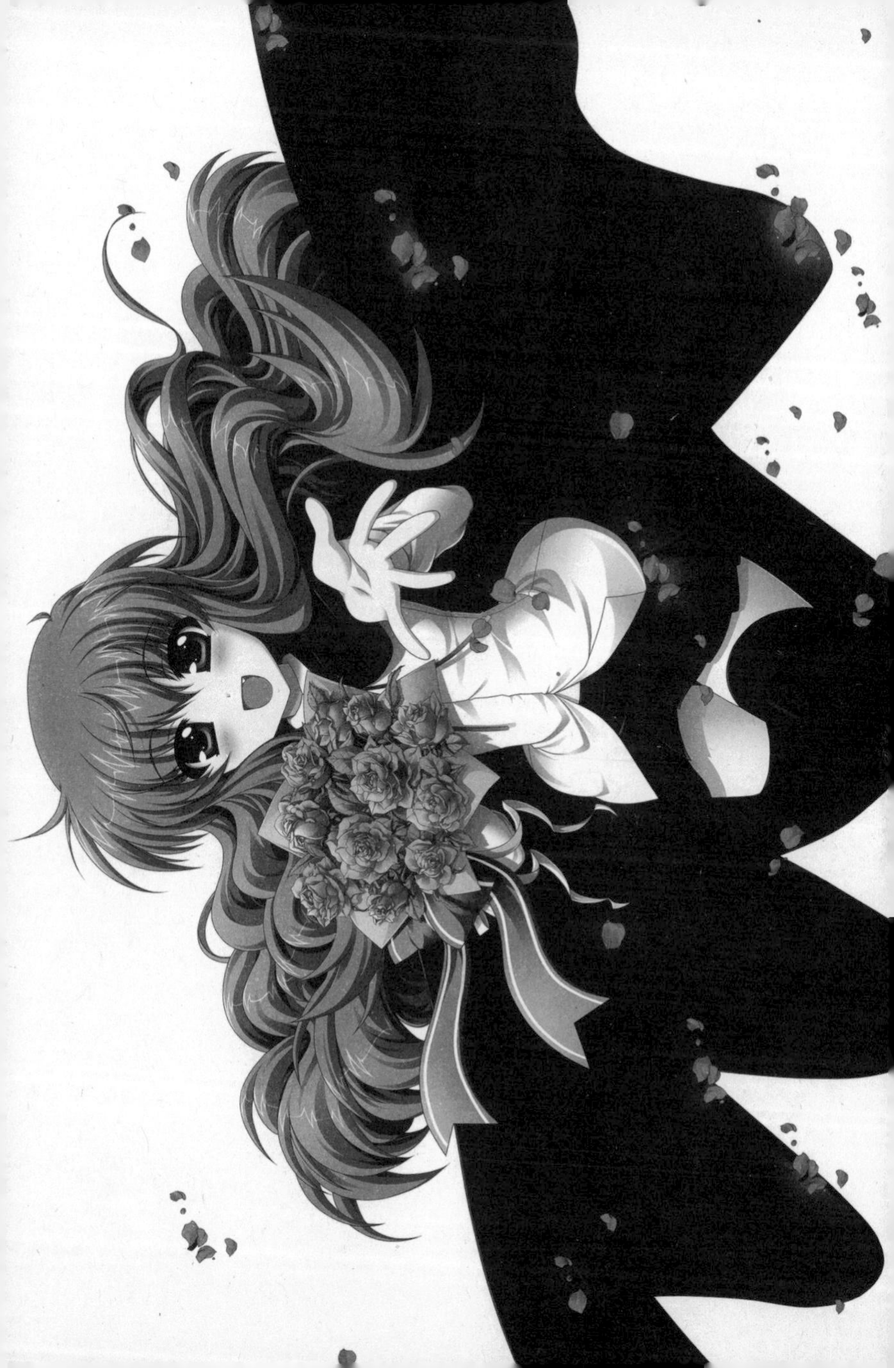

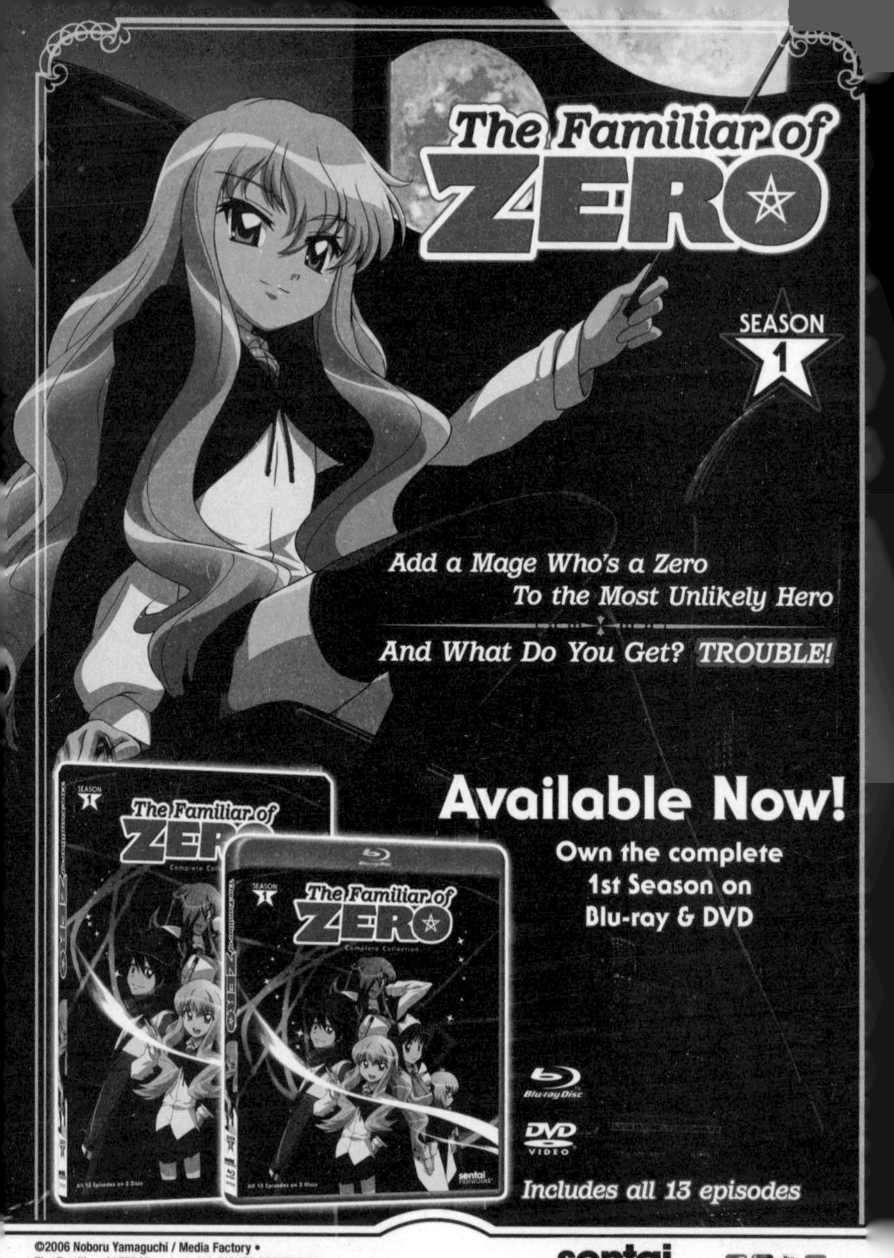
The Familiar of ZERO
SEASON 1
Add a Mage Who's a Zero
To the Most Unlikely Hero
And What Do You Get? TROUBLE!
Available Now!
Own the complete
1st Season on
Blu-ray & DVD
Includes all 13 episodes

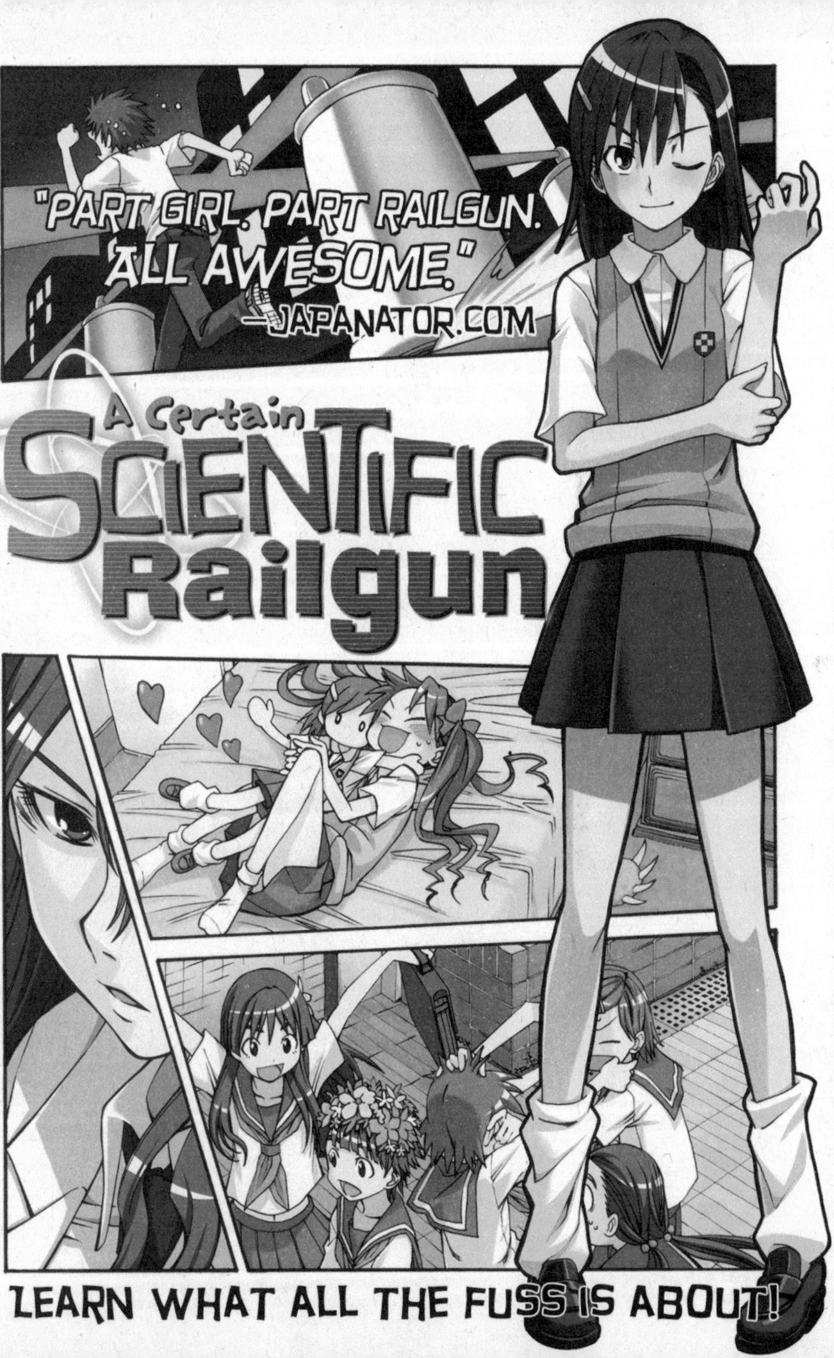
"PART GIRL. PART RAILGUN.
ALL AWESOME."
—JAPANATOR.COM
A Certain
SCIENTIFIC
Railgun
LEARN WHAT ALL THE FUSS IS ABOUT!

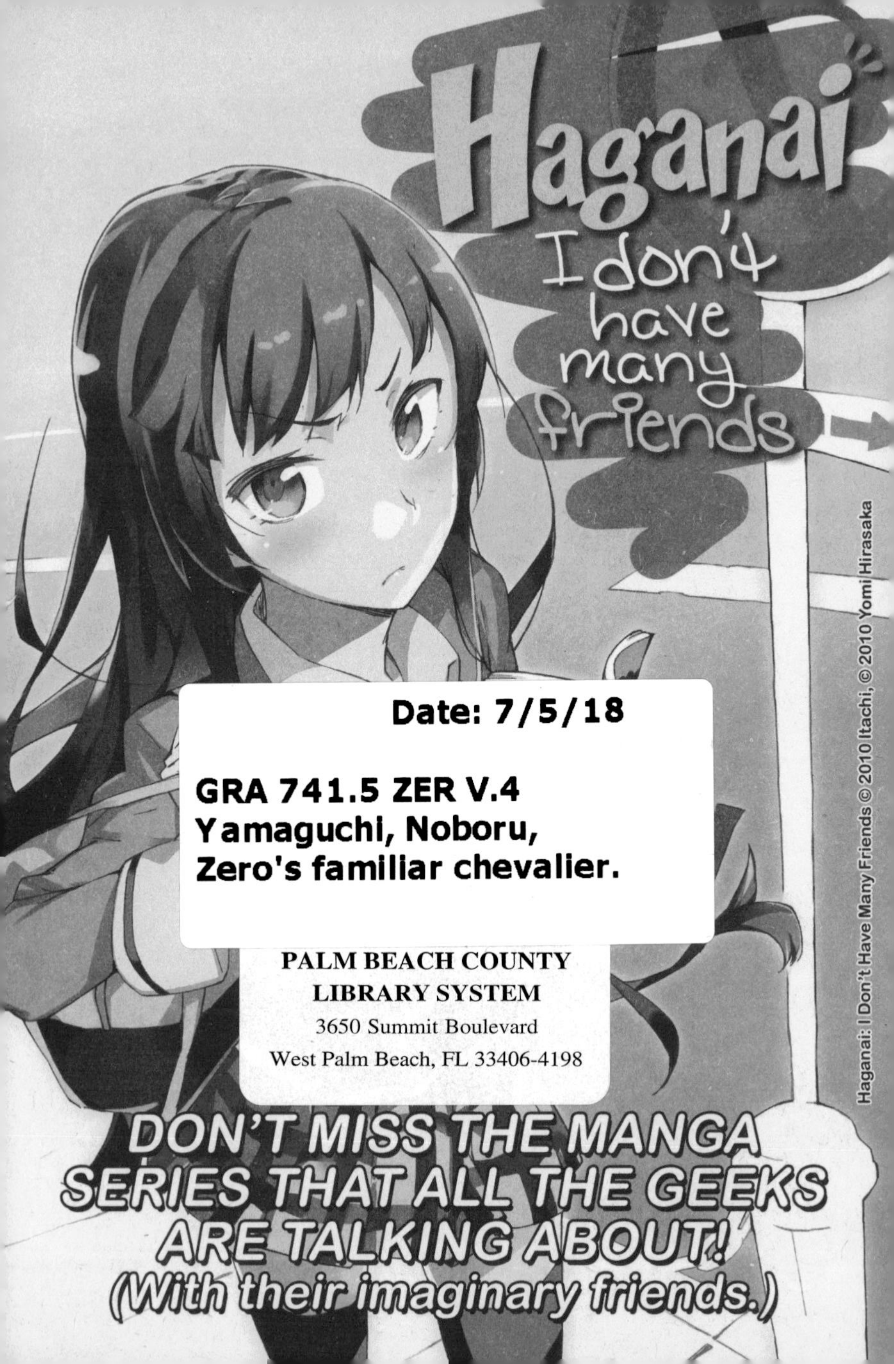
Haganai
I don't have many friends
DON'T MISS THE MANGA SERIES THAT ALL THE GEEKS ARE TALKING ABOUT!
(With their imaginary friends.)
Haganai: I Don't Have Many Friends © 2010 Itachi, © 2010 Yomi Hirasaka

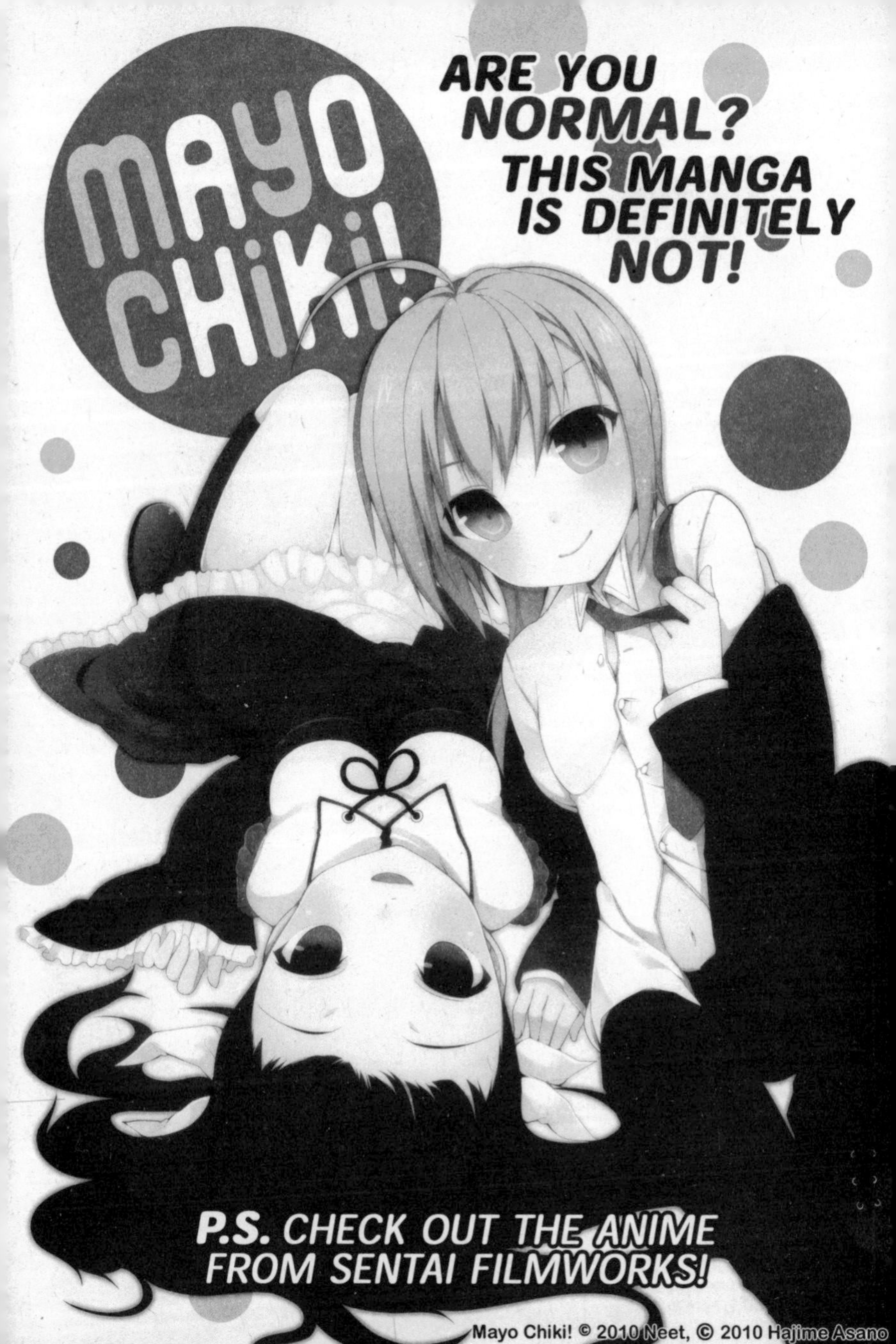
MAYO CHiKi!
ARE YOU NORMAL? THIS MANGA IS DEFINITELY NOT!
P.S. CHECK OUT THE ANIME FROM SENTAI FILMWORKS!

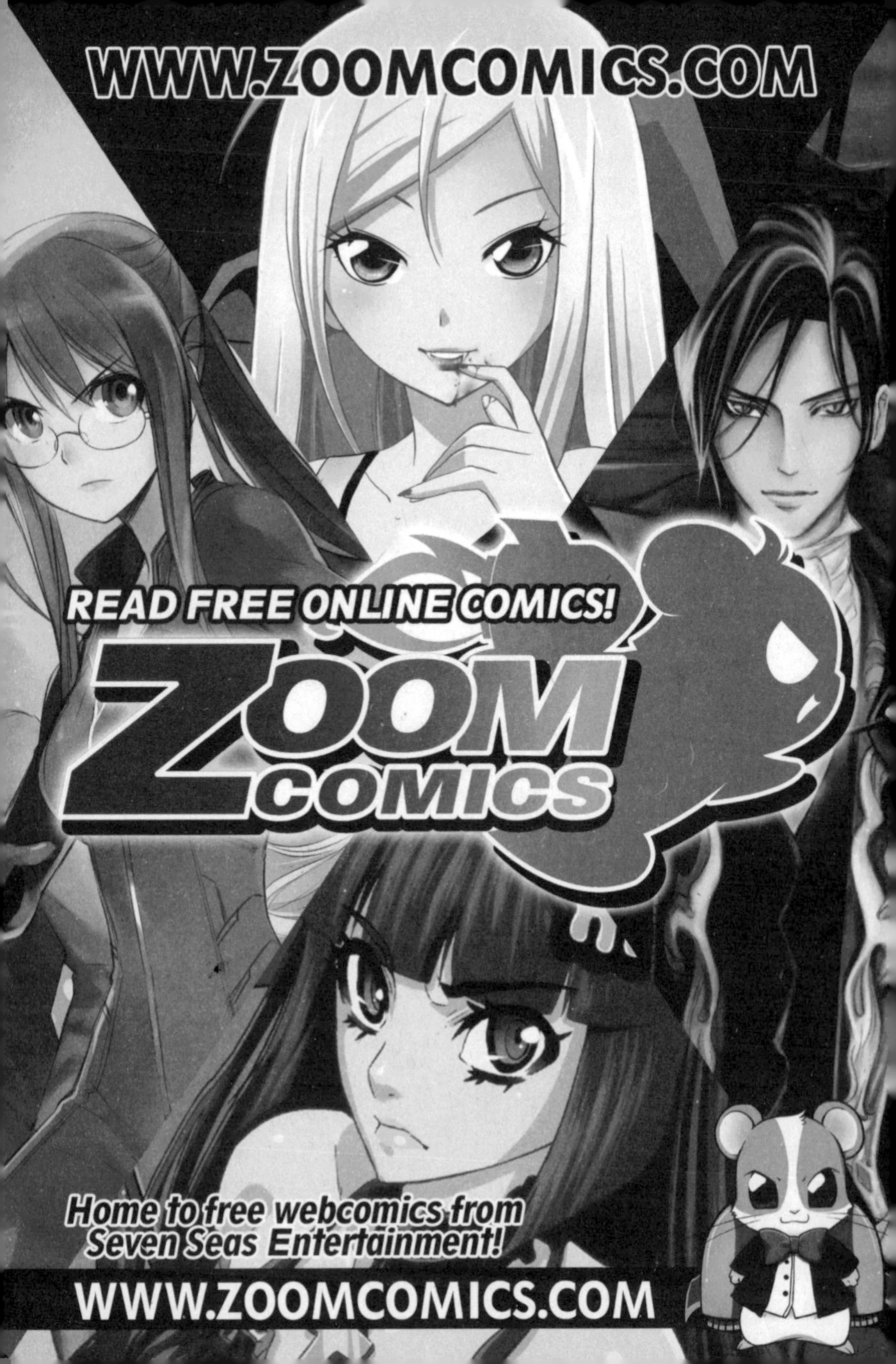